Fodor's

OAHU

4th Edition

Fodor's Travel Publications   New York, Toronto, London, Sydney, Auckland
www.fodors.com

Portions of this book appear in *Fodor's Hawaii.*

FODOR'S OAHU

Writers: Melissa Chang, Michael Levine, Catherine E. Toth

Editors: Jess Moss, Douglas Stallings, Mark Sullivan

Production Editor: Jennifer DePrima
Maps & Illustrations: David Lindroth, Ed Jacobus, William Wu, with additional cartography provided by Henry Columb, Mark Stroud, and Ali Baird, Moon Street Cartography, *cartographers;* Rebecca Baer, *map editor;* William Wu, *information graphics*
Design: Fabrizio La Rocca, *creative director;* Tina Malaney, Chie Ushio, Jessica Walsh, *designers;* Melanie Marin, *associate director of photography;* Jennifer Romains, *photo research*
Cover Photo: (Waimea Bay) Rick Doyle/Corbis
Production Manager: Angela L. McLean

4th Edition

ISBN 978–0–307–92921–1

ISSN 1559–0771

SPECIAL SALES

This book is available at special discounts for bulk purchases for sales promotions or premiums. Special editions, including personalized covers, excerpts of existing books, and corporate imprints, can be created in large quantities for special needs. For more information, write to Special Markets/Premium Sales, 1745 Broadway, MD 3-1, New York, NY 10019, or e-mail specialmarkets@randomhouse.com.

AN IMPORTANT TIP & AN INVITATION

Although all prices, opening times, and other details in this book are based on information supplied to us at press time, changes occur all the time in the travel world, and Fodor's cannot accept responsibility for facts that become outdated or for inadvertent errors or omissions. So **always confirm information when it matters,** especially if you're making a detour to visit a specific place. Your experiences—positive and negative—matter to us. If we have missed or misstated something, **please write to us.** Share your opinion instantly through our online feedback center at fodors.com/contact-us.

PRINTED IN COLOMBIA

10 9 8 7 6 5 4 3 2 1

CONTENTS

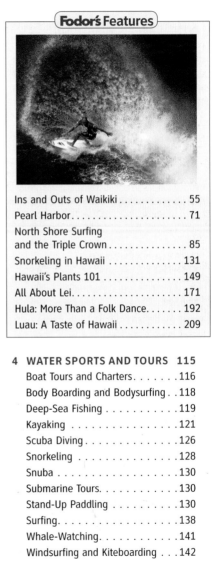

Fodor's Features

MAPS

ABOUT
THIS BOOK

Our Ratings

As travelers we've all discovered a place so wonderful that its worthiness is obvious. And sometimes that place is so unique that superlatives don't do it justice: you just have to be there to know. These sights, properties, and experiences get our highest rating, **Fodor's Choice,** indicated by orange stars throughout this book. Black stars highlight sights and properties we deem **Highly Recommended.** By default, there's another category: any place we include in this book is by definition worth your time, unless we say otherwise. And we will. Disagree with any of our choices? Care to nominate a place or suggest that we rate one more highly? Visit our feedback center at www.fodors.com/feedback.

> For expanded hotel reviews, visit **Fodors.com**

Hotels

Hotels have private bath, phone, TV, and air-conditioning, and do not offer meals unless we specify that in the review. We always list facilities but not whether you'll be charged an extra fee to use them.

Restaurants

Unless we state otherwise, restaurants are open for lunch and dinner daily. We mention dress only when there's a specific requirement and reservations only when they're essential or not accepted—it's always best to book ahead.

Credit Cards

We assume that restaurants and hotels accept credit cards. If not, we'll note it in the review.

Budget Well

Hotel and restaurant price categories from $ to $$$$ are defined in the opening pages of the respective chapters. For attractions, we always give standard adult admission fees; reductions are usually available for children, students, and senior citizens.

Listings
★ Fodor's Choice
★ Highly recommended
✉ Physical address
✛ Directions or Map coordinates
📬 Mailing address
☎ Telephone
🖷 Fax
⊕ On the Web

✍ E-mail
✉ Admission fee
⊙ Open/closed times
Ⓜ Metro stations
▭ No credit cards

Hotels & Restaurants
🏨 Hotel
🛏 Number of rooms
♨ Facilities
🍽 Meal plans
✕ Restaurant
♨ Reservations
🏛 Dress code
🚭 Smoking

Outdoors
⛳ Golf
⛺ Camping
Other
🧒 Family-friendly
⇨ See also
✉ Branch address
☞ Take note

Experience
Oahu

WHAT'S WHERE

1 Honolulu. The vibrant capital city holds the nation's only royal palace, free concerts under the tamarind trees in the financial district, and the art galleries, hipster bars, and open markets of Nuuanu and Chinatown.

2 Waikiki. This is the city from postcards, dressed in lights at the base of Diamond Head, famous for its world-class shopping, restaurants, and surf.

3 Pearl Harbor. Hawaii's largest natural harbor is also the resting place of the USS *Arizona*, sunk on December 7, 1941. A memorial pays tribute to the 2,390 dead and hundreds wounded in the attack that led the United States into World War II.

4 Southeast Oahu. Honolulu's main bedroom communities crawl up the steep-sided valleys that flow into Maunalua Bay. Also here are snorkelers' favorite Hanauma Bay and a string of wild and often hidden beaches.

5 Windward Oahu. The sleepy neighborhoods at the base of the majestic Koolau Mountains offer a respite from the bustling city with long stretches of sandy beaches, charming eateries, ancient Hawaiian fishponds, and offshore islands to explore.

6 The North Shore. Best known for its miles of world-class surf breaks and green sea-turtle sightings, this plantation town also boasts farms, restaurants, and hiking trails.

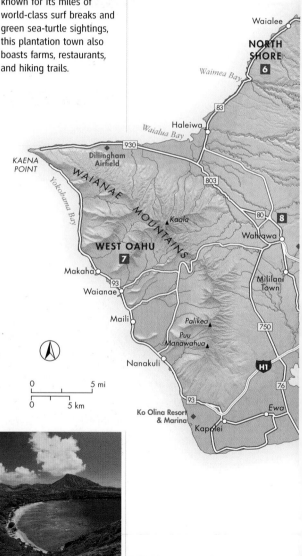

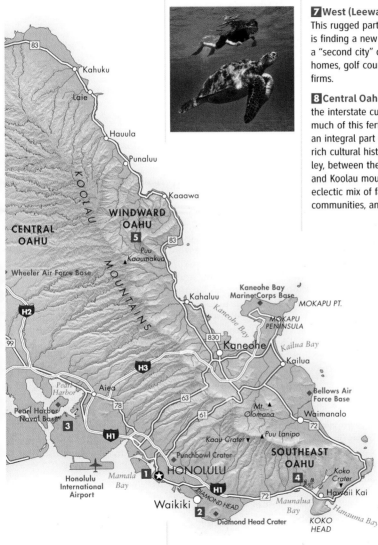

7 West (Leeward) Oahu. This rugged part of the island is finding a new identity as a "second city" of suburban homes, golf courses, and tech firms.

8 Central Oahu. Though the interstate cuts through much of this fertile region, it's an integral part of Hawaii's rich cultural history. This valley, between the Waianae and Koolau mountains, is an eclectic mix of farms, planned communities, and strip malls.

83

Kahuku

Laie

Hauula

Punaluu

Kaaawa

KOOLAU

WINDWARD OAHU 5

83

CENTRAL OAHU

Puu Kaaumakua

Wheeler Air Force Base

MOUNTAINS

Kahaluu

Kaneohe Bay Marine Corps Base

MOKAPU PT.

H2

MOKAPU PENINSULA

99

Kaneohe Bay

830

Kaneohe

Kailua Bay

H3

Kailua

Aiea

Pearl Harbor

78

63

Mt. Olomana

Bellows Air Force Base

Pearl Harbor Naval Base

3

61

Waimanalo

72

H1

Puu Lanipo

Kaau Crater

Punchbowl Crater

SOUTHEAST OAHU

4

Koko Crater

Honolulu International Airport

Mamala Bay

1

HONOLULU

H1

Hawaii Kai

Waikiki

DIAMOND HEAD

72

Maunalua Bay

Hanauma Bay

2

Diamond Head Crater

KOKO HEAD

OAHU AND HAWAII TODAY

Nicknamed "The Gathering Place," Oahu is the third-largest Hawaiian island and has 75% of the state's population. Honolulu is the perfect place to experience the state's indigenous culture, the hundred years of immigration that resulted in today's blended society, and the tradition of aloha. The museums and historic and cultural sites will ground you, at least a bit, in Hawaii's history. Honolulu has everything from award-winning restaurants to farmers' markets, from legendary surf breaks to trendy nightclubs. But Oahu is not just Honolulu and Waikiki. It's looping mountain trails on the western Waianae and eastern Koolau ranges. It's monster waves breaking on the golden beaches of the North Shore. It's country stores and beaches where turtles are your swimming companions.

Hawaiian culture and tradition here have experienced a renaissance over the last few decades. There's a real effort to revive traditions and to respect history as the Islands go through major changes. New developments often have a Hawaiian cultural expert on staff to ensure cultural sensitivity and to educate newcomers.

Nonetheless, development remains a huge issue for all Islanders—land prices are skyrocketing, putting many areas out of reach for the native population. Traffic is becoming a problem on roads that were not designed to accommodate all the new drivers, and the Islands' limited natural resources are being seriously tapped. The government, though sluggish to respond at first, is trying to make development in Hawaii as sustainable as possible.

Sustainability

Although sustainability is an effective buzzword and authentic direction for the Islands' dining establishments, 90% of Hawaii's food and energy is imported.

Most of the land was used for mono-cropping of pineapple or sugarcane, both of which have all but vanished. Sugarcane is now produced in only two plants on Kauai and Maui, while pineapple production has dropped precipitously. Dole, once the largest pineapple company in Hawaii, closed its plants in 1991, and after 90 years, Del Monte stopped pineapple production in 2008. The next year, Maui Land and Pineapple Company also ceased its Maui Gold pineapple operation, although in early 2010 a group of executives took over one third of the land and created a new company. Low cost of labor and transportation from Latin American and Southeast Asian pineapple producers are factors contributing to the industry's demise in Hawaii. Although this proves daunting, it also sets the stage for great agricultural change to be explored.

Back-to-Basics Agriculture

Emulating how the Hawaiian ancestors lived and returning to their simple ways of growing and sharing a variety of foods has become a statewide initiative. Hawaii has the natural conditions and talent to produce far more diversity in agriculture than it currently does.

The seed of this movement thrives through various farmers' markets and partnerships between restaurants and local farmers. Localized efforts such as the Hawaii Farm Bureau Federation are collectively leading the organic and sustainable agricultural renaissance. From home-cooked meals to casual plate lunches to fine-dining cuisine,

these sustainable trailblazers enrich the culinary tapestry of Hawaii and uplift the Islands' overall quality of life.

Tourism and the Economy

The over-$10 billion tourism industry represents a third of Hawaii's state income. Naturally, this dependency causes economic hardship as the financial meltdown of recent years affects tourists' ability to visit and spend.

One way the industry has changed has been to adopt more eco-conscious practices, as many Hawaiians feel that development shouldn't happen without regard for impact to local communities and their natural environment.

Belief that an industry based on the Hawaiians' *aloha* should protect, promote, and empower local culture and provide more entrepreneurial opportunities for local people has become more important to tourism businesses. More companies are incorporating authentic Hawaiiana in their programs and aim not only to provide a commercially viable tour but also to ensure that the visitor leaves feeling connected to his or her host.

The concept of *kuleana*, a word for both privilege and responsibility, is upheld. Having the privilege to live in such a sublime place comes with the responsibility to protect it.

Sovereignty

Political issues of sovereignty continue to divide Native Hawaiians, who have formed myriad organizations, each operating with a separate agenda and lacking one collectively defined goal. Ranging from achieving complete independence to solidifying a nation within a nation, existing sovereignty models remain fractured and their future unresolved.

The introduction of the Native Hawaiian Government Reorganization Act of 2009 attempts to set up a legal framework in which Native Hawaiians can attain federal recognition and coexist as a self-governed entity. Also known as the Akaka Bill after Senator Daniel Akaka of Hawaii, this pending bill has been presented before Congress and is still awaiting a vote at the time of this writing.

Rise of Hawaiian Pride

After Hawaii became a state in 1959, a process of Americanization began. Traditions were duly silenced in the name of citizenship. Teaching Hawaiian language was banned from schools and children were distanced from their local customs.

But Hawaiians are resilient people, and with the rise of the civil rights movement they began to reflect on their own national identity, bringing an astonishing renaissance of the Hawaiian culture to fruition.

The people rediscovered language, hula, chanting, and even the traditional Polynesian arts of canoe building and wayfinding (navigation by the stars without use of instruments). This cultural resurrection is now firmly established in today's Hawaiian culture, with a palpable pride that exudes from Hawaiians young and old.

The election of President Barack Obama definitely increased Hawaiian pride and inspired a ubiquitous hope for a better future. The president's strong connection and commitment to Hawaiian values of diversity, spirituality, family, and conservation have restored confidence that Hawaii can inspire a more peaceful, tolerant, and environmentally conscious world.

WELCOME TO OAHU

When You Arrive

Honolulu International Airport is 20 minutes (40 during rush hour) from Waikiki. Car-rental companies have booths at baggage claim; shuttle buses then take you to the car pickup areas. An inefficient airport taxi system requires you to line up to a taxi wrangler who radios for cars (about $25 to Waikiki). Other options include the city's reliable bus system ($2.50) with stops throughout Honolulu and Waikiki, or the Airport Waikiki Express shuttle ($9), which transports you to any hotel in Waikiki. Ask the driver to take Interstate H1, not Nimitz Highway, or your introduction to paradise will be via Honolulu's industrial back side.

Visitor Information

Hawaii Visitors and Convention Bureau ⊠ 2270 *Kalakaua Ave., Suite 801, Honolulu* ☏ 808/923–1811, *800/464–2924 for brochures* ⊕ *www.gohawaii.com.*

Oahu Visitors Bureau ⊠ 733 *Bishop St., Suite 1520, Honolulu* ☏ 808/524–0722 ⊕ *www. visit-oahu.com.*

Getting Here and Around

You can get away without renting a car if you plan on staying in Waikiki. But if you want to explore the rest of the island, there's no substitute for having your own wheels. Avoid the obvious tourist cars—candy-colored convertibles, for example—and never leave anything valuable inside, even if you locked the car. Get a portable GPS navigator, as Oahu's streets can be confusing.

Reserve your vehicle in advance, especially when traveling during the Christmas holidays and summer breaks. This will not only ensure that you get a car but also that you get the best rates. ⇨ *See "Travel Smart Oahu" for more information on renting a car and driving.*

Island Driving Times

Don't let maps fool you. While the distance between Waikiki and, say, the North Shore is roughly 40 miles, it may take more than an hour to get there, thanks to heavy traffic, construction, and other factors. Many of Oahu's main roads are a single lane in each direction, with no alternate routes. So if you're stuck behind a slow-moving vehicle, you may have no other choice than to hope it turns soon. Heavy traffic moving toward downtown can begin as early as 6 am, with after-work traffic starting at 3 pm.

Here are some average driving times—without traffic—that will help you plan your excursions.

Waikiki to Ko Olina	1 hour
Waikiki to Haleiwa	45 minutes
Waikiki to Hawaii Kai	25 minutes
Waikiki to Kailua	30 minutes
Waikiki to downtown Honolulu	10 minutes
Waikiki to airport	25 minutes
Kaneohe to Turtle Bay	1 hour
Hawaii Kai to Kailua	25 minutes
Haleiwa to Turtle Bay	20 minutes

Money-Saving Tips

A vacation to Hawaii doesn't have to break the bank. Take advantage of coupons in the free publications stacked at the airport and in racks all over Waikiki. Online sources like Groupon or Living Social offer discounted rates for everything from dinner cruises to massages.

Access to beaches and most hiking trails on the island is free to the public. For inexpensive fresh fruit and produce, check out farmers' markets and farm stands along the road—they'll often let you try before you buy.

For cheap and quick lunches, consider a food truck. Part of the culinary landscape of Oahu for generations, these lunch wagons—which rove around downtown and other areas—charge substantially less than restaurants.

Dining and Lodging on Oahu

If you want to see Hawaii's cultural blending, look no further than its cuisine. From traditional local-style plate lunches to sushi bars to high-end steak houses, there's no shortage of interesting flavors and cuisines.

Whether you're looking for a quick snack or a multicourse meal, turn to Chapter 8 to find the best eating experiences the island has to offer. And bring your appetite.

Choosing vacation lodging is a tough decision, but fret not—our expert writers and editors have done most of the legwork.

Looking for a tropical forest retreat, a luxurious resort, or a private vacation rental? Chapter 9 will give you all the details you need to book a place that suits your style. Quick tips: Reserve your room far in advance. Be sure to ask about discounts and special packages. (Some hotel Web sites have Internet-only deals).

WHAT IT COSTS

	$	$$	$$$	$$$$
Restaurants	Under $17	$17–$26	$27–$35	over $35
Hotels	Under 180	$180–$260	$261–$340	over $340

Restaurant prices are for a main course at dinner. Hotel prices are for two people in a standard double room in high season. Condo price categories reflect studio and one-bedroom rates.

Seeing Pearl Harbor

Pearl Harbor is a must-see for many, but there are things to know before you go.

Consider whether you want to see only the USS *Arizona* Memorial, or the USS *Bowfin* and USS *Missouri* as well. Allow approximately an hour and 15 minutes for the USS *Arizona* tour, which includes a 23-minute documentary of the Pearl Harbor attack and a ferry ride to the memorial itself.

Plan to arrive early—tickets for the USS *Arizona* Memorial are free and given out on a first-come, first-served basis. They can disappear within an hour. Take some time to enjoy the newly upgraded visitor center, which houses two exhibits using state-of-the-art technology to tell the story of the attack on December 7, 1941.

Strict security measures prohibit purses, backpacks, diaper bags, and camera cases (although cameras are allowed). Strollers are allowed in the visitor center but not in the theaters or on the shuttle boats. Baggage lockers are available for a small fee. Also, don't forget your ID.

Children under four years of age are not allowed on the USS *Bowfin* for safety reasons, and may not enjoy the crowds or waiting in line at other sights.

Older kids are likely to find the more experiential, hands-on history of the USS *Bowfin* and USS *Missouri* memorable.

For more information, visit ⊕ *www.nps.gov/valr.*

OAHU
TOP ATTRACTIONS

That Beach
(A) Kailua is the beach you came to Hawaii for—and the reason why many have never left. This popular stretch of white, sandy beach on Oahu's windward side is wide and inviting, with several small offshore islands perfect for exploring on kayaks. The waves are gentle and forgiving, and the beach is within walking distance of small convenience stores and friendly eateries.

Finding Shangri La
(B) Built atop the cliffs of Diamond Head, Shangri La is the lavish oceanfront home of American philanthropist Doris Duke. It houses an extensive collection of Islamic art, much of which was collected during her world travels. But the sprawling 5-acre estate—with its sweeping views, exotic gardens, and 75-foot saltwater pool—is an architectural wonder in its own right. It's open to the public for small group tours.

Oahu After Hours
(C) Nightlife in Hawaii may conjure up visions of mai tais by the hotel pool at sunset. But in the multicultural metropolis of Honolulu, there's so much more to it than that. Sip one of 17 different sparkling wines at Brasserie Du Vin in downtown Honolulu. Nosh on deep-fried potato cakes at Genius Lounge Sake Bar & Grill in Waikiki. Sing karaoke and munch on fried pork chops at the Side Street Inn near the Ala Moana Center. Or listen to jazz with a glass of wine—and maybe some artichoke-and-crabmeat fondue on crostini—at Formaggio Wine Bar.

Hiking to Kaena Point
(D) On the westernmost point of the island, magical Kaena Point is one of the last intact dune ecosystems in the Hawaiian Islands and is home to a growing population of wedge-tailed shearwaters and other rare and endangered seabirds. Hawaiian green sea turtles and monk seals

often rest along the shore, and in winter you can often see migrating humpback whales offshore. While you can't access all 850 acres of this culturally significant place—this area has long been known as the leaping place of souls—you can walk or bike along the coastline. A trek through this protected area may change your mind about Oahu being "too crowded."

Catching a Wave

(E) Since the turn of the 20th century, Waikiki beach boys like the famed Duke Kahanamoku have been teaching visitors how to ride the waves. Even today you can walk the beach along Kalakaua Avenue and find a tanned instructor to get you up on your board. Waikiki is one of the best spots to catch that first wave. The surf here is rolling and gentle (except during south swells in the summer). You might forget the name of the break, but you'll never forget the feeling of catching that first wave.

Exploring Chinatown

(F) Over the past few years, Chinatown has been transformed into the center of Oahu's arts scene. This vibrant neighborhood, which pours into downtown Honolulu, boasts art galleries, eclectic restaurants, hip bars, trendy boutiques, and the historic Hawaii Theatre. There are a few guided tours of the cultural attractions, but you can easily wander the area on your own. Every first Friday of the month there's a block party of sorts, when art galleries and restaurants stay open late and bars feature live music. It's well worth the cab fare.

Hula with Heart

(G) Professional hula dancers—the ones in poolside hotel shows and dinner extravaganzas—are perfection: hands like undulating waves, smiles that never waiver. But if you want to experience hula with heart, scan the newspapers for a hula school fundraiser or ask the activities desk about

local festivals. You may see some missteps and bumbles, but you'll also experience different hula styles and hear songs and chants deeply rooted in the culture, all the while surrounded by the scents of a hundred homemade lei.

A Sail on the Wild Side

(H) Who wouldn't want these memory snapshots to take home: the unblinking and seemingly amused eye of a spinner dolphin as it arcs through the wake of the catamaran in which you're riding; the undulating form of an endangered Hawaiian green sea turtle swimming below you; the slap and splash and whoosh of a humpback whale breaching in full view on indigo seas. Wild Side Specialty Tours can't promise these specific encounters, but their ecologically conscious daily excursions in a quiet, uncrowded catamaran do guarantee good memories.

A Day on the North Shore

(I) Head north along Oahu's eastern coastline toward the famed North Shore, where professional surfers nab some of the world's best waves. You'll pass through quaint residential areas and fruit stands on the side of the road. (Stop and buy bananas in Kahuku.) While you'll be tempted to try one of the famous shrimp trucks—plates of garlic shrimp hover around $20—consider the variety of eats on the North Shore, from old-school bakeries to burger joints to sit-down restaurants. In Haleiwa town, cool off at Matsumoto Shave Ice or Aoki's Shave Ice. If you're visiting in the summer, head to Three Tables or Shark's Cove for some stellar snorkeling. Or spend a lazy day at Sunset Beach, good book optional.

A Trip to Japan

(J) Little known outside Oahu's growing community of Japanese nationals is a class of small restaurant-bars called *izakaya*, or

Japanese taverns. Grilled, fried, and raw dishes are perfect with beer, sake, or *sho-chu* (a liquor distilled from barley, sweet potato, or rice). Even newer on the scene are *okonomi*, hip spots that specialize in Osaka-style grilled omelets and potent Japanese spirits. Both are like a visit to Japan, minus the long plane ride. They are a must-notch in any foodie's belt.

A Plate-Lunch Picnic

(K) Grab a plate lunch—typically meat with two scoops of macaroni salad and two scoops of white rice—and head to the nearest beach or park. Eat, *talk story* (local slang for chatting), and relax. You can find plate lunches at restaurants or from lunch wagons all over town. Some options: Rainbow Drive-In on Kapahulu Avenue; Sugoi on Kalani Street in Kapalama; Dean's Drive-Inn in Kaneohe; and Diamond Head Market and Grill near Kapiolani Park.

Walking in the Rain Forest or to a Waterfall

(L) Wend your way through the hillside neighborhood of Aiea, northwest of Honolulu, and suddenly you're in a cool, green park, scented with astringent eucalyptus. This is the 3½-mile Aiea Loop Trail, and if you're committed to squeezing a hike into a short Oahu stay, you couldn't do better for glimpses of hidden valleys and the experience of an island forest.

If waterfalls are more your speed, then head straight to the back of Manoa Valley, 3 miles *mauka* (toward the mountains from Waikiki) and you'll find a 1½-mile trail along a well-worn path following Manoa stream through native trees and flowers to the Manoa Falls.

GREAT ITINERARIES

To experience even a fraction of Oahu's charms, you need a minimum of four days and a bus pass. Five days and a car is better: Waikiki is at least a day, Honolulu and Chinatown another, Pearl Harbor the better part of another. Each of the rural sections can swallow a day each, just for driving, sightseeing, and stopping to eat. And that's before you've taken a surf lesson, hung from a parasail, hiked a loop trail, or visited a botanical garden. The following itineraries will take you to our favorite spots on the island.

First Day in Waikiki

You'll be up at dawn due to the time change and dead on your feet by afternoon due to jet lag. Have a dawn swim, change into walking gear, and head east along Kalakaua Avenue to Monsarrat Avenue toward Diamond Head. Either climb to the summit (about 1½ hours round-trip) or enjoy the view from the lookout. After lunch—there are plenty of options along Monsarrat—take a nap in the shade, do some shopping, or visit the nearby East Honolulu neighborhoods of Moiliili and Kaimuki, rife with small shops and quaint restaurants. End the day with an early and inexpensive dinner at one of these neighborhood spots.

Southeast and Windward Exploring

For sand, sun, and surf, follow H1 east to the keyhole-shaped Hanauma Bay for picture-perfect snorkeling, then round the southeast tip of the island with its windswept cliffs and the famous Halona Blowhole. Watch bodysurfers at Sandy Beach or walk up the trail leading to the Makapuu Point Lighthouse. If you like, stop in at Sea Life Park. In Waimanalo, stop for local-style plate lunch or punch on through to Kailua, where there's intriguing shopping and good eating.

Lounge at Lanikai Beach until sunset, then grab dinner at one of the area's many restaurants.

The North Shore

Hit H1 westbound and then H2 to get to the North Shore. You'll pass through pineapple fields before dropping down a scenic winding road to Waialua and Haleiwa. Stop in Haleiwa town to shop, enjoy shave ice, and pick up a guided dive or snorkel trip. On winding Kamehameha Highway, stop at famous big-wave beaches, take a dip in a cove with a turtle, and buy fresh island fruit from roadside stands.

Pearl Harbor

Pearl Harbor is almost an all-day investment. Be on the grounds by 7:30 am to line up for USS *Arizona* Memorial tickets. Clamber all over the USS *Bowfin* submarine. Finally, take the free trolley to see the "Mighty Mo" battleship. If it's Wednesday, Saturday, or Sunday, make the five-minute drive *mauka* (toward the mountains) for bargain-basement shopping at the sprawling Aloha Stadium Swap Meet.

Town Time

If you are interested in history, devote a day to Honolulu's historic sites. Downtown, see Iolani Palace, the Kamehameha Statue, and Kawaiahao Church. A few blocks east, explore Chinatown, gilded Kuan Yin Temple, and artsy Nuuanu with its galleries. On the water is the informative Hawaii Maritime Center. Hop west on H1 to the Bishop Museum, the state's anthropological and archaeological center. And 1 mile up Pali Highway is Queen Emma Summer Palace, whose shady grounds were a royal retreat. The Foster Botanical Garden is worth a visit for plant lovers.

THE HAWAIIAN ISLANDS

Oahu. The state's capital, Honolulu, is on Oahu; this is the center of Hawaii's economy and by far the most populated island in the chain—953,000 residents add up to 71% of the state's population. At 597 square miles Oahu is the third largest island in the chain; the majority of residents live in or around Honolulu, so the rest of the island still fits neatly into the tropical, untouched vision of Hawaii. Situated southeast of Kauai and northwest of Maui, Oahu is a central location for island hopping. Pearl Harbor, iconic Waikiki Beach, and surfing contests on the legendary North Shore are all here.

Maui. The second largest island in the chain, Maui is northwest of the Big Island and close enough to be visible from its beaches on a clear day. The island's 729 square miles are home to only 155,000 people but host more than 2 million tourists every year. With its restaurants and lively nightlife, Maui is the only island that competes with Oahu in terms of entertainment; its charm lies in the fact that although entertainment is available, Maui's towns still feel like island villages compared to the heaving modern city of Honolulu.

Hawaii (The Big Island). The Big Island has the second largest population of the Islands (almost 190,000) but feels sparsely settled due to its size. It's 4,038 square miles and growing—all the other Islands could fit onto the Big Island and there would still be room left over. The southernmost island in the chain (slightly southeast of Maui), the Big Island is home to Kilauea, the most active volcano on the planet. It percolates within Volcanoes National Park, which draws nearly 3 million visitors every year.

Kauai. The northernmost island in the chain (northwest of Oahu), Kauai is, at approximately 622 square miles, the fourth largest of all the Islands and the least populated of the larger Islands, with 64,000 residents. Known as the Garden Isle, this island is home to lush botanical gardens as well as the stunning Napali Coast and Waimea Canyon. The island is a favorite with honeymooners and others wanting to get away from it all—lush and peaceful, it's the perfect escape from the modern world.

Molokai. North of Lanai and Maui, and east of Oahu, Molokai is Hawaii's fifth-largest island, encompassing 260 square miles. On a clear night, the lights of Honolulu are visible from Molokai's western shore. Molokai is sparsely populated, with about 7,300 residents, the majority of whom are Native Hawaiians. Most of the island's 79,000 annual visitors travel from Maui or Oahu to spend the day exploring its beaches, cliffs, and former leper colony on Kalaupapa Peninsula.

Lanai. Lying just off Maui's western coast, Lanai looks nothing like its sister Islands, with pine trees and deserts in place of palm trees and beaches. Still, the tiny 140-square-mile island is home to about 3,200 residents and draws an average of 75,000 visitors each year to two resorts (one in the mountains and one at the shore), both operated by Four Seasons.

Hawaii's Geology

The Hawaiian Islands comprise more than just the islands inhabited and visited by humans. A total of 19 islands and atolls constitute the State of Hawaii, with a total landmass of 6,423.4 square miles.

The Islands are actually exposed peaks of a submersed mountain range called the Hawaiian Ridge-Emperor Seamounts

chain. The range was formed as the Pacific plate moves very slowly (around 32 miles every million years—or about as much as your fingernails grow in one year) over a hot spot in the Earth's mantle. Because the plate moves northwestwardly, the Islands in the northwest portion of the archipelago (chain) are older, which is also why they're smaller—they have been eroding longer and have actually sunk back into the sea floor.

The Big Island is the youngest, and thus the largest, island in the chain. It is built from five different volcanoes, including Mauna Loa, which is the largest mountain on the planet (when measured from the bottom of the sea floor). Mauna Loa and Kilauea are the only Hawaiian volcanoes still erupting with any sort of frequency. Mauna Loa last erupted in 1984. Kilauea has been continuously erupting since 1983.

Mauna Kea (Big Island), Hualalai (Big Island), and Haleakala (Maui) are all in what's called the post-shield-building stage of volcanic development—eruptions decrease steadily for up to a million years before ceasing entirely. Kohala (Big Island), Lanai (Lanai), and Waianae (Oahu) are considered extinct volcanoes, in the erosional stage of development; Koolau (Oahu) and West Maui (Maui) volcanoes are extinct volcanoes in the rejuvenation stage—after lying dormant for hundreds of thousands of years, they began erupting again, but only once every several thousand years.

There is currently an active undersea volcano to the south and east of the Big Island called Kamaehu that has been erupting regularly. If it continues its current pattern, it should breach the ocean's surface in tens of thousands of years.

Hawaii's Flora and Fauna

More than 90% of native Hawaiian flora and fauna are endemic (they evolved into unique species here), like the koa tree and the yellow hibiscus. Long-dormant volcanic craters are perfect hiding places for rare native plants. The silversword, a rare cousin of the sunflower, grows on Hawaii's three tallest peaks: Haleakala, Mauna Kea, and Mauna Loa, and nowhere else on Earth. Ohia trees—thought to be the favorite of Pele, the volcano goddess—bury their roots in fields of once-molten lava, and one variety sprouts ruby pom-pom-like lehua blossoms. The deep yellow petals of ilima (once reserved for royalty) are tiny discs, which make the most elegant lei.

But most of the plants you see while walking around, however, aren't Hawaiian at all and came from Tahitian, Samoan, or European visitors. Plumeria is ubiquitous; alien orchids run rampant on the Big Island; bright orange relatives of the ilima light up the mountains of Oahu. Though these flowers are not native, they give the Hawaiian lei their color and fragrance.

Hawaii's state bird, the nene goose, is making a comeback from its former endangered status. It roams freely in parts of Maui, Kauai, and the Big Island. Rare Hawaiian monk seals breed in the northwestern Islands. With only 1,500 left in the wild, you probably won't catch many lounging on the beaches, though they have been spotted on the shores of Kauai in recent years. Spinner dolphins and sea turtles can be found off the coast of all the Islands; and every year from November to April, the humpback whales migrate past Hawaii in droves.

WHEN TO GO

Long days of sunshine and fairly mild year-round temperatures make Hawaii an all-season destination. Most resort areas are at sea level, with average afternoon temperatures of 75°F to 80°F during the coldest months of December and January; during the hottest months of August and September, the temperature often reaches 90°F. Higher upcountry elevations typically have cooler and often misty conditions. Only at mountain summits does it reach freezing.

Moist trade winds drop their precipitation on the north and east sides of the Islands, creating tropical climates, whereas the south and west sides remain hot and dry with desertlike conditions. Rainfall can be high in winter, particularly on the north and east shores.

Most travelers head to the Islands in winter, specifically from mid-December through mid-April. This high season means that fewer travel bargains are available; room rates average 10% to 15% higher during this season than the rest of the year.

Winter on Oahu is whales (November through March) and waves (surf competitions December through February). In September, the Aloha Festivals celebrate island culture. In summer, the Islands honor the king who made them a nation, Kamehameha I, on June 11, with parades and events on all islands. Oahu's one-of-a-kind Pan-Pacific Festival follows the Kamehameha Day, bringing together hundreds of performers from Japan's seasonal celebrations. And summer swells bring waves (and surf contests) to southern beaches.

Hawaiian Holidays

If you happen to be in the Islands on March 26 or June 11, you'll notice light traffic and busy beaches—these are state holidays not celebrated anywhere else. March 26 recognizes the birthday of Prince Jonah Kuhio Kalanianaole, a member of the royal line who served as a delegate to Congress and spearheaded the effort to set aside homelands for Hawaiian people. June 11 honors the first island-wide monarch, Kamehameha I; locals drape his statues with lei and stage elaborate parades. May 1 isn't an official holiday, but it's the day when schools and civic groups celebrate the quintessential Island gift, the flower lei, with lei-making contests and pageants. Statehood Day is celebrated on the third Friday in August (admission to the Union was August 21, 1959). Most Japanese and Chinese holidays are widely observed. On Chinese New Year, homes and businesses sprout bright-red good-luck mottoes, lions dance in the streets, and everybody eats *gau* (steamed pudding) and *jai* (vegetarian stew). Good Friday is a state holiday in spring, a favorite for family picnics.

Climate

The following are average maximum and minimum temperatures for Honolulu; the temperatures throughout the Hawaiian Islands are similar.

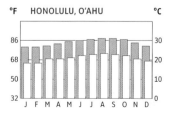

°F HONOLULU, O'AHU °C

86

68

50

32

J F M A M J J A S O N D

30

20

10

0

HAWAIIAN HISTORY

Hawaiian history is long and complex; a brief survey can put into context the ongoing renaissance of native arts and culture.

The Polynesians

Long before both Christopher Columbus and the Vikings, Polynesian seafarers set out to explore the vast stretches of the open ocean in double-hulled canoes. From western Polynesia, they traveled back and forth between Samoa, Fiji, Tahiti, the Marquesas, and the Society Isles, settling on the outer reaches of the Pacific, Hawaii, and Easter Island, as early as AD 300. The golden era of Polynesian voyaging peaked around AD 1200, after which the distant Hawaiian Islands were left to develop their own unique cultural practices and subsistence in relative isolation.

The Islands' symbiotic society was deeply intertwined with religion, mythology, science, and artistry. Ruled by an *alii*, or chief, each settlement was nestled in an *ahupuaa*, a pie-shaped land division from the uplands where the alii lived, through the valleys and down to the shores where the commoners resided. Everyone contributed, whether it was by building canoes, catching fish, making tools, or farming land.

A United Kingdom

When the British explorer Captain James Cook arrived in 1778, he was revered as a god upon his arrival and later killed over a stolen boat. With guns and ammunition purchased from Cook, the Big Island chief, Kamehameha the Great, gained a significant advantage over the other alii. He united Hawaii into one kingdom in 1810, bringing an end to the frequent interisland battles that dominated Hawaiian life.

Tragically, the new kingdom was beset with troubles. Native religion was abandoned, and *kapu* (laws and regulations) were eventually abolished. The European explorers brought foreign diseases with them, and within a few short decades the Native Hawaiian population was decimated.

New laws regarding land ownership and religious practices eroded the underpinnings of pre-contact Hawaii. Each successor to the Hawaiian throne sacrificed more control over the Island kingdom. As Westerners permeated Hawaiian culture, Hawaii became more riddled with layers of racial issues, injustice, and social unrest.

Modern Hawaii

Finally in 1893, the last Hawaiian monarch, Queen Liliuokalani, was overthrown by a group of Americans and European businessmen and government officials, aided by an armed militia. This led to the creation of the Republic of Hawaii, and it became a U.S. territory for the next 60 years. The loss of Hawaiian sovereignty and the conditions of annexation have haunted the Hawaiian people since the monarchy was deposed.

Pearl Harbor was attacked in 1941, which engaged the United States immediately into World War II. Tourism, from its beginnings in the early 1900s, flourished after the war and naturally inspired rapid real estate development in Waikiki. In 1959, Hawaii officially became the 50th state. Statehood paved the way for Hawaiians to participate in the American democratic process, which was not universally embraced by all Hawaiians. With the rise of the civil rights movement in the 1960s, Hawaiians began to reclaim their own identity, from language to hula.

HAWAIIAN PEOPLE AND THEIR CULTURE

By October 2010, Hawaii's population was more than 1.3 million with the majority of residents living on Oahu. Nine percent are Hawaiian or other Pacific Islander, almost 40% are Asian American, 9% are Latino, and about 25% Caucasian. Nearly a fifth of the population list two or more races, making Hawaii the most diverse state in the United States.

Among individuals 18 and older, about 84% finished high school, half attained some college, and 26% completed a bachelor's degree or higher.

The Role of Tradition

The kingdom of Hawaii was ruled by a spiritual class system. Although the *alii*, or chief, was believed to be the direct descendent of a deity or god, high priests, known as *kahuna*, presided over every imaginable aspect of life and *kapu* (taboos) that strictly governed the commoners.

Each part of nature and ritual was connected to a deity—Kane was the highest of all deities, symbolizing sunlight and creation; Ku was the god of war; Lono represented fertility, rainfall, music, and peace; Kanaloa was the god of the underworld or darker spirits. Probably the most well known by outsiders is Pele, the goddess of fire.

The kapu not only provided social order, they also swayed the people to act with reverence for the environment. Any abuse was met with extreme punishment, often death, as it put the land and people's *mana*, or spiritual power, in peril.

Ancient deities play a huge role in Hawaiian life today—not just in daily rituals, but in the Hawaiians' reverence for their land. Gods and goddesses tend to be associated with particular parts of the land, and most of them are connected with many places, thanks to the body of stories built up around each.

One of the most important ways the ancient Hawaiians showed respect for their gods and goddesses was through the hula. Various forms of the hula were performed as prayers to the gods and as praise to the chiefs. Performances were taken very seriously, as a mistake was thought to invalidate the prayer, or even to offend the god or chief in question. Hula is still performed both as entertainment and as prayer; it is not uncommon for a hula performance to be included in an official government ceremony.

Who Are the Hawaiians Today?

To define the Hawaiians in a page, let alone a paragraph, is nearly impossible. Those considered to be indigenous Hawaiians are descendants of the ancient Polynesians who crossed the vast ocean and settled Hawaii. According to the government, there are Native Hawaiians or native Hawaiians (note the change in capitalization), depending on a person's background.

Federal and state agencies apply different methods to determine Hawaiian lineage, from measuring blood percentage to mapping genealogy. This has caused turmoil within the community because it excludes many who claim Hawaiian heritage. It almost guarantees that, as races intermingle, even those considered Native Hawaiian now will eventually disappear on paper, displacing generations to come.

Modern Hawaiian Culture

Perfect weather aside, Hawaii might be the warmest place anyone can visit. The Hawaii experience begins and ends with *aloha*, a word that envelops love, affection, and mercy, and has become a salutation for hello and good-bye. Broken down, *alo* means "presence" and *ha* means "breath"—the presence of breath. It's to live with love and respect for self and others with every breath. Past the manicured resorts and tour buses, aloha is a moral compass that binds all of Hawaii's people.

Hawaii is blessed with some of the most unspoiled natural wonders, and aloha extends to the land, or *aina*. Hawaiians are raised outdoors and have strong ties to nature. They realize as children that the ocean and land are the delicate source of all life. Even ancient gods were embodied by nature, and this reverence has been passed down to present generations who believe in *kuleana*, their privilege and responsibility.

Hawaii's diverse cultures unfold in a beautiful montage of customs and arts—from music, to dance, to food. Musical genres range from slack key to *Jawaiian* (Hawaiian reggae) to *hapa-haole* (Hawaiian music with English words). From George Kahumoku's Grammy-worthy laid-back strumming, to the late Iz Kamakawiwoole's "Somewhere over the Rainbow," to Jack Johnson's more mainstream tunes, contemporary Hawaiian music has definitely carved its ever-evolving niche.

The Merrie Monarch Festival is celebrating almost 50 years of worldwide hula competition and education. The fine-dining culinary scene, especially in Honolulu, has a rich tapestry of ethnic influences and talent. But the real gems are the humble hole-in-the-wall eateries that serve authentic cuisines of many ethnic origins in one plate, a deliciously mixed plate indeed.

And perhaps, the most striking quality in today's Hawaiian culture is the sense of family, or *ohana*. Sooner or later, almost everyone you meet becomes an uncle or auntie, and it is not uncommon for near strangers to be welcomed into a home as a member of the family.

Until the last century, the practice of *hanai*, in which a family essentially adopts a child, usually a grandchild, without formalities, was still prevalent. While still practiced to a somewhat lesser degree, the *hanai*, which means to feed or nourish, still resonates within most families and communities.

How to Act Like a Local

Adopting local customs is a firsthand introduction to the Islands' unique culture. So live in T-shirts and shorts. Wear cheap rubber flip-flops, but call them slippers. Wave people into your lane on the highway, and, when someone lets you in, give them a wave of thanks in return. Never, ever blow your horn, even when the pickup truck in front of you is stopped for a long session of "talk story" right in the middle of the road.

Holoholo means to go out for the fun of it—an aimless stroll, ride, or drive. "Wheah you goin', braddah?" "Oh, holoholo." It's local speak for Sunday drive, no plan, it's not the destination but the journey. Try setting out without an itinerary. Learn to *shaka*: pinky and thumb extended, middle fingers curled in, waggle sideways. Eat white rice with everything. When someone says, "Aloha!" answer, "Aloha no!" ("And a real big aloha back to you"). And, as the locals say, "No make big body" ("Try not to act like you own the place").

KIDS AND FAMILIES

With dozens of adventures, discoveries, and fun-filled beach days, Hawaii is a blast for kids of all ages. Even better, the things to do here do not appeal only to small fry. The entire family, parents included, will enjoy surfing, discovering a waterfall in the rain forest, and snorkeling with sea turtles. And there are plenty of organized activities for kids that will free parents' time for a few romantic beach strolls.

Choosing a Place to Stay

Resorts: All the big resorts make kids' programs a priority, and it shows. When you are booking your room, ask about *keiki* (children's) menus at restaurants, free activities on the property, and pools and water parks built specifically for the younger set.

In Waikiki, your best bet for kids is the Hilton Hawaiian Village, where there's a large beach and loads of kids' programs. Another good choice is the Waikiki Beach Marriott Resort, which has a variety of programs for kids as well. Other options include the Waikiki Beach Hotel and the Sheraton Princess Kaiulani.

Condos: Condo and vacation rentals are a fantastic value for families vacationing in Hawaii. You can cook your own food, which is cheaper than eating out and sometimes easier (especially if you have a finicky eater in your group), and you'll get twice the space of a hotel room for about a quarter of the price. If you decide to go the condo route, be sure to ask about the size of the complex's pool (some try to pawn off a tiny soaking tub as a pool) and whether barbecues are available. One of the best parts of staying in your own place is having a sunset family barbecue by the pool or overlooking the ocean.

For the ultimate condo experience on Oahu, Marriott's Ko Olina Beach Club can't be beat. Sheltered beaches, four pools, barbecues, and children's play areas, combined with large kitchens and an on-site grocery store make this the best condo option for families. In Waikiki, the Castle Waikiki Shore is the only beach-front condo property. Outrigger Luana Waikiki offers barbecues, a pool, and recreational areas near Fort DeRussy on Waikiki Beach.

Ocean Activities

Hawaii is all about getting your kids outside—away from TV and video games. And who could resist the turquoise water, the promise of spotting dolphins or whales, or the fun of body boarding or surfing?

On the Beach: Most people like being in the water, but toddlers and school-age kids tend to be especially enamored of it. The swimming pool at your condo or hotel is always an option, but don't be afraid to hit the beach with a little one in tow. There are several beaches in Hawaii that are nearly as safe as a pool—completely protected bays with pleasant white-sand beaches and staffed by lifeguards. As always, use your judgment, and heed all posted signs and warnings.

In Waikiki, your best bets for young children are Kuhio Beach Park and Fort DeRussy Beach Park. Both are protected from a strong shore break and offer a wide stretch of sand. (And lifeguards are on duty.) On the windward side, your best bets are Kailua Beach Park, with its shady trees and good bathroom and shower facilities, or laid-back Lanikai Beach. North Shore beaches are recommended for children only in the summer months, and of these, Waimea Bay, with its wide stretch of sand and good facilities, ranks as the best for kids. (Don't let your kids

jump off the rock—a popular but very dangerous pastime.) On the leeward side of the island, KoOlina's protected coves are great for families with small children.

On the Waves: Surf lessons are a great idea for older kids, especially if mom and dad want a little quiet time. Beginner lessons are always on safe and easy waves and last anywhere from two to four hours.

Waikiki is *the* place for everyone to learn to surf, including kids. Some hotels, including the Waikiki Beach Marriott Resort & Spa, offer in-house surf schools. Or, for a unique experience, try Hawaiian Fire. These off-duty Honolulu firefighters teach water safety in addition to surfing in their two-hour lessons near Barber's Point (starting at $99).

The Underwater World: If your kids are ready to try snorkeling, Hawaii is a great place to introduce them to the underwater world. Even without the mask and snorkel, they'll be able to see colorful fish darting around coral reefs, and they may also spot endangered Hawaiian green sea turtles and dolphins at many of the island beaches.

On Oahu the quintessential snorkeling experience can be had at Hanauma Bay. After viewing an educational film about Hawaii's underwater world, and descending into a half-submerged volcano, kids have an opportunity not only to see hundreds of species of fish in protected waters but to enjoy a wide stretch of beach as well. In summer months only, Shark's Cove on the North Shore is an interesting experience for older kids who have learned the basics of snorkeling at Hanauma Bay.

Land Activities

In addition to beach experiences, Hawaii has rain forests, botanical gardens, numerous aquariums (Oahu and Maui take the cake), and even petting zoos and hands-on children's museums that will keep your kids entertained and out of the sun for a day.

Oahu is fortunate to have the largest variety of land-based experiences in the Islands. Kids can visit the Honolulu Zoo for a sleepover, touch fishy friends at the Waikiki Aquarium, help in a dolphin training session at Sea Life Park, or even learn to husk a coconut at the Polynesian Culture Center. For kids who need some room to roam, Hoomaluhia Botanical Garden offers wide-open spaces and a pond complete with ducks, while Kualoa Ranch is the place for horseback riding.

After Dark

At night, younger kids get a kick out of luau, and many of the shows incorporate young audience members, adding to the fun. The older kids might find it all a bit lame, but there are a handful of new shows in the Islands that are more modern, incorporating acrobatics, lively music, and fire dancers. If you're planning on hitting a luau with a teen in tow, we highly recommend going the modern route.

OAHU'S BEST BEACHES

The best thing about Oahu's beautiful beaches? Like snowflakes, no two are exactly alike. Some are wide, others are narrow. Some are protected by fringing reefs, and others have huge waves breaking right on shore. *All* are special.

Here are some of our favorite stretches of sand, where you can make your home away from home:

Best for Families

KoOlina, West (Leeward) Oahu. Four man-made lagoons are totally protected and offer great grassy spots to grab a nap. Plus, Disney's new resort is nearby if the kids get restless and need a Mickey fix.

White Plains, West (Leeward) Oahu. Not only are there are bathrooms, barbecues, and picnic tables here—there are even sleeping seals. What more could a kid want?

Best for Big Waves

Waimea Bay, the North Shore. In summer, snorkeling is great at this beach. But in winter, surf's up, so be careful if you don't know what you're doing. Pros flock here for contests—"the Eddie," a competition honoring big-wave-surfer Eddie Aikau, is held here only when waves are at least 20 feet—and fans flock to watch. Come early in the morning when there are waves and claim your seat on the dunes.

Haleiwa Alii Beach Park, the North Shore. The Vans Triple Crown of Surfing kicks off at this beach in November, and the small town of Haleiwa is a surf mecca. From board shops to galleries devoted to inside-the-tube photos, you'll experience the full range of surf lifestyle.

Best for Flying a Kite

Sandy Beach, Southeast Oahu. If you're afraid you'll break your neck bodysurfing in the waves here, retire to the shoreline and watch kites perform acrobatics in the gusts.

Kualoa Regional Park, Windward Oahu. This expansive park gives campers and others plenty of space to spread out and take advantage of the wind with two-handed kites. Chinaman's Hat, an offshore island, provides a great backdrop.

Best for Soft Sand

Ala Moana Beach Park, Honolulu. Just steps away from food and shopping outlets, this beach offers extraordinarily fine sand, though there's little shade. When you get warm, the equally smooth water beckons.

Lanikai Beach Park, Windward Oahu. This spot and adjacent Kailua Beach Park have powdery white sand and some trees for shade. But good luck finding a parking spot on weekends.

Best for Watching the Sun Rise and Set

Bellows Beach, Southeast Oahu (Sunrise). Try camping out (weekends only) at this eastward-facing beach so you can catch the earliest rays. Nearby Waimanalo Beach Park offers another option.

Sunset Beach, the North Shore (Sunset). The name says it all. From here, you can see all the way down the North Shore toward Kaena Point in the west, and enjoy the last rays before the sun dips below the horizon.

TOP 10 HAWAIIAN FOODS TO TRY

Food in Hawaii is a reflection of the state's diverse cultural makeup and tropical location. Fresh seafood, organic fruits and vegetables, free-range beef, and locally grown products are the hallmarks of Hawaii regional cuisine. Its preparations are drawn from across the Pacific Rim, including Japan, the Philippines, Korea, and Thailand—and "local food" is a cuisine in its own right. Don't miss Hawaiian-grown coffee, either, whether it's smooth Kona from the Big Island or coffee grown on other islands.

Saimin

The ultimate hangover cure and the perfect comfort food during Hawaii's mild winters, *saimin* ranks at the top of the list of local favorites. In fact, it's one of the few dishes deemed truly local, having been highlighted in cookbooks since the 1930s. Saimin is an Asian-style noodle soup so ubiquitous, it's even on McDonald's menus statewide. In mom-and-pop shops, a large melamine bowl is filled with homemade *dashi*, or chicken broth, and wheat-flour noodles and then topped off with strips of omelet, green onions, bright pink fish cake and *char siu* (Chinese roast pork) or canned luncheon meat, such as SPAM. Add shoyu and chili pepper water, lift your chopsticks and slurp away.

SPAM

Speaking of SPAM, Hawaii's most prevalent grab-and-go snack is SPAM *musubi*. Often displayed next to cash registers at groceries and convenience stores, the glorified rice ball is rectangular, topped with a slice of fried SPAM and wrapped in *nori* (seaweed). Musubi is a bite-sized meal in itself. But just like sushi, the rice part hardens when refrigerated. So it's best to gobble it up, right after purchase.

Hormel Company's SPAM actually deserves its own recognition—way beyond as a mere musubi topping. About 5 million cans are sold per year in Hawaii and the Aloha State even hosts a festival in its honor. It's inexpensive protein and goes a long way when mixed with rice, scrambled eggs, noodles or, well, anything. The spiced luncheon meat gained popularity in World War II days, when fish was rationed. Gourmets and those with aversions to salt, high cholesterol, or high blood pressure may cringe at the thought of eating it, but SPAM in Hawaii is here to stay.

Manapua

Another savory snack is *manapua*, fist-sized dough balls fashioned after Chinese *bao* (a traditional Chinese bun) and stuffed with fillings such as *char siu* (Chinese barbeque) pork and then steamed. Many mom-and-pop stores sell them in commercial steamer display cases along with pork hash and other dim sum. Modern-day fillings include curry chicken.

Fresh Ahi or Tako Poke

There's nothing like fresh ahi or *tako* (octopus) *poke* to break the ice at a backyard party, except, of course, the cold beer handed to you from the cooler. The perfect pupu, poke (pronounced poh-kay) is basically raw seafood cut into bite-sized chunks and mixed with everything from green onions to roasted and ground kukui nuts. Other variations include mixing the fish with chopped round onion, sesame oil, seaweed, and chili pepper water. Shoyu is the constant. These days, grocery stores sell a rainbow of varieties such as kimchi crab and anything goes, from adding mayonnaise to tobiko caviar. Fish lovers who want to take it to the next level order

sashimi, the best cuts of ahi sliced and dipped in a mixture of shoyu and wasabi.

Tropical Fruits

Tropical fruits such as apple banana and strawberry papaya are plucked from trees in Island neighborhoods and eaten for breakfast—plain or with a squeeze of fresh lime. Give them a try; the banana tastes like an apple and the papaya's rosy flesh explains its name. Locals also love to add their own creative touches to exotic fruits. Green mangoes are pickled with Chinese five spice, and Maui Gold pineapples are topped with li hing mui powder (heck, even margarita glasses are rimmed with it). Green papaya is tossed in a Vietnamese salad with fish paste and fresh prawns.

Plate Lunch

It would be remiss not to mention the plate lunch as one of the most beloved dishes in Hawaii. It generally includes two scoops of sticky white rice, a scoop of macaroni or macaroni-potato salad, heavy on the mayo, and perhaps kimchi or *koko* (salted cabbage). There are countless choices of main protein such as chicken *katsu* (fried cutlet), fried mahimahi and beef tomato. The king of all plate lunches is the Hawaiian plate. The main item is laulau or kalua pig and cabbage along with poi, *lomilomi* salmon, chicken long rice, and sticky white rice.

Bento Box

The bento box gained popularity back in the plantation days, when workers toiled in the sugarcane fields. No one brought sandwiches to work then. Instead it was a lunch box with the ever-present steamed white rice, pickled *ume* (plum) to preserve the rice, and main meats such as fried chicken or fish. Today, many stores sell prepackaged bentos or you may go to an *okazuya* (Japanese deli) with a hot buffet counter and create your own.

Malasadas

The Portuguese have contributed much to Hawaii cuisine in the form of sausage, soup, and sweetbread. But their most revered food is *malasadas*, hot, deep-fried doughnuts rolled in sugar. Malasadas are crowd-pleasers. Buy them by the dozen, hot from the fryer, placed in brown paper bags to absorb the grease. Or bite into gourmet malasadas at restaurants, filled with vanilla or chocolate cream.

Shave Ice

Much more than just a snow cone, shave ice is what locals crave after a blazing day at the beach or a hot-as-Hades game of soccer. If you're lucky, you'll find a neighborhood store that hand-shaves the ice, but it's rare. Either way, the counter person will ask you first if you'd like ice cream and/or adzuki beans scooped into the bottom of the cone or cup. Then they shape the ice to a giant mound and add colorful fruit syrups. First-timers should order the Rainbow, of course.

Crack Seed

There are dozens of varieties of crack seed in dwindling specialty shops and at the drug stores. Chinese call the preserved fruits and nuts *see mui* but somehow the Pidgin English version is what Hawaiians prefer. Those who like hard candy and salty foods will love li hing mangoes and rock salt plums, and those with an itchy throat will feel relief from the lemon strips. Peruse large glass jars of crack seed sold in bulk or smaller hanging bags—the latter make good gifts to give to friends back home.

HAWAII AND THE ENVIRONMENT

Sustainability. It's a word rolling off everyone's tongues these days. In a place known as the most remote island chain in the world (check your globe), Hawaii relies heavily on the outside world for food and material goods—estimates put the percentage of food arriving on container ships as high as 90. Like many places, though, efforts are afoot to change that. And you can help.

Shop Local Farms and Markets

From Kauai to the Big Island, farmers' markets are cropping up, providing a place for growers to sell fresh fruits and vegetables. There is no reason to buy imported mangoes, papayas, avocadoes, and bananas at grocery stores, when the ones you'll find at farmers' markets are not only fresher and bigger but tastier, too. Some markets allow the sale of fresh-packaged foods—salsa, say, or smoothies—and the on-site preparation of food—like pork *laulau* (pork, beef and fish or chicken with taro, or luau, leaves wrapped and steamed in *ti* leaves) or roasted corn on the cob—so you can make your run to the market a dining experience.

Not only is the locavore movement vibrantly alive at farmers' markets, but Hawaii's top chefs are sourcing more of their produce—and fish, beef, chicken, and cheese—from local providers as well. You'll notice this movement on restaurant menus, featuring Kilauea greens or Hamakua tomatoes or locally caught mahimahi.

And while most people are familiar with Kona coffee farm tours on Big Island, if you're interested in the growing slow-food movement in Hawaii, you'll be heartened to know many farmers are opening up their operations for tours—as well as sumptuous meals.

Support Hawaii's Merchants

Food isn't the only sustainable effort in Hawaii. Buying local goods like art and jewelry, Hawaiian heritage products, crafts, music, and apparel is another way to "green up" the local economy. The County of Kauai helps make it easy with a program called **Kauai Made** (⊕ *www.kauaimade.net*), which showcases products made on Kauai, by Kauai people, using Kauai materials. The Maui Chamber of Commerce does something similar with **Made in Maui** (⊕ *www.madeinmaui.com*). Think of both as the Good Housekeeping Seal of Approval for locally made goods.

Then there are the crafty entrepreneurs who are diverting items from the trash heap by repurposing garbage. Take Oahu's **Muumuu Heaven** (⊕ *www.muumuuheaven.com*). They got their start by reincarnating vintage aloha apparel into hip new fashions. **Kini Beach** (⊕ *www.kinibeach.com*) collects discarded grass mats and plastic inflatables from Waikiki hotels and uses them to make pricey bags and totes.

Choose Green Tour Operators

Conscious decisions when it comes to Island activities go a long way to protecting Hawaii's natural world. The **Hawaii Ecotourism Association** (⊕ *www.hawaiiecotourism.org*) recognizes tour operators for, among other things, their environmental stewardship. The **Hawaii Tourism Authority** (⊕ *www.hawaiitourismauthority.org*) recognizes outfitters for their cultural sensitivity. Winners of these awards are good choices when it comes to guided tours and activities.

OAHU'S BEST OUTDOOR ADVENTURES

In a place surrounded by the ocean, water sports abound. Surfing. Snorkeling. Scuba diving. Hawaii has it all—and more. But that's just the sea. Interior mountains and valleys offer a never-ending stream of other outdoor adventures. Here are our picks for the best water and land adventures.

✷ Take in the View atop Diamond Head
You won't get off the beaten path on this hike, but the well-worn route to the top of Hawaii's most famous crater will get your heart racing, especially when you reach the steep stairs near the top. The views are worth the climb—on clear days you'll gaze over Honolulu, Waikiki, and the Pacific Ocean. Bring water, as this trail is hot and sunny.

Dive and Snorkel at Shark's Cove
Some of the best things in life require a wait. That's the case with Shark's Cove—you have to wait for summer until it's safe to enter the water and swim with an amazing array of marine life, thanks to the large boulders and coral heads dotting the seafloor and forming small caves and ledges. This is both a spectacular shore dive and snorkeling destination in one—perfect for the diver–snorkeler couple.

Bike the Aiea Loop Trail
This 4.5-mile, single-track loop trail offers some of the most fun mountain biking in central Oahu. Although it's listed as an intermediate trail, some sections are a bit technical, with steep drop-offs. We recommend it for the weekend warrior who has a bit more experience. Caution: do not attempt in wet weather.

Golf at The Royal Hawaiian Golf Club
Carved out of the middle of a tropical rain forest, this peaceful setting offers an antidote to the hustle and bustle of Waikiki. Bring your A game and a full bag, because club selection is key here. You'll want to hit every fairway.

Learn to Surf at Waikiki Beach
You've heard the age-old saying that goes, "When in Rome, do as the Romans do"? Well, when in Hawaii, surf. Surfing was once reserved for *alii* (royalty), but today it knows no class barrier. And there is no better place to learn than Waikiki, with its long and gentle rolling swells.

Hike to Kaena Point
For a raw and rugged look at Oahu's coastline, head to hot, dry Kaena Point. The 5-mile round-trip hike—you can also bike it—ends at the westernmost tip of the island, known in Hawaiian culture as the jumping-off point for souls departing this world for the next. Today, Laysan albatrosses nest here.

Watch Monster Waves at Waimea Bay
This is the beach that makes Hawaii famous every winter when monster waves and the world's best surfers roll in. Show up to watch, not partake. If the rest of us want to get in the water here, we have to wait until summer when the safe onshore break is great for novice bodysurfers.

ONLY IN HAWAII

Traveling to Hawaii is as close as an American can get to visiting another country while staying within the United States. There's much to learn and understand about the state's indigenous culture, the hundred years of immigration that resulted in today's blended society, and the tradition of aloha that has welcomed millions of visitors over the years.

Aloha Shirt

To go to Hawaii without taking an aloha shirt home is almost sacrilege. The first aloha shirts from the 1920s and 1930s—called "silkies"—were classic canvases of art and tailored for the tourists. Popular culture caught on in the 1950s, and they became a fashion craze. With the 1960s' more subdued designs, Aloha Friday was born, and the shirt became appropriate clothing for work, play, and formal occasions. Because of its soaring popularity, cheaper and mass-produced versions became available.

Hawaiian Quilt

Although ancient Hawaiians were already known to produce fine *kapa* (bark) cloth, the actual art of quilting originated from the missionaries. Hawaiians have created designs to reflect their own aesthetic, and bold patterns evolved over time. They can be pricey because the quilts are intricately made by hand and can take years to finish. These masterpieces are considered precious heirlooms that reflect the history and beauty of Hawaii.

Popular Souvenirs

Souvenir shopping can be intimidating. There's a sea of Island-inspired and often kitschy merchandise, so we'd like to give you a breakdown of popular and fun gifts that you might encounter and consider bringing home. If authenticity is important to you, be sure to check labels and ask shopkeepers. Museum shops are good places for authentic, Hawaiian-made souvenirs.

Fabrics. Purchased by the yard or already made into everything from napkins to bedspreads, modern Hawaiian fabrics make wonderful keepsakes.

Home accessories. Deck out your kitchen or dining room in festive luau style with bottle openers, pineapple mugs, tiki glasses, shot glasses, slipper and surfboard magnets, and salt-and-pepper shakers.

Lei and shell necklaces. From silk or polyester flower lei to kukui or puka shell necklaces, lei have been traditionally used as a welcome offering to guests (although the artificial ones are more for fun, as real flowers are always preferable).

Lauhala products. *Lauhala* weaving is a traditional Hawaiian art. The leaves come from the hala, or pandanus, tree and are hand-woven to create lovely gift boxes, baskets, bags, and picture frames.

Spa products. Relive your spa treatment at home with Hawaiian bath and body products, many of them manufactured with ingredients found only on the Islands.

Vintage Hawaii. You can find vintage photos, reproductions of vintage postcards or paintings, heirloom jewelry, and vintage aloha wear in many specialty stores.

Luau

The luau's origin, which was a celebratory feast, can be traced back to the earliest Hawaiian civilizations. In the traditional luau, the taboo or *kapu* laws were very strict, requiring men and women to eat separately. However, in 1819 King Kamehameha II broke the great taboo and shared a feast with women and commoners ushering in the modern-era luau. Today, traditional luau usually

commemorate a child's first birthday, graduation, wedding, or other family occasion. They also are a Hawaiian experience that most visitors enjoy, and resorts and other companies have incorporated the fire-knife dance and other Polynesian dances into their elaborate presentations.

Nose flutes

The nose flute is an instrument used in ancient times to serenade a lover. For the Hawaiians, the nose is romantic, sacred, and pure. The Hawaiian word for kiss is *honi*. Similar to an Eskimo's kiss, the noses touch on each side sharing one's spiritual energy or breath. The Hawaiian term, *ohe hano ihu*, simply translated to "bamboo," with which the instrument is made; "breathe," because one has to gently breathe through it to make soothing music; and "nose," as it is made for the nose and not the mouth.

Slack-Key Guitar and the Paniolo

Kihoalu, or slack-key music, evolved in the early 1800s when King Kamehameha III brought in Mexican and Spanish vaqueros to manage the overpopulated cattle that had run wild on the Islands. The vaqueros brought their guitars and would play music around the campfire after work. When they left, supposedly leaving their guitars to their new friends, the Hawaiian *paniolo*, or cowboys, began to infuse what they learned from the vaqueros with their native music and chants, and so the art of slack-key music was born.

Today, the paniolo culture thrives where ranchers have settled.

Ukulele

The word *ukulele* literally translates to the "the jumping flea" and came to Hawaii in the 1880s by way of the Portuguese and Spanish. Once a fading art form, today it brings international kudos as a solo instrument, thanks to tireless musicians and teachers who have worked hard to keep it by our fingertips.

One such teacher is Roy Sakuma. Founder of four ukulele schools and a legend in his own right, Sakuma and his wife Kathy produced Oahu's first Ukulele Festival in 1971. Since then, they've brought the tradition to the Big Island, Kauai, and Maui. The free event annually draws thousands of artists and fans from all over the globe.

Hula

"Hula is the language of the heart, therefore the heartbeat of the Hawaiian people." —Kalakaua, the Merrie Monarch. Thousands—from tots to seniors—devote hours each week to hula classes. All these dancers need some place to show off their stuff. The result is a network of hula competitions (generally free or very inexpensive) and free performances in malls and other public spaces. Many resorts offer hula instruction.

WEDDINGS AND HONEYMOONS

There's no question that Hawaii is one of the country's foremost honeymoon destinations. Romance is in the air here, and the white, sandy beaches, turquoise water, swaying palm trees, balmy tropical breezes, and perpetual sunshine put people in the mood for love. It's easy to understand why Hawaii is fast becoming a popular wedding destination as well, especially as the cost of airfare is often discounted, new resorts and hotels entice visitors, and as of January 2012 the state now recognizes and grants civil unions. A destination wedding is no longer exclusive to celebrities and the superrich. You can plan a traditional ceremony in a place of worship followed by a reception at an elegant resort, or you can go barefoot on the beach and celebrate at a luau. There are almost as many wedding planners in the Islands as real estate agents, which makes it oh-so-easy to wed in paradise, and then, once the knot is tied, stay and honeymoon as well.

The Big Day

Choosing the Perfect Place. When choosing a location, remember that you really have two choices to make: the ceremony location and where to have the reception, if you're having one. For the former, there are beaches, bluffs overlooking beaches, gardens, private residences, resort lawns, and, of course, places of worship. As for the reception, there are these same choices, as well as restaurants and even luau. If you decide to go outdoors, remember the seasons—yes, Hawaii has seasons. If you're planning a winter wedding outdoors, be sure you have a backup plan (such as a tent), in case it rains. Also, if you're planning an outdoor wedding at sunset—which is very popular—be sure you match the time of your ceremony to the time the sun sets at that time of year. If

you choose an indoor spot, be sure to ask for pictures of the location when you're planning. You don't want to plan a pink wedding, say, and wind up in a room that's predominantly red. Or maybe you do. The point is, it should be your choice.

Finding a Wedding Planner. If you're planning to invite more than a minister and your loved one to your wedding ceremony, seriously consider an on-island wedding planner who can help select a location, help design the floral scheme and recommend a florist as well as a photographer, help plan the menu and choose a restaurant, caterer, or resort, and suggest any Hawaiian traditions to incorporate into your ceremony. And more: Will you need tents, a cake, music? Maybe transportation and lodging? Many planners have relationships with vendors, providing packages—which mean savings.

If you're planning a resort wedding, most have on-site wedding coordinators; however, there are many independents around the Islands and even those who specialize in certain types of ceremonies—by locale, size, religious affiliation, and so on. A simple "Hawaii weddings" Google search will reveal dozens. What's important is that you feel comfortable with your coordinator. Ask for references—and call them. Share your budget. Get a proposal—in writing. Ask how long they've been in business, how much they charge, how often you'll meet with them, and how they select vendors. Request a detailed list of the exact services they'll provide. If your idea of your wedding doesn't match their services, try someone else. If you can afford it, you might want to meet the planner in person.

Getting Your License. The good news about marrying in Hawaii is that no waiting period, no residency or citizenship requirements, and no blood tests or shots are required. However, both the bride and groom must appear together in person before a marriage-license agent to apply for a marriage license. You'll need proof of age—the legal age to marry is 18. (If you're 19 or older, a valid driver's license will suffice; if you're 18, a certified birth certificate is required.) Upon approval, a marriage license is immediately issued and costs $60, cash only. After the ceremony, your officiant will mail the marriage license to the state. Approximately four months later, you will receive a copy in the mail. (For $10 extra, you can expedite this process. Ask your marriage-license agent when you apply.) For more detailed information, visit ⊕ *www.ehawaii.gov.*

Also—this is important—the person performing your wedding must be licensed by the Hawaii Department of Health, even if he or she is a licensed minister. Be sure to ask.

Wedding Attire. In Hawaii, basically anything goes, from long, formal dresses with trains to white bikinis. Floral sundresses are fine, too. For the men, tuxedos are not the norm; a pair of solid-colored slacks with a nice aloha shirt is. In fact, tradition in Hawaii for the groom is a plain white aloha shirt (they do exist) with slacks or long shorts and a colored sash around the waist. If you're planning a wedding on the beach, barefoot is the way to go.

If you decide to marry in a formal dress and tuxedo, you're better off making your selections on the mainland and hand-carrying them aboard the plane. Yes, it can be a pain, but ask your wedding-gown retailer to provide a special carrying bag.

After all, you don't want to chance losing your wedding dress in a wayward piece of luggage. And when it comes to fittings, again, that's something to take care of before you arrive in Hawaii.

Local customs. The most obvious traditional Hawaiian wedding custom is the lei exchange in which the bride and groom take turns placing a lei around the neck of the other—with a kiss. Bridal lei are usually floral, whereas the groom's is typically made of *maile*, a green leafy garland that drapes around the neck and is open at the ends. Brides often also wear a *lei poo*—a circular floral headpiece. Other Hawaiian customs include the blowing of the conch shell, hula, chanting, and Hawaiian music.

The Honeymoon

Do you want champagne and strawberries delivered to your room each morning? A breathtaking swimming pool in which to float? A five-star restaurant in which to dine? Then a resort is the way to go. If, however, you prefer the comforts of a home, try a bed-and-breakfast. A small inn is also good if you're on a tight budget or don't plan to spend much time in your room. On the other hand, maybe you want your own private home in which to romp naked—or just laze around recovering from the wedding planning. Maybe you want your own kitchen so you can whip up a gourmet meal for your loved one. In that case, a private vacation-rental home is the answer. Or maybe a condominium resort. That's another beautiful thing about Hawaii: the lodging accommodations are almost as plentiful as the beaches, and there's one that will perfectly match your tastes and your budget.

CRUISING THE ISLANDS

Cruising has become extremely popular in Hawaii. For first-time visitors, it's an excellent way to get a taste of all the Islands; and if you fall in love with one or even two Islands, you know how to plan your next trip.

Cruising to Hawaii

Carnival Cruises. They call them "fun ships" for a reason—Carnival is all about keeping you busy and showing you a good time, both on board and on shore. Great for families, Carnival always plans plenty of kid-friendly activities, and their children's program rates high with the little critics. Carnival offers itineraries starting in Los Angeles, Ensenada, Vancouver, and Honolulu. Their ships stop on Maui (Kahului), the Big Island (Kailua-Kona and Hilo), Oahu, and Kauai. ☎ 888/227–6482 ⊕ www.carnival.com.

Holland America. The grande dame of cruise lines, Holland America has a reputation for service and elegance. Holland America's Hawaii cruises leave from and return to San Diego, California, with a brief stop at Ensenada. In Hawaii, the ship ties up at port in Maui (Lahaina), the Big Island (Hilo), Oahu, and Kauai (Nawiliwili). Holland America also offers longer itineraries (30-plus days) that include Hawaii, Tahiti, and the Marquesas and depart from or return to San Diego, Seattle, or Vancouver. ☎ 877/932–4259 ⊕ www.hollandamerica.com.

Princess Cruises. Princess strives to offer affordable luxury. Their prices start out a little higher, but you get more bells and whistles (affordable balcony rooms, nicer decor, more restaurants to choose from, personalized service). They're not fantastic for kids, but they do a great job of keeping teenagers occupied. *Golden Princess, Sapphire Princess,* and *Star Princess*

sail from Los Angeles on a 14-day round-trip voyage with calls at Hilo on the Big Island, Honolulu, Kauai, and Lahaina on Maui, plus Ensenada, Mexico. There are also 15-day cruises out of San Francisco. In addition, the line offers longer cruises—up to 29 day—that include stops in Hawaii and the South Pacific. ☎ 800/774–6237 ⊕ www.princess.com.

Cruising within Hawaii

American Safari Cruises. Except for the summer months when its yachts cruise Alaska, American Safari Cruises offers round-trip, eight-day, seven-night interisland cruises departing from Lahaina, Maui. The *Safari Explorer* accommodates only 36 passengers; its smaller size allows it to dock at Moloka'i and Lana'i in addition to a stop on the island of Hawaii. The cruise is all-inclusive, with even shore excursions, water activities, and a massage included as part of the deal. ☎ 888/862–8881 ⊕ www.americansafaricruises.com.

Hawaii Nautical. Offering a completely different sort of experience, Hawaii Nautical provides private multiple-day interisland cruises on their catamarans, yachts, and sailboats. Prices are higher, but service is completely personal, right down to the itinerary. ☎ 808/234–7245 ⊕ www.hawaiinautical.com.

Norwegian Cruise Lines. Norwegian is the only major operator to offer interisland cruises in Hawaii. *Pride of America* sails year-round and offers seven day itineraries within the Islands stopping on Maui, Oahu, the Big Island (Hilo), and overnighting on Kauai. The ship has a vintage Americana theme and a big family focus with lots of connecting staterooms and suites. ☎ 800/327–7030 ⊕ www.ncl.com.

Exploring Oahu

WORD OF MOUTH

"[W]e rented a car for just one day and were able to drive all the way around the island stopping here and there. [We w]ent to the Pineapple plantation, Haleiwa, Waimea, then around the other side and back to Honolulu. [It was w]orth the time to see more than just the million souvenir shops in Waikiki."

—oregonmom

Updated by
Michael Levine

Oahu is one-stop Hawaii—all the allure of the Islands in a chop-suey mix that has you kayaking around offshore islets by day and sitting in a jazz club 'round midnight, all without ever having to take another flight or repack your suitcase. It offers both the buzz of modern living in jam-packed Honolulu (the state's capital) and the allure of slow-paced island life on its northern and eastern shores. It is, in many ways, the center of the Hawaiian universe.

There are more museums, staffed historic sites, and walking tours here than you'll find on any other island. And only here do a wealth of renovated buildings and well-preserved neighborhoods so clearly spin the story of Hawaii's history. It's the only place to experience island-style urbanity, since there are no other true cities in the state. And yet you can get as lost in the rural landscape and be as laid-back as you wish.

Oahu is home to Waikiki, the most famous Hawaiian beach, as well as some of the world's most famous surf on the North Shore and the Islands' best known historical site—Pearl Harbor. If it's isolation, peace, and quiet you want, Oahu might not be for you, but if you'd like a bit of spice with your piece of paradise, this island provides it.

GEOLOGY

Encompassing 597 square miles, Oahu is the third-largest island in the Hawaiian chain. Scientists believe the island was formed about 4 million years ago by two volcanoes: Waianae and Koolau. Waianae, the older of the two, created the mountain range on the western side of the island, whereas Koolau shapes the eastern side. Central Oahu is an elevated plateau bordered by the two mountain ranges, with Pearl Harbor to the south. Several of Oahu's most famous natural landmarks, including Diamond Head and Hanauma Bay, are tuff rings and cinder cones formed during a renewed volcanic stage (roughly 1 million years ago).

Kick back in a hammock and gaze off at Diamond Head in the distance.

FLORA AND FAUNA

The eastern (Koolau) side of Oahu is much cooler and wetter than the western side of the island, which tends to be dry and arid. The island's official flower, the little orange *ilima,* grows predominantly in the east, but lei throughout the island incorporate *ilima.* Numerous tropical fish call the reef at Hanauma Bay home, migrating humpback whales can be spotted off the coast past Waikiki and Diamond Head from December through April, spinner dolphins pop in and out of the island's bays, and dozens of islets off Oahu's eastern coast provide refuge for endangered seabirds.

HISTORY

Oahu is the most populated island because early tourism to Hawaii started here. Although Kilauea volcano on Hawaii was a tourist attraction in the late 1800s, it was the building of the Moana Hotel on Waikiki Beach in 1901 and subsequent advertising of Hawaii to wealthy San Franciscans that really fueled tourism in the islands. Oahu was drawing tens of thousands of guests yearly when, on December 7, 1941, Japanese Zeros appeared at dawn to bomb Pearl Harbor. Though tourism understandably dipped during the war (Waikiki Beach was fenced with barbed wire), the subsequent memorial only seemed to attract more visitors, and Oahu remains hugely popular with tourists—especially the Japanese—to this day.

GUIDED TOURS

Guided tours are convenient; you don't have to worry about finding a parking spot or getting admission tickets. Most of the tour guides have taken special classes in Hawaiian history and lore, and many are certified by the state of Hawaii. On the other hand, you won't have the freedom to proceed at your own pace, nor will you have the ability to take a detour trip if something else catches your attention.

BUS AND VAN TOURS

Polynesian Adventure. This company leads tours of Pearl Harbor and also offers a circle-island tour by motor coach, van, and minicoach. Best of all, kids are free on many tours. ☎ *808/833–3000* ⊕ *www.polyad.com.*

Roberts Hawaii. Choose from a large selection of tours, including downtown Honolulu ghost tours, underwater submarine tours, and the more traditional Pearl Harbor excursions. Tours are conducted via everything from vans to president-worthy limousines. ☎ *808/539–9400* ⊕ *www.robertshawaii.com.*

THEME TOURS

Discover Hawaii Tours. In addition to circle-island and other Oahu-based itineraries on motor and minicoaches, this company can also get you from Waikiki to the lava flows of the Big Island or to Maui's Hana Highway and back in one day. ☎ *808/690–9050* ⊕ *www.discoverhawaiitours.com.*

E Noa Tours. Certified tour guides conduct circle-island, Pearl Harbor, and shopping tours. ☎ *808/591–2561* ⊕ *www.enoa.com.*

Home of the Brave Hawaii Victory Tour. Perfect for military history buffs, these narrated tours visit Oahu's military bases and the National Memorial Cemetery of the Pacific. Tours also include a visit to the company's private museum, which displays artifacts and memorabilia from World War II. ☎ *808/396–8112* ⊕ *www.pearlharborhq.com.*

HONOLULU

Here is Hawaii's only true metropolis, its seat of government, center of commerce and shipping, entertainment and recreation mecca, a historic site and an evolving urban area—conflicting roles that engender endless debate and controversy. For the visitor, Honolulu is an everyman's delight: hipsters and scholars, sightseers and foodies, nature lovers and culture vultures all can find their bliss.

Once there was the broad bay of Mamala and the narrow inlet of Kou, fronting a dusty plain occupied by a few thatched houses and the great Pakaka *heiau* (shrine). Nosing into the narrow passage in the early 1790s, British sea captain William Brown named the port Fair Haven. Later, Hawaiians would call it Honolulu, or "sheltered bay." As shipping traffic increased, the settlement grew into a Western-style town of streets and buildings, tightly clustered around the single freshwater source, Nuuanu Stream. Not until piped water became available in the early 1900s did Honolulu spread across the greening plain. Long before that, however, Honolulu gained importance when King Kamehameha

I reluctantly abandoned his home on the Big Island to build a chiefly compound near the harbor in 1804 to better protect Hawaiian interests from the Western incursion.

Two hundred years later, the entire island is, in a sense, Honolulu—the City and County of Honolulu. The city has no official boundaries, extending across the flatlands from Pearl Harbor to Waikiki and high into the hills behind.

DOWNTOWN HONOLULU

Honolulu's past and present play a delightful counterpoint throughout the downtown sector, which is approximately 6 miles east of Honolulu International Airport. Postmodern glass-and-steel office buildings look down on the Aloha Tower, built in 1926 and, until the early 1960s, the tallest structure in Honolulu. Hawaii's history is told in the architecture of these few blocks: the cut-stone turn-of-the-20th-century storefronts of Merchant Street, the gracious white-columned American-Georgian manor that was the home of the Islands' last queen, the jewel-box palace occupied by the monarchy before it was overthrown, the Spanish-inspired stucco and tile-roofed Territorial Era government buildings, and the 21st-century glass pyramid of the First Hawaiian Bank Building.

GETTING HERE AND AROUND

To reach downtown Honolulu from Waikiki by car, take Ala Moana Boulevard to Alakea Street and turn right; three blocks up on the right, between South King and Hotel, there's a municipal parking lot in Alii Place on the right. There are also public parking lots (75¢ per half hour for the first two hours) in buildings along Alakea, Smith, Beretania, and Bethel streets (Gateway Plaza on Bethel Street is a good choice). The best parking downtown, however, is metered street parking along Punchbowl Street—when you can find it.

Another option is to take Route 19 or 20 of highly popular and convenient TheBus to the Aloha Tower Marketplace, or take a trolley from Waikiki.

WALKING TOURS

American Institute of Architects (AIA) Downtown Walking Tour. See Downtown Honolulu from an architectural perspective. Advance reservations are required. Tours are offered only on Saturday. ☎ *808/545–4242* ⊕ *www. aiahonolulu.org.*

Hawaii Geographic Society. A number of downtown Honolulu historic-temple and archaeology walking tours are available from the society. Email the organization for more information. ☎ *808/538–3952* ✑ *hawaiigeographicsociety@gmail.com* ✉ *$15.*

TIMING

Plan a couple of hours for exploring downtown's historic buildings, more if you're taking a guided tour or walk. The best time to visit is in the cool and relative quiet of morning or on the weekends when downtown is all but deserted except for the historic sites.

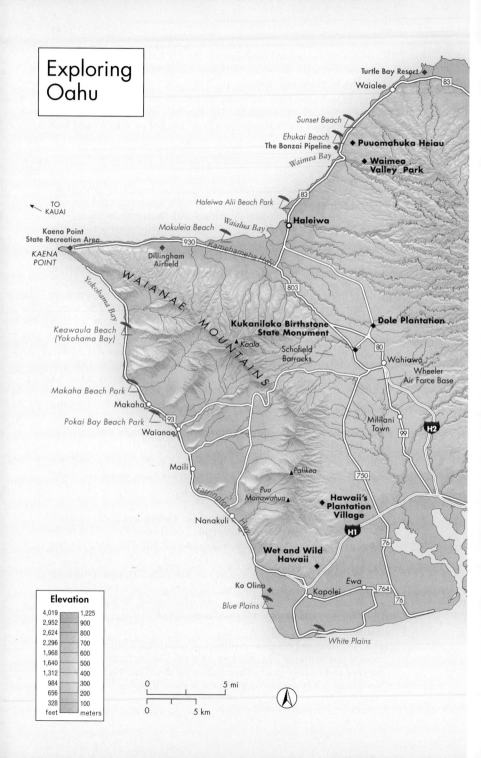

Exploring Oahu

Turtle Bay Resort ◆
Waialee ○   83

Sunset Beach

Ehukai Beach
The Bonzai Pipeline   ◆ **Puuomahuka Heiau**

Waimea Bay   ◆ **Waimea
                              Valley Park**

← TO
KAUAI

Haleiwa Alii Beach Park
                            83
Waialua Bay
Mokuleia Beach   ○ **Haleiwa**

**Kaena Point
State Recreation Area**   930
*KAENA
POINT*   *Kamehameha Hwy*

◆ *Dillingham
Airfield*   803

Yokohama Bay

W A I A N A E   **Dole Plantation** ◆

*Keawaula Beach
(Yokohama Bay)*   **Kukaniloko Birthstone
                             State Monument**   80
              Kaala   ○ Wahiawa
         M O U N T A I N S   Schofield
                                  Barracks   Wheeler
                                                       Air Force Base

Makaha Beach Park
                Makaha ○   Mililani
                                                  Town   H2
Pokai Bay Beach Park   93
         Waianae ○   99

                Maili ○   ▲ *Palikea*
                                                   750
                        Farrington Hwy
                                  *Puu
                              Manawahua* ▲   **Hawaii's
                                                   Plantation
              Nanakuli ○   Village**
                                                   H1
                                                        76
                         **Wet and Wild
                            Hawaii**   ◆

                Ko Olina ◆   *Ewa*   764
                         Kapolei ○
            Blue Plains   76

                        White Plains

Elevation

feet	meters
4,019	1,225
2,952	900
2,624	800
2,296	700
1,968	600
1,640	500
1,312	400
984	300
656	200
328	100
feet	meters

0   5 mi

0   5 km

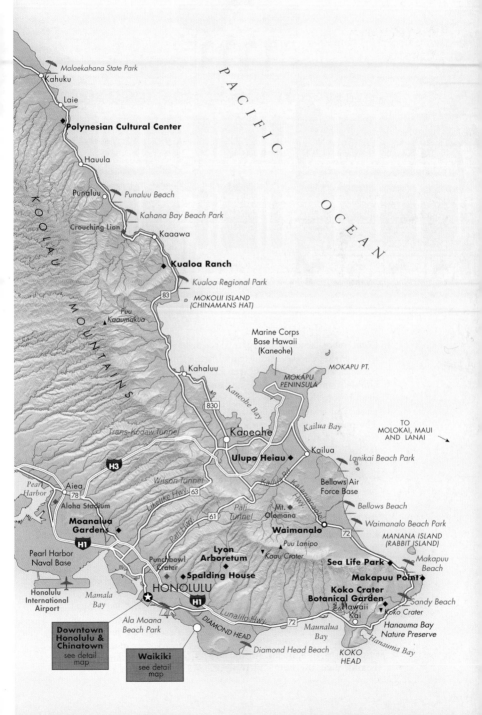

Maloekahana State Park

Kahuku

Laie

Polynesian Cultural Center

Hauula

Punaluu   Punaluu Beach

Kahana Bay Beach Park

Crouching Lion   Kaaawa

Kualoa Ranch

83   Kualoa Regional Park

MOKOLII ISLAND
(CHINAMANS HAT)

Puu
Kaaumakua

KOOLAU   MOUNTAINS

PACIFIC

OCEAN

Marine Corps
Base Hawaii
(Kaneohe)

MOKAPU PT.

MOKAPU
PENINSULA

Kahaluu

830

Kaneohe Bay

Kailua Bay

TO
MOLOKAI, MAUI
AND LANAI

Trans-Koolau Tunnel

Kaneohe

Ulupo Heiau   Kailua

Lanikai Beach Park

H3

Wilson Tunnel

Likelike Hwy   63

Pali
Tunnel

Bellows Air
Force Base

Pearl
Harbor

Aiea

78

Pali Hwy

61

Mt.
Olomana

Waimanalo

Bellows Beach

Waimanalo Beach Park

72

Aloha Stadium

**Moanalua
Gardens**

H1

Puu Lanipo

Puu Lanipo

Kaau Crater

MANANA ISLAND
(RABBIT ISLAND)

Pearl Harbor
Naval Base

Punchbowl
Crater

**Lyon
Arboretum**

Spalding House

Sea Life Park

Makapuu
Beach

Makapuu Point

Honolulu
International
Airport

Mamala
Bay

HONOLULU

H1

**Koko Crater
Botanical Garden**

Hawaii
Kai

Sandy Beach

Koko Crater

Ala Moana
Beach Park

DIAMOND HEAD

Lunalilo Hwy

72

Maunalua
Bay

Hanauma Bay
Nature Preserve

**Downtown
Honolulu &
Chinatown**
see detail
map

Waikiki
see detail
map

Diamond Head Beach

KOKO
HEAD

Hanauma Bay

Take a guided tour of Iolani Palace, said to be America's only royal residence, built in 1882.

TOP ATTRACTIONS

Fodor's Choice ★

Iolani Palace. America's only royal residence was built in 1882 on the site of an earlier palace, and it contains the thrones of King Kalakaua and his successor (and sister) Queen Liliuokalani. Bucking the stereotype of simple island life, the palace had electricity and telephone lines installed even before the White House. Downstairs galleries showcase the royal jewelry and kitchen and offices restored to the glory of the monarchy. The palace is open for guided or self-guided audio tours, and reservations are recommended. ■ TIP→ **If you're set on taking a guided tour, call for reservations a few days in advance.** The gift shop was formerly the Iolani Barracks, built to house the Royal Guard. ⊠ *King and Richards Sts., Downtown Honolulu* 🕿 *808/522–0832* ⊕ *www.iolanipalace. org* 🖂 *$20 guided tour, $12 audio tour, $6 downstairs galleries only* 🕑 *Mon.–Sat. 9–4, guided tours every 15 min 9–11:15, self-guided audio tours 11:45–3:30.*

Kamehameha I Statue. Paying tribute to the Big Island chieftain who united all the warring Hawaiian Islands into one kingdom at the turn of the 18th century, this statue, which stands with one arm outstretched in welcome, is one of three originally cast in Paris, France, by American sculptor T. R. Gould. The original statue, lost at sea and replaced by this one, was eventually salvaged and is now in Kapaau, on the Big Island, near the king's birthplace.

WORD OF MOUTH

"My kids enjoyed the Bishop Museum and Iolani Palace, which bills itself as 'the only official state residence of royalty in the United States.'" —Anonymous

FUN THINGS TO DO IN HONOLULU

- Grab some green tea in Chinatown.

- Tickle a tiki at La Mariana Sailing Club bar and restaurant.

- Visit a goddess at Kuan Yin Temple.

- Bow to the throne in the only royal palace in the United States.

- Encounter an artist at First Friday in Nuuanu's gallery district.

- Shop 'til you drop in the funky neighborhoods of Moiliili and Kaimuki.

- Study the Hawaiian stars at Bishop Museum planetarium.

- Hum along with a Hawaiian hymn during Sunday services at Kawaiahao Church.

- Hang from the heavens parasailing off the Honolulu shore.

- Eat Navy-style grub on the "Mighty Mo."

Each year on the king's birthday, June 11, the more famous copy is draped in fresh lei that reach lengths of 18 feet and longer. A parade proceeds past the statue, and Hawaiian civic clubs, the women in hats and impressive long *holoku* dresses and the men in sashes and cummerbunds, pay honor to the leader whose name means "The Lonely One." ⊠ *417 S. King St., outside Aliiolani Hale, Downtown Honolulu.*

Kawaiahao Church. Fancifully called Hawaii's Westminster Abbey, this 14,000-coral-block house of worship witnessed the coronations, weddings, and funerals of generations of Hawaiian royalty. Each of the building's coral blocks was quarried from reefs offshore at depths of more than 20 feet and transported to this site. Interior woodwork was created from the forests of the Koolau Mountains. The upper gallery has an exhibit of paintings of the royal families. The graves of missionaries and of King Lunalilo are adjacent. Services in English and Hawaiian are held each Sunday, and the church members are exceptionally welcoming, greeting newcomers with lei; their affiliation is United Church of Christ. Although there are no guided tours, you can look around the church at no cost. ⊠ *957 Punchbowl St., at King St., Downtown Honolulu* ☎ *808/522–1333* ☜ *Free* ⊙ *Service in English and Hawaiian Sun. at 9 am.*

WORTH NOTING

Aloha Tower Marketplace. In two stories of shops and kiosks you can find Island-inspired clothing, jewelry, art, and home furnishings. The Marketplace also has indoor and outdoor restaurants and live entertainment. For a bird's-eye view of this working harbor, take a free ride up to the observation deck of Aloha Tower. Cruise ships dock at piers 9 and 10 alongside the Marketplace and are often greeted and sent out to sea with music and hula dancing at the piers' end. ⊠ *1 Aloha Tower Dr., at Piers 10 and 11, Downtown Honolulu* ☎ *808/528–5700 entertainment info* ⊕ *www.alohatower.com* ⊙ *Mon.–Sat. 9–9, Sun. 9–6; restaurants open later.*

Murphy's Bar & Grill. In a vintage brick building at the corner of Nuuanu Street and Merchant, Murphy's Bar & Grill is an old-fashioned Irish pub, sports bar, and kamaaina-style family restaurant. Comfort food is the order of the day. ⊠ *2 Merchant St., Downtown Honolulu* 🕾 *808/531–0422.*

Hawaii State Art Museum. Hawaii was one of the first states in the nation to legislate that a portion of the taxes paid on commercial building projects be set aside for the purchase of artwork. A few years ago, the state purchased an ornate period-style building (built to house the headquarters of a prominent developer) and dedicated 12,000 feet on the second floor to the art of Hawaii in all its ethnic diversity. The **Diamond Head Gallery** features new acquisitions and thematic shows from the State Art Collection and the State Foundation on Culture and the Arts. The **Ewa Gallery** houses more than 150 works documenting Hawaii's visual-arts history since becoming a state in 1959. Also included are a sculpture gallery as well as a café serving tasty, locally grown food, a gift shop, and educational meeting rooms. Check for occasional evening events. ⊠ *250 S. Hotel St., 2nd fl., Downtown Honolulu* 🕾 *808/586–0900 museum, 808/536–5900 restaurant* ⊕ *www.hawaii.gov/sfca* 🎫 *Free* ☉ *Tues.–Sat. 10–4.*

Hawaii State Capitol. The capitol's architecture is richly symbolic: the columns resemble palm trees, the legislative chambers are shaped like volcanic cinder cones, and the central court is open to the sky, representing Hawaii's open society. Replicas of the Hawaii state seal, each weighing 7,500 pounds, hang above both its entrances. The building, which in 1969 replaced Iolani Palace as the seat of government, is surrounded by reflecting pools, just as the Islands are embraced by water. A pair of statues, often draped in lei, flank the building: one of the beloved queen Liliuokalani and the other of the sainted Father Damien de Veuster. ⊠ *415 S. Beretania St., Downtown Honolulu* 🕾 *808/586–0178* 🎫 *Free* ☉ *Guided tours Mon., Wed., Fri. 1:30.*

Hawaii State Library. This beautifully renovated main library was built in 1913. Its Samuel M. Kamakau Reading Room, on the first floor in the Mauka (Hawaiian for "mountain") Courtyard, houses an extensive Hawaii and Pacific book collection and pays tribute to Kamakau, a missionary student whose 19th-century writings in English offer rare and vital insight into traditional Hawaiian culture. ⊠ *478 King St., Downtown Honolulu* 🕾 *808/586–3500* 🎫 *Free* ☉ *Mon. and Wed. 10–5, Tues., Fri., and Sat. 9–5, Thurs. 9–8.*

Historic Washington Place. For many years the home of Hawaii's governors, this white-columned mansion was built by sea captain John Dominis, whose son married the woman who became the Islands' last queen, Liliuokalani. Deposed by American-backed forces, the queen returned to the home—which is in sight of the royal palace—and lived there until her death. The nonprofit Washington Place Foundation operates the gracious estate now, opening it for tours weekday mornings and on special occasions. ⊠ *320 S. Beretania St., Downtown Honolulu* 🕾 *808/586–0248* ⊕ *www.washingtonplacefoundation.org* 🎫 *Donations accepted* ☉ *By appointment only, at least 48 hrs in advance Mon.–Fri. only.*

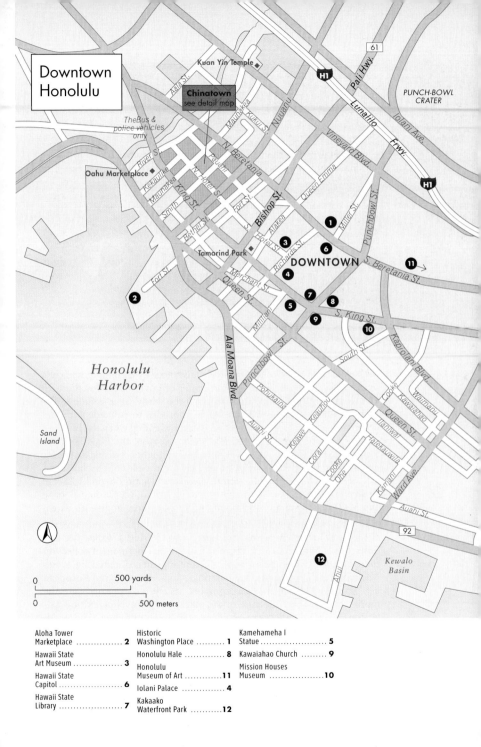

Downtown Honolulu

Kuan Yin Temple

Chinatown
see detail map

PUNCH-BOWL CRATER

61

H1

Pali Hwy.

Lunalilo Frwy.

Iolani Ave.

TheBus & police vehicles only

Vineyard Blvd.

H1

Aala St.

Maunakea St.

Kukui St.

Nuuanu

Queen Emma

River St.

N. Beretania

Pauahi

Oahu Marketplace

Kekaulike

N. Hotel St.

Miller St.

Punchbowl St.

Maunakea

King St.

Fort St.

Bishop St.

❶

Smith

Bethel St.

Alakea

S. Beretania St.

Tamarind Park

❸

Hotel St.

Richards St.

❻

⓫

Fort St.

❹

DOWNTOWN

❷

Merchant St.

Queen St.

❼

❺

❽

Militani

❾

S. King St.

Ala Moana Blvd.

South St.

Kapiolani Blvd.

❿

Honolulu Harbor

Punchbowl St.

Pohukaina

Keawe

Keaulou

Cooke

Queen St.

Kawaiahao

Waimanu

Ilaniwai

Halekauwila

Sand Island

Auahi St.

Coral

Cooke

Ohe

Kamani

Kamani

Ward Ave.

Auahi St.

92

⓬

Kewalo Basin

Auahi

0	500 yards
0	500 meters

Waikiki and Honolulu, looking west to Diamond Head, as seen from above.

Honolulu Hale. This Mediterranean Renaissance–style building was constructed in 1929 and serves as the center of government for the City and County of Honolulu. Stroll through the shady, open-ceiling lobby with exhibits of local artists, and time your visit to coincide with one of the free concerts sometimes offered in the evening, when the building stays open late. During the winter holiday season, the Hale becomes the focal point for the annual Honolulu City Lights, a display of lighting and playful holiday scenes spread around the Honolulu Hale campus. ⊠ *530 S. King St., Downtown Honolulu* ☎ *808/768–6622* ☜ *Free* ⏱ *Weekdays 8–4:30.*

Honolulu Museum of Art. Originally built around the collection of a Honolulu matron who donated much of her estate to the museum, the academy is housed in a maze of courtyards, cloistered walkways, and quiet, low-ceilinged spaces. There's an impressive permanent collection that includes Hiroshige's *ukiyo-e* Japanese prints, donated by James Michener; Italian Renaissance paintings; and American and European art. The newer Luce Pavilion complex, nicely incorporated into the more traditional architecture of the place, has a traveling-exhibit gallery, a Hawaiian gallery, an excellent café, and a gift shop. The Academy Theatre screens art films. This is also the jumping-off place for tours of Doris Duke's estate, Shangri-La (these tours are very much in demand and should be reserved far in advance). Call or check the website for special exhibits, concerts, and films. ⊠ *900 S. Beretania St., Downtown Honolulu* ☎ *808/532–8700* ⊕ *www.honolulumuseum.org* ☜ *$10, free 1st Wed. and 3rd Sun. of month; tours of Shangri-La $25 (includes transportation)* ⏱ *Tues.–Sat. 10–4:30, Sun. 1–5; Shangri-La tours Wed.–Sat. 8:30–1:30 by reservation only.*

Kakaako Waterfront Park. Rolling hills carpeted in lush green grass greet the visitor to Kakaako park. Popular with local families and perfect for watching the sunset or the Friday evening sailboat races, it has a seaside promenade following a lava-rock wall. Though it has no beach access, the Diamond Head end of the promenade is a great spot to watch surfers and Friday-evening fireworks off of Waikiki. ✉ *677 Ala Moana Blvd., Kakaako* ☎ *No phone* ☉ *7–7daily.*

Mission Houses Museum. The determined Hawaii missionaries arrived in 1820, gaining royal favor and influencing every aspect of island life. Their descendants became leaders in government and business. You can walk through their original dwellings, including Hawaii's oldest wooden structure, a white-frame house that was prefabricated in New England and shipped around the Horn. Certain areas of the museum may be seen only on a one-hour guided tour. Costumed docents give an excellent picture of what mission life was like. Rotating displays showcase such arts as Hawaiian quilting, portraits, even toys. ✉ *553 S. King St., Downtown Honolulu* ☎ *808/531–0481* ⊕ *www. missionhouses.org* 🖅 *$10* ☉ *Tues.–Sat. 10–4; guided tours hourly 11–3.*

> **BEST SNACKS IN CHINATOWN**
>
> A world of small, inexpensive restaurants exists within Chinatown, among them:
>
> ■ **Golden Palace:** $1.50 dim sum
>
> ■ **Yusura:** Homey Japanese
>
> ■ **Ba-Le:** Vietnamese sandwiches
>
> ■ **Urumi:** Japanese noodles
>
> ■ **Grand Café & Bakery:** Retro diner
>
> ■ **Mabuhay:** Filipino standards
>
> ■ **Sweet Basil:** Thai buffet

CHINATOWN

Chinatown's original business district was made up of dry-goods and produce merchants, tailors and dressmakers, barbers, herbalists, and dozens of restaurants. The meat, fish, and produce stalls remain, but the mix is heavier now on gift and curio stores, lei stands, jewelry shops, and bakeries, with a smattering of noodle makers, travel agents, Asian-language video stores, and dozens of restaurants.

The name *Chinatown* here has always been a misnomer. Though three-quarters of Oahu's Chinese lived closely packed in these 25 acres in the late 1800s, even then the neighborhood was half Japanese. Today, you hear Vietnamese and Tagalog as often as Mandarin and Cantonese, and there are voices of Japan, Singapore, Malaysia, Korea, Thailand, Samoa, and the Marshall Islands, as well.

Perhaps a more accurate name is the one used by early Chinese: *Wah Fau* ("Chinese port"), signifying a landing and jumping-off place. Chinese laborers, as soon as they completed their plantation contracts, hurried into the city to start businesses here. It's a launching point for today's immigrants, too: Southeast Asian shops almost outnumber Chinese; stalls carry Filipino specialties like winged beans and goat meat; and in one tiny space, knife-wielding Samoans skin coconuts to order.

In the half century after the first Chinese laborers arrived in Hawaii in 1851, Chinatown was a link to home for the all-male cadre of workers who planned to return to China rich and respected. Merchants not only sold supplies, they held mail, loaned money, wrote letters, translated documents, sent remittances to families, served meals, offered rough bunkhouse accommodations, and were the center for news, gossip, and socializing.

Though much happened to Chinatown in the 20th century—beginning in January 1900, when almost the entire neighborhood was burned to the ground to halt the spread of bubonic plague—it remains a bustling, crowded, noisy, and odiferous place bent primarily on buying and selling, and sublimely oblivious to its status as a National Historic District or the encroaching gentrification on nearby Nuuanu Avenue.

GETTING HERE AND AROUND

Chinatown occupies 15 blocks immediately north of downtown Honolulu—it's flat, compact, and very walkable.

TIMING

This area is easily explored in half a day. The best time to visit is morning, when the *popos* (grandmas) shop—it's cool out, and you can enjoy a cheap dim-sum breakfast. Chinatown is a seven-days-a-week operation. Sundays are especially busy with families sharing dim sum in raucous dining hall–size restaurants.

If you're here between January 20 and February 20, check local newspapers for Chinese New Year activities. Bakeries stock special sweets, stores and homes sprout bright-red scrolls, and lion dancers cavort through the streets feeding on *li-see* (money envelopes). The Narcissus Queen is chosen, and an evening street fair draws crowds.

GUIDED TOURS

Matthew Gray's Hawaii Food Tours. Gray's "Hole in the Wall Tour" culinary tour includes discussion of Hawaiian culinary history and the diversity of the food culture on the island, along with enjoying samples of local favorites from a variety of ethnic restaurants, markets, and bakeries as you walk through Chinatown. It's a great way to get a delicious taste of Hawaii's culture. ☎ *808/926–3663* ⊕ *www.hawaiifoodtours.com.*

TOP ATTRACTIONS

Chinatown Cultural Plaza. This sprawling multistory shopping square surrounds a courtyard with an incense-wreathed shrine and Moongate stage for holiday performances. The Chee Kung Tong Society has a beautifully decorated meeting hall here; a number of such *tongs* (meeting places) are hidden on upper floors in Chinatown. Outside, near the canal, local members of the community play cards and mah-jongg. ⊠ *100 N. Beretania St., Chinatown* ⊕ *www.chinatownhi.com/.*

Hawaiian Chinese Cultural Museum and Archives. Within the Maunakea Marketplace, the Hawaiian Chinese Cultural Museum and Archives displays historic photographs and artifacts. ⊠ *Maunakea Marketplace, 1120 Maunakea St., Chinatown* ☎ *808/524–3409* ▨ *$2* ☉ *Mon.–Sat. 10–2.*

Izumo Taisha Shrine. From Chinatown Cultural Plaza, cross a stone bridge to visit Okuninushi No Mikoto, a *kami* (god) who is believed in Shinto

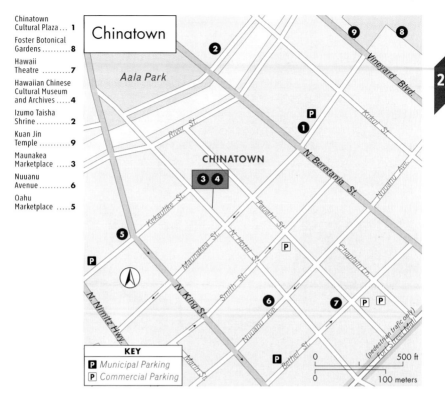

Chinatown

Aala Park

CHINATOWN

KEY
P *Municipal Parking*
P *Commercial Parking*

0   500 ft

0   100 meters

tradition to bring good fortune if properly courted (and thanked afterward). ⊠ *N. Kukui and Canal, Chinatown* ☎ *No phone.*

Kuan Yin Temple. A couple of blocks *mauka* (toward the mountains) from Chinatown is the oldest Buddhist temple in the Islands. Mistakenly called a goddess by some, Kuan Yin, also known as Kannon, is a *bodhisattva*—one who chose to remain on earth doing good even after achieving enlightenment. Transformed from a male into a female figure centuries ago, she is credited with a particular sympathy for women. You will see representations of her all over the Islands: holding a lotus flower (beauty from the mud of human frailty), as at the temple; pouring out a pitcher of oil (like mercy flowing); or as a sort of Madonna with a child. Visitors are permitted but be aware this is a practicing place of worship. ⊠ *170 N. Vineyard, Chinatown* ☎ *No phone.*

Maunakea Marketplace. On the corner of Maunakea and Hotel streets is this plaza surrounded by shops, an indoor market, and a food court. ■ **TIP**➔ **If you appreciate fine tea, visit the Tea Hut, an unpretentious counter inside a curio shop.** ⊠ *1120 Maunakea St., Chinatown* ☎ 808/524–3409.

★ **Oahu Marketplace.** Here is a taste of old-style Chinatown, where you're likely to be hustled aside as a whole pig (dead, of course) is wrestled through the crowd and where glassy-eyed fish of every size and hue lie stacked forlornly on ice. Try the bubble tea (juices and flavored teas

DID YOU KNOW?

Just north of downtown Honolulu is Chinatown, where you can explore temples, eat authentic cuisine, and watch Chinese New Year festivities.

2

SHOPPING IN CHINATOWN

Chinatown is rife with ridiculously inexpensive gifts: folding fans for $1 and coconut purses for $5 at **Maunakea Marketplace,** for example.

Curio shops sell everything from porcelain statues to woks, ginseng to Mao shoes. If you like to sew, or have a yen for a brocade cheongsam, visit the Hong Kong Supermarket in the Wo Fat Chop Sui building (at the corner of N. Hotel and Maunakea) for fresh fruit, crack seed (Chinese dried fruit popular for snacking), and row upon row of boxed, tinned delicacies with indecipherable names.

Chinatown Cultural Plaza offers fine-quality jade. Chinatown is Honolulu's lei center, with shops strung along Beretania and Maunakea; the locals have favorite shops where they're greeted by name. In spring, look for gardenia nosegays wrapped in ti leaves.

with tapioca bubbles inside) or pick up a bizarre magenta dragonfruit for breakfast. ⊠ *N. King St. at Kekaulike, Chinatown.*

WORTH NOTING

Foster Botanical Garden. Some of the trees in this botanical garden, open since 1931, date back to 1853 when Queen Kalama allowed a young German doctor to lease a portion of her land. Over 150 years later, you can see these trees and countless others along with bromeliads, orchids, and other tropical plants, some of which are rare or endangered. Look out in particular for the cannonball tree and the redwood-size Quipo tree. A docent-led tour is available Monday through Saturday at 1 pm (call for reservations). ⊠ *50 N. Vineyard Blvd., Chinatown* ☎ *808/522–7065* ⊕ *www1.honolulu.gov/parks/hbg/fbg.htm* 🎫 *$5* ☉ *Daily 9–4.*

Hawaii Theatre. Opened in 1922, this theater earned rave reviews for its neoclassical design, with Corinthian columns, marble statues, and plush carpeting and drapery. Nicknamed the "Pride of the Pacific," the facility was rescued from demolition in the early 1980s and underwent a $30 million renovation. Listed on both the State and National Register of Historic Places, it has become the centerpiece of revitalization efforts of Honolulu's downtown area. The 1,200-seat venue hosts concerts, theatrical productions, dance performances, and film screenings. ⊠ *1130 Bethel St., Chinatown* ☎ *808/528–0506* ⊕ *www.hawaiitheatre. com* 🎫 *$10* ☉ *1-hr guided tours Tues. at 11 am.*

Nuuanu Avenue. Here on Chinatown's main mauka-makai drag and on Bethel Street, which runs parallel, are clustered art galleries, restaurants, a wine shop, an antiques auctioneer, a dress shop or two, one tiny theater space (the Arts at Mark's Garage), and one historic stage (the Hawaii Theatre). **First Friday** art nights, when galleries stay open until 9 pm, draw crowds. Many stay later and crowd Chinatown's bars. If you like art and people-watching and are fortunate enough to be on Oahu the first Friday of the month, this event shouldn't be missed. ⊠ *Nuuanu Ave., Chinatown.*

WAIKIKI

Waikiki is approximately 3 miles east of downtown Honolulu.

A short drive from downtown Honolulu, Waikiki is Oahu's primary resort area. A mix of historic and modern hotels and condos front the sunny 2-mile stretch of beach, and many have clear views of Diamond Head to the west. The area is home to much of the island's dining, nightlife, and shopping scene—from posh boutiques to hole-in-the-wall eateries to craft booths at the International Marketplace.

Waikiki was once a favorite retreat for Hawaiian royalty. In 1901 the Moana Hotel debuted, introducing Waikiki as an international travel destination. The region's fame continued to grow when Duke Kahanamoku helped popularize the sport of surfing, offering lessons to visitors at Waikiki. You can see Duke immortalized in a bronze statue, with a surfboard, on Kuhio Beach. Today, there is a decidedly "urban resort" vibe here; streets are clean, gardens are manicured, and the sand feels softer than at beaches farther down the coast. There isn't much of a local culture—it's mainly tourist crowds—but you'll still find the relaxed surf-y vibe that has drawn people here for more than a century.

Diamond Head Crater (*see ⇨ Greater Honolulu and Diamond Head*) is perhaps Hawaii's most recognizable natural landmark. It got its name from sailors who thought they had found precious gems on its slopes; these later proved to be calcite crystals, or fool's gold. Hawaiians saw a resemblance in the sharp angle of the crater's seaward slope to the oddly shaped head of the ahi fish and so called it Leahi, though later they Hawaiianized the English name to Kaimana Hila. It is commemorated in a widely known hula—*"A ike i ka nani o Kaimana Hila, Kaimana Hila, kau mai i luna"* ("We saw the beauty of Diamond Head, Diamond Head set high above").

Kapiolani Park lies in the shadow of the crater. King David Kalakaua established the park in 1887, named it after his queen, and dedicated it "to the use and enjoyment of the people." Kapiolani Park is a 500-acre expanse where you can play all sorts of field sports, enjoy a picnic, see wild animals at the Honolulu Zoo, or hear live music at the Waikiki Shell or the Kapiolani Bandstand.

GETTING HERE AND AROUND

Bounded by the Ala Wai Canal on the north and west, the beach on the south, and the Honolulu Zoo to the east, Waikiki is compact and easy to walk around. TheBus runs multiple routes here from the airport and downtown Honolulu. By car, finding Waikiki from H1 can be tricky; look for the Punahou exit for the west end of Waikiki, and the King Street exit for the eastern end.

EXLPORING

Honolulu Zoo. To get a glimpse of the endangered *nene,* the Hawaii state bird, check out the zoo's Kipuka Nene Sanctuary. Though many animals prefer to remain invisible, particularly the elusive big cats, the monkeys appear to enjoy being seen and are a hoot to watch. It's best to get to the zoo right when it opens, since the animals are livelier in the cool of the morning. There are bigger and better zoos, but this one,

Continued on page 61

INS & OUTS OF WAIKIKI

Waikiki is all that is wonderful about a resort area, and all that is regrettable. It's where beach culture meets city life, with water sports, dining, shopping, and hotels—and crowds, too.

On the wonderful side: swimming, surfing, parasailing, and catamaran-riding steps from the street; the best nightlife in Hawaii; shopping from designer to dime stores; and experiences to remember: the heart-lifting rush the first time you stand up on a surfboard, and eating fresh grilled snapper as the sun slips into the sea. As to the regrettable: clogged streets, body-lined beaches, $5 cups of coffee, tacky T-shirts, $20 parking stalls, schlocky artwork, drunks, ceaseless construction—all rather brush the bloom from the plumeria.

Modern Waikiki is nothing like its original self, a network of streams, marshes, and islands that drained the inland valleys. The Ala Wai Canal took care of that in the 1920s. More recently, new landscaping, walkways, and a general attention to infrastructure have brightened a façade that had begun to fade.

But throughout its history, Waikiki has retained its essential character: an enchantment that cannot be fully explained and one that, though diminished by highrises, traffic, and noise, has not yet disappeared. Hawaiian royalty came here, and visitors continue to follow, falling in love with sharp-prowed Diamond Head, the sensuous curve of shoreline with its babysafe waves, and the strong-footed surfers like moving statues in the golden light.

WAIKIKI WEST

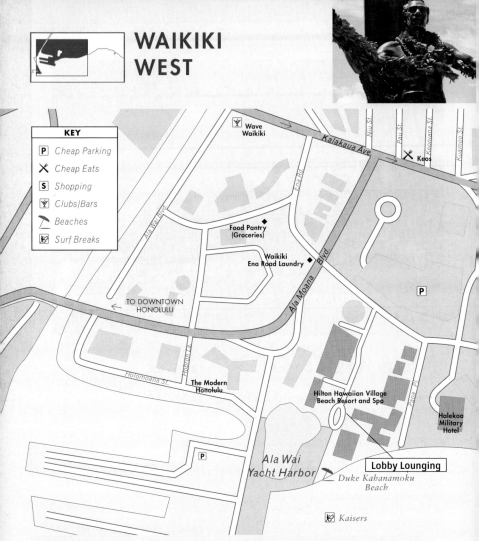

KEY

P	*Cheap Parking*
✗	*Cheap Eats*
S	*Shopping*
♆	*Clubs/Bars*
⚓	*Beaches*
🏄	*Surf Breaks*

Wave Waikiki

Kalakaua Ave.

Niu St.

Pau St.

Keoniana St.

Kuamoo St.

✗ Keos

Ena Rd.

Ala Wai Blvd.

Food Pantry (Groceries)

Waikiki Ena Road Laundry

Ala Moana Blvd.

P

TO DOWNTOWN HONOLULU ←

Holomoana La.

Holomoana St.

The Modern Honolulu

Hilton Hawaiian Village Beach Resort and Spa

Paoa Pl.

Halekoa Military Hotel

P

Ala Wai Yacht Harbor

Lobby Lounging

⚓ Duke Kahanamoku Beach

🏄 Kaisers

CHEAP EATS
Keo's, 2028 Kuhio: Breakfast.

Pho Old Saigon, 2270 Kuhio: Vietnamese.

Japanese noodle shops: Try Menchanko-Tei, Waikiki Trade Center; Ezogiku, 2164 Kalakaua.

■ **TIP→** Thanks to the many Japanese nationals who stay here, Waikiki is blessed with lots of cheap, authentic Japanese food, particularly noodles. Plastic representations of food in the window are an indicator of authenticity and a help in ordering.

SHOP, SHOP, SHOP/PARTY, PARTY, PARTY
2100 Kalakaua: Select high-end European boutiques (Chanel, Gucci, Yves Saint Laurent).

Waikiki Beach Walk: Dine and shop for gifts and apparel from locally-owned stores. 227 Lewers St. 808/931-3591.

Zanzabar: Upscale Zanzabar is a different club every night–Latin, global, over 30. Waikiki Trade Center, 2255 Kuhio Ave. 808/924-3939. Check www.zanzabarhawaii.com for events or call.

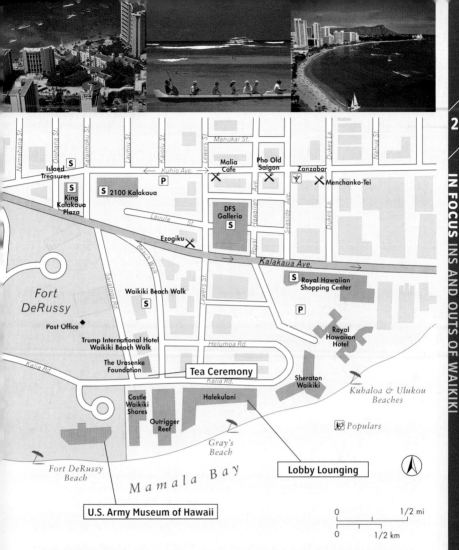

RAINY DAY IDEAS

Bliss Out: Relax at one of Waikiki's luxurious hotel spas. Most treatments feature Hawaiian ingredients.

Lobby Lounging: Among Waikiki's great gathering spots are Halekulani's tranquil courtyards with gorgeous flower arrangements and glimpses of the famous and the Hilton Hawaiian Village's flagged pathways with koi ponds, squawking parrots, and great shops.

Tea Ceremony, Urasenke Foundation: Japan's mysterious tea ceremony is demonstrated. 245 Saratoga Rd. 808/923-3059. $3 donation. Wed., Fri. 10–11 AM.

U.S. Army Museum of Hawaii: Exhibits, including photographs and military equipment, trace the history of Army in the Islands. Battery Randolph, Kalia Rd., Fort DeRussy. 808/955-9552. Free. Tues.–Sat. 9-5.

WAIKIKI EAST

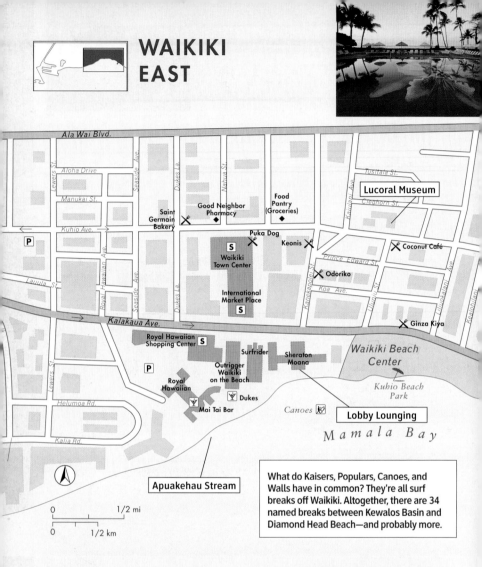

Lucoral Museum

Coconut Café

Keonis

Odoriko

Ginza Kiya

Saint Germain Bakery

Good Neighbor Pharmacy

Food Pantry (Groceries)

Puka Dog

Waikiki Town Center

International Market Place

Royal Hawaiian Shopping Center

Surfrider

Sheraton Moana

Outrigger Waikiki on the Beach

Royal Hawaiian

Mai Tai Bar

Dukes

Canoes

Waikiki Beach Center

Kuhio Beach Park

Lobby Lounging

Apuakehau Stream

M a m a l a   B a y

Ala Wai Blvd.
Aloha Drive
Manukai St.
Kuhio Ave.
Lauula St.
Kalakaua Ave.
Helumoa Rd.
Kalia Rd.
Lewers St.
Seaside Ave.
Royal Hawaiian Ave.
Dukes La.
Nahua St.
Kaiulani Ave.
Prince Edward St.
Kanekapolei St.
Koa Ave.
Uluniu Ave.
Liliuokalani Ave.
Kealohilani
Tusitala St.
Cleghorn St.
Kaunapou St.

0   1/2 mi
0   1/2 km

What do Kaisers, Populars, Canoes, and Walls have in common? They're all surf breaks off Waikiki. Altogether, there are 34 named breaks between Kewalos Basin and Diamond Head Beach—and probably more.

CHEAP EATS

Coconut Café, 2441 Kuhio: Burgers, sandwiches under $5; fresh fruit smoothies.

Ginza Kiya, 2464 Kalakaua: Japanese noodle shop.

Keoni's, Outrigger East Hotel, 150 Kaiulani Ave.: Breakfasts at rock-bottom prices.

Odoriko, King's Village, 131 Kaiulani Ave.: Japanese noodle shop.

Puka Dog, 2301 Kuhio #334: Delicious hot dogs baked into their buns.

■ **TIP→** To save money, go inland. Kuhio, one block toward the mountains from the main drag of Kalakaua, is lined with less expensive restaurants, hotels, and shops.

SHOP, SHOP, SHOP/PARTY, PARTY, PARTY

Sheraton Moana Surfrider: Pick up a present at Nohea Gallery or Sand People. Then relax with a drink at the venerable Banyan Veranda. The radio program *Hawaii Calls* first broadcast to a mainland audience from here in 1935.

Duke's Canoe Club, Outrigger Waikiki: Beach party central.

Mai Tai Bar at the Royal Hawaiian: Birthplace of the Mai Tai.

KEY

P	Cheap Parking
X	Cheap Eats
S	Shopping
Y	Clubs/Bars
⚓	Beaches
🏄	Surf Breaks

Ala Wai Blvd.

Liliuokalani Garden

Waimanu Way

Pualani Way

Kanekoa

Kuhio Ave.

Ohua Ave.

Paoakalani Ave.

Cartwright Rd.

Lemon Rd.

Kapahulu Ave.

Honolulu Zoo

Kalakaua Ave.

TO DIAMOND HEAD →

🏄 *Walls*

Queens Surf

Sans Souci

WHAT THE LOCALS LOVE

Paid-parking–phobic Islanders usually avoid Waikiki, but these attractions are juicy enough to lure locals:

■ **Royal Hawaiian Park Band,** free concerts every Sunday at the Kapiolani Bandstand.

■ **Pan-Pacific Festival-Matsuri in Hawaii,** a summer cultural festival that's as good as a trip to Japan.

■ **Aloha Festivals in September,** the legendary floral parade and evening show of contemporary Hawaiian music.

■ **The Wildest Show in Town,** $1 summer concerts at the Honolulu Zoo.

■ **Sunset on the Beach,** free films projected on an outdoor screen at Queen's Beach, with food and entertainment.

APUAKEHAU STREAM

Wade out just in front of the Outrigger Waikiki on the Beach and feel a current of chilly water curling around your ankles. This is the last remnant of three streams that once drained the inland valleys behind you, making of Waikiki a place of swamps, marshes, taro and rice paddies, and giving it the name "spouting water." High-ranking chiefs surfed in a legendary break gouged out by the draining freshwater and rinsed off afterward in the stream whose name means "basket of dew." The Ala Wai Canal, completed in the late 1920s, drained the land, reducing proud Apuakehau Stream to a determined phantom passing beneath Waikiki's streets.

RAINY DAY IDEAS

Lobby lounging: Check out the century-old, period-furnished lobby and veranda of the Sheraton Moana Surfrider Hotel on Kalakaua.

Lucoral Museum: Exhibit and shop explores the world of coral and other semi-precious stones; wander about or take $2 guided tour and participate in jewelry-making activity. 2414 Kuhio.

WHAT'S NEW & CHANGING

Waikiki, which was looking a bit shop-worn, is in the midst of many makeovers. Ask about noise, disruption, and construction when booking.

In addition to fresh landscaping and period light fixtures along Kalakaua and a pathway that encircles Ala Wai Canal, expect:

BEACH WALK: After ten years of planning, the Waikiki Beach Walk—a pedestrian walkway lined with restaurants and shops—opened in 2007 to rave reviews. It was a massive project for the city, costing about $535 million and taking up nearly 8 acres of land. It's a great place to spend the afternoon, but be warned: this place gets packed on weekends.

ROYAL HAWAIIAN SHOPPING CENTER: The fortress-like Royal Hawaiian Shopping Center in the center of Kalakaua Avenue is an open, inviting space with a palm grove and a mix of shops and restaurants.

GETTING THERE

It can seem impossible to figure out how to get to Waikiki from H-1. The exit is far inland, and even when you follow the signs, the route jigs and jogs; it sometimes seems a wonder that more tourists aren't found starving in Kaimuki.

FROM EASTBOUND H-1 (COMING FROM THE AIRPORT):
1. To western Waikiki (Ft. DeRussy and most hotels): Take the Punahou exit from H-1, turn right on Punahou and get in the center lane. Go right on Beretania and almost immediately left onto Kalakaua, which takes you into Waikiki.

2. To eastern Waikiki (Kapiolani Park): Take the King Street exit, and stay on King for two blocks. Go right on Kapahulu, which takes you to Ala Wai Boulevard.

FROM WESTBOUND H-1:
Take the Kapiolani Boulevard exit. Follow Kapiolani to McCully, and go left on McCully. Follow McCully to Kalakaua, and you're in Waikiki.

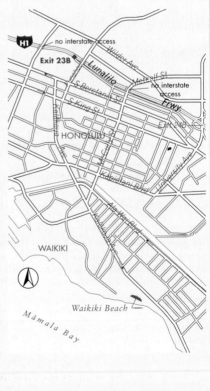

though showing signs of neglect due to budget constraints, is a lush garden and has some great programs. There is a lot of work going on, including the creation of a new elephant enclosure with more space for the pachyderms to roam. The Wildest Show in Town, a series of concerts ($2 donation), takes place on Wednesday evenings in summer. You can have a family sleepover inside the zoo during Snooze in the Zoo on a Friday or Saturday night every month. Or just head for the petting zoo, where kids can make friends with a llama or stand in the middle of a koi pond. There's an exceptionally good gift shop. On weekends, the Zoo Fence Art Mart, on Monsarrat Avenue on the Diamond Head side outside the zoo, has affordable artwork by contemporary artists. Metered parking is available all along the *makai* (ocean) side of the park and in the lot next to the zoo—but it can fill up early. TheBus, Oahu's only form of public transportation, makes stops here along the way to and from Ala Moana Center and Sea Life Park (routes 22 and 58). ⊠ *151 Kapahulu Ave., Waikiki* ☏ *808/971–7171* ⊕ *www. honoluluzoo.org* ⊠ *$14* ⊙ *Daily 9–4:30.*

> **WAIKIKI'S BEST FREE ENTERTAINMENT**
>
> Waikiki's entertainment scene isn't just dinner shows and lounge acts. There are plenty of free or nearly free offerings right on the beach and at Kapiolani Park. Queen's Surf Beach hosts the popular Sunset on the Beach, which brings big-screen showings of recent Hollywood blockbusters to the great outdoors. Also, during the summer months, the Honolulu Zoo has weekly concerts, and admission is just $1.

Kapiolani Bandstand. Victorian-style Kapiolani Bandstand, which was originally built in the late 1890s, is Kapiolani Park's stage for community entertainment and concerts. The nation's only city-sponsored band, the Royal Hawaiian Band, performs free concerts on Sunday afternoon. Local newspapers list event information. ⊠ *2805 Monsarrat Ave., Waikiki* ☏ *808/922–5331* ⊕ *www.rhb-music.com.*

Waikiki Aquarium. This amazing little attraction harbors more than 3,000 organisms and 500 species of Hawaiian and South Pacific marine life, endangered Hawaiian monk seals, sharks, and the only chambered nautilus living in captivity. The Edge of the Reef exhibit showcases five different types of reef environments found along Hawaii's shorelines. Check out the small new Northwestern Hawaiian Islands exhibit that explains the formation of the island chain, the Ocean Drifters jellyfish exhibit, outdoor touch pool, and the self-guided audio tour, which is included with admission. The aquarium offers programs of interest to adults and children alike, including the Aquarium After Dark when visitors grab a flashlight and view fish going about their rarely observable nocturnal activities. Plan to spend at least an hour at the aquarium, including 10 minutes for a film in the Sea Visions Theater. ⊠ *2777 Kalakaua Ave., Waikiki* ☏ *808/923–9741* ⊕ *www.waquarium. org* ⊠ *$9* ⊙ *Daily 9–4:30.*

Waikiki Shell. Locals bring picnics and grab one of the 6,000 "grass seats" (lawn seating) for music under the stars (there are actual seats, as well). Concerts are held May 1 to Labor Day, with a few winter dates,

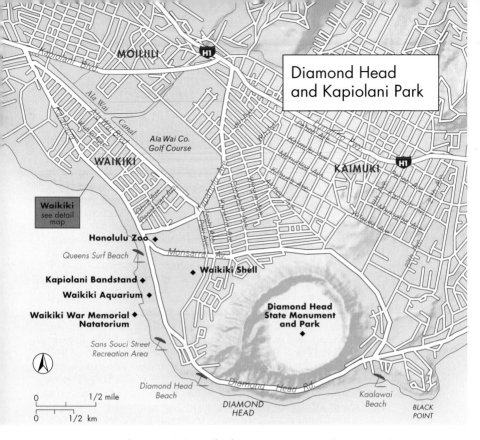

MOILIILI

Ala Wai Co.
Golf Course

WAIKIKI

KAIMUKI

Waikiki
see detail
map

Honolulu Zoo ◆

Queens Surf Beach

Monsarrat Av.

◆ Waikiki Shell

Kapiolani Bandstand ◆

Waikiki Aquarium ◆

Diamond Head
State Monument
and Park
◆

Waikiki War Memorial ◆
Natatorium

Sans Souci Street
Recreation Area

0   1/2 mile

0   1/2 km

Diamond Head
Beach

Diamond Head Rd.

DIAMOND
HEAD

Kaalawai
Beach

BLACK
POINT

weather permitting. Check newspaper entertainment sections to see
who is performing. ⊠ *2805 Monsarrat Ave., Waikiki* ☎ *808/768–5252*
⊕ *www.blaisdellcenter.com.*

Waikiki War Memorial Natatorium. This 1927 World War I monument,
dedicated to the 102 Hawaiian servicemen who lost their lives in battle,
stands proudly—its 20-foot archway, which was completely restored in
2002, is floodlit at night. Despite a face-lift in 2000, the 100-meter saltwater swimming pool, the training spot for Olympians Johnny Weiss-
muller and Buster Crabbe and the U.S. Army during World War II, is
closed as the pool needs repair. The city has commissioned a study of
the natatorium's future while a nonprofit group fights to save the facility. ⊠ *2777 Kalakaua Ave., Waikiki.*

GREATER HONOLULU AND DIAMOND HEAD

Downtown Honolulu and Chinatown can easily swallow up a day's
walking, sightseeing, and shopping. Another day's worth of attractions surrounds the city's core. To the north, just off H1 in the tightly
packed neighborhood of Kalihi, explore a museum given to the Islands
in memory of a princess. Immediately *mauka*, off Pali Highway, are a
renowned resting place and a carefully preserved home where royal
families retreated during the doldrums of summer. To the south, along

King Street and Waialae Avenue, are a pair of neighborhoods chocka-block with interesting restaurants and shops. Down the shore a bit from Diamond Head, visit Oahu's ritziest address and an equally upscale shopping center.

One reason to venture farther afield is the chance to glimpse Hono-lulu's residential neighborhoods. Species of classic Hawaii homes include the tiny green-and-white plantation-era house with its corru-gated tin roof, two windows flanking a central door and small porch; the breezy bungalow with its swooping Thai-style roofline and two wings flanking screened French doors through which breezes blow into the living room. Note the tangled "Grandma-style" gardens and many *ohana* houses—small homes in the backyard of a larger home or built as apartments perched over the garage, allowing extended families to live together. Carports, which rarely house cars, are the island's version of rec rooms, where parties are held and neighbors sit to "talk story." Sometimes you see gallon jars on the flat roofs of garages or carports: these are pickled lemons fermenting in the sun. Also in the neighborhoods, you find the folksy restaurants and takeout spots favored by the islanders.

GETTING HERE AND AROUND

For those with a Costco card, the cheapest gas on the island is at the Costco station on Arakawa Street between Dillingham Boulevard and Nimitz Highway.

TOP ATTRACTIONS

★ **Bishop Museum.** Founded in 1889 by Charles R. Bishop as a memorial to his wife, Princess Bernice Pauahi Bishop, the museum began as a repository for the royal possessions of this last direct descendant of King Kamehameha the Great. Today it's the Hawaii State Museum of Natural and Cultural History. Its five exhibit halls house almost 25 million items that tell the history of the Hawaiian Islands and their Pacific neighbors. The latest addition to the complex is a 16,500 square-foot natural-science wing with a three-story simulated volcano at its center. The recently renovated Hawaiian Hall, with state-of-the art and often interactive displays, teaches about the Hawaiian cul-ture. Spectacular Hawaiian artifacts—lustrous feather capes, bone fish hooks, the skeleton of a giant sperm whale, photography and crafts displays, and an authentic, well-preserved grass house—are displayed inside a three-story 19th-century Victorian-style gallery. The build-ing alone, with its huge Victorian turrets and immense stone walls, is worth seeing. Also check out the planetarium, daily tours, hula and science demonstrations, special exhibits, and the Shop Pacifica. ⊠ *1525 Bernice St., Kalihi* ☎ *808/847–3511* ⊕ *www.bishopmuseum. org* ⊡ *$17.95* ⊘ *Wed.–Mon. 9–5.*

Diamond Head State Monument and Park. Panoramas from this 760-foot extinct volcanic peak, once used as a military fortification, extend from Waikiki and Honolulu in one direction and out to Koko Head in the other, with surfers and windsurfers scattered like confetti on the cresting waves below. This 360-degree perspective is a great orienta-tion for first-time visitors. On a clear day, look east past Koko Head to

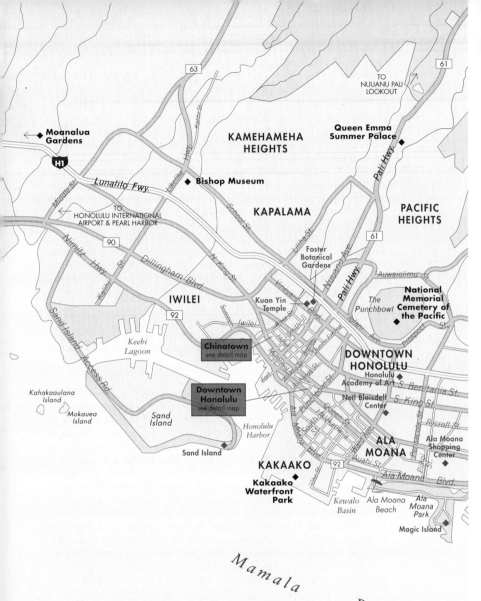

To NUUANU PALI LOOKOUT

61

63

Moanalua Gardens

H1

Lunalilo Fwy.

TO
HONOLULU INTERNATIONAL
AIRPORT & PEARL HARBOR

90

Nimitz Hwy.

Dillingham Blvd.

N. King St.

Bishop Museum

KAMEHAMEHA HEIGHTS

Queen Emma
Summer Palace

Pali Hwy.

KAPALAMA

PACIFIC HEIGHTS

61

Foster
Botanical
Gardens

Auwaiolimu St.

IWILEI

92

Keehi Lagoon

Kuan Yin Temple

Nuuanu Ave.

The
Punchbowl

National
Memorial
Cemetery of
the Pacific

Prospect St.

Chinatown
see detail map

DOWNTOWN
HONOLULU

Honolulu
Academy of Art
S. Beretania St.

Kahakaaulana
Island

Mokauea
Island

Sand
Island

Downtown
Honolulu
see detail map

Honolulu
Harbor

Neil Blaisdell
Center

S. King St.

Rycroft St.

Ala Moana
Shopping
Center

Sand Island

KAKAAKO

92

Kakaako
Waterfront
Park

Kewalo
Basin

Ala Moana
Beach

ALA
MOANA

Ala Moana Blvd.

Ala
Moana
Park

Magic Island

Mamala Bay

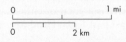

0   1 mi

0   2 km

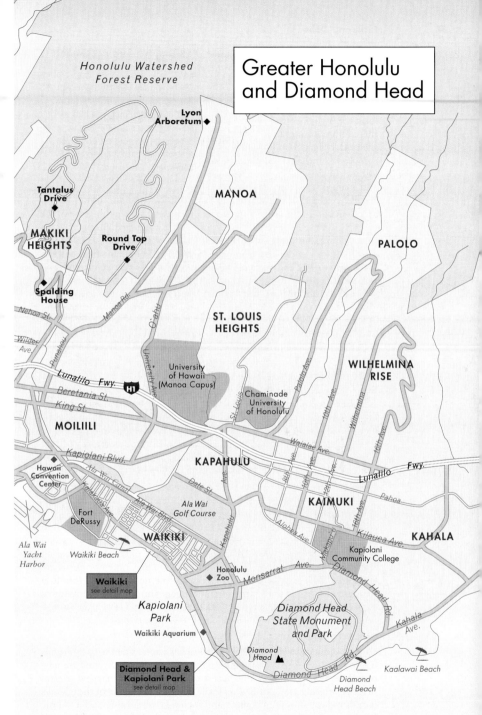

Greater Honolulu and Diamond Head

Honolulu Watershed Forest Reserve

Lyon Arboretum ◆

MANOA

Tantalus Drive ◆

MAKIKI HEIGHTS

Round Top Drive ◆

PALOLO

Spalding House ◆

Nehoa St.

Wilder Ave.

ST. LOUIS HEIGHTS

Lunalilo Fwy. **H1**

Manoa Rd.

O'ahu

University Ave.

Beretania St.

King St.

University of Hawaii (Manoa Capus)

Chaminade University of Honolulu

St. Louis

Palolo Ave.

WILHELMINA RISE

10th Ave.

Wilhemina

MOILIILI

Kapiolani Blvd.

Hawaii Convention Center

Ala Wai Canal

Kalakaua Ave.

Ala Wai Blvd.

KAPAHULU

Date St.

Ala Wai Golf Course

Kapahulu

Waialae Ave.

9th Ave.

12th Ave.

Lunalilo Fwy.

Pahoa

KAIMUKI

Aloha Ave.

Kilauea Ave.

Kapiolani Community College

KAHALA

Fort DeRussy

WAIKIKI

Ala Wai Yacht Harbor

Waikiki Beach

Waikiki see detail map

Kapiolani Park

Waikiki Aquarium ◆

Honolulu Zoo ◆

Monsarrat Ave.

Mariani D.

Diamond Head State Monument and Park

Diamond Head Rd.

Kahala Ave.

Diamond Head & Kapiolani Park see detail map

Diamond Head ▲

Diamond Head Rd.

Diamond Head Beach

Kaalawai Beach

glimpse the outlines of the islands of Maui and Molokai. To enter the park from Waikiki, take Kalakaua Avenue east, turn left at Monsarrat Avenue, head a mile up the hill, and look for a sign on the right. Drive through the tunnel to the inside of the crater. The ¾-mile trail to the top begins at the parking lot. New lighting inside the summit tunnel and a spiral staircase eases the way,

WORD OF MOUTH

"Since you are visiting the Iolani Palace, you might also enjoy a tour of Queen Emma's Summer Palace. If you go to the Pali (it is quite an experience) it is near the summer palace and could be combined." —Giovanna

but be aware that the hike to the crater is an upward climb; if you aren't in the habit of getting occasional exercise, this might not be for you. At the top, you'll find a somewhat awkward climb out into the open air, but the view is worth it. Take bottled water with you to stay hydrated under the tropical sun. ■ TIP➜ **To beat the heat and the crowds, rise early and make the hike before 8 am.** As you walk, note the color of the vegetation; if the mountain is brown, Honolulu has been without significant rain for a while; but if the trees and undergrowth glow green, you'll know it's the wet season (winter) without looking at a calendar. This is when rare Hawaiian marsh plants revive on the floor of the crater. Keep an eye on your watch if you're here at day's end: the gates close promptly at 6. ⊠ *Diamond Head Rd. at 18th Ave., Waikiki* 🕾 *808/587–0300* ⊕ *www.hawaiistateparks.org/parks/oahu* ⌦ *$1 per person, $5 per vehicle* ☉ *Daily 6–6.*

★ **Queen Emma Summer Palace.** Queen Emma and her family used this stately white home, built in 1848, as a retreat from the rigors of court life in hot and dusty Honolulu during the mid-1800s. It has an eclectic mix of European, Victorian, and Hawaiian furnishings and has excellent examples of Hawaiian quilts and koa-wood furniture. ⊠ *2913 Pali Hwy., Nuuanu* 🕾 *808/595–3167* ⊕ *www.queenemmasummerpalace. org* ⌦ *$6* ☉ *Self-guided or guided tours daily 9–4.*

Spalding House. In the exclusive Makiki Heights neighborhood, just minutes from downtown Honolulu, The Contemporary Museum houses collections of modern art dating from 1940. Situated in the 3.5-acre Alice Cooke Spalding home and estate (built in 1925), the museum boasts ever-changing exhibitions as well as a peaceful sculpture garden with breathtaking views of Diamond Head and Waikiki. A fun gift shop features jewelry and other art by local artists. The Contemporary Café is popular with locals for lunch. It recently merged with the Honolulu Academy of Arts, so a single admission gets you into both museums. ⊠ *2411 Makiki Heights Dr., Makiki Heights* 🕾 *808/526–1322* ⊕ *honolulumuseum.org* ⌦ *$10* ☉ *Tues.–Sat. 10–4, Sun. noon–4.*

WORTH NOTING

Kahala. Oahu's wealthiest neighborhood has streets lined with multimillion-dollar homes. At intervals along tree-lined Kahala Avenue are narrow lanes that provide public access to Kahala's quiet, narrow coastal beaches offering views of Koko Head. Kahala Mall is one of the island's largest indoor shopping centers and includes restaurants and a Whole Foods grocery store. Kahala is also the home of the private Waialae Golf

DID YOU KNOW?

The Bishop Museum in Honolulu is the state's natural and cultural heritage museum, and has more than 24.7 million items inside.

Course, site of the annual Sony Open PGA golf tournament in January. ⊠ *East of Diamond Head, Kahala Ave., Kahala.*

Lyon Arboretum. Tucked all the way back in Manoa Valley, this is a gem of an arboretum operated by the University of Hawaii. Hike to a waterfall or sit and enjoy beautiful views of the valley. You'll also see an ethnobotanical garden and one of the largest palm collections anywhere—all within a parklike setting. Its educational mission means there are regular talks and walks with university faculty. Docents give 60- to 90-minute tours weekdays at 10 am. There are also self-guided audio tours. ⊠ *3860 Manoa Rd., Manoa* ☎ *808/988–0456* ⊕ *www. hawaii.edu/lyonarboretum* ⊠ *$5 donation* ⊙ *Mon.–Fri. 8–4; Sat. 9–3.*

Moanalua Gardens. This lovely park is the site of the internationally acclaimed Prince Lot Hula Festival on the third weekend in July. Throughout the year, the Moanalua Gardens Foundation sponsors 3-mile guided hikes into Kamananui Valley, usually on Sunday; call for times. Self-guided tour booklets ($5) are also available from the Moanalua Gardens Foundation office. To reach Moanalua Gardens, take the Moanalua Freeway westbound (78). Take the Tripler exit, then take a right on Mahiole Street. Pineapple Place is just after Moanalua Elementary School. ⊠ *1352 Pineapple Pl., Salt Lake* ☎ *808/833–1944* ⊕ *www.mgf-hawaii.org* ⊠ *Free, guided hikes $5* ⊙ *Weekdays 8–4:30.*

Moiliili. Packed into the neighborhood of Moiliili are flower and lei shops, restaurants (Spices, Fukuya Delicatessen, Sweet Home Café), and little stores such as Kuni Island Fabrics, a great source for Hawaiian quilting and other crafting materials; Siam Imports, for goodies from Thailand; and Revolution Books, Honolulu's only leftist book shop. ⊠ *S. King St., between Isenberg and Waialae Ave., Moiliili.*

National Memorial Cemetery of the Pacific. Nestled in the bowl of Puowaina, or Punchbowl Crater, this 112-acre cemetery is the final resting place for more than 50,000 U.S. war veterans and family members and is a solemn reminder of their sacrifice. Among those buried here is Ernie Pyle, the famed World War II correspondent who was killed by a Japanese sniper on Ie Shima, an island off the northwest coast of Okinawa. There are intricate stone maps providing a visual military history lesson. Puowaina, formed 75,000–100,000 years ago during a period of secondary volcanic activity, translates as "Hill of Sacrifice." Historians believe this site once served as an altar where ancient Hawaiians offered sacrifices to their gods. ■ **TIP➜ The entrance to the cemetery has unfettered views of Waikiki and Honolulu—perhaps the finest on Oahu.** ⊠ *2177 Puowaina Dr., Nuuanu* ☎ *808/532–3720* ⊕ *www.cem.va.gov/cem/ cems/nchp/nmcp.asp* ⊠ *Free* ⊙ *Mar.–Sept., daily 8–6:30; Oct.–Feb., daily 8–5:30.*

**OFF THE
BEATEN
PATH**

Tantalus and Round Top Scenic Drive. A few minutes and a world away from Waikiki and Honolulu, this scenic drive shaded by vine-draped trees has frequent pullouts with views of Diamond Head and the *Ewa* side of Honolulu. It's a nice change of pace from urban life below. At Puu Ualakaa Park, stop to see the sweeping view from Manoa Valley to Honolulu. To start the drive, go to Punchbowl Memorial Cemetery

If you're a snorkeler, head straight for Hanauma Bay, the best and most popular place to snorkel on Oahu.

and follow Tantalus Drive as it climbs uphill. ✉ *3200 Round Top Dr., Tantalus.*

PEARL HARBOR

Pearl Harbor is approximately 9 miles west of downtown Honolulu, beyond Honolulu International Airport.

December 7, 1941. Every American then alive recalls exactly what he or she was doing when the news broke that the Japanese had bombed Pearl Harbor, the catalyst that brought the United States into World War II. More than 2,000 people died that day, and a dozen ships were sunk.

Here, in what is still a key Pacific naval base, the attack is remembered every day by thousands of visitors. In recent years, the memorial has been the site of reconciliation ceremonies involving Pearl Harbor veterans from both sides.

Fodor's Choice **Pearl Harbor National Memorial Museum and Visitor Center.** The Pearl Har-
★ bor visitor center, recently reopened after a $58 million renovation and now part of the World War II Valor In the Pacific National Monument, is open from 7 am to 5 pm. For more information, visit ⊕ *www.nps.gov/ valr/index.htm.* The site is a must-see for many, but there are things to know before you go. Consider whether you want to see only the *Arizona* Memorial, or the USS *Bowfin* and USS *Missouri* as well (the latter two sights charge admission fees). Allow approximately an hour and 15 minutes for the USS *Arizona* tour. Arrive early—the free, first-come, first-served tickets for the *Arizona* Memorial can disappear within an hour. There are restrictions on what you can bring with you: not

rmitted are purses, backpacks, and camera cases (although cameras e allowed). Baggage lockers are available for a small fee. Also, don't rget ID. ⇨ *For much more detailed information, see the highlighted eature in this chapter.* ⊠ *World War II Valor in the Pacific National Monument, 1 Arizona Memorial Pl., Pearl Harbor* ☎ *808/422–3300* ⊕ *www.nps.gov/valr/index.htm* ✉ *Free (timed tickets required for Arizona Memorial)* ☉ *Daily 7–5; Arizona Memorial tours daily 8–3.*

SOUTHEAST OAHU

Approximately 10 miles southeast of Waikiki.

Driving southeast from Waikiki on busy four-lane Kalanianaole Highway, you'll pass a dozen bedroom communities tucked into the valleys at the foot of the Koolau Range, with fleeting glimpses of the ocean from a couple of pocket parks. Suddenly, civilization falls away, the road narrows to two lanes, and you enter the rugged coastline of Koko Head and Ka Iwi.

This is a cruel coastline: dry, windswept, and rocky shores, with untamed waves that are notoriously treacherous. While walking its beaches, do not turn your back on the ocean, don't venture close to wet areas where high waves occasionally reach, and be sure to heed warning signs.

At this point, you're passing through Koko Head Regional Park. On your right is the bulging remnant of a pair of volcanic craters that the Hawaiians called Kawaihoa, known today as Koko Head. To the left is Koko Crater and an area of the park that includes a hiking trail, a dryland botanical garden, a firing range, and a riding stable. Ahead is a sinuous shoreline with scenic pullouts and beaches to explore. Named the Ka Iwi Coast (*iwi,* "ee-vee," are bones—sacred to Hawaiians and full of symbolism) for the channel just offshore, this area was once home to a ranch and small fishing enclave that were destroyed by a tidal wave in the 1940s.

EXPLORING

QUICK BITES

Kokonuts Shave Ice and Snacks. Stop for shave ice on the South Shore? President Barack Obama did while visiting the island after the 2008 election. Kokonuts Shave Ice and Snacks in Koko Marina Center serves, arguably, the best shave ice this side of Haleiwa. ⊠ *7192 Kalanianaole Hwy., Hawaii Kai* ☎ *808/396–8809* ☉ *10:30 am–9 pm.*

Halona Blowhole. Below a scenic turnout along the Koko Head shoreline, this oft-photographed lava tube sucks the ocean in and spits it out. Don't get too close, as conditions can get dangerous. ■ **TIP➔ Look to your right to see the tiny beach below that was used to film the wave-washed love scene in From Here to Eternity.** In winter this is a good spot to watch whales at play. Offshore, the islands of Molokai and Lanai call like distant sirens, and every once in a while Maui is visible in blue silhouette. Take your valuables with you and lock your car, because this scenic location is overrun with tourists and therefore a hot spot for petty thieves. ⊠ *Kalanianaole Hwy., 1 mile east of Hanauma Bay.*

Continued on page 77

USS *West Virginia* (BB48), 7 December 1941

PEARL HARBOR

December 7, 1941. Every American then alive recalls exactly what he or she was doing when the news broke that the Japanese had bombed Pearl Harbor, the catalyst that brought the United States into World War II.

Although it was clear by late 1941 that war with Japan was inevitable, no one in authority seems to have expected the attack to come in just this way, at just this time. So when the Japanese bombers swept through a gap in Oahu's Koolau Mountains in the hazy light of morning, they found the bulk of America's Pacific fleet right where they hoped it would be: docked like giant stepping stones across the calm waters of the bay named for the pearl oysters that once prospered there. More than 2,000 people died that day, including 49 civilians. A dozen ships were sunk. And on the nearby air bases, virtually every American military aircraft was destroyed or damaged. The attack was a stunning success, but it lit a fire under America, which went to war with "Remember Pearl Harbor" as its battle cry. Here, in what is still a key Pacific naval base, the attack is remembered every day by thousands of visitors, including many curious Japanese, who for years heard little World War II history in their own country. In recent years, the memorial has been the site of reconciliation ceremonies involving Pearl Harbor veterans from both sides.

GETTING AROUND

Pearl Harbor is both a working military base and the most-visited Oahu attraction. Four distinct destinations share a parking lot and are linked by footpath, shuttle, and ferry.

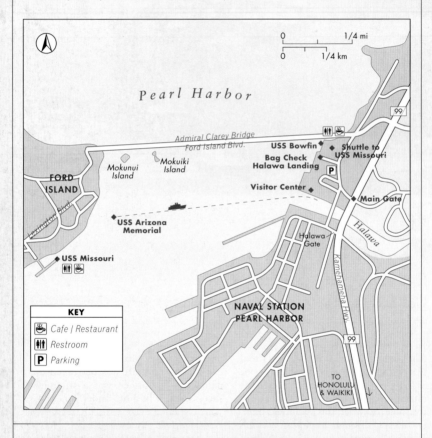

The visitor center is accessible from the parking lot. The USS *Arizona* Memorial itself is in the middle of the harbor; get tickets for the ferry ride at the visitor center. The USS *Bowfin* is also reachable from the parking lot.

The USS *Missouri* is docked at Ford Island, a restricted area of the naval base. Vehicular access is prohibited. To get there, take a shuttle bus from the station near the *Bowfin*.

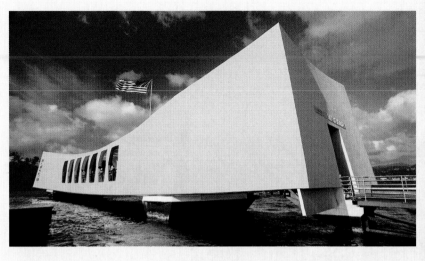

ARIZONA MEMORIAL

Snugged up tight in a row of seven battleships off Ford Island, the USS *Arizona* took a direct hit that December morning, exploded, and rests still on the shallow bottom where she settled.

The swooping, stark-white memorial, which straddles the wreck of the USS *Arizona*, was designed to represent both the depths of the low-spririted, early days of the war, and the uplift of victory.

A visit here begins at the Pearl Harbor Visitor Center, which recently underwent a $58 million renovation. High definition projectors and interactive exhibits were installed, and the building was modernized. From the visitor center, a ferry takes you to the memorial itself, and a new shuttle hub now gives access to sites that were previously inaccessible, like the USS *Utah* and USS *Oklahoma*.

A somber, contemplative mood descends upon visitors during the ferry ride to the *Arizona*; this is a place where 1,177 crewmen lost their lives. Gaze at the names of the dead carved into the wall of white marble. Scatter flowers (but no lei—the string is bad for the fish). Salute the flag. Remember Pearl Harbor.

☎ *808/422–0561*
⊕ *www.nps.gov/valr*

USS *MISSOURI* (BB63)

Together with the *Arizona* Memorial, the *Missouri's* presence in Pearl Harbor perfectly bookends America's WWII experience that began December 7, 1941, and ended on the "Mighty Mo's" starboard deck with the signing of the Terms of Surrender.

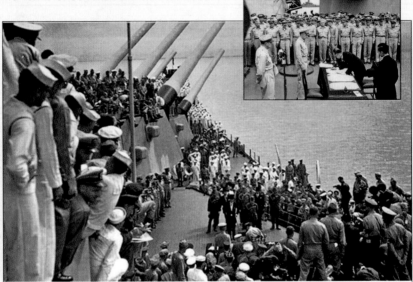

Surrender of Japan, USS *Missouri*, 2 September 1945

In the parking area behind the USS *Bowfin* Museum, board a shuttle for a breezy, eight-minute ride to Ford Island and the teak decks and towering superstructure of the *Missouri*, docked for good in the very harbor from which she first went to war on January 2, 1945. The last battleship ever built, the *Missouri* famously hosted the final act of WWII, the signing of the Terms of Surrender. The commission that governs this floating museum has surrounded her with buildings tricked out in WWII style—a canteen that serves as an orientation space for tours, a WACs and WAVEs lounge with a flight simulator the kids will love ($10 per person), Truman's Line restaurant serving Navy-style meals, and a Victory Store housing a souvenir shop and covered with period mottos ("Don't be a blabateur").

■**TIP→** Definitely hook up with a tour guide (additional charge) or audio tour —these add a great deal to the experience.

The *Missouri* is all about numbers: 209 feet tall, six 239,000-pound guns, capable of firing up to 23 mi away. Absorb these during the tour, then stop to take advantage of the view from the decks. The Mo is a work in progress, with only a handful of her hundreds of spaces open to view.

☎ *808/423–2263* or ☎ *888/877–6477*
⊕ *www.ussmissouri.com*

USS *BOWFIN* (SS287)

SUBMARINE MUSEUM & PARK

Launched one year to the day after the Pearl Harbor attack, the USS *Bowfin* sank 44 enemy ships during WWII and now serves as the centerpiece of a museum honoring all submariners.

Although the *Bowfin* no less than the *Arizona* Memorial commemorates the lost, the mood here is lighter. Perhaps it's the childlike scale of the boat, a metal tube just 16 feet in diameter, packed with ladders, hatches, and other obstacles, like the naval version of a jungle gym. Perhaps it's the World War II-era music that plays in the covered patio. Or it might be the museum's touching displays—the penciled sailor's journal, the Vargas girlie posters. Aboard the boat nicknamed "Pearl Harbor Avenger," compartments are fitted out as though "Sparky" was away from the radio room just for a moment, and "Cooky" might be right back to his pots and pans. The museum includes many artifacts to spark family conversations, among them a vintage dive suit that looks too big for Shaquille

O'Neal. A caution: The *Bowfin* could be hazardous for very young children; no one under four allowed.

☏ *808/423–1341*
⊕ *www.bowfin.org*

THE PACIFIC AVIATION MUSEUM

This museum opened on December 7, 2006, as phase one of a four-phase tribute to the air wars of the Pacific. Located on Ford Island in Hangar 37, an actual seaplane hangar that survived the Pearl Harbor attack, the museum is made up of a theater where a short film on Pearl Harbor kicks off the tour, an education center, a shop, and a restaurant. Exhibits—many of which are interactive and involve sound effects—include an authentic Japanese Zero in a diorama setting a chance to don a flight suit and play the role of a World War II pilot using one of six flight simulators. Various aircrafts are employed to narrate the great battles: the Doolittle Raid on Japan, the Battle of Midway, Guadalcanal, and so on. The actual Stearman N2S-3 in which President George H. W. Bush soloed is another exhibit. ☏ *808/441–1000* ⊕ *www.pacificaviationmuseum.org* ▨ $20.

PLAN YOUR PEARL HARBOR DAY LIKE A MILITARY CAMPAIGN

DIRECTIONS

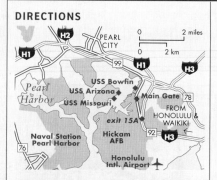

Take H–1 west from Waikiki to Exit 15A and follow signs. Or take The-Bus route 20 or 47 from Waikiki. Beware high-priced private shuttles. It's a 30-minute drive from Waikiki.

WHAT TO BRING

Picture ID is required during periods of high alert; bring it just in case.

You'll be standing, walking, and climbing all day. Wear something with lots of pockets and a pair of good walking shoes. Carry a light jacket, sunglasses, hat, and sunscreen.

No purses, packs, or bags are allowed. Take only what fits in your pockets. Cameras are okay but without the bags. A private bag storage booth is located in the parking lot near the visitors' center. Leave nothing in your car; theft is a problem despite bicycle security patrols.

HOURS

Hours are 7 AM to 5 PM for the visitor center, though the attractions open at 8 AM. The *Arizona* Memorial starts giving out tickets on a first-come, first-served basis at 7:30 AM; the last tickets are given out at 3 PM. Spring break, summer, and holidays are busiest, and tickets sometimes run out by noon or earlier.

TICKETS

Arizona: Free. Add $7.50 for museum audio tours.

Aviation: $20 adults, $10 children. Add $10 for aviator's guided tour.

Missouri: $20 adults, $10 children. Add $25 for in-depth, behind-the-scenes tours.

Bowfin: $10 adults, $4 children. Add $2 for audio tours. Children under 4 may go into the museum but not aboard the *Bowfin.*

KIDS

This might be the day to enroll younger kids in the hotel children's program. Preschoolers chafe at long waits, and attractions involve some hazards for toddlers. Older kids enjoy the *Bowfin* and *Missouri,* especially.

MAKING THE MOST OF YOUR TIME

Expect to spend at least half a day; a whole day is better if you're a military history buff.

At the *Arizona* Memorial, you'll get a ticket, be given a tour time, and then have to wait anywhere from 15 minutes to 3 hours. You must pick up your own ticket so you can't hold places. If the wait is long, skip over to the *Bowfin* to fill the time.

SUGGESTED READING

Pearl Harbor and the USS Arizona Memorial, by Richard Wisniewski. $5.95. 64-page magazine-size quick history.

Bowfin, by Edwin P. Hoyt. $14.95. Dramatic story of undersea adventure.

The Last Battleship, by Scott C. S. Stone. $11.95. Story of the Mighty Mo.

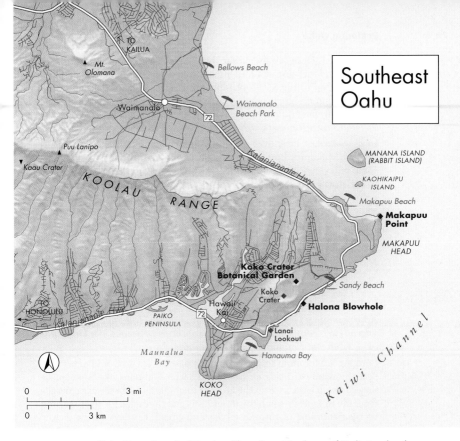

Koko Crater Botanical Garden. If you've visited any of Oahu's other botanical gardens, this one will be in stark contrast. Inside the tallest tuff
cone on Oahu, in one of the hottest and driest areas on the island,
Koko Crater Botanical Garden allows visitors the opportunity to see
dryland species of plants including baobab trees, cacti, plumeria, and
bougainvillea. ✉ *Entrance off of Kealahou St., near Hawaii Kai Dr.,
Hawaii Kai* ☎ *808/522–7063* ⊕ *www1.honolulu.gov/parks/hbg/kcbg.
htm* ✦ *Free* ☺ *Daily sunrise–sunset.*

Makapuu Point. This spot has breathtaking views of the ocean, mountains, and the Windward Islands. The point of land jutting out in the
distance is **Mokapu Peninsula,** site of a U.S. Marine base. The spired
mountain peak is **Mt. Olomana.** In front of you on the long pier is part
of the **Makai Undersea Test Range,** a research facility that's closed to
the public. Offshore is **Manana Island (Rabbit Island),** a picturesque
cay said to resemble a swimming bunny with its ears pulled back. Ironically enough, Manana Island was once overrun with rabbits, thanks to
a rancher who let a few hares run wild on the land. They were eradi-
cated in 1994 by biologists who grew concerned that the rabbits were
destroying the island's native plants.

Nestled in the cliff face is the **Makapuu Lighthouse,** which became
operational in 1909 and has the largest lighthouse lens in America. The

lighthouse is closed to the public, but near the Makapuu Point turnout you can find the start of a mile-long paved road (closed to traffic). Hike up to the top of the 647-foot bluff for a closer view of the lighthouse and, in winter, a great whale-watching vantage point. ⊠ *Ka Iwi State Scenic Shoreline, Kalanianaole Hwy., above Makapuu Beach, Kaneohe* ⊕ *www.hawaiistateparks.org.*

Lanai Lookout. A little over a half-mile past Hanauma Bay as you head toward Makapuu Point, you'll see a turnout on the ocean side with some fine views of the coastline. In winter, you'll have an opportunity to see storm-generated waves crashing against lava cliffs. This is also a popular place for winter whale-watching so bring your binoculars, some sunscreen, and a picnic lunch and join the small crowd scanning for telltale white spouts of water only a few hundred yards away. On clear days, you should be able to see the islands of Molokai and Lanai off in the distance, hence the name. ⊠ *Kalanianaole Hwy., just past Hanauma Bay, Koko Head.*

WINDWARD OAHU

Approximately 15 miles northeast of downtown Honolulu (20–25 minutes by car), approximately 25 miles southeast of downtown Honolulu via Ka Iwi and Waimanalo (35–45 minutes by car).

Looking at Honolulu's topsy-turvy urban sprawl, you would never suspect the windward side existed. It's a secret Oahuans like to keep, so they can watch the awe on the faces of their guests when the car emerges from the tunnels through the mountains and they gaze for the first time on the panorama of turquoise bays and emerald valleys watched over by the knife-edged Koolau ridges. Jaws literally drop. Every time. And this just a 15-minute drive from downtown.

It's on this side of the island where many native Hawaiians live. Evidence of traditional lifestyles is abundant in crumbling fishponds, rock platforms that once were altars, taro patches still being worked, and thrown-net fishermen posed stock-still above the water (though today, they're invariably wearing polarized sunglasses, the better to spot the fish).

Here, the pace is slower, more oriented toward nature. Beach-going, hiking, diving, surfing, and boating are the draws, along with a visit to the Polynesian Cultural Center, and poking through little shops and wayside stores.

GETTING HERE AND AROUND

For a driving experience you won't soon forget, take the H3 freeway over to the windward side. As you pass through the tunnels, be prepared for one of the most breathtaking stretches of road anywhere. Flip a coin before you leave to see who will drive and who will gape.

TIMING

You can easily spend an entire day exploring Windward Oahu, or you can just breeze on through, nodding at the sights on your way to the North Shore. Waikiki to Windward is a drive of less than half an hour; to the North Shore via Kamehameha Highway along the Windward Coast is one hour, minimum.

Shangri La

The marriage of heiress Doris Duke, at age 23, to a much older man didn't last. But their around-the-world honeymoon did leave her with two lasting loves: Islamic art and architecture, which she first encountered on that journey; and Hawaii, where the honeymooners made an extended stay while Doris learned to surf and befriended Islanders unimpressed by her wealth.

Today visitors to her beloved Islands—where she spent most winters—can share both loves by touring her home. The sought-after tours, which are coordinated by and begin at the Honolulu Museum of Art in downtown Honolulu, start with a visit to the Arts of the Islamic World Gallery. A short van ride then takes small groups on to the house itself, on the far side of Diamond Head.

In 1936, heiress Doris Duke bought 5 acres at Black Point, down the coast from Waikiki, and began to build and furnish the first home that would be all her own. She called it **Shangri-La.** For more than 50 years, the home was a work in progress as Duke traveled the world, buying art and furnishings, picking up ideas for her Mughul garden, for the Playhouse in the style of a 17th-century Irani pavilion, and for the water terraces and tropical gardens. When she died in 1993, Duke left instructions that her home was to become a public center for the study of Islamic art.

To walk through the house and its gardens—which have remained much as Duke left them with only some minor conservation-oriented changes—is to experience the personal style of someone who saw everything as raw material for her art. With her trusted houseman, Jin de Silva, she helped build the elaborate Turkish Room, trimming tiles and painted panels to retrofit the existing space (including raising the ceiling and lowering the floor) and building a fountain of her own design. Among many aspects of the home inspired by the Muslim tradition is the entry: an anonymous gate, a blank white wall, and a wooden door that bids you "Enter herein in peace and security" in Arabic characters. Inside, tiles glow, fountains tinkle, and shafts of light illuminate artworks through arches and high windows. This was her private world, entered only by trusted friends.

Guided tours take 2½ hours including transportation from the Honolulu Museum of Art (*see the listing in Exploring Honolulu*). Children under 12 are not admitted. The tours cost $25 and are offered Wednesday–Saturday (first tour 8:30 am, last tour 1:30 pm). They should be reserved far in advance. For more information, see ⊕ *www.shangrilahawaii.org.*

TOP ATTRACTIONS

Byodo-In Temple. Tucked away in the back of the Valley of the Temples cemetery is a replica of the 11th-century Temple at Uji in Japan. A 2-ton carved wooden statue of the Buddha presides inside the main temple building. Next to the temple building are a meditation pavilion and gardens set dramatically against the sheer, green cliffs of the Koolau Mountains. You can ring the 5-foot, 3-ton brass bell for good luck and

Windward Oahu Villlages

Tiny villages—generally consisting of a sign, store, a beach park, possibly a post office, and not much more—are strung along Kamehameha Highway on the windward side. Each has something to offer. In **Waiahole**, look for fruit stands and an ancient grocery store. In **Kaaawa**, there's a lunch spot and convenience store–gas station. In **Punaluu**, stop at the gallery of fanciful landscape artist Lance Fairly and the woodworking shop, Kahaunani Woods & Crafts, plus venerable Ching

General Store or the Shrimp Shack. Kim Taylor Reece's photo studio, featuring haunting portraits of hula dancers, is between Punaluu and Hauula. **Hauula** has Hauula Gift Shop and Art Gallery, formerly yet another Ching Store, now a clothing shop where sarongs wave like banners, and, at Hauula Kai Shopping Center, Tamura Market, with excellent seafood and the last liquor before Mormon-dominated Laie.

feed some of the hundreds of carp, ducks, and turtles that inhabit the garden's 2-acre pond. Or you can enjoy the peaceful surroundings and just relax. ⊠ *47-200 Kahekili Hwy., Kaneohe* ☎ *808/239–9844* ⊕ *www.byodo-in.com* ⊑ *$3* ⊘ *Daily 9–5.*

NEED A BREAK?

Kalapawai Market. Generations of children have purchased their beach snacks and sodas at Kalapawai Market, near Kailua Beach. A Windward landmark since 1932, the green-and-white market has distinctive charm. You'll see slipper-clad locals sitting in front sharing a cup of coffee and talking story at picnic tables or in front of the market. It's a good source for your carryout lunch, since there's no concession stand at the beach. With one of the better selections of wine on the island, the market is also a great place to pick up a bottle. ⊠ *306 S. Kalaheo Ave., Kailua* ☎ *808/262–4359* ⊕ *www.kalapawaimarket.com* ⊘ *Daily 6 am–9 pm; deli closes at 8 pm.*

Nuuanu Pali Lookout. This panoramic perch looks out to Windward Oahu. It was in this region that King Kamehameha I drove defending forces over the edges of the 1,000-foot-high cliffs, thus winning the decisive battle for control of Oahu. ■**TIP→** From here you can see views that stretch from Kaneohe Bay to Mokolii (little lizard), a small island off the coast, and beyond. Temperatures at the summit are several degrees cooler than in warm Waikiki, so bring a jacket along. And hang on tight to any loose possessions; it gets extremely windy at the lookout. Lock your car; break-ins have occurred here (this lookout is in the most trafficked state park in Hawaii). ⊠ *Top of Pali Hwy., Kaneohe* ⊕ *www.hawaiistateparks.org/parks/oahu/nuuanu.cfm* ⊘ *Daily during daylight hours.*

EN ROUTE

Mokolii. As you drive the Windward and North shores along Kamehameha Highway, you'll note a number of interesting geological features. At Kualoa look to the ocean and gaze at the uniquely shaped little island of Mokolii (little lizard), a 206-foot-high sea stack also known as Chinaman's Hat. According to Hawaiian legend, the goddess Hiiaka, sister of Pele, slew the dragon Mokolii and flung its tail into the sea,

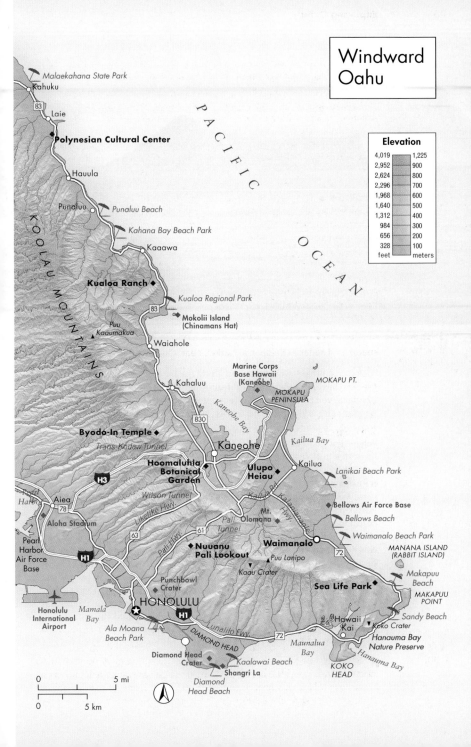

Windward Oahu

Elevation

feet	meters
4,019	1,225
2,952	900
2,624	800
2,296	700
1,968	600
1,640	500
1,312	400
984	300
656	200
328	100
feet	meters

Malaekahana State Park
Kahuku
Laie
Polynesian Cultural Center
Hauula
Punaluu
Punaluu Beach
Kahana Bay Beach Park
Kaaawa
Kualoa Ranch
Kualoa Regional Park
Mokolii Island
(Chinamans Hat)
Puu
Kaaumakua
Waiahole
Marine Corps
Base Hawaii
(Kaneohe)
MOKAPU PT.
MOKAPU
PENINSULA
Kahaluu
Kaneohe Bay
Kailua Bay
Byodo-In Temple
Trans-Koolau Tunnel
Kaneohe
Kailua
Lanikai Beach Park
**Hoomaluhia
Botanical
Garden**
**Ulupo
Heiau**
Aiea
Wilson Tunnel
Likelike Hwy.
Bellows Air Force Base
Pearl
Harbor
Air Force
Base
Mt.
Olomana
Bellows Beach
Waimanalo Beach Park
**Nuuanu
Pali Lookout**
Pali
Tunnel
Pali Hwy.
Waimanalo
Puu Lanipo
Kaau Crater
MANANA ISLAND
(RABBIT ISLAND)
Punchbowl
Crater
Sea Life Park
Makapuu
Beach
MAKAPUU
POINT
HONOLULU
Honolulu
International
Airport
Mamala
Bay
Ala Moana
Beach Park
Lunalilo Hwy.
DIAMOND HEAD
Maunalua
Bay
Hawaii
Kai
Koko Crater
Sandy Beach
Hanauma Bay
Nature Preserve
KOKO
HEAD
Hanauma Bay
Diamond Head
Crater
Kaalawai Beach
Shangri La
Diamond
Head Beach

PACIFIC
OCEAN

KOOLAU MOUNTAINS

Pearl
Harbor

0		5 mi

0		5 km

You can catch a great sunrise over Manana Island, otherwise known as Rabbit Island, located on the windward side of Oahu.

forming the distinct islet. Other dragon body parts—in the form of rocks, of course—were scattered along the base of nearby Kualoa Ridge. ■ **TIP** → **In Laie, if you turn right on Anemoku Street, and right again on Naupaka, you come to a scenic lookout where you can see a group of islets, dramatically washed by the waves.** ✉ *49-479 Kamehameha Highway, Kaneohe* ⊕ *www1.honolulu.gov/parks/programs/beach/kualoa.htm.*

🙂 **Polynesian Cultural Center.** Re-created individual villages showcase the lifestyles and traditions of Hawaii, Tahiti, Samoa, Fiji, the Marquesas Islands, New Zealand, and Tonga. Focusing on individual Islands within its 42-acre center, 35 miles from Waikiki, the Polynesian Cultural Center was founded in 1963 by the Church of Jesus Christ of Latter-day Saints. It houses restaurants, hosts luau, and demonstrates cultural traditions such as tribal tattooing, fire dancing, and ancient customs and ceremonies. The expansive open-air shopping village carries Polynesian handicrafts. ■ **TIP** → **If you're staying in Honolulu, see the center as part of a van tour so you won't have to drive home late at night after the two-hour evening show.** More than 10 different packages are available, from basic admission to an all-inclusive deal. Every May, the PCC hosts the World Fire-Knife Dance Competition, an event that draws the top fire-knife dance performers from around the world. Get tickets for that event in advance. ✉ *55-370 Kamehameha Hwy., Laie* ☎ *808/293–3333, 800/367–7060* ⊕ *www.polynesia.com* 💲 *$45–$225* 🕐 *Mon.–Sat. noon–9:30. Islands close at 6.*

WORTH NOTING

Hoomaluhia Botanical Garden. The name, which means "to make a place of peace and tranquility," describes the serenity and feeling of endless space you find in this verdant garden framed by the stunning Koolau mountain range. Inside its 400 acres are plant collections from such tropical areas as the Americas, Africa, Melanesia, the Philippines, and Hawaii. Not just for the botanist, Hoomaluhia also has a 32-acre lake and open lawns ideal for picnicking. ⊠ *45-680 Luluku Rd., Kaneohe* ☎ *808/233–7323* ⊕ *www1. honolulu.gov/parks/hbg/hmbg.htm* ☐ *Free* ☉ *Daily 9–4.*

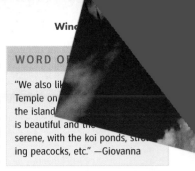

WORD O
"We also li[ke]
Temple on
the island
is beautiful and th[e]
serene, with the koi ponds, str[oll]
ing peacocks, etc." —Giovanna

Kualoa Ranch. Encompassing 4,000 acres about 45 minutes by car from Waikiki, this working ranch offers a wide range of activities—from ATV and horseback tours to hula lessons or jungle expeditions in six-wheel-drive vehicles. The mountains, which serve as the backdrop of this scenic ranch, may seem familiar as the ranch has served as the set for movies such as *Jurassic Park* and *Wind Talkers*, and TV shows *Magnum PI* and *Lost*. From the grounds, you'll have a wonderful view of the ocean and Chinaman's Hat. ⊠ *49-560 Kamehameha Highway, Kaaawa* ☎ *808/237–7321* ⊕ *www.kualoa.com* ☐ *Admission varies based on activity* ☉ *Book activities 2–3 days in advance.*

☺ **Sea Life Park.** Dolphins leap and spin and penguins frolic at this marine-life attraction 15 miles from Waikiki at scenic Makapuu Point. The park has a 300,000-gallon Hawaiian reef aquarium, the Hawaiian Monk Seal Care Center, and a breeding sanctuary for Hawaii's endangered *honu* sea turtle. Join the Stingray or Dolphin Encounter and get up close and personal in the water with these sea creatures (don't worry, the rays' stingers have been removed) or go on an underwater photo safari. ⊠ *41-202 Kalanianaole Hwy., Waimanalo* ☎ *808/259–2500, 866/365–7446* ⊕ *www.sealifeparkhawaii.com* ☐ *$30* ☉ *Daily 10:30–5.*

Ulupo Heiau. Though they may look like piles of rocks to the uninitiated, *heiau* are sacred stone platforms for the worship of the gods and date from ancient times. *Ulupo* means "night inspiration," referring to the legendary *Menehune*, a mythical race of diminutive people who are said to have built the *heiau* under the cloak of darkness. ⊠ *Kalanianaole Hwy. and Kailua Rd., behind the YMCA, Kailua* ⊕ *www. hawaiistateparks.org/parks/oahu/ulupo.cfm.*

Waimanalo. This modest little seaside town flanked by chiseled cliffs is worth a visit. Home to more local families than Kailua to the north or Hawaii Kai to the south, Waimanalo's biggest draws are its beautiful beaches, offering glorious views to the Windward side. **Bellows Beach** is great for swimming and bodysurfing, and **Waimanalo Beach Park** is also safe for swimming. Down the side roads, as you head *mauka* (toward the mountains), are little farms that grow a variety of fruits and flowers. Toward the back of the valley are small ranches with grazing horses. ■ **TIP→** If you see any trucks selling corn and you're staying at a

Stroll along Kailua Beach, which many consider to be Oahu's best beach, as well as the hottest place to windsurf on the island.

place where you can cook it, be sure to get some in Waimanalo. It may be the sweetest you'll ever eat, and the price is the lowest on Oahu. ⊠ *Kalanianaole Hwy., Waimanalo.*

THE NORTH SHORE

Approximately 35 miles (one hour) north of downtown Honolulu, approximately 25 miles (one hour by car) from Kualoa Regional Park (Chinaman's Hat) in Windward Oahu.

An hour from town and a world away in atmosphere, Oahu's North Shore, roughly from Kahuku Point to Kaena Point, is about small farms and big waves, tourist traps and otherworldly landscapes. Parks and beaches, roadside fruit stands and shrimp shacks, a bird sanctuary, and a valley preserve offer a dozen reasons to stop between the onetime plantation town of Kahuku and the surf mecca of Haleiwa.

Haleiwa has had many lives, from resort getaway in the 1900s to plantation town through the 20th century to its life today as a surf and tourist magnet. Beyond Haleiwa is the tiny village of Waialua, a string of beach parks, an airfield where gliders, hang gliders, and parachutists play, and, at the end of the road, Kaena Point State Recreation Area, which offers a brisk hike, striking views, and whale-watching in season.

Pack wisely for a day's North Shore excursion: swim and snorkel gear, light jacket and hat (the weather is mercurial, especially in winter), sunscreen and sunglasses, bottled water and snacks, towels and a picnic blanket, and both sandals and close-toed shoes for hiking. A small cooler is

Continued on page 90

Imagine picking your seat for free at the Super Bowl or wandering the grounds of Augusta National at no cost during The Masters, and you glimpse the opportunity you have when attending the Vans Triple Crown of Surfing on the North Shore.

NORTH SHORE SURFING & THE TRIPLE CROWN

10-FOOT WAVES.
10,000 FANS.
TOP 50 SURFERS.

Long considered the best stretch of surf breaks on Earth, the North Shore surf area encompasses 6 miles of coastline on the northwestern tip of Oahu from Haleiwa to Sunset Beach. There are over 20 major breaks within these 6 miles. Winter storms in the North Pacific send huge swells southward which don't break for thousands of miles until they hit the shallow reef of Oahu's remote North Shore. This creates optimum surfing all winter long and was the inspiration for having surf competitions here each holiday season.

Every November and December the top 50 surfers in world rankings descend on "The Country" to decide who is the best all-around surfer in the world. Each of the three invitation-only contests that make up the Triple Crown has its own winner; competitors also win points based on the final standings. The surfer who excels in all three contests, racking up the most points overall, wins the Vans Triple Crown title. The first contest is held at **Haleiwa Beach,** the second at **Sunset Beach.** The season reaches its crescendo at the most famous surf break in the world, the **Banzai Pipeline.**

The best part is the cost to attend the events—nothing; your seat for the show—wherever you set down your beach towel. Just park your car, grab your stuff, and watch the best surfers in the world tame the best waves in the world.

The only surfing I understand involves the TV.

The contests were created not only to name an overall champion, but to attract the casual fan to the sport. Announcers explain each ride over the loudspeakers, discussing the nuances and values being weighed by the judges. A scoreboard displays points and standings during the four days of each event.

If this still seems incomprehensible to you, the action on the beach can also be exciting as some of the most beautiful people in the world are attracted to these contests.

For more information, see www.triplecrownofsurfing.com.

What should I bring?

Pack for a day at the Triple Crown the way you would for any day at the beach—sun block, beach towel, bottled water, and if you want something other than snacks, food.

These contests are held in rural neighborhoods (read: few stores), so pack anything you might need during the day. Also, binoculars are suggested, especially for the contest at Sunset. The pros will be riding huge outside ocean swells, and it can be hard to follow from the beach without binoculars. Haleiwa's breaks and Pipeline are considerably closer to shore, but binoculars will let you see the intensity on the contestants' faces.

Haleiwa Alii Beach Park
Vans Triple Crown Contest #1: Reef Pro Hawaii

The Triple Crown gets underway with high-performance waves (and the know-how to ride them) at Haleiwa. Though lesser known than the other two breaks of the Triple Crown, it is the perfect wave for showing off: the contest here is full of sharp cutbacks (twisting the board dramatically off the top or bottom of the wave), occasional barrel rides, and a crescendo of floaters (balancing the board on the top of the cresting wave) before the wave is destroyed on the shallow tabletop reef called the Toilet Bowl. The rider who can pull off the most tricks will win this leg, evening the playing field for the other two contests, where knowledge of the break is the key. Also, the beach park is walking distance from historic Haleiwa town, a mecca to surfers worldwide who make their pilgrimage here every winter to ride the waves. Even if you are not a fan, immersing yourself in their culture will make you one by nightfall.

Sunset Beach
Vans Triple Crown Contest #2: Vans World Cup of Surfing

At Sunset, the most guts and bravado win the day. The competition is held when the swell is at 8 to 12 feet and from the northwest. Sunset gets the heaviest surf because it is the exposed point on the northern tip of Oahu. Surfers describe the waves here as "moving mountains." The choice of waves is the key to this contest as only the perfect one will give the competitor a ride through the jigsaw-puzzle outer reef, which can kill a perfect wave instantly, all the way into the inner reef. Big bottom turns (riding all the way down the face of the wave before turning dramatically back onto the wave) and slipping into a super thick tube (slowing down to let the wave catch you and riding inside its vortex) are considered necessary to carry the day.

Banzai Pipeline

Vans Triple Crown Contest #3: Billabong Pipeline Masters

Surfing competitions are generally judged on the top three waves ridden by the competitors. In the Pipeline Masters, however, instead of accruing points through tricks and jumps, the surfers score high by dropping in the deepest and staying inside the tube the longest. The best trick at Pipeline is surviving this incredibly hollow and heavy wave, no other artistry is necessary.

How does the wave become hollow in the first place? When the deep ocean floor ascends steeply to the shore, the waves that meet it will pitch over themselves sharply, rather than rolling. This pitching causes a tube to form, and in most places in the world that tube is a mere couple of feet in diameter. In the case of Pipeline, however, its unique, extremely shallow reef causes

■**TIP→** The **Banzai Pipeline is a surf break, not a beach. The best place to catch a glimpse of the break is from Ehukai Beach.**

the swells to open into 10-foot-high moving hallways that surfers can pass through. Only problem: a single slip puts them right into the raggedly sharp coral heads that caused the wave to pitch in the first place. Broken arms and boards are the rule rather than the exception for those who dare to ride and fail.

When Are the Contests?

The first contests at Haleiwa begin the second week of November, and the Triple Crown finishes up right before Christmas.

Surfing, more so than any other sport, relies on Mother Nature to allow competition. Each contest in the Triple Crown requires only four days of competition, but each is given a window of twelve days. Contest officials decide by 7 AM of each day whether the contest will be held or not, and they release the information to radio stations and via a hotline (the number changes each year, unfortunately). By 7:15, you will know if it is on or not. Consult the local paper's sports section for the hotline number or listen to the radio announcement. The contests run from 8:30 to 4:30, featuring half-hour heats with four to six surfers each.

If big crowds bother you, go early on in the contests, within the first two days of each one. While the finale of the Pipeline Masters may draw about 10,000 fans, the earlier days have the same world-class surfers with fewer than a thousand fans.

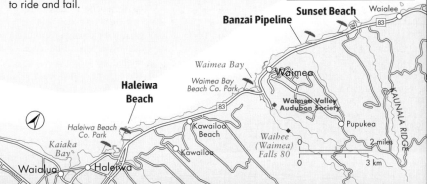

How Do I Get There?

If you hate dealing with parking and traffic, take TheBus. It will transport you from Waikiki to the contest sites in an hour for two bucks and no hassle.

If you must drive, watch the news the night before. If they are expecting big waves that night, there is a very good chance the contest will be on in the morning. Leave by 6 AM to beat the crowd. When everybody else gets the news at 7:15 AM that the show is on, you will be parking your car and taking a snooze on the beach waiting for the surfing to commence.

Parking is limited so be prepared to park alongside Kamehameha Highway and trek it in.

But I'm not coming until Valentine's Day.

There doesn't need to be a contest underway for you to enjoy these spots from a spectator's perspective. The North Shore surf season begins in October and concludes at the end of March. Only the best can survive the wave at Pipeline. You may not be watching 11-time world champ Kelly Slater ripping, but, if the waves are up, you will still see surfing that will blow your mind. Also, there are surf contests year-round on all shores of Oahu, so check the papers to see what is going on during your stay. A few other events to be on the lookout for:

Buffalo's Annual Big Board Surfing Classic

Generally held in March at legendary waterman "Buffalo" Keaulana's home beach of Makaha, this is the Harlem Globetrotters of surfing contests. You'll see tandem riding, headstands, and outrigger canoe surfing. The contest is more about making the crowds cheer than beating your competitors, which makes it very accessible for the casual fan.

Converse Hawaiian Open

During the summer months, the waves switch to the south shore, where there are surf contests of one type or another each week. The Open is one of the biggest and is a part of the US Professional Longboard Surfing Championships. The best shoot it out every August on the waves Duke Kahanamoku made famous at Queen's Beach in Waikiki.

Quiksilver in Memory of Eddie Aikau Big Wave Invitational

The granddaddy of them all is a one-day, winner-take-all contest in 25-foot surf at Waimea Bay. Because of the need for huge waves, it can be held only when there's a perfect storm. That could be at any time in the winter months, and there have been many years when it didn't happen at all. When Mother Nature does comply, however, it is not to be missed. You can hear the waves from the road, even before you can see the beach or the break.

BOARD SHAPES

Longboard: Lengthier (about 2.5–3 m/9–10.5 feet), wider, thicker, and more buoyant than the often-miniscule shortboards. Offers more flotation and speedier paddling, which makes it easier to get into waves. Great for beginners and those with relaxed surf styles. Skill level: Beginner to Intermediate.

Funboard: A little shorter than the longboard with a slightly more acute nose and blunt tail, the Funboard combines the best attributes of the longboards with some similar characteristics of the shorter boards. Good for beginners or surfers looking for a board more maneuverable and faster than a longboard. Skill level: Beginner to Intermediate.

Fishboard: A stumpy, blunt-nosed, twin-finned board that features a "V" tail (giving it a "fish" like look, hence the name) and is fast and maneuverable. Good for catching small, steep, slow waves and pulling tricks. At one point this was the world's best-selling surfboard. Skill level: Intermediate to Expert.

Shortboard: Shortboards came on the scene in 1967-70 when the average board length dropped from 9'6" to 6'6" (2.9m to 2m) and changed the wave riding styles in the surf world forever. This board is a short, light, high-performance stick that is designed for carving the wave with a high amount of maneuverability. These boards need a fast steep wave, completely different than a longboard break, which tends to be slower with shallower wave faces. Skill level: Expert.

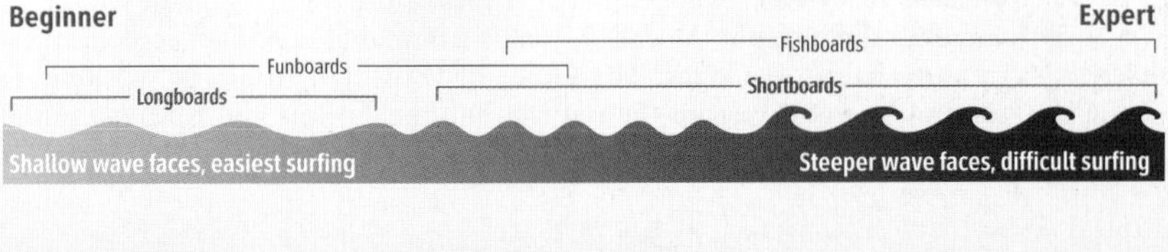

Beginner   Expert

Funboards

Fishboards

Longboards

Shortboards

Shallow wave faces, easiest surfing   Steeper wave faces, difficult surfing nice; you may want to pick up some fruit or fresh corn. As always, leave valuables in the hotel safe and lock the car whenever you park.

GETTING HERE AND AROUND

From Waikiki, the quickest route to the North Shore is H1 east to H2 north, and then the Kamehameha Highway past Wahiawa; you'll hit Haleiwa in less than an hour. The windward route (H1 east, H3, Like Like or Pali Highway, through the mountains, or Kamehameha Highway north) takes at least 90 minutes to Haleiwa, but the drive is far prettier.

TIMING

It's best to dedicate an entire day for an excursion to the North Shore, as it's about an hour from downtown Honolulu, depending on traffic.

TOP ATTRACTIONS

Haleiwa. During the 1920s this seaside hamlet boasted a posh hotel at the end of a railroad line (both long gone). During the 1960s, hippies gathered here, followed by surfers from around the world. Today Haleiwa is a fun mix, with old general stores and contemporary boutiques, galleries, and eateries. Be sure to stop in at **Liliuokalani Protestant Church,** founded by missionaries in the 1830s. It's fronted by a large stone archway built in 1910 and covered with night-blooming cereus. ⊠ *Haleiwa* ✥ *Follow H1 west from Honolulu to H2 north, exit at Wahiawa, follow Kamehameha Hwy. 6 miles, turn left at signaled intersection, then right into Haleiwa.*

NEED A BREAK?   **Matsumoto's.** For a real slice of Haleiwa life, stop at Matsumoto's, a family-run business in a building dating from 1910, for shave ice in every flavor imaginable. For something different, order a shave ice with adzuki beans— the red beans are boiled until soft, mixed with sugar, and then placed in the cone with the ice on top. ⊠ *66-087 Kamehameha Hwy., Haleiwa* ☎ *808/637-4827* ⊕ *www.matsumotoshaveice.com* ⊘ *Daily 9–6.*

Kaena Point State Recreation Area. The name means "the heat" and, indeed, this windy barren coast lacks both shade and fresh water (or any man-made amenities). Pack water, wear sturdy closed-toed shoes, don sunscreen and a hat, and lock the car. The hike is along a rutted dirt road, mostly flat and 3 miles long, ending in a rocky, sandy headland. It is here that Hawaiians believed the souls of the dead met with their family gods, and, if judged worthy to enter the afterlife, leaped off into eternal darkness at Leinaakauane, just south of the point. In summer and at low tide, the small coves offer bountiful shelling; in winter, don't venture near the water. Rare native plants dot the landscape. November through March, watch for humpbacks, spouting and breaching. Binoculars and a camera are highly recommended. ⊠ *69-385 Farrington Hwy., Makua* ⊕ *www.hawaiistateparks.org/parks/oahu/index.cfm?park_id=19.*

☺ ★ **Waimea Valley Park.** Waimea may get lots of press for the giant winter waves in the bay, but the valley itself is a newsmaker and an ecological treasure in its own right. The Office of Hawaiian Affairs is working to conserve and restore the natural habitat. Follow the Kamananui Stream up the valley through the 1,800 acres of gardens. The botanical collections here include more than 5,000 species of tropical flora, including a superb gathering of Polynesian plants. It's the best place on the island to see native species, such as the endangered Hawaiian moorhen. You can also see the remains of the Hale O Lono *heiau* (temple) along with other ancient archaeological sites; evidence suggests that the area was an impor-

WORD OF MOUTH

"The Waimea Audubon Center [now known as Waimea Valley Park] was very nice. It has paved trails through beautiful gardens; there are also some other trails. It was very peaceful! Peacocks run around the property." —Kerry392

tant spiritual center. Daily activities between 10 and 2 include hula lessons, native plant walks, lei-making lessons, kapa cloth-making demonstrations, depending on how many staff members are working on a given day. At the back of the valley, **Waihi Falls** plunges 45 feet into a swimming pond. ■TIP➜ Bring your board shorts—a swim is the perfect way to end your hike. Be sure to bring mosquito repellent, too; it gets buggy. ✉ 59–864 *Kamehameha Hwy., Haleiwa* ☎ 808/638–7766 ⊕ *www.waimeavalley.net* 🎫 $15 ⊗ *Daily 9–5.*

QUICK BITES

Ted's Bakery. The chocolate *haupia* (coconut pudding) pie at Ted's Bakery is legendary. Stop in for a take-out pie or for a quick plate lunch or sandwich. ✉ 59-024 Kamehameha Hwy., near Sunset Beach, Haleiwa ☎ 808/638-8207 ⊕ www.tedsbakery.com ⊗ Mon.–Tues. 7–6, Wed.–Sun. 7 am–8 pm.

WORTH NOTING

Puuomahuka Heiau. Worth a stop for its spectacular views from a bluff high above the ocean overlooking Waimea Bay, this sacred spot was once the site of human sacrifices. It's now on the National Register of Historic Places. ✉ *Pupukea Rd., ½ mile north of Waimea Bay, Haleiwa* ✛ *From Rte. 83, turn right on Pupukea Rd. and drive 1 mile uphill.*

CENTRAL OAHU

Wahiawa is approximately 20 miles (30–35 minutes by car) north of downtown Honolulu, 15 miles (20–30 minutes by car) south of the North Shore.

Oahu's central plain is a patchwork of old towns and new residential developments, military bases, farms, ranches, and shopping malls, with a few visit-worthy attractions and historic sites scattered about. Central Oahu encompasses the Moanalua Valley, residential Pearl City and Mililani, and the old plantation town of Wahiawa, on the uplands halfway to the North Shore.

GETTING HERE AND AROUND

For central Oahu, all sights are most easily reached by either the H1 or H2 freeway.

TIMING

In Central Oahu, check out the Dole Plantation for all things pineapple. This area is about 35 minutes' drive from downtown Honolulu and might make a good stop on the drive to the North Shore or after a

DID YOU KNOW?

Waikiki beach stretches from Hilton Hawaiian Village to Kapiolani Park and Diamond Head, and if you surf here you'll be hanging 10 with the best of 'em.

morning at Pearl Harbor, but the area is probably not worth a separate visit, particularly if you're short on time.

EXPLORING

Dole Plantation. Celebrate Hawaii's famous golden fruit at this promotional center with exhibits, a huge gift shop, a snack concession, educational displays, and the world's largest maze. Take the self-guided Garden Tour, plant your own pineapple, or hop aboard the *Pineapple Express* for a 20-minute train tour to learn a bit about life on a pineapple plantation. Kids love the more than 3-acre Pineapple Garden Maze, made up of 14,000 tropical plants and trees. This is about a 40-minute drive from Waikiki, a suitable stop on the way to or from the North Shore. ⌧ *64-1550 Kamehameha Hwy., Wahiawa* ☎ *808/621–8408* ⊕ *www.dole-plantation.com* ✉ *Pavilion free, maze $6, train $8, garden tour $5* ☉ *Daily 9:30–5:30; train, maze, and garden 9:30–5.*

Kukaniloko Birthstone State Monument. In the cool uplands of Wahiawa is haunting Kukaniloko, where noble chieftesses went to give birth to high-ranking children. One of the most significant cultural sites on the island, the lava-rock stones here were believed to possess the power to ease the labor pains of childbirth. The site is marked by approximately 180 stones covering about a half-acre. It's about a 40- to 45-minute drive from Waikiki. ⌧ *Kamehameha Hwy. and Whitmore Ave., north side of Wahiawa town, Wahiawa* ⊕ *www.hawaiistateparks.org/parks/oahu/index.cfm?park_id=24.*

WEST (LEEWARD) OAHU

Kapolei is approximately 20 miles (30 minutes by car) west of downtown Honolulu, and 12 miles (20 minutes by car) from Mililani; traffic can add significantly to driving time.

West (or Leeward) Oahu has the island's fledgling "second city"—the planned community of Kapolei, where the government hopes to attract enough jobs to lighten inbound traffic to downtown Honolulu—then continues on past a far-flung resort to the Hawaiian communities of Nanakuli and Waianae, to the beach and the end of the road at Keaweula, aka Yokohama Bay.

A couple of cautions as you head to the leeward side: Highway 93 is a narrow, winding, two-lane road notorious for accidents. There's an abrupt transition from freeway to highway at Kapolei, and by the time you reach Nanakuli, it's a country road, so *slow down*. ⚠ **Car break-ins and beach thefts are common here.**

GETTING HERE AND AROUND
West Oahu begins at folksy Waipahu and continues past Makakilo and Kapolei on H1 and Highway 93, Farrington Highway.

TIMING
If you've got to leave one part of this island for the next trip, this is the part to skip. It's a longish drive to West Oahu by island standards—45 minutes to Kapolei from Waikiki and 90 minutes to Waianae—and Central Oahu has little to offer. The Waianae Coast is naturally beautiful, but the area doesn't have the tourist amenities you'll find elsewhere on the

island. The attraction most worth the trek to West Oahu is Hawaii's Plantation Village in Waipahu, about a half hour out of town; it's a living-history museum built from actual homes of turn-of-the-20th-century plantation workers.

WORD OF MOUTH

"[We] typically visit in winter months and have found that when weather is rough elsewhere on the island, the Ko Olina lagoons almost always have nice weather conditions." —JohnD

EXPLORING

Hawaii's Plantation Village. Starting in the 1800s, immigrants seeking work on the sugar plantations came to these islands like so many waves against the shore. At this living museum 30 minutes from downtown Honolulu, visit authentically furnished buildings, original and replicated, that re-create and pay tribute to the plantation era. See a Chinese social hall; a Japanese shrine, sumo ring, and saimin stand; a dental office; and historic homes. The village is open for guided tours only. ⊠ *Waipahu Cultural Gardens Park, 94-695 Waipahu St., Waipahu* ☎ *808/677–0110* ⊕ *www.hawaiiplantationvillage.org* ⊠ *$13* ☉ *Tours on the hr, Mon.–Sat. 10–2.*

Ⓒ **Wet and Wild Hawaii.** This 25-acre family attraction has waterslides, water cannons, and waterfalls. ⊠ *400 Farrington Hwy., off H1 at Exit 1, Kapolei* ☎ *808/674–9283* ⊕ *www.wetnwildhawaii.com* ⊠ *$42* ☉ *M, Th, F 10:30–3:30; weekend 10:30–4.*

3

Beaches

WORD OF MOUTH

"Hanauma Bay was beautiful with blue, blue waters. I got some very nice shots. We were there for just 30 minutes (cheap parking at $1). The sun was out on this side of the island. We stopped at Sandy Beach where I used to body surf and watched the people in the water. Also stopped at Makapuu point. Fabulous scenery!"

—monicapileggi

Updated by
Michael Levine

Tropical sun mixed with cooling trade winds and pristine waters make Oahu's shores a literal heaven on earth. But contrary to many assumptions, the island is not one big beach. There are miles and miles of coastline without a grain of sand, so you need to know where you're going to fully enjoy the Hawaiian experience.

Much of the island's southern and eastern coast is protected by inner reefs. The reefs provide still coastline water but not much as far as sand is concerned. However, where there are beaches on the south and east shores, they are mind-blowing. In West Oahu and on the North Shore you can find the wide expanses of sand you would expect for enjoying the sunset. Sandy bottoms and protective reefs make the water an adventure in the winter months. Most visitors assume the seasons don't change a bit in the Islands, and they would be mostly right—except for the waves, which are big on the South Shore in summer and placid in winter. It's exactly the opposite on the north side, where winter storms bring in huge waves, but the ocean becomes glass-like come May and June.

HONOLULU

Downtown Honolulu has only one beach, the monstrous Ala Moana. It hosts everything from Dragon Boat competitions to the Aloha State Games.

☾ **Ala Moana Beach Park.** Ala Moana has a protective reef, which makes it essentially a ½-mile-wide saltwater swimming pool. Very smooth sand and no waves make it a haven for families and stand-up paddle surfers. After Waikiki, this is the most popular beach among visitors, and the free parking area can fill up quickly on sunny weekend days. On the Waikiki side is a peninsula called Magic Island, with shady trees and paved sidewalks ideal for jogging. Ala Moana also has playing fields, tennis courts, and a couple of small ponds for sailing toy boats. This beach is for everyone, but only in the daytime. It's a high-crime area,

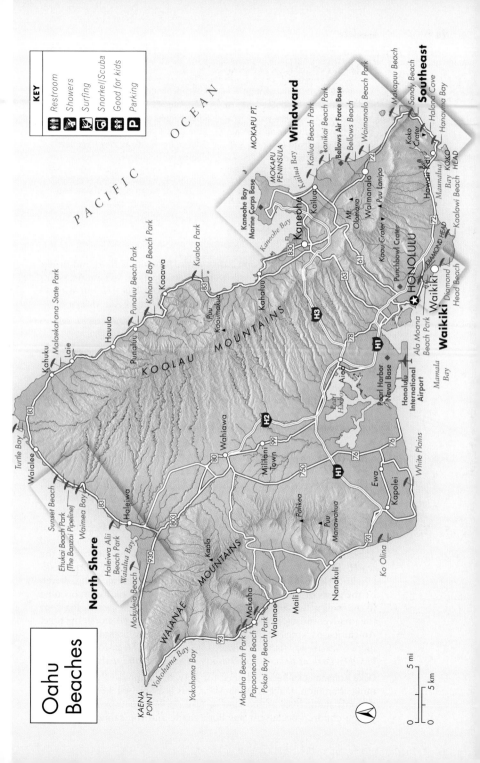

OUTRIGGER CANOES

Outrigger canoes are a simple, cheap, but often-overlooked way to have fun in Waikiki. Everyone clamors to be on the water off Waikiki, and most people go for pricey sailing trips or surf lessons.

The long, funny-looking boats in front of Duke's Canoe Club allow you to get out on the water for much less money. At $10 for three rides, the price hasn't changed in a decade, and the thrill hasn't changed in centuries. You can get a paddle, but no one expects you to use it— the beach boys negotiate you in and out of the break as they have been doing all their lives.

If you think taking off on a wave on a 10-foot board is a rush, wait until your whole family takes off on one in a 30-foot boat!

with lots of homeless people, after dark. **Amenities:** food and drink; lifeguards; parking (no fee); showers; toilets. **Best for:** swimming; walking. ⊠ *1201 Ala Moana Blvd., Downtown Honolulu ✦ From Waikiki take Bus 8 to Ala Moana Shopping Center and cross Ala Moana Blvd.*

WAIKIKI

The 2-mile strand called Waikiki Beach extends from Hilton Hawaiian Village on one end to Kapiolani Park and Diamond Head on the other. Although it's one contiguous piece of beach, it's as varied as the people that inhabit the Islands. Whether you're an old-timer looking to enjoy the action from the shade or a sports nut wanting to do it all, you can find every beach activity here without ever jumping in the rental car.

■ **TIP→** If you're staying outside the area, our best advice is to park at either end of the beach and walk in. Plenty of parking exists on the west end at the Ala Wai Marina, where there are myriad free spots on the beach as well as metered stalls around the harbor. For parking on the east end, Kapiolani Park and the Honolulu Zoo both have metered parking for $1 an hour—more affordable than the $10 per hour the resorts want.

Diamond Head Beach. You have to like a little hiking to like Diamond Head Beach. This beautiful, remote spot is at the base of Diamond Head crater. The beach is just a small strip of sand with lots of coral in the water. This said, the views looking out from the point are breathtaking, and it's amazing to watch the windsurfers skimming along, driven by the gusts off the point. From the parking area, look for an opening in the wall where an unpaved trail leads down to the beach. Even for the unadventurous, a stop at the lookout point is well worth the time. **Amenities:** parking (free); showers. **Best for:** surfing; solitude; windsurfing. ⊠ *At base of Diamond Head, 3500 Diamond Head Rd., Diamond Head ✦ Park at the crest of Diamond Head Rd. and walk down.*

☾ **Duke Kahanamoku Beach.** Named for Hawaii's famous Olympic swimming champion, Duke Kahanamoku, this is a hard-packed beach with the only shade trees on the sand in Waikiki. It's great for families with young children because it has both shade and the calmest waters in

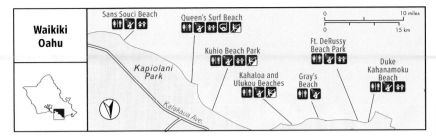

Waikiki, thanks to a rock wall that creates a semiprotected cove. The ocean clarity here is not as brilliant as most of Waikiki because of the stillness of the surf, but it's a small price to pay for peace of mind about youngsters. The beach fronts the Hilton Hawaiian Village Beach Resort and Spa. **Amenities:** food and drink; showers; toilets. **Best for:** walking; sunset. ⊠ *2005 Kalia Rd.*

Fort DeRussy Beach Park. This is one of the finest beaches on the south side of Oahu. A wide, soft, ultrawhite beachfront with gently lapping waves makes it a family favorite for running-jumping-frolicking fun (this also happens to be where the NFL holds its rookie sand football game every year). The new, heavily shaded grass grilling area, sand volleyball courts, and aquatic rentals make this a must for the active visitor. The beach fronts Hale Koa Hotel as well as Fort DeRussy. **Amenities:** food and drink; lifeguards; showers; toilets; water sports. **Best for:** swimming; walking. ⊠ *2161 Kalia Rd.*

Gray's Beach. A little guesthouse called Gray's-by-the-Sea stood here in the 1920s; now it's a gathering place for eclectic beach types from sailing pioneers like George Parsons to the "bird men" of Waikiki: stop and watch the show as up to six parrots are placed on the heads, shoulders, and arms of squealing tourists waiting impatiently for their photos to be taken. The tides often put sand space at a premium, but if you want a look back into old Waikiki, have a mai tai at the Shorebird and check out a time gone by. The Halekulani Hotel and Outrigger Reef hotel are on this beach. **Amenities:** food and drink; lifeguards; parking (fee); showers; toilets. **Best for:** partiers; walking. ⊠ *2199 Kalia Rd.*

Kahaloa and Ulukou Beaches. The beach widens back out here, creating the "it" spot for the bikini crowd. Beautiful bodies abound. This is where you find most of the sailing catamaran charters for a spectacular sail out to Diamond Head, or surfboard and outrigger canoe rentals for a ride on the rolling waves of the Canoe surf break. Great music and outdoor dancing beckon the sand-bound visitor to Duke's Canoe Club, where shirt and shoes not only aren't required, they're discouraged. The Hawaiian Hotel and the Moana Surfrider are both on this beach. **Amenities:** food and drink; lifeguards; parking (fee); showers; toilets; water sports. **Best for:** partiers; surfing. ⊠ *2259 Kalakaua Ave.*

Kuhio Beach Park. This beach has experienced a renaissance after a recent face-lift. Now bordered by a landscaped boardwalk, it's great for romantic walks any time of day. Check out the Kuhio Beach hula mound Tuesday to Sunday at 6:30 for free hula and Hawaiian-music

If you've never been on a surfboard before, Oahu is the place to give it a try, just like these students on Waikiki Beach.

performances and a torch-lighting ceremony at sunset. Surf lessons for beginners are available from the beach center every half hour. **Amenities:** food and drink; lifeguards; showers; toilets; water sports. **Best for:** walking; surfing. ⊠ *2461 Kalakaua Ave.* ⊹ *Go past the Moana Surfrider Hotel to the Kapahulu Ave. pier.*

Queen's Surf. So named as it was once the site of Queen Liliuokalani's beach house, this beach draws a mix of families and gay couples—and it seems as if someone is always playing a steel drum. Many weekends, movie screens are set up on the sand, and major motion pictures are shown after the sun sets (⊕ *www.sunsetonthebeach.net*). In the daytime, there are banyan trees for shade and volleyball nets for pros and amateurs alike (this is where Misty May and Kerri Walsh play while in town). The water fronting Queen's Surf is an aquatic preserve, providing the best snorkeling in Waikiki. **Amenities:** lifeguards; showers; toilets. **Best for:** snorkeling; swimming; walking. ⊠ *2598 Kalakaua Ave., across from the entrance to Honolulu Zoo.*

Sans Souci. Nicknamed Dig-Me Beach because of its outlandish display of skimpy bathing suits, this small rectangle of sand is nonetheless a good sunning spot for all ages. Children enjoy its shallow, safe waters, which are protected by the walls of the historic natatorium, an Olympic-size saltwater swimming arena that's been closed for decades. Serious swimmers and triathletes also swim in the channel here, beyond the reef. Sans Souci is favored by locals wanting to avoid the crowds while still enjoying the convenience of Waikiki. The New Otani Kaimana Beach Hotel is next door. **Amenities:** lifeguards; parking (fee and no fee); showers; toilets. **Best for:** swimming; walking. ⊠ *2776 Kalakaua Ave.,*

across from Kapiolani Park, between the New Otani Kaimana Beach Hotel and the Waikiki War Memorial Natatorium.

SOUTHEAST OAHU

Much of Southeast Oahu is surrounded by reef, making most of the coast uninviting to swimmers, but the spots where the reef opens up are true gems. The drive along this side of the island is amazing, with its sheer lava-rock walls on one side and deep-blue ocean on the other. There are plenty of restaurants in the suburb of Hawaii Kai, so you can make a day of it, knowing that food isn't far away.

Halona Cove. Also known as *From Here to Eternity Beach* and "Pounders," this little beauty is never crowded due to the short, treacherous climb down to the sand. But for the intrepid, what a treat this spot can be. It's in a break in the ocean cliffs, with the surrounding crags providing protection from the wind. Open-ocean waves roll up onto the beach (thus the second nickname), but unlike at Sandy Beach, a gently sloping sand bottom takes much of the punch out of them before they hit the shore. Turtles frequent the small cove, seeking respite from the otherwise blustery coast. It's great for packing a lunch and holing up for the day. ■ **TIP→** **The current is mellow inside the cove but dangerous once you get outside it.** **Amenities:** parking (no fee). **Best for:** sunrise; solitude. ⊠ *8699 Kalanianaole Hwy., below the Halona Blow Hole Lookout parking lot, Hawaii Kai.*

Hanauma Bay Nature Preserve. Picture this as the world's biggest open-air aquarium. You go here to see fish, and fish you'll see. Due to their exposure to thousands of visitors every week, these fish are more like family pets than the skittish marine life you might expect. An old volcanic crater has created a haven from the waves where the coral has thrived. There's an educational center where you must watch a nine-minute video about the nature preserve before being allowed down to the bay. ■ **TIP→** **The bay is best early in the morning (around 7), before the crowds arrive; it can be difficult to park later in the day.** There's an entry fee for nonresidents. Smoking is not allowed, and the beach is closed on Tuesday. Wednesday to Monday, the beach is open from 6 am to 6 pm. There's a tram from the parking lot to the beach. Need transportation? Hanauma Bay Dive Tours runs snorkeling, snuba, and scuba tours to Hanauma Bay with transportation from Waikiki hotels on Monday, Wednesday, Thursday, and Friday only. ⇨ *See Scuba Diving in Chapter*

BEACH SAFETY ON OAHU

Hawaii's world-renowned, beautiful beaches can be dangerous at times due to large waves and strong currents—so much so that the state rates wave hazards using three signs: a yellow square (caution), a red stop sign (high hazard), and a black diamond (extreme hazard). Signs are posted and updated three times daily or as conditions change.

Visiting beaches with lifeguards is strongly recommended, and you should swim only when there's a normal caution rating. Never swim alone or dive into unknown water or shallow breaking waves. If you're unable to swim out of a rip current, don't fight the pull but instead tread water and wave your arms in the air to signal for help.

Even in calm conditions, there are other dangerous things in the water to be aware of, including razor-sharp coral, jellyfish, eels, and sharks.

Jellyfish cause the most ocean injuries, and signs are posted along beaches when they're present. Reactions to a sting are usually mild (burning sensation, redness, welts); however, in some cases they can be severe (breathing difficulties). If you're stung, pick off the tentacles, rinse the affected area with water, and apply ice.

The chances of getting bitten by a shark in Hawaiian waters are very low; sharks attack swimmers or surfers fewer than three or four times per year. Of the 40 species of sharks found near Hawaii, tiger sharks are considered the most dangerous because of their size and indiscriminate feeding behavior. They're easily recognized by their blunt snouts and vertical bars on their sides. Here are a few tips to reduce your shark-attack risk:

■ Swim, surf, or dive with others at beaches patrolled by lifeguards.

■ Avoid swimming at dawn, dusk, and night, when some shark species may move inshore to feed.

■ Don't enter the water if you have open wounds or are bleeding.

■ Avoid murky waters, harbor entrances, areas near stream mouths (especially after heavy rains), channels or steep drop-offs.

■ Don't wear high-contrast swimwear or shiny jewelry.

■ Don't swim near dolphins, which are often prey for large sharks.

■ If you spot a shark, leave the water quickly and calmly; never provoke or harass a shark, no matter how small.

The website ⊕ *oceansafety.soest. hawaii.edu* provides statewide beach-hazard maps as well as weather and surf advisories, listings of closed beaches, and safety tips.

4, *Water Sports and Tours*. **Amenities:** food and drink; lifeguards; parking (fee); showers; toilets. **Best for:** snorkeling; swimming. ⊠ *7455 Kalanianaole Hwy., Hawaii Kai* ☎ *808/396–4229* ⊠ *Nonresident fee $7.50; parking $1; mask, snorkel, and fins rental $12; tram from parking lot to beach $1.75 round-trip* ☉ *Wed.–Mon. 6–6.*

★ **Sandy Beach.** Probably the most popular beach with locals on this side of Oahu, the broad, sloping beach is covered with sunbathers there to

Not a water baby? Come to Sandy Beach—otherwise known as Break-Neck Beach—to watch the massive ocean swells and awesome pounding surf.

watch the "Show" and soak up rays. The Show is a shore break that's like no other in the Islands. Monster ocean swells rolling into the beach combined with the sudden rise in the ocean floor causes waves to jack up and crash magnificently on the shore. Expert surfers and body boarders young and old brave this danger to get some of the biggest barrels you can find for bodysurfing. ■TIP→ **But keep in mind that the beach is nicknamed "Break-Neck Beach" for a reason: many neck and back injuries are sustained here each year.** Use extreme caution when swimming here, or just kick back and watch the drama unfold from the comfort of your beach chair. **Amenities:** lifeguards; parking (no fee); showers; toilets. **Best for:** surfing; walking. ⊠ *7850 Kalanianaole Hwy., makai of Kalanianaole Hwy., 2 miles east of Hanauma Bay., Hawaii Kai.*

WINDWARD OAHU

The Windward side lives up to its name, with ideal spots for windsurfing and kiteboarding, or for the more intrepid, hang gliding. For the most part the waves are mellow, and the bottoms are all sand—making for nice spots to visit with younger kids. The only drawback is that this side does tend to get more rain. But the vistas are so beautiful that a little sprinkling of "pineapple juice" shouldn't dampen your experience; plus, it benefits the waterfalls that cascade down the Koolaus.

Bellows Beach. Bellows is the same beach as Waimanalo, but it's under the auspices of the military, making it more friendly for visitors—though that also limits public beach access to weekends. The park area is excellent for camping, and ironwood trees provide plenty of shade.

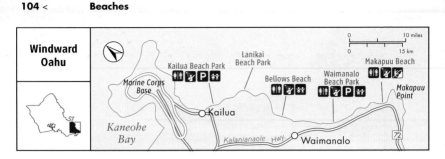

■**TIP→** **The beach is best before 2 pm.** After 2, the trade winds bring clouds that get hung up on steep mountains nearby, causing overcast skies until midafternoon. There are no food concessions, but McDonald's and other takeout fare, including *huli huli* (rotisserie) chicken on weekends, are right outside the entrance gate. **Amenities:** lifeguards; parking (no fee); showers; toilets. **Best for:** camping; solitude; swimming. ⊠ *520 Tinker Rd., Waimanalo* ✦ *Entrance on Kalanianaole Hwy. near Waimanalo town center.*

☾ **Kahana Bay Beach Park.** Local parents often bring their children here to wade in safety in the very shallow, protected waters. This pretty beach cove, surrounded by mountains, has a long arc of sand that is great for walking and a cool, shady grove of tall ironwood and pandanus trees that is ideal for a picnic. An ancient Hawaiian fishpond, which was in use into the 1920s, is visible nearby. The water here is not generally a clear blue due to the runoff from heavy rains in the valley. **Amenities:** lifeguards; parking (no fee); showers; toilets. **Best for:** walking; swimming. ⊠ *52-201 Kamehameha Hwy., north of Kualoa Park, Kaneohe.*

☾ **Kailua Beach Park.** A cobalt-blue sea and a wide continuous arc of pow-
Fodor's Choice dery sand make Kailua Beach Park one of the island's best beaches,
★ illustrated by the crowds of local families who spend their weekend days here. This is like a big Lanikai Beach, but a little windier and a little wider, and a better spot for spending a full day. Kailua Beach has calm water, a line of palms and ironwoods that provide shade on the sand, and a huge park with picnic pavilions where you can escape the heat. This is the "it" spot if you're looking to try your hand at windsurfing or kiteboarding. You can rent kayaks nearby at Kailua Sailboards and Kayaks (*130 Kailua Rd.*) and take them to the Mokulua Islands for the day. Two-seaters cost $55 for four hours or $65 for a full day. ⇨ *See Windsurfing and Kiteboarding in Chapter 4.* **Amenities:** lifeguards; parking (no fee); showers; toilets; water sports. **Best for:** walking; windsurfing. ⊠ *437 Kawailoa Rd., Kailua* ✦ *Near Kailua town, turn right on Kailua Rd. At market, cross bridge, then turn left into beach parking lot.*

Kualoa Park. Grassy expanses border a long, narrow stretch of beach with spectacular views of Kaneohe Bay and the Koolau Mountains, making Kualoa one of the island's most beautiful picnic, camping, and beach areas. Dominating the view is an islet called Mokolii, better known as Chinaman's Hat, which rises 206 feet above the water. You can swim in the shallow areas year-round. The one drawback is that it's

Kailua Beach is an ideal place for a picnic, as nearby pavilions and palm trees provide a break from the strong Hawaiian sun.

usually windy here, but the wide-open spaces are ideal for kite flying. **Amenities:** lifeguards; showers; toilets. **Best for:** solitude; swimming. ⊠ *49-479 Kamehameha Hwy., north of Waiahole, Kaaawa.*

★ **Lanikai Beach Park.** Think of the beaches you see in commercials: peaceful jade green waters, powder-soft white sand, families and dogs frolicking mindlessly, offshore islands in the distance. It's an ideal spot for camping out with a book. Though the beach hides behind multimillion-dollar houses, by state law there is public access every 400 yards. You'll find street parking on Mokulua Drive for the various public-access points to the beach. ■ **TIP→ Look for walled or fenced pathways every 400 yards, leading to the beach. Be sure not to park in the marked bike/jogging lane.** There are no shower or bathroom facilities here—they are a two-minute drive away at Kailua Beach Park. **Amenities:** None. **Best for:** walking; swimming. ⊠ *974 Mokulua Dr., past Kailua Beach Park, Kailua.*

Fodor's Choice **Makapuu Beach.** A magnificent beach protected by Makapuu Point wel-
★ comes you to the Windward side. Hang gliders circle above the beach, and the water is filled with body boarders. Just off the coast you can see Bird Island, a sanctuary for aquatic fowl, jutting out of the blue. The currents can be heavy, so check with a lifeguard if you're unsure of safety. Before you leave, take the prettiest (and coldest) outdoor shower available on the island. Being surrounded by tropical flowers and foliage while you rinse off that sand will be a memory you will cherish from this side of the rock. **Amenities:** lifeguards; parking (no fee); showers; toilets. **Best for:** swimming; walking. ⊠ *41-095 Kalanianaole Hwy, across from Sea Life Park, 2 miles south of Waimanalo, Waimanalo.*

DID YOU KNOW?

Windward Oahu's Makapuu Beach is protected by Makapuu Point, but currents are still strong, so take caution when in the water.

Malaekahana Beach Park. The big attraction here is tiny Goat Island, a bird sanctuary just offshore. At low tide the water is shallow enough—never more than waist-high—so that you can wade out to it. Wear sneakers or aqua socks so you don't cut yourself on the coral. The beach itself is fairly narrow but long enough for a 20-minute stroll, one-way. The waves are

never too big, and sometimes they're just right for the beginning body-surfer. The entrance gates, which close at 6:45 pm, are easy to miss, and you can't see the beach from the road. Families love to camp in the groves of ironwood trees at Malaekahana State Park. Cabins are also available here, making a perfect rural getaway. **Amenities:** parking (no fee); showers; toilets. **Best for:** walking; swimming. ⊠ *56-207 Kamehameha Hwy., Kahuku ✛ Entrance gates are ½ mile north of Laiie on Kamehameha Hwy.*

Punaluu Beach Park. If you're making a circle of the island, this is a great stopping point to jump out of your car and stretch your legs. It's easy, because the sand literally comes up to your parked car, and nice, because there is a sandy bottom and mostly calm conditions. Plus there are full facilities and lots of shade trees. Often overlooked, and often overcast, Punaluu can afford you a moment's fresh air before you get back to your sightseeing. **Amenities:** parking (no fee); showers; toilets. **Best for:** solitude; swimming. ⊠ *53-400 Kamehameha Hwy., Hauula.*

Waimanalo Beach Park. One of the most beautiful beaches on the island, Waimanalo is a local beach, busy with picnicking families and active sports fields. Expect a wide stretch of sand; turquoise, emerald, and deep blue seas; and gentle shore-breaking waves that are fun for all ages. Theft is an occasional problem, so lock your car. **Amenities:** lifeguards; parking (no fee); showers; toilets. **Best for:** sunrise; walking; swimming. ⊠ *41-849 Kalanianaole Hwy., south of Waimanalo town center, Waimanalo.*

NORTH SHORE

"North Shore, where the waves are mean, just like a washing machine," sing the Kaau Crater Boys about this legendary side of the island. And in winter they are absolutely right. At times the waves overtake the road, stranding tourists and locals alike. When the surf is up, there are signs on the beach telling you how far to stay back so that you aren't swept out to sea. The most prestigious big-wave contest in the world, the Eddie Aikau, is held at Waimea Bay on waves the size of a five- or six-story building. The Triple Crown of Surfing roams across three North Shore beaches in the winter months.

All this changes come summer when this tiger turns into a kitten, with water smooth enough to water-ski on and ideal for snorkeling. The

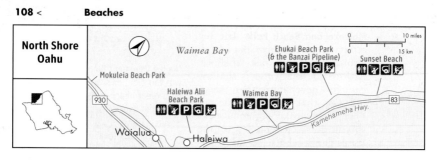

fierce Banzai Pipeline surf break becomes a great dive area, allowing you to explore the coral heads that, in winter, have claimed so many lives on the ultra-shallow but big, hollow tubes created here. Even with the monster surf subsided, this is still a time for caution: lifeguards are scarce, and currents don't subside just because the waves do.

That said, it's a place like no other on earth, and must be explored. From the turtles at Mokuleia to the tunnels at Shark's Cove, you could spend your whole trip on this side and not be disappointed.

Ehukai Beach Park. What sets Ehukai apart is the view of the famous Banzai Pipeline, where the winter waves curl into magnificent tubes, making it an experienced wave-rider's dream. It's also an inexperienced swimmer's nightmare, though spring and summer waves are more accommodating to the average swimmer, and there's good snorkeling. Except when the surf contests are going on, there's no reason to stay on the central strip. Travel in either direction from the center, and the conditions remain the same but the population thins out, leaving you with a magnificent stretch of sand all to yourself. **Amenities:** lifeguards; parking (no fee); showers; toilets. **Best for:** surfing; snorkeling. ⊠ *59-406 Kamehameha Hwy., 1 mile north of Foodland at Pupukea, Haleiwa.*

Haleiwa Alii Beach Park. The winter waves are impressive here, but in summer the ocean is like a lake, ideal for family swimming. The beach itself is big and often full of locals. Its broad lawn off the highway invites volleyball and Frisbee games and groups of barbecuers. This is also the opening break for the Triple Crown of Surfing, and the grass is often filled with art festivals or carnivals. **Amenities:** lifeguards; parking (no fee); showers; toilets. **Best for:** surfing; swimming. ⊠ *66-162 Haleiwa Rd., north of Haleiwa town center and past harbor, Haleiwa.*

Mokuleia Beach Park. There is a reason why the producers of the TV show *Lost* chose this beach for their set. On the remote northwest point of the island, it is about 10 miles from the closest store or public restroom; you could spend a day here and not see another living soul. And that is precisely its beauty—all the joy of being stranded on a deserted island without the trauma of the plane crash. The beach is wide and white, the waters bright blue (but a little choppy) and full of sea turtles and other marine life. Mokuleia is a great secret find; just remember to pack supplies and use caution, as there are no lifeguards. **Amenities:** None. **Best for:** solitude. ⊠ *68-67 Farrington Hwy., east of Haleiwa town center, across from Dillingham Airfield, Haleiwa.*

DID YOU KNOW?

If you're vacationing with kids, Lanikai Beach is a good choice, with calm water and soft sand.

Sunset Beach on Oahu's North Shore is known for its ample supply of puka shells, which are a staple of Hawaiian jewelry.

★ **Sunset Beach.** The beach is broad, the sand is soft, the summer waves are gentle, making for good snorkeling, and the winter surf is crashing. Many love searching this shore for the puka shells that adorn the necklaces you see everywhere. Carryout truck stands selling shave ice, plate lunches, and sodas usually line the adjacent highway. **Amenities:** food and drink; lifeguards; parking (no fee); showers; toilets. **Best for:** snorkeling; sunset. ⊠ *59 Kamehameha Hwy., 1 mile north of Ehukai Beach Park, Haleiwa.*

Turtle Bay. Now known more for its resort (the Turtle Bay Resort) than its magnificent beach, Turtle Bay is mostly passed over on the way to the better-known beaches of Sunset and Waimea. But for the average visitor with the average swimming capabilities, this is the place to be on the North Shore. The crescent-shaped beach is protected by a huge sea wall. You can see and hear the fury of the northern swell, while blissfully floating in cool, calm waters. The convenience of this spot is also hard to pass up—there is a concession selling sandwiches and sunblock right on the beach. **Amenities:** food and drink; parking (no fee); showers; toilets. **Best for:** swimming; sunset. ⊠ *57-20 Kuilima Dr., 4 miles north of Kahuku, Kahuku ✛ Turn into Turtle Bay Resort, and let guard know where you are going.*

Fodor's Choice **Waimea Bay.** Made popular in that old Beach Boys song "Surfin' U.S.A.," ★ Waimea Bay is a slice of big-wave heaven, home to king-size 25- to 30-foot winter waves. Summer is the time to swim and snorkel in the calm waters. The shore break is great for novice bodysurfers. Due to its popularity, the postage-stamp parking lot is quickly filled, but everyone parks along the side of the road and walks in. **Amenities:** lifeguards;

SUN SAFETY ON OAHU

Hawaii's weather—seemingly never-ending warm, sunny days with gentle trade winds—can be enjoyed year-round with good sun sense. Because of Hawaii's subtropical location, the length of daylight here changes little throughout the year. The sun is particularly strong, with a daily UV average of 14. Visitors should take extra precaution to avoid sunburns and long-term cancer risks due to sun exposure.

The Hawaii Dermatological Society recommends these sun safety tips:

■ Plan your beach, golf, hiking, and other outdoor activities for the early morning or late afternoon, avoiding the sun between 10 am and 4 pm, when it's the strongest.

■ Apply a broad-spectrum sunscreen with a sun protection factor (SPF) of at least 15. Hawaii lifeguards use sunscreens with an SPF of 30. Cover areas that are most prone to burning, like your nose, shoulders, tops of feet, and ears. And don't forget to use sun-protection products on your lips.

■ Apply sunscreen at least 30 minutes before you plan to be outdoors and reapply every two hours, even on cloudy days. Clouds scatter sunlight so you can still burn on an overcast day.

■ Wear light, protective clothing, such as a long-sleeve shirt and pants, broad-brimmed hat, and sunglasses.

■ Stay in the shade whenever possible—especially on the beach—by using an umbrella. Remember that sand and water can reflect up to 85% of the sun's damaging rays.

■ Children need extra protection from the sun. Apply sunscreen frequently and liberally on children over six months of age and minimize their time in the sun. Sunscreen is not recommended for children under six months.

parking (no fee); showers; toilets. **Best for:** surfing (in winter); swimming and snorkeling (in summer). ⊠ *61-31 Kamehameha Hwy., across from Waimea Valley, 3 miles north of Haleiwa, Haleiwa.*

WEST (LEEWARD) OAHU

The North Shore may be known as "Country," but the west side is truly the rural area on Oahu. There are commuters from this side to Honolulu, but many are born, live, and die on this side with scarcely a trip to town. For the most part, there's little hostility toward outsiders, but occasional problems have flared up, mostly due to drug abuse that has ravaged the fringes of the island. The problems have generally been car break-ins, not violence. So, in short, lock your car, don't bring valuables, and enjoy the amazing beaches.

The beaches on the west side are expansive and empty. Most Oahu residents and tourists don't make it to this side simply because of the drive; in traffic it can take almost 90 minutes to make it to Kaena Point from downtown Honolulu. But you'll be hard-pressed to find a better sunset anywhere.

DID YOU KNOW?

Beach Boys fans flock to Waimea Bay, the beach with winter waves reaching 30 feet, made popular in "Surfin' U.S.A."

☺ **Ko Olina.** This is the best spot on the island if you have small kids. The
★ resort commissioned a series of four man-made lagoons, but, as it has
to provide public beach access, you are the winner. Huge rock walls
protect the lagoons, making them into perfect spots for the kids to get
their first taste of the ocean without getting bowled over. The large
expanses of seashore grass and hala trees that surround the semicircle
beaches are made-to-order for naptime. A 1½-mile jogging track con-
nects the lagoons. Due to its appeal for *keiki* (children), Ko Olina is
popular, and the parking lot fills up quickly when school is out and on
weekends, so try to get here before 10 am. The biggest parking lot is at
the farthest lagoon from the entrance. There are actually three resorts
here: Aulani (the Disney resort), the J.W. Marriott Ihilani Resort & Spa,
and the Ko Olina Beach Villas Resort (which has a time-share section as
well). **Amenities:** food and drink; parking (no fee); showers; toilet. **Best
for:** swimming; walking. ✉ *92 Aliinui Dr., 23 miles west of Honolulu,
Kapolei* ✛ *Take Ko Olina exit off H1 West and proceed to guard shack.*

Makaha Beach Park. This beach provides a slice of local life most visitors
don't see. Families string up tarps for the day, fire up hibachis, set up
lawn chairs, get out the fishing gear, and strum ukulele while they "talk
story" (chat). Legendary waterman Buffalo Kaeulana can be found in
the shade of the palms playing with his grandkids and spinning yarns of
yesteryear. In these waters Buffalo not only invented some of the most
outrageous methods of surfing, but also raised his world-champion son,
Rusty. He also made Makaha the home of the world's first international
surf meet in 1954 and still hosts his Big Board Surfing Classic. With
its long, slow-building waves, it's a great spot to try out longboarding.
The swimming is generally decent in summer, but avoid the big winter
waves. The only parking is along the highway, but it's free. **Amenities:**
lifeguards; showers; toilets. **Best for:** swimming; surfing. ✉ *84-450 Farrington Hwy., Waianae* ✛ *Go 32 miles west of Honolulu on the H1,
then exit onto Farrington Hwy. The beach will be on your left.*

Pokai Bay Beach Park. This gorgeous swimming and snorkeling beach
is protected by a long breakwater left over from a now-defunct boat
harbor. The beach's entire length is sand, and a reef creates smallish
waves perfect for novice surfers. **Amenities:** parking (no fee); toilets.
Best for: snorkeling; swimming; surfing. ✉ *85-027 Waianae Valley Rd.,
off Farrington Hwy., Waianae.*

Papaoneone Beach. You may have to do a little exploring to find Papaoneone Beach, which is tucked away behind three condos. Duck through
a wide, easy-to-spot hole in the fence, and you find an extremely wide,
sloping beach that always seems to be empty. You'll have to park on
the street. The waters are that eerie blue found only on the west side.
The waves can get high here (it faces the same direction as the famed
Makaha Beach), but, for the most part, the shore break makes for great
easy rides on your boogie board or belly. The only downside is that,
with the exception of a shower, all the facilities are for the condos at
the adjacent Beach Lovers Hawaii, so it's just you and the big blue.
Amenities: showers. **Best for:** solitude; swimming (carefully). ✉ *84-946
Farrington Hwy, in Makaha, across from Jade St., Waianae.*

White Plains. Concealed from the public eye for many years as part of the former Barbers Point Naval Air Station, this beach is reminiscent of Waikiki but without the condos and the crowds. It is a long, sloping beach with numerous surf breaks, but it is also mild enough at shore for older children to play freely. It has views of Pearl Harbor and, over that, Diamond Head. Although the sand lives up to its name, the real joy of this beach comes from its history as part of a military property for the better part of a century. Expansive parking, great restroom facilities, and numerous tree-covered barbecue areas make it a great day-trip spot. As a bonus, a Hawaiian monk seal takes up residence here several months out of the year (seals are rare in the Islands). **Amenities:** lifeguards; parking (no fee); showers; toilets. **Best for:** swimming; surfing. ✉ *Essex Rd. and Tripoli Rd., off H1 W., Kapolei ✛ Take the Makakilo exit off H1 West, then turn left. Follow it into base gates, make a left. Blue signs lead to beach.*

Yokohama Bay. You'll be one of the few outsiders at this Waianae Coast beach at the very end of the road. If it weren't for the little strip of paved road, it would feel like a deserted isle: no stores, no houses, just a huge sloping stretch of beach and some of the darkest-blue water off the island. Locals come here to fish and swim in waters that are calm enough for children in summer. Early morning brings with it spinner dolphins by the dozens just offshore. Though Makua Beach up the road is the best spot to see these animals, it's not nearly as beautiful or sandy as "Yokes." **Amenities:** parking (no fee); showers; toilets. **Best for:** solitude; sunset; swimming. ✉ *81-780 Farrington Hwy., about 7 miles north of Makaha, Waianae.*

Water Sports and Tours

WORD OF MOUTH

"I could not believe the clarity of the water and how warm it was. We jump in, stick our heads in the water and are rewarded with colorful fish. Then I see what I came here to see. A sea turtle!"

—GypsyGurl

Updated by
Catherine E.
Toth

From snorkeling on the North Shore to kayaking to small islands off Kailua Beach to stand-up paddleboarding in Waikiki—when you're on Oahu, there's always a reason to get wet. You can swim with native fish in a protected bay, surf waves in an outrigger canoe, take to the skies in a parasail above Diamond Head, or enjoy panoramic views of Waikiki aboard a 45-foot catamaran. Diving into the ocean—whether in a boat, on a board, or with your own finned feet—is a great way to experience Oahu.

But as with any physical activity, heed the warnings. The ocean is unpredictable and unforgiving, and it can be as dangerous as it can be awe-inspiring. But if you respect it, it can offer you the kind of memories that last well after your vacation.

BOAT TOURS AND CHARTERS

Being on the water can be the best way to enjoy the Islands. Whether you want to see the fish in action or experience how they taste, there is a tour for you.

For a sailing experience in Oahu, you need go no farther than the beach in front of your hotel in Waikiki. Strung along the sand are seven beach catamarans that will provide you with one-hour rides during the day and 90-minute sunset sails. Look for $23 to $25 for day sails and $30 to $34 for sunset rides. ■TIP➜ **Feel free to haggle, especially with the smaller boats.** Some provide drinks for free, some charge for them, and some let you pack your own, so keep that in mind when pricing the ride.

Hawaii Nautical. Catamaran cruises lead to snorkeling with dolphins, gourmet-dinner cruises head out of beautiful Kalaeloa harbor, and sailing lessons are available on a 20-foot sailboat and a 50-foot cat. If you're driving out from Waikiki, you may want to make a day of it, with sailing in the morning, then 18 holes on one of the five golf courses in the area in the afternoon. Three-hour cruise rates with snacks and two drinks begin at $109 per person. There's a second location at 91-607 Malakole Street in Kapolei. ⊠ *Kewalo Basin Harbor, 1125 Ala Moana Blvd., Kapolei* ☎ *808/234–7245* ⊕ *www.hawaiinautical.com.*

Maitai Catamaran. Taking off from the stretch of sand between the Sheraton Waikiki and the Halekulani Hotel, this 44-foot twin-hull cat is the fastest and sleekest on the beach. If you have a need for speed and enjoy a little more upscale experience, this is the boat for you. ⊠ *Waikiki Beach, between the Sheraton Waikiki and the Halekulani Hotel, Waikiki, Honolulu* ☎ *808/922–5665, 800/462–7975* ⊕ *www. maitaicatamaran.net* ☜ *$28–$45.*

Makani Catamaran. This 64-foot Makani catamaran is the tops in Hawaii for luxury, from its Bose stereo system to its LCD TVs to its freshwater bathrooms. It sails out of Kewalo Basin three times daily. Breakfast cruises start at $42, while "city lights" dinner cruises start at $53. ⊠ *Kewalo Basin Harbor, 1125 Ala Moana Blvd., Honolulu* ☎ *808/591–9000* ⊕ *www.sailmakani.com.*

Na Hoku II Catamaran. The boat's motto is "Free drinks, easy crew." It features thumping reggae music and includes free booze in its $25 price tag ($30 for sunset cruises). The 45-foot catamaran is tied up near Duke's Barefoot Bar and sails five times daily. ⊠ *Waikiki Beach, between the Sheraton Moana Surfrider Hotel and Duke's Barefoot Bar, Honolulu* ☎ *No phone* ⊕ *www.nahokuii.com* ☜ *$25–$30.*

Red Dolphin. Despite its name, the Red Dolphin is actually a yellow, blue, and green floating platform anchored off Waikiki. It's like an 11,000-square-foot playground with diving platforms, waterslides, trampoline, and floating bar and grill. Admission is $49, with activities like snorkeling, kayaking, paddleboarding, and parasailing costing extra. The platform holds up to 400 people and is open daily. There are eight pickup points throughout Waikiki. ⊠ *1025 Ala Moana Blvd., Honolulu* ☎ *808/753–9446* ⊕ *www.reddolphin.net* ☜ *$49.*

Star of Honolulu Cruises. Founded in 1957, this company recently expanded its fleet to include the 65-foot *Hoku Naia*, docked on Oahu's west coast. It offers everything from snorkeling cruises in the pristine waters off the Waianae coast to gourmet-dinner cruises with live entertainment to seasonal whale-watching sails on one of two vessels. Popular cruises teach you how to string lei and dance hula. Two-hour whale-watching-excursion rates begin at $30 per person, while dinner cruises start at $175. The company has a second location at 85-371 Farrington Highway in Waianae. ⊠ *Aloha Tower Marketplace, 1 Aloha Tower Dr., Honolulu* ☎ *808/983–7827* ⊕ *www.starofhonolulu.com* ☜ *$30–$175.*

Tradewind Charters. This company's half-day excursions feature sailing, snorkeling, and whale-watching. Traveling on these luxury yachts not only gets you away from the crowds, but also gives you the opportunity to "take the helm" if you wish. The cruise includes snorkeling at an exclusive anchorage, as well as hands-on snorkeling and sailing instruction. Charter prices are about $495 for up to six passengers.

Sail around the island to spot wildlife and deserted beaches.

✉ *Kewalo Basin Harbor, 1125 Ala Moana Blvd., Ala Moana, Honolulu*
☎ *800/829–4899* ⊕ *www.tradewindcharters.com.*

BODY BOARDING AND BODYSURFING

Body boarding (or sponging) has long been a popular alternative to surfing for a couple of reasons. First, the start-up cost is much less—a usable board can be purchased for $30 to $40 or can be rented on the beach for $5 an hour. Second, it's a whole lot easier to ride a body board than to tame a surfboard. All you have to do is paddle out to the waves, then turn toward the beach as the wave approaches and kick like crazy.

Most grocery and convenience stores sell body boards. Though these boards don't compare to what the pros use, beginners won't notice a difference in their handling on smaller waves. ■**TIP➔ Another small investment you'll want to make is surf fins.** These smaller, sturdier versions of dive fins sell for $25 to $60 at surf and dive stores, and sporting-goods stores. Most beach stands don't rent fins with the boards. Though they are not necessary for body boarding, fins do give you a tremendous advantage when you're paddling. If you plan to go out into bigger surf, we would also suggest getting a leash, which reduces the chance you'll lose your board.

Bodysurfing requires far less equipment—just a pair of swim fins with heel straps—but it can be a lot more challenging to master. Typically, surf breaks that are good for body boarding are good for bodysurfing.

If the direction of the current or dangers of the break are not readily apparent to you, don't hesitate to ask a lifeguard for advice.

BEST SPOTS

Body boarding and bodysurfing can be done anywhere there are waves, but due to the paddling advantage surfers have over spongers, it's usually more fun to go to surf breaks exclusively for body boarding.

Bellows Field Beach. On Oahu's windward side, Bellows Field Beach has shallow waters and a consistent break that makes it an ideal spot for body boarders and bodysurfers. (Surfing isn't allowed between the two lifeguard towers.) But take note: the Portuguese man-o-war, a blue jellyfish-like invertebrate that delivers painful and powerful stings, is often seen here. ✉ *41-043 Kalanianaole Hwy., Waimanalo.*

Kuhio Beach. This beach is an easy spot for first-timers to check out the action. The Wall, a break near the large pedestrian walkway called Kapahulu Groin, is the quintessential body-boarding spot. The soft, rolling waves make it perfect for beginners. Even during summer's south swells, it's relatively tame because of the outer reefs. ✉ *Waikiki Beach, between the Sheraton Moana Surfrider Hotel and the Kapahulu Groin, Honolulu.*

Makapuu Beach. With its extended waves, Makapuu Beach is a sponger's dream. If you're a little more timid, go to the far end of the beach to **Keiki's,** where the waves are mellowed by Makapuu Point. Although the main break at Makapuu is much less dangerous than Sandy's, check out the ocean floor—the sands are always shifting, sometimes exposing coral heads and rocks. Always check (or ask lifeguards about) the currents, which can get pretty strong. ✉ *41-095 Kalanianaole Hwy., across from Sea Life Park.*

EQUIPMENT

There are more than 30 rental spots along Waikiki Beach, all offering basically the same prices. But if you plan to body board for more than just an hour, we would suggest buying an inexpensive board for $20 to $40 at an ABC Store—there are more than 30 in the Waikiki area—and giving it to a kid at the end of your vacation. It will be more cost-effective for you, and you'll be passing along some aloha spirit in the process.

DEEP-SEA FISHING

Fishing isn't just a sport in Hawaii, it's a way of life. A number of charter boats with experienced crews can take you on a sportfishing adventure throughout the year. Sure, the bigger yellowfin tuna (ahi) are generally caught in summer, and the coveted spearfish are more frequent in winter, but you can still hook them any day of the year. You can also find dolphinfish (mahimahi), wahoo (ono), skip jacks, and the king—Pacific blue marlin—ripe for the picking on any given day. The largest marlin ever caught, weighing in at 1,805 pounds, was reeled in along Oahu's coast.

The windward side has many good spots for body boarding.

When choosing a fishing boat in the Islands, keep in mind the immensity of the surrounding ocean. Look for veteran captains who have decades of experience. Better yet, find those who care about Hawaii's fragile marine environment. Many captains now tag and release their catches to preserve the state's fishing grounds.

The general rule for the catch is an even split with the crew. Unfortunately, there are no "freeze-and-ship" providers in the state, so unless you plan to eat the fish while you're here, you'll probably want to leave it with the boat. Most boats do offer mounting services for trophy fish; ask your captain.

Besides the gift of fish, a gratuity of 10% to 20% is standard, but use your own discretion depending on how you felt about the overall experience.

BOATS AND CHARTERS

Hawaii Fishing Charters. Based out of Ko Olina resort, Captain Jim and his crew try to bring the full Hawaiian experience to their fishing trips. While most fishing boats head straight out to the open ocean, Captain Jim trolls along the leeward coast, giving visitors a nice sense of the island while stalking the fish. The company also offers an overnighter to Molokai's Penguin Banks, reputed to be some of Hawaii's best fishing grounds, starting at $2,000. ⊠ *Ko Olina Resort and Marina, 92 Aliinui Dr., Kapolei* ☎ *808/783–9274* ⊕ *www.hawaiifishingcharters.net.*

Maggie Joe Sport Fishing. The oldest sportfishing company on Oahu also boasts landing one of the largest marlins every caught out of Kewalo Basin. With two smaller boats and the 53-foot custom *Maggie Joe* (which can hold up to 25 anglers), it has air-conditioned cabins, hot showers, and cutting-edge fishing equipment. A marine taxidermist can mount the monster you reel in. Half-day exclusive charter rates for groups of six begin at $652 on the 41-foot *Sea Hawk* or the 38-foot *Ruckus*. Charters on the *Maggie Joe* start at $890. ⊠ *Kewalo Basin, 1025 Ala Moana Blvd., Honolulu* ☎ *808/591–8888, 877/806–3474* ⊕ *www.maggiejoe.com.*

Magic Sportfishing. This 50-foot Pacifica fishing yacht, aptly named *Magic*, boasts a slew of sportfishing records, including some of largest marlins caught in local tournaments and the most mahimahi hooked during a one-day charter. This yacht is very comfortable, with twin diesel engines that provide a smooth ride, air-conditioning, and a cozy seating area. The boat can accommodate up to six passengers. ⊠ *Kewalo Basin Harbor, 1025 Ala Moana Blvd., Honolulu* ☎ *808/596–2998, 808/286–2998* ⊕ *www.magicsportfishing.com.*

Sashimi Fun Fishing. A combination trip suits those who aren't quite ready to troll for big game in the open-ocean swells. Sashimi Fun Fishing runs a dinner cruise with fishing and music. The boat keeps close enough to shore so that while you're hooking reef fish, you can still see Oahu. The cruise includes a local barbecue dinner, and you can also cook what you catch. With hotel transportation included, the rates begin at $63 per person. ⊠ *Kewalo Basin Harbor, 1125 Ala Moana Blvd., Honolulu* ☎ *808/955–3474* ⊕ *www.808955fish.com.*

KAYAKING

Kayaking is an easy way to explore the ocean—and Oahu's natural beauty—without much effort or skill. It offers a vantage point not afforded by swimming or surfing, and a workout you won't get lounging on a catamaran. Even novices can get in a kayak and enjoy the island's scenery.

The ability to travel long distances can also get you into trouble. ⚠ **Experts agree that rookies should stay on the windward side.** Their reasoning is simple: if you get tired, break or lose an oar, or just plain pass out, the onshore winds will eventually blow you back to the beach. The same cannot be said for the offshore breezes of the North Shore and West Oahu.

Kayaks are specialized: some are better suited for riding waves while others are designed for traveling long distances. Your outfitter can address your needs depending on your skill level. Sharing your plans with your outfitter can lead to a more enjoyable—and safer—experience.

BEST SPOTS

★ If you want to try your hand at surfing kayaks, **Bellows Field Beach** (near Waimanalo Town Center, entrance on Kalanianaole Highway) on the windward side and **Mokuleia Beach** (across from Dillingham Airfield) on the North Shore are two great spots. Hard-to-reach breaks, the ones that surfers exhaust themselves trying to reach, are easily accessed by kayak. The buoyancy of the kayak also allows you to catch the wave earlier and get out in front of the white wash. One reminder on these spots: if you're a little green, stick to Bellows Field Beach

OAHU'S TOP WATER ACTIVITIES

Tour Company/ Outfitter	Length	AM/ PM	Departure Point	Adult/Kid Price	Ages	Snack vs. Meal	Alcoholic Beverages	Boat Type	Worth Noting
Sailing									
Pirate Bar Cruise	2 hrs	PM	Honolulu	Free	Adults only	N/A	Yes	80-foot maxi	Departs from Kewalo Basin, sail is free, drinks to be purchased
Hawaii Nautical	3 hrs	AM/ PM	West Side	$99	All ages	Snack	Yes	50-foot cat	Leaves from Ko Olina resort, lots of whales in the wintertime
Makani	2 hrs	AM/ PM	South Shore	$39	All ages	Snack	Yes	64-foot catamaran	Offers all variety of sails, from sunset to snorkel sails
Hawaii Sailing Adventure	2 hrs	PM	South Shore	$119	Adults	Full dinner	All drinks included	80-foot single hull	Luxury cruise
Tradewind Charters	Half day	AM/ PM	South Shore	$495 for 6 people	All Ages	Upon request	Yes	Variety of vessels	Great for weddings or private parties
Deep Sea Fishing									
Maggie Joe	3/4 day	AM	South Side	$890 for 6 people	N/A	N/A	BYOB	53-foot deep-sea fishing boat	Oldest running sports-fishing company on Oahu
Magic Sportfishing	Full day	AM	South Side	$950	N/A	N/A	BYOB	50-foot fishing yacht	Boat is built for comfort
Sashimi Fun Fishing	4 hrs	PM	South Side	$63 a person	N/A	Meal	BYOB	50-foot fishing boat	Reef fishing for those not ready for the open ocean

Deep Sea Fishing cont'd.

Hawaii Fishing Charters	6 hrs	AM/PM	West Side	$775	N/A	N/A	N/A	44-foot luxury boat	Sails out of Ko Olina Resort

Diving

Captain Bruce's Hawaii	2 hrs	AM/PM	West/East Shore	$115	N/A	N/A	N/A	Pro 42 Jet Boat	Hot showers on board
Ocean Concepts Hawaii	2 hrs	AM/PM	West Shore	$110	N/A	Snack	N/A	Variety of Vessels	Only full-service diving company on Leeward side
Oahu Diving	3 hrs	AM/PM	South Shore	$115	N/A	N/A	N/A	Variety of Vessels	Good for first-time divers
Surf-N-Sea	2 hrs	AM/PM	North Shore	$120	N/A	N/A	N/A	Variety of Vessels	Cameraman available to shoot your dive

DID YOU KNOW?

Inexperienced kayakers should stick to Windward Oahu, where calmer waters allow you to relax and check out what's down below.

with those onshore winds. Generally speaking, you don't want to be catching waves where surfers are; in Waikiki, however, pretty much anything goes.

Kahana River. For something a little different, try the Kahana River on the island's windward side. The river may not have the blue water of the ocean, but the majestic Koolau Mountains, with waterfalls during rainy months, make for a picturesque backdrop. It's a short jaunt, about 2 miles round-trip, but it's tranquil and packed with rain-forest foliage. Bring mosquito repellent. ⊠ *Kamehameha Hwy., 8 miles east of Kaneohe.*

Lanikai Beach. The perennial favorite of kayakers is Lanikai Beach, on the island's windward side. Tucked away in an upscale residential area, this award-winning beach has become a popular spot for amateur kayakers because of its calm waters and onshore winds. More adventurous paddlers can head to the Mokulua Islands, two islets less than 1 mile from the beach. You can land on Moku Nui, which has surf breaks and small beaches great for picnicking. Take a dip in Queen's Bath, a small saltwater swimming hole. ⊠ *Mokulua Dr., past Kailua Beach Park, Kailua.*

> **KAYAKING TO THE MOKES**
>
> The Mokulua Islands—commonly referred to as "The Mokes"—are two islets off Lanikai Beach. The larger of the islands, Moku Niu, is a perfect kayaking destination and a popular place for picnics. The islands are state-protected bird sanctuaries, and sometimes you can catch a glimpse of one of the 11 different kinds of seabirds that nest there. Some outfitters offer guided tours. But since the water between the islets and Lanikai is typically calm and as it would be impossible to miss them, spend your money on sunscreen and snacks instead and enjoy the paddle.

EQUIPMENT, LESSONS, AND TOURS

Go Bananas. Staffers make sure that you rent the appropriate kayak for your abilities, and can also outfit your rental car with soft racks to transport your boat to the beach. (The racks are included in the rental fee.) The store also carries clothing and kayaking accessories. Full-day rates begin at $30 for single kayaks, $45 for doubles. ⊠ *799 Kapahulu Ave., Kapahulu, Honolulu* ☎ *808/737–9514* ⊕ *www.gobananaswatersports.com.*

Kailua Sailboards and Kayaks. One of the best places for beginners to rent kayaks is Kailua Beach. Kailua Sailboards and Kayaks has an ideal location just across the street. More adventurous kayakers can venture to the Mokulua Islands off Lanikai. This one-stop shop also provides kayak tours starting at $69 per person. Half-day kayak rentals start at $39 for a single, $55 for a double. ⊠ *130 Kailua Rd., Kailua* ☎ *808/262–2555* ⊕ *www.kailuasailboards.com.*

Surf 'N Sea. This outfitter is located in a rustic wooden building on the beach, so in minutes you can start paddling. Keep in mind that these plastic boats are great from spring to fall, but winter weather can be hazardous for even veteran kayakers. Full-day rates begin at $60 for single kayaks, $75 for doubles. ⊠ *62-595 Kamehameha Hwy., Haleiwa* ☎ *808/637–7973, 800/899–7873* ⊕ *www.surfnsea.com.*

Twogood Kayaks Hawaii. The outfitter offers kayak rentals, lessons, guided tours, and even weeklong camps if you want to immerse yourself in the sport. Guides are trained in the history, geology, and birds of the area. Full-day rental rates begin at $55 for single kayaks, $65 for doubles. Full-day kayak excursions are $125, including lunch, snorkeling gear, and transportation to and from Waikiki. Although the prices are slightly higher than average, this outfitter puts the boats in the water for you and gives you a crash course in ocean safety. ⊠ *134B Hamakua Dr., Kailua* ☎ *808/262–5656* ⊕ *www.twogoodkayaks.com.*

SCUBA DIVING

Not all of Hawaii's beauty is above water. What lurks below can be just as magnificent.

While snorkeling and snuba (more on that later) provide adequate access to this underwater world, nothing gives you the freedom—or depth, quite literally—as scuba.

The diving on Oahu is comparable with any you might do in the tropics, but its uniqueness comes from the isolated environment of the Islands. There are literally hundreds of species of fish and marine life that you can find only in this chain. In fact, about 25% of Hawaii's marine life can be seen here only—nowhere else in the world. Adding to the singularity of diving off Oahu is the human history of the region. Military activities and tragedies of the 20th century filled the waters surrounding Oahu with wreckage that the ocean creatures have since turned into their homes.

Although instructors certified to license you in scuba are plentiful in the Islands, we suggest that you get your PADI certification before coming, as a week of classes may be a bit of a commitment on a short vacation. ■ **TIP➜ You can go on introductory dives without the certification, but the best dives require it.**

BEST SPOTS

Hanauma Bay Nature Preserve. On Oahu's southeast shore, Hanauma Bay Nature Preserve is home to more than 250 different species of fish, of which a quarter can be found nowhere else in the world. This has made this volcanic crater bay one of the most popular dive sites in the state. It's a long walk from the parking lot to the beach—even longer lugging equipment—so consider hooking up with a licensed dive-tour operator. Preservation efforts have aided the bay's delicate ecosystem, so expect to see various butterfly fish, surgeonfish, tangs, parrot fish, and endangered Hawaiian sea turtles. ⊠ *7455 Kalanianaole Hwy., Honolulu* ☎ *808/396–4229.*

Hundred Foot Hole. Once an ancient Hawaiian fishing ground reserved for royalty, the Hundred Foot Hole is a cluster of volcanic boulders that have created ledges, caves, and a large open-ended cavern perfect for diving. Accessible from shore, this spot near Diamond Head attracts octopus, manta rays, and the occasional white-tip shark. ⊠ *Honolulu.*

Mahi Waianae. Hawaii's waters are littered with shipwrecks, but one of the most intact and accessible is the *Mahi Waianae*, a 165-foot minesweeper that was sunk in 1982 off the Waianae Coast. It lays upright in about 90 feet of calm and clear water, encrusted in coral and patrolled by white spotted eagle rays and millet seed butterfly fish. The wreck serves as an artificial reef for such Hawaii aquatic residents as blue-striped snappers, puffer fish, lionfish, moray eels, and octopus. Visibility averages about 100 feet, making this one of the most popular dives on the island. ✉ *Waianae.*

Maunalua Bay. The bay stretches about 7 miles, from Portlock Point to Black Point on Oahu's southeastern shore. Teeming with marine life, this spot has several accessible dive sites of varying difficulty. The shallow-water Turtle Canyon is home to endangered Hawaiian green sea turtles. Fantasy Reef is another shallow dive with three plateaus of volcanic rock lined with coral that is home to fish, eels, and sea turtles. In about 85 feet of water, Baby Barge is an easy-to-penetrate sunken vessel encrusted in coral. An advanced dive, the wreck of a Vought F4U Corsair gives you a close-up look at garden eels and stingrays. ✉ *Honolulu.*

Fodor's Choice **Shark's Cove.** Oahu's best shore dive is accessible only during the sum-
★ mer months. Shark's Cove, on Oahu's North Shore, churns with monster surf during the winter, making this popular snorkeling and diving spot extremely dangerous. In summer, the cavernous lava tubes and tunnels are great for both novices and experienced divers. Some dive-tour companies offer round-trip transportation from Waikiki. ✉ *Haleiwa.*

Three Tables. A short walk from Shark's Cove is Three Tables, named for a trio of flat rocks running perpendicular to shore. There are lava tubes to the right of these rocks that break the surface and then extend out about 50 feet. While this area isn't as active as Shark's Cove, you can still spot octopus, moray eels, parrot fish, green sea turtles, and the occasional shark. ✉ *Haleiwa.*

EQUIPMENT, LESSONS, AND TOURS

Captain Bruce's Hawaii. Focusing on the island's western and eastern shores, this full-service company offers refresher and introductory dives as well as more advanced drift and night dives. Everything is provided, including transportation to and from Waikiki. Most importantly, the boat has hot showers. Two-tank dives begin at $115 per person. ✉ *86-222 Moeha St., Waianae* ☎ *808/373–3590, 800/535–2487* ⊕ *www.captainbruce.com.*

Hanauma Bay Dive Tours. You can guess the specialty here. This tour operator offers introductory courses in the federally protected reserve for divers aged 12 and above, with snuba available for younger kids. The charge is $115 for a one-tank dive. ✉ *460 Ena Rd., Honolulu* ☎ *808/256–8956, 800/505–8956* ⊕ *www.hanaumabaydivetours.com.*

Oahu Scuba Diving Tours. Veteran instructor Andre Huste leads small-group and private dives around Oahu. With no overhead costs and a real passion for diving, Huste believes his job is to ensure that you have a good, safe time—and that you get your money's worth. Introductory and two-tank dives are $125 per person, and certification dives are

Here in the warm waters off the coast of Oahu, there's a good chance you'll find yourself swimming alongside a green sea turtle.

$325. ✉ *1778 Ala Moana Blvd., Honolulu* ☎ *808/450–8046* ⊕ *www. oahuscubadivingtours.com.*

Surf 'N Sea. The North Shore headquarters for all things water related is also great for diving. An interesting perk—a cameraman can shoot a video of you diving. It's hard to see facial expressions under the water, but it still might be fun for those who want to prove that they took the plunge. Two-tank boat-dive rates begin at $100 per certified diver (prices are higher for noncertified divers). ✉ *62-595 Kamehameha Hwy., Haleiwa* ☎ *800/899–7873* ⊕ *www.surfnsea.com.*

SNORKELING

If you can swim, you can snorkel. And you don't need any formal training, either.

Snorkeling is a favorite pastime for both visitors and residents, and can be done anywhere there's enough water to stick your face in. Each spot will have its great days depending on the weather and time of year, so consult with the purveyor of your gear for tips on where the best viewing is that day. Keep in mind that the North Shore should be attempted only when the waves are calm, namely in the summertime.

■ **TIP➔** Think of buying a mask and snorkel as a prerequisite for your trip— they make any beach experience better. Just make sure you put plenty of sunscreen on your back because once you start gazing below, your head may not come back up for hours.

BEST SPOTS

Electric Beach. Directly across from the electricity plant—hence the name—Electric Beach is a haven for tropical fish, making it a great snorkeling spot. The expulsion of hot water from the plant raises the temperature of the ocean, attracting Hawaiian green sea turtles, spotted moray eels, and spinner dolphins. Although the visibility is not always the best, the crowds are small and the fish are guaranteed. ⊠ *Farrington Hwy., 1 mile west of Ko Olina Resort, Kapolei.*

Hanauma Bay. What Waimea Bay is to surfing, Hanauma Bay in southeast Oahu is to snorkeling. Easily the most popular snorkeling spot on the island, it's home to more more than 250 different species of marine life. Due to the protection of the narrow mouth of the cove and the prodigious reef, you will be hard-pressed to find a place you will feel safer while snorkeling. ⊠ *7455 Kalanianaole Hwy., Honolulu* ☎ *808/396–4229.*

Queen's Surf. On the edge of Waikiki, Queen's Surf is a marine reserve located between Kapahulu Groin and the Waikiki Aquarium. It's not as chock-full of fish as Hanauma Bay, but it has its share of colorful reef fish and the occasional Hawaiian green sea turtle. Just yards from shore, it's a great spot for an escape if you're stuck in Waikiki and have grown weary of watching the surfers. ⊠ *Kalakaua Ave., Honolulu.*

Fodor'sChoice
★

Shark's Cove. Great shallows protected by a huge reef make Shark's Cove on the North Shore a prime spot for snorkelers, even young ones, in the summer. You'll find a plethora of critters, from crabs to octopus, in water that's no more than waist deep. When the winter swells come, this area can turn treacherous. ⊠ *Kamehameha Hwy., across from Foodland, Haleiwa.*

EQUIPMENT AND TOURS

Hanauma Bay Rental Stand. You can get masks, fins, and snorkels right at the park. ⊠ *7455 Kalanianaole Hwy, Honolulu* ☎ *808/395–4725.*

Hanauma Bay Snorkeling Excursions. For those who are a little timid about entering these waters, this outfitter provides a tour with a guide to help alleviate your fears. For just $18, this tour package includes all your snorkeling needs, including transportation to and from Waikiki hotels. ☎ *808/306–3393* ⊕ *www.hanaumabaysnorkel.com.*

Hawaii Nautical. The dock in Ko Olina harbor is a little more out of the way, but this is a much more luxurious option than the town snorkel cruises. Two-hour morning and afternoon tours of the west side of Oahu are punctuated with stops for observing dolphins from the boat and to a snorkel spot well populated with fish. All gear, snacks, sandwiches, and two alcoholic beverages make for a more complete experience, but also a pricier one (starting at $109 per person). ⊠ *91-607 Malakole St., Kapolei* ☎ *808/234–7245* ⊕ *www.hawaiinautical.com.*

Honolulu Sailing Company. The *Kahala Kai* sails out of Kewalo Basin Harbor in Honolulu—very convenient if you have other plans in town. Take a two-hour sail out to sea turtle breeding grounds, where 50-foot-plus visibility makes for great snorkeling. There's loads of sea life, from turtles and reef fish to dolphins and, in the winter, whales. ⊠ *Kewalo*

Basin Harbor, 1125 Ala Moana Blvd., Honolulu ☎ *808/239–3900* ⊕ *www.honsail.com.*

Snorkel Bob's. This place has all the stuff you'll need—and more—to make your water adventures more enjoyable. Feel free to ask the staff about good snorkeling spots, as the best ones can vary with weather and the seasons. ✉ *700 Kapahulu Ave., Honolulu* ☎ *808/735–7944, 800/262–7725* ⊕ *www.snorkelbob.com.*

SNUBA

Snuba, the combination of scuba and snorkeling, gives the nondiving set its first glimpse into the freedom of scuba. Snuba utilizes a raft with a standard air tank on it and a 20-foot air hose that hooks up to a regulator. Once attached to the hose, you can swim, unfettered by heavy tanks and weights, up to 15 feet down to chase fish and examine the reef. If you need a rest, the raft is right there, ready to support you. Kids eight years and older can use the equipment. It can be pricey, but, then again, how much is it worth to be able to sit face to face with a 6-foot Hawaiian green sea turtle and not have to rush to the surface to get another breath?

Hawaii Nautical. Not confident enough for scuba diving? Add snuba— a cross between snorkeling and scuba diving—to any snorkel or dive tour with Hawaii Nautical for an additional $59. No certification is required. ✉ *Kewalo Basin Harbor, 1125 Ala Moana Blvd., Honolulu* ☎ *808/234–7245* ⊕ *www.hawaiinautical.com.*

SUBMARINE TOURS

★ **Atlantis Submarines.** This is the underwater adventure for the unadventurous. Not fond of swimming but want to see what you've been missing? Board this 64-passenger vessel for a ride past shipwrecks, turtle breeding grounds, and coral reefs. The tours, which depart from the pier at the Hilton Hawaiian Village, are available in several languages and start at $119. ✉ *Hilton Hawaiian Village Beach Resort and Spa, 2005 Kalia Rd., Honolulu* ☎ *808/973–1296, 800/548–6262* ⊕ *www. atlantisadventures.com.*

STAND-UP PADDLING

From the lakes of Wisconsin to the coast of Lima, Peru, stand-up paddling (or SUP, for short) is taking the sport of surfing to the most unexpected places. Still, the sport remains firmly rooted in the Hawaiian Islands.

Back in the 1960s, Waikiki beach boys would paddle out on their longboards using a modified canoe paddle. It was longer than a traditional paddle, enabling them to stand up and stroke. It was easier this way to survey the ocean and snap photos of tourists learning how to surf. Eventually it became a sport unto itself, with professional contests at world-class surf breaks and long-distance races across treacherous waters.

Continued on page 136

SNORKELING IN HAWAII

The waters surrounding the Hawaiian Islands are filled with life—from giant manta rays cruising off the Big Island's Kona Coast to humpback whales giving birth in Maui's Maalaea Bay. Dip your head beneath the surface to experience a spectacularly colorful world: pairs of milletseed butterflyfish dart back and forth, redlipped parrotfish snack on coral algae, and spotted eagle rays flap past like silent spaceships. Sea turtles bask at the surface while tiny wrasses give them the equivalent of a shave and a haircut. The water quality is typically outstanding; many sites afford 30-foot-plus visibility. On snorkel cruises, you can often stare from the boat rail right down to the bottom.

Certainly few destinations are as accommodating to every level of snorkeler as Hawaii. Beginners can tromp in from sandy beaches while more advanced divers descend to shipwrecks, reefs, craters, and sea arches just offshore. Because of Hawaii's extreme isolation, the island chain has fewer fish species than Fiji or the Caribbean—but many of the fish that are here exist nowhere else. The Hawaiian waters are home to the highest percentage of endemic fish in the world.

The key to enjoying the underwater world is slowing down. Look carefully. Listen. You might hear the strange crackling sound of shrimp tunneling through coral, or you may hear whales singing to one another during winter. A shy octopus may drift along the ocean's floor beneath you. If you're hooked, pick up a waterproof fishkey from Long's Drugs. You can brag later that you've looked the Hawaiian turkeyfish in the eye.

Picasso Triggerfish	Milletseed Butterflyfish*	Yellow Tang
Moorish Idol	Hawaiian Whitespotted Toby*	Saddleback Wrasse*
Redlip Parrotfish	Hawaiian Turkeyfish*	Zebra Moray Eel
Stocky Hawkfish	Green Sea Turtle (Honu)	Spotted Eagle Ray

*endemic to Hawaii

POLYNESIA'S FIRST CELESTIAL NAVIGATORS: HONU

Honu is the Hawaiian name for two native sea turtles, the hawksbill and the green sea turtle. Little is known about these dinosaur-age marine reptiles, though snorkelers regularly see them foraging for *limu* (seaweed) and the occasional jellyfish in Hawaiian waters. Most female honu nest in the uninhabited Northwestern Hawaiian Islands, but a few sociable ladies nest on Maui and Big Island beaches. Scientists suspect that they navigate the seas via magnetism—sensing the earth's poles. Amazingly, they will journey up to 800 miles to nest—it's believed that they return to their own birth sites. After about 60 days of incubation, nestlings emerge from the sand at night and find their way back to the sea by the light of the stars.

SNORKELING

Many of Hawaii's reefs are accessible from shore.

The basics: Sure, you can take a deep breath, hold your nose, squint your eyes, and stick your face in the water in an attempt to view submerged habitats . . . but why not protect your eyes, retain your ability to breathe, and keep your hands free to paddle about when exploring underwater? That's what snorkeling is all about.

Equipment needed: A mask, snorkel (the tube attached to the mask), and fins. In deeper waters (any depth over your head), life jackets are advised.

Steps to success: If you've never snorkeled before, it's natural to feel a bit awkward at first, so don't sweat it. Breathing through a mask and tube, and wearing a pair of fins take getting used to. Like any activity, you build confidence and comfort through practice.

If you're new to snorkeling, begin by submerging your face in shallow water or a swimming pool and breathing calmly through the snorkel while gazing through the mask.

Next you need to learn how to clear water out of your mask and snorkel, an essential skill since splashes can send water into tube openings and masks can leak. Some snorkels have built-in drainage valves, but if a tube clogs, you can force water up and out by exhaling through your mouth. Clearing a mask is similar: lift your head from water while pulling forward on mask to drain. Some masks have built-in purge valves, but those without can be cleared underwater by pressing the top to the forehead and blowing out your nose (charming, isn't it?), allowing air to bubble into the mask, pushing water out the bottom. If it sounds hard, it really isn't. Just try it a few times and you'll soon feel like a pro.

Now your goal is to get friendly with fins—you want them to be snug but not too tight—and learn how to propel yourself with them. Fins won't help you float, but they will give you a leg up, so to speak, on smoothly moving through the water or treading water (even when upright) with less effort.

Flutter stroking is the most efficient underwater kick, and the farther your foot bends forward the more leg power you'll be able to transfer to the water and the farther you'll travel with each stroke. Flutter kicking movements involve alternately separating the legs and then drawing them back together. When your legs separate, the leg surface encounters drag from the water, slowing you down. When your legs are drawn back together, they produce a force pushing you forward. If your kick creates more forward force than it causes drag, you'll move ahead.

Submerge your fins to avoid fatigue rather than having them flailing above the water when you kick, and keep your arms at your side to reduce drag. You are in the water—stretched out, face down, and snorkeling happily away—but that doesn't mean you can't hold your breath and go deeper in the water for a closer look at some fish or whatever catches your attention. Just remember that when you do this, your snorkel will be submerged, too, so you won't be breathing (you'll be holding your breath). You can dive head-first, but going feet-first is easier and less scary for most folks, taking less momentum. Before full immersion, take several long, deep breaths to clear carbon dioxide from your lungs.

If your legs tire, flip onto your back and tread water with inverted fin motions while resting. If your mask fogs, wash condensation from lens and clear water from mask.

TIPS FOR SAFE SNORKELING

■ Snorkel with a buddy and stay together.

■ Plan your entry and exit points prior to getting in the water.

■ Swim into the current on entering and then ride the current back to your exit point.

■ Carry your flippers into the water and then put them on, as it's difficult to walk in them.

■ Make sure your mask fits properly and is not too loose.

■ Pop your head above the water periodically to ensure you aren't drifting too far out, or too close to rocks.

■ Think of the water as someone else's home—don't take anything that doesn't belong to you, or leave any trash behind.

■ Don't touch any sea creatures; they may sting.

■ Wear a T-shirt over your swimsuit to help protect you from being fried by the sun.

■ When in doubt, don't go without a snorkeling professional; try a guided tour.

Green sea turtle (Honu)

Stand-up paddling is easy to learn—though riding waves takes some practice—and most outfitters on Oahu offer lessons for all skill levels. It's also a great workout; you can burn off yesterday's dinner buffet, strengthen your core, and experience the natural beauty of the island's coastlines all at once.

If you're looking to learn, go where there's already an SUP presence. Avoid popular surf breaks, unless you're an experienced stand-up paddle surfer, and be wary of ocean and wind conditions. You'll want to find a spot with calm waters, easy access in and out of the ocean, and a friendly crowd that doesn't mind the occasional stand-up paddler.

BEST SPOTS

Ala Moana Beach Park. About a mile west of Waikiki, Ala Moana is the most SUP-friendly spot on the island. In fact, the state installed a series of buoys in the flat-water lagoon to separate stand-up paddlers and swimmers. There are no waves here, making it a great spot to learn, but beware of strong trade winds, which can push you into the reef.

Anahulu Stream. Outfitters on the North Shore like to take SUP beginners to Anahulu Stream, which empties into Waialua Bay near the Haleiwa Boat Harbor. This area is calm and protected from winds, plus there's parking at the harbor, and surf shops nearby rent boards.

Waikiki. There are a number of outfitters on Oahu's south shore that take beginners into the waters off Waikiki. **Canoes,** the surf break fronting the Duke Kahanamoku statute, and the channels between breaks are often suitable for people learning how to maneuver their boards in not-so-flat conditions. But south swells here can be deceptively menacing, and ocean conditions can change quickly. Check with lifeguards before paddling out and be mindful of other surfers in the water.

EQUIPMENT AND LESSONS

Hawaiian Watersports. Paddle in the picturesque Kailua Bay or in the waters off Waikiki with Hawaiian Watersports. Two-hour lessons are $99 for groups and $179 for private sessions. If you book eight hours of lessons you get a discounted rate. Rentals start at $49 for a half day. There's also a branch in Kailua. ✉ *415 Kapahulu Ave., Honolulu* ☎ *808/262–5483, 808/739–5483* ⊕ *www.hawaiianwatersports.com.*

Paddle Core Fitness. Paddling is a way of life for Reid Inouye, who now shares his passion for the sport with students. (He's also the publisher of *Standup Paddle Magazine.*) His company offers introductory classes as well as fitness programs for serious paddlers. Lesssons are held in the flat waters of Ala Moana Beach, where there's a designated area for paddling. Prices range from $50 for group lessons to $75 for private lessons. ✉ *Ala Moana Beach Park, Ala Moana Blvd., Honolulu* ☎ *808/723–5357* ⊕ *www.paddlecorefitness.com.*

Rainbow Watersports Adventures. When you spot this company's rainbow van you'll know you're in the right place. A two-hour group lesson on Oahu's North Shore costs $79 per person. Semiprivate lessons—two paddlers, one instructor—are $89 per person. One-on-one lessons cost $99. A two- to three-hour coastal-adventure trip costs $197. ✉ *Ha-*

DID YOU KNOW?

Shark's Cove is a wonderful place for young snorkelers to spend time exploring the ocean's bottom in shallow waters, as the area is protected by a huge reef just offshore.

leiwa Beach Park, Kamehameha Hwy., Haleiwa ☎ 800/470–4964, 808/372–9304 ⊕ www.rainbowwatersports.com.

SURFING

Perhaps no word is more associated with Hawaii than surfing. Every year the best of the best gather on Oahu's North Shore to compete in their version of the Super Bowl: the prestigious Vans Triple Crown of Surfing. The pros dominate the waves for a month, but the rest of the year belongs to folks just trying to have fun.

Oahu is unique because it has so many famous spots: Banzai Pipeline, Waimea Bay, Kaiser Bowls, and Sunset Beach. But the island also has miles of coastline with surf spots that are perfect for everyday surfers. But remember this surfer's credo: when in doubt, don't go out. If you're unsure about conditions, stay on the beach.

If you're nervous and don't want to run the risk of a confrontation, try some of the alternate spots listed below. They may not have the name recognition, but the waves can be just as great.

BEST SPOTS

Makaha Beach. If you like to ride waves, try Makaha Beach on Oahu's west side. It has legendary, interminable rights that allow riders to perform all manner of stunts: from six-man canoes with everyone doing headstands to bully boards (oversize boogie boards) with whole families along for the ride. Mainly known as a longboarding spot, it's predominantly local but respectful to outsiders. Use caution in the winter, as the surf can get huge. It's not called Makaha—which means "fierce"—for nothing. ⊠ *84-369 Farrington Hwy., Waianae.*

Sunset Beach. If you want to impress your surfing buddies back home, catch a wave at the famous Sunset Beach on Oahu's North Shore. Two of the more manageable breaks are **Kammie Land** (or Kammie's) and **Sunset Point.** For the daring, Sunset is part of the Vans Triple Crown of Surfing for a reason. Thick waves and long rides await, but you're going to want to have a thick board and a thicker skull. Surf etiquette here is a must, as it's mostly local. ⊠ *59-104 Kamehameha Hwy., 1 mile north of Ehukai Beach Park, Haleiwa.*

Ulukou Beach. In Waikiki you can paddle out to **Populars,** a break at Ulukou Beach. Nice and easy, Populars—or Pops—never breaks too hard and is friendly to both newbies and veterans. It's one of the best places to surf during pumping south swells, as this thick wave breaks in open ocean, making it more rideable. The only downside is the long paddle out to the break from Kuhio Beach, but that keeps the crowds manageable. ⊠ *Waikiki Beach, in front of the Sheraton Waikiki hotel, Honolulu.*

White Plains Beach. Known among locals as "mini Waikiki," the surf at White Plains breaks in numerous spots, preventing the logjams that are inevitable at many of Oahu's more popular spots. It's a great break for novice to intermediate surfers, though you do have to keep a lookout for wayward boards. From the H1, take the Makakilo exit. ⊠ *Off H1, Kapolei.*

This surfer is doing a stellar job of surfing the infamous Banzai Pipeline on Oahu's North Shore.

EQUIPMENT AND LESSONS

Aloha Beach Services. It may sound like a cliché, but there's no better way to learn to surf than from a beach boy in Waikiki. And there's no one better than Harry "Didi" Robello, a second-generation beach boy and owner of Aloha Beach Services. Learn to surf for $30 in an hour-long group lesson, $50 for a semiprivate lesson, or $80 with just you and an instructor. You can also rent a board for $15 an hour. ⊠ *2365 Kalakaua Ave., on the beach near the Moana Surfrider, Honolulu* ☎ *808/922–3111* ⊕ *www.alohabeachservices.com.*

Faith Surf School. Professional surfer Tony Moniz started his own surf school in 2000, and since then he and his wife, Tammy, have helped thousands of people catch their first waves in Waikiki. The 90-minute group lessons are $60 per person and include all equipment and transportation. Semiprivate lessons with up to three people are $100 per person, and private lessons are $125. For $500 per person you can book an all-day surf tour with Moniz, riding waves with him at his favorite breaks. ⊠ *Sheraton Waikiki, 2255 Kalakaua Ave., Honolulu* ☎ *808/931–6262* ⊕ *www.faithsurfschool.com.*

Hans Hedemann Surf School. Hans Hedemann spent 17 years on the professional surfer circuit. He and his staff offer surfing, bodysurfing, and stand-up paddleboard instruction, four-day intensive surf camps, and fine-tuning courses with Hedemann himself. One-hour group lessons begin at $75 per person, and private lessons are $150 per person. There's a second location at Turtle Bay Resort in Kahuku. ⊠ *Park Shore Waikiki, 2586 Kalakaua Ave., Honolulu* ☎ *808/924–7778, 808/447–6755* ⊕ *www.hhsurf.com.*

DID YOU KNOW?

Windsurfing is a sport some say was born on the Hawaiian islands. Newbies looking for gentle breezes can give it a shot on the windward side of Oahu.

SURF SMART

A few things to remember when surfing in Oahu:

■ The waves switch with the seasons—they're big in the south in summer and loom large in the north in winter. If you're not experienced, it's best to go where the waves are small. There will be smaller crowds, and your chances of injury will dramatically decrease.

■ Always wear a leash. It may not look the coolest, but when your board gets swept away from you and you're swimming a half mile after it, you'll remember this advice.

■ Watch where you're going. Take a few minutes and scan the surf from the shore. Observe how big it is, where it's breaking, and how quickly the sets are coming. This will allow you to get in and out more easily and to spend more time riding waves and less time paddling.

4

☼ **Hawaiian Fire.** Learn how to surf from some of Hawaii's most knowledgeable water-safety experts at this school, owned and operated by Honolulu firefighters. Lessons include two hours of surfing time (with a lunch break) at a secluded beach near Barbers Point. Transportation is available to and from Waikiki. Two-hour group lessons begin at $109 per person, while private lessons are $189 per person. ✉ *3318 Campbell Ave., Honolulu* ☎ *808/737–3473, 888/955–7873* ⊕ *www. hawaiianfire.com.*

★ **Surf 'N Sea.** This is a one-stop shop for water-sports enthusiasts on the North Shore. Rent a shortboard for $5 an hour or a longboard for $7 an hour ($24 and $30 for full-day rentals). Lessons start at $85 for three hours. Surf safaris, which can last between four to five hours, are $220 per person. ✉ *62-595 Kamehameha Hwy., Haleiwa* ☎ *808/637–7973, 800/899–7873* ⊕ *www.surfnsea.com.*

WHALE-WATCHING

November is marked by the arrival of snow in much of America, but in Hawaii it marks the return of the humpback whale. These migrating behemoths move south from their North Pacific homes during the winter months for courtship and calving, and they put on quite a show. Watching males and females alike throwing themselves out of the ocean and into the sunset awes even the saltiest of sailors. Newborn calves riding gently next to their two-ton mothers will stir you to your core. These gentle giants can be seen from the shore as they make a splash, but there is nothing like having your boat rocking beneath you in the wake of a whale's breach.

★ **Wild Side Specialty Tours.** Boasting a marine-biologist crew, this company takes you to undisturbed snorkeling areas. Along the way you can view dolphins, turtles, and, in winter, migrating humpback whales. The tours depart at 7:30 am, so it's important to plan ahead. Four-hour whale-watching cruises on a 42-foot catamaran start at $115. There's a second location in Waianae. ⊠ *Kewalo Basin Harbor, 1125 Ala Moana Blvd., Honolulu* ☎ *808/306–7273* ⊕ *www.sailhawaii.com.*

WINDSURFING AND KITEBOARDING

Those who call windsurfing and kiteboarding cheating because they require no paddling have never tried hanging on to a sail or kite. It will turn your arms to spaghetti quicker than paddling ever could, and the speeds you generate earn these sports the label of "extreme."

Windsurfing was born here in the Islands. For amateurs, the windward side is best because the onshore breezes will bring you back to land even if you don't know what you're doing. The newer sport of kiteboarding is tougher but more exhilarating, as the kite will sometimes take you in the air for hundreds of feet. We suggest only those in top shape try the kites, but windsurfing is fun for all ages.

EQUIPMENT AND LESSONS

Kailua Sailboards and Kayaks. This company offers both beginner and high-performance gear. You can also take lessons, either at $129 for a four-hour group lesson or $109 for a one-hour individual lesson. ■TIP➜ Since both options are around the same price, we suggest the one-hour individual lesson; then you have the rest of the day to practice what these instructors preach. Half-day rentals for the more experienced run from $59 for the standard board to $79 for a high-performance board. ⊠ *130 Kailua Rd., Kailua* ☎ *808/262–2555* ⊕ *www.kailuasailboards.com.*

Golf, Hiking, and Outdoor Activities

WORD OF MOUTH

"IMO, you can't beat the neighbor islands for picturesque golf courses. But on Oahu, I'd recommend the Palmer course at Turtle Bay. The pros play there couple times a year. Wonderful scenery and you'll enjoy the drive."

—travelinandgolfin

Updated by
Michael Levine

Although much is written about the water surrounding this little rock known as Oahu, there is as much to be said for the rock itself. It's a wonder of nature, thrust from the ocean floor thousands of millennia ago by a volcanic hot spot that is still spitting out islands today. Hawaii is the most remote island chain on earth, and there are creatures and plants that can be seen here and nowhere else. And there are dozens of ways for you to check them all out.

From the air you can peer down into nooks and crannies in the mountains—where cars cannot reach and hikers don't dare. Whether flitting here and there amidst a helicopter's rush and roar, or sailing by in the silence of a glider's reverie, you glimpse sights that few have experienced. Or if you would rather, take a step back in time and take off from the waters of Keehi Lagoon in a World War II–era seaplane. Follow the flight path flown by the Japanese Zeros as they attempted to destroy Pearl Harbor and the American spirit.

Would you prefer the ground tour, where you and gravity are no longer at odds? Oahu is covered in hikes that vary from tropical rain forest to arid desert. Even when in the bustling city of Honolulu, you are but minutes from hidden waterfalls and bamboo forests. Out west you can wander a dusty path that has long since given up its ability to accommodate cars but is perfect for hikers. You can splash in tidal pools, admire sea arches, and gape at caves opened by the rock slides that closed the road. You can camp out for free on many of these treks and beaches.

If somewhat less rugged and less vigorous exploration is more your style, how about letting horses do your dirty work? You can ride them on the beaches and in the valleys, checking out ancient holy sites, movie sets, and brilliant vistas.

Finally, there is the ancient sport of Scotland. Why merely hike into the rain forest when you can slice a 280-yard drive through it and then hunt for your Titleist in the bushy leaves instead? Almost 40 courses

Ka'ena Point in the northwestern corner of the island is windy and dry, and is where rare, native Hawaiian plants grow.

cover this tiny expanse, ranging from the target jungle golf of the Royal Hawaiian Golf Club to the pro-style links of Turtle Bay. There is no off-season in the tropics, and no one here knows your real handicap.

AERIAL TOURS

Taking an aerial tour of the Islands opens up a world of perspective. Look down from the sky at the outline of the USS *Arizona* where it lies in its final resting place below the waters of Pearl Harbor, or get a glimpse of the vast carved expanse of a volcanic crater—here are views only seen by an "eye in the sky." Don't forget your camera.

Blue Hawaiian Helicopters. This company stakes its claim as Hawaii's largest 'copter company, with tours on all the major islands and more than two dozen choppers in its fleet. The Oahu tour, with six seats and narration from your friendly pilot, takes a little less than an hour and includes sweeping views of Waikiki, the beautiful windward coast, and the North Shore. If you like to see the world from above or are just pinched for time and want to get a quick overview of the whole island without renting a car, this is the way to go. Tours are $233 per person. ⊠ *99 Kaulele Pl., Honolulu* ☎ *808/831–8800* ⊕ *www.bluehawaiian.com.*

★ **Island Seaplane Service.** Harking back to the days of the earliest air visitors to Hawaii, the seaplane has always had a special spot in island lore. The only seaplane service still operating in Hawaii takes off from Keehi Lagoon. Flight options are either a half-hour south and eastern Oahu shoreline tour or an hour island circle tour. The *Pan Am Clipper*

Take a helicopter tour for a unique perspective of the island.

may be gone, but you can revisit the experience for $149 to $269. ✉ *85 Lagoon Dr., Honolulu* ☎ *808/836–6273* ⊕ *www.islandseaplane.com.*

Makani Kai Helicopters. This may be the best way to see the beautiful Sacred Falls on the windward side of the island, as the park around the falls was closed to hikers after a deadly 1999 rock slide. Makani Kai dips the helicopter down to show you one of Hawaii's former favorite trails and the pristine waterfall it leads to. Half-hour tour rates begin at $155 per person, and full-hour tours are $263. Customized private charters are available starting at $1,750 per hour. ✉ *130 Iolana Pl., Honolulu* ☎ *808/834–5813* ⊕ *www.makanikai.com.*

★ **The Original Glider Rides.** "Mr. Bill" has been offering piloted glider (sailplane) rides over the northwest end of Oahu's North Shore since 1970. These are piloted scenic rides for one or two passengers in sleek, bubbletop, motorless aircraft. You'll get aerial views of mountains, shoreline, coral pools, windsurfing sails, and, in winter, humpback whales. Reservations are recommended; flights range from 10 to 60 minutes long and depart continuously from 10 to 5 daily. The charge for one passenger is $79–$215, depending on the length of the flight; two people fly for $128–$390. ✉ *Dillingham Airfield, 68 Farrington Hwy., Waialua* ☎ *808/677–3404* ⊕ *www.honolulusoaring.com.*

BIKING

Oahu's coastal roads are flat, well paved, and unfortunately, awash in vehicular traffic. Frankly, biking is no fun in either Waikiki or Honolulu, but things are a bit better outside the city. Your best bet is to get off the road and check out the island's bike trails.

Honolulu City and County Bike Coordinator. This office can answer all your biking questions concerning trails, permits, and state laws. ☎ 808/768–8335 ⊕ www1.honolulu.gov/dts/bikepage.htm.

BEST SPOTS

Fodor'sChoice

★

Aiea Loop Trail. Our favorite ride is in central Oahu on the Aiea Loop Trail. There's a little bit of everything you expect to find in Hawaii— wild pigs crossing your path, an ancient Hawaiian *heiau* (holy ground), and the remains of a World War II crashed airplane. Campsites and picnic tables are available along the way and, if you need a snack, strawberry guava trees abound. Enjoy the foliage change from bamboo to Norfolk pine in your climb along this 4½-mile track. ⊠ *End of Aiea Heights Dr., just past Keaiwa Heiau State Park, Aiea.*

Kaena Point Trail. If going up a mountain is not your idea of mountain biking, then perhaps Kaena Point Trail is better suited to your needs. A longer ride (10 miles) but much flatter, this trail takes you oceanside around the westernmost point on the island. You pass sea arches and a mini-blowhole, then finish up with some motocross jumps right before you turn around. There's no drinking water available on this ride, but at least at the end you have the Yokohama beach showers to cool you off. ⊠ *69–385 Farrington Hwy., Waialua.*

Waimanalo Demonstration Trail. Locals favor biking this 10-mile trail that has breathtaking views as you descend into Waimanalo. There are many flat portions but also some uneven ground to negotiate unless you're willing to carry your bike for small stretches. ⊠ *Begins at the Pali Lookout on the blacktop of Old Pali Rd., Nuuanu Pali Dr., Honolulu.*

West Kaunala Trail. Biking the North Shore may sound like a great idea, but the two-lane road is narrow and traffic-heavy. We suggest you try the West Kaunala Trail. It's a little tricky at times, but with the rainforest surroundings and beautiful ocean vistas you'll hardly notice your legs burning on the steep ascent at the end. It's about 5½ miles round-trip. Bring water because there's none on the trail unless it comes from the sky. ⊠ *59-777 Pupukea Rd., end of Pupukea Rd. This road is next to Foodland, the only grocery store on North Shore, Haleiwa.*

EQUIPMENT AND TOURS

Bike Hawaii. Whether it's road tours of the North Shore or muddy off-road adventures in Kaaawa Valley, this is the company to get you there. They'll even pick you up at your hotel. There are also combination packages that pair cycling with kayaking, snorkeling, or hiking. Three-hour road tours start out at $60, with the six-hour mountain-biking foray running $125. Tours include equipment, transportation, water, and lunch. ✑ *Box 240170, Honolulu 96824* ☎ *877/682–7433* ⊕ *www. bikehawaii.com.*

Blue Sky Rentals & Sports Center. Known more for motorcycles than for man-powered bikes, Blue Sky does rent bicycles for $20 for eight hours, $25 for a day, and $75 per week—no deposit is required. The prices include a bike, a helmet, and a lock. ⊠ *1920 Ala Moana Blvd., Across from Hilton Hawaiian Village, Waikiki, Honolulu* ☎ *808/947–0101.*

Boca Hawaii LLC. If you want to do intense riding this is your first stop. The triathlon shop, owned and operated by top athletes, has full-suspension Fuji road and mountain bikes, both for $40 a day and $175 a week. Call ahead and reserve a bike, as supplies are limited. The shop is closed Sunday. ⊠ *330 Cooke St., Next to Bike Factory, Kakaako, Honolulu* ☎ *808/591–9839* ⊕ *www.bocahawaii.com.*

Hawaii Bicycling League. Don't want to go cycling by yourself? Visit this shop online and you can get connected with rides and contests. ⊡ *Box 4403, 3442 Waialae Ave., Kaimuki, Honolulu 96813* ☎ *808/735–5756* ⊕ *www.hbl.org.*

CAMPING

For a more rugged escape from the resorts of Waikiki, consider pitching a tent on the beach or in the mountains, where you have easy access to hiking trails and the island's natural features. ■TIP→ Camping here is not as highly organized as it is on the mainland: expect few marked sites, scarce electrical outlets, and nary a ranger station. What you find instead are unblemished spots in the woods and on the beach. With price tags ranging from free to $5, it's hard to complain about the lack of amenities.

There are four state recreation areas at which you can camp, one in the mountains and three on the beach. All state parks' campsites can now be reserved up to a year in advance online at ⊕ *www.hawaiistateparks. org.* The fee is $18 a night per campsite for up to six people. As for the county spots, there are 15 currently available and all require a permit. The good news is that the permits are free and are easy to obtain, as long as you're not trying to go on a holiday weekend. Visit ⊕ *www1. honolulu.gov/parks/* for more information.

GOLF

Unlike on the Neighbor Islands, the majority of Oahu's golf courses are not associated with hotels and resorts. In fact, of the island's three dozen–plus courses, only five are tied to lodging and none of them are in the tourist hub of Waikiki.

Municipal courses are a good choice for budget-conscious golfers. Your best bet is to call the day you want to play and inquire about walk-on availability. Greens fees are standard at city courses: walking rate, $49 for visitors; riding cart $20 for 18 holes; pull carts $4.

Greens fees listed here are the highest course rates per round on weekdays and weekends for U.S. residents. (Some courses charge non-U.S. residents higher prices.) Discounts are often available for resort guests

Continued on page 152

HAWAII'S PLANTS 101

Hawaii is a bounty of rainbow-colored flowers and plants. The evening air is scented with their fragrance. Just look at the front yard of almost any home, travel any road, or visit any local park and you'll see a spectacular array of colored blossoms and leaves. What most visitors don't know is that many of the plants they are seeing are not native to Hawaii; rather, they were introduced during the last two centuries as ornamental plants, or for timber, shade, or fruit.

Hawaii boasts nearly every climate on the planet, excluding the two most extreme: arctic tundra and arid desert. The Islands have wine-growing regions, cactus-speckled ranchlands, icy mountaintops, and the rainiest forests on earth.

Plants introduced from around the world thrive here. The lush lowland valleys along the windward coasts are predominantly populated by non-native trees including yellow- and red-fruited **guava**, silvery-leafed **kukui**, and orange-flowered **tulip trees**.

The colorful **plumeria flower**, very fragrant and commonly used in lei making, and

the giant multicolored **hibiscus flower** are both used by many women as hair adornments, and are two of the most common plants found around homes and hotels. The umbrella-like **monkeypod tree** from Central America provides shade in many of Hawaii's parks including Kapiolani Park in Honolulu. Hawaii's largest tree, found in Lahaina, Maui, is a giant **banyan tree.** Its canopy and massive support roots cover about two-thirds of an acre. The native **ohia tree**, with its brilliant red brush-like flowers, and the **hapuu**, a giant tree fern, are common in Hawaii's forests and are also used ornamentally in gardens.

Bougainvillea

Guava

Monkeypod

Banyan

Ohia Lehua*

Tulip Tree

Plumeria

Pandanus

Hibiscus

Anthurium

Kukui

Hapuu

*endemic to Hawaii

5

IN FOCUS HAWAII'S PLANTS 101

DID YOU KNOW?

More than 2,200 plant species are found in the Hawaiian Islands, but only about 1,000 are native. Of these, 320 are so rare, they are endangered. Hawaii's endemic plants evolved from ancestral seeds arriving in the Islands over thousands of years as baggage with birds, floating on ocean currents, or drifting on winds from continents thousands of miles away. Once here, these plants evolved in isolation, creating many new species known nowhere else in the world.

TIPS FOR THE GREEN

Before you head out to the first tee, there are a few things you should know about golf in Hawaii:

■ All resort courses and many daily-fee courses provide rental clubs. In many cases, they're the latest lines from Titleist, Ping, Callaway, and the like. This is true for both men and women, as well as left-handers, which means you don't have to schlep clubs across the Pacific.

■ Most courses offer deals varying from twilight deep-discount rates to frequent-visitor discounts, even for tourists. Ask questions when calling pro shops, and don't just accept the first quote—deals abound if you persist.

■ Pro shops at most courses are well stocked with balls, tees, and other accoutrements, so even if you bring your own bag, it needn't weigh a ton.

■ Come spikeless—very few Hawaii courses still permit metal spikes.

■ Sunscreen. Buy it, apply it (minimum 30 SPF). The subtropical rays of the sun are intense, even in December.

■ Resort courses, in particular, offer more than the usual three sets of tees, sometimes four or five. So bite off as much or little challenge as you can chew. Tee it up from the tips and you'll end up playing a few 600-yard par-5s and see a few 250-yard forced carries.

■ In theory, you can play golf in Hawaii 365 days a year. But there's a reason the Hawaiian Islands are so green. Better to bring an umbrella and light jacket and not use them than not to bring them and get soaked.

■ Unless you play a muni or certain daily-fee courses, plan on taking a cart. Riding carts are mandatory at most courses and are included in the greens fees.

and for those who book tee times online. Twilight fees are usually offered; call individual courses for information.

WAIKIKI

There is only one spot to golf near Waikiki and it is the busiest course in America. While not a very imaginative layout, the price is right and the advantage of walking from your hotel to the course is not to be overlooked. Just make sure you bring a newspaper because it will be a little while before you tee off.

Ala Wai Municipal Golf Course. Just across the Ala Wai Canal from Waikiki, Ala Wai is said to host more rounds than any other U.S. course—up to 500 per day. Not that it's a great course, just really convenient. Although residents can obtain a city golf card that allows automated tee-time reservation over the phone, the best bet for a visitor is to show up and expect to wait at least an hour. The course itself is flat. Robin Nelson did some redesign work in the 1990s, adding mounding, trees, and a lake. The Ala Wai Canal comes into play on several holes on the back nine, including the treacherous 18th. ⊠ *404 Kapahulu Ave., Waikiki* ☎ *808/733–7387 starter's office, 808/738–4652 golf shop*

⊕ www1.honolulu.gov/des/golf/alawai.htm ⌘ 18 holes. 5,861 yds. Par 70. Greens fee: $49 ⌨ Facilities: Driving range, putting green, golf carts, pull carts, rental clubs, pro shop, lessons.

HONOLULU

Moanalua Country Club. Said to be (but not without dispute) the oldest golf club west of the Rockies, this 9-holer is private but allows public play except on weekend and holiday mornings. Nestled in the hardwoods, the only course in Honolulu will remind you more of golf in Pennsylvania than the tropics, but it offers the cheapest greens fees in the area, and by the time you get here, you'll probably be over the whole palm-tree theme anyway. The course is a bit quirky, but the final two holes, a par-3 off a cliff to a smallish tree-rimmed green and a par-4 with an approach to a green set snugly between stream and jungle, are classic. Play early in the week and get unlimited golf for the price of 18 holes. ✉ *1250 Ala Aolani St.* ☎ *808/839–2411* ⌘ *9 holes. 2,972 yds. Par 36. Greens fee: $35* ⌨ *Facilities: Putting green, golf carts, restaurant, bar.*

SOUTHEAST OAHU

Prepare to keep your ball down on this windy corner of Oahu. You'll get beautiful ocean vistas, but you may need them to soothe you once your perfect drive gets blown 40 yards off course by a gusting trade wind.

Hawaii Kai Golf Course. The Championship Golf Course (William F. Bell, 1973) winds through a Honolulu suburb at the foot of Koko Crater. Homes (and the liability of a broken window) come into play on many holes, but they are offset by views of the nearby Pacific and a crafty routing of holes. With several lakes, lots of trees, and bunkers in all the wrong places, Hawaii Kai really is a "championship" golf course, especially when the trade winds howl. The **Executive Course** (1962), a par-55 track, is the first of only three courses in Hawaii built by Robert Trent Jones Sr. Although a few changes have been made to his original design, you can find the usual Jones attributes, including raised greens and lots of risk-reward options. ✉ *8902 Kalanianaole Hwy., Hawaii Kai* ☎ *808/395–2358* ⊕ *www.hawaiikaigolf.com* ⌘ *Championship Course: 18 holes. 6,222 yds. Par 72. Greens fee: $100. Executive Course: 18 holes. 2,223 yds. Par 55. Greens fee: $39* ⌨ *Facilities: Driving range, putting green, golf carts, pull carts, rental clubs, pro shop, lessons, restaurant, bar.*

WINDWARD OAHU

Windward Oahu is what you expect when you think of golfing in the Islands. Lush, tropical foliage will surround you, with towering mountains framing one shot and the crystal blue Pacific framing the next. While it's a bit more expensive to golf on this side, and a good deal wetter, the memories and pictures you take on these courses will last a lifetime.

Koolau Golf Club. Koʻolau Golf Club is marketed as the toughest golf course in Hawaii and one of the most challenging in the country. Dick

Nugent and Jack Tuthill (1992) routed 10 holes over jungle ravines that require at least a 110-yard carry. The par-4 18th may be the most difficult closing hole in golf. The tee shot from the regular tees must carry 200 yards of ravine, 250 from the blue tees. The approach shot is back across the ravine, 200 yards to a well-bunkered green. Set at the Windward base of the Koolau Mountains, the course is as much beauty as beast. Kaneohe Bay is visible from most holes, orchids and yellow ginger bloom, the shama thrush (Hawaii's best singer since Don Ho) chirrups, and waterfalls flute down the sheer, green mountains above. ⊠ *45-550 Kionaole Rd., Kaneohe* ☎ *808/236–4653* ⊕ *www. koolaugolfclub.com* ⚑ *18 holes. 6,406 yds. Par 72. Greesn fee: $145* ⚐ *Facilities: Driving range, putting green, golf carts, rental clubs, pro shop, golf academy, restaurant, bar.*

★ **Olomana Golf Links.** Bob and Robert L. Baldock are the architects of record for this layout, but so much has changed since it opened in 1969 that they would recognize little of it. A turf specialist was brought in to improve fairways and greens, tees were rebuilt, new bunkers added, and mangroves cut back to make better use of natural wetlands. But what really puts Olomana on the map is that this is where wunderkind Michelle Wie learned the game. ⊠ *41-1801 Kalanianaole Hwy., Waimanalo* ☎ *808/259–7926* ⊕ *www.olomanagolflinks.com* ⚑ *18 holes. 5,896 yds. Par 72. Greens fee: $95* ⚐ *Facilities: Driving range, putting green, golf carts, pull carts, rental clubs, pro shop, lessons, restaurant, bar.*

Fodor'sChoice **Royal Hawaiian Golf Club.** In the cool, lush Maunawili Valley, Pete and ★ Perry Dye created what can only be called target jungle golf. In other words, the rough is usually dense jungle, and you may not hit a driver on three of the four par-5s, or several par-4s, including the perilous 18th that plays off a cliff to a narrow green protected by a creek. Mt. Olomana's twin peaks tower over Luana Hills. ■TIP➜ **The back nine wanders deep into the valley, and includes an island green (par-3 11th) and perhaps the loveliest inland hole in Hawaii (par-4 12th).** ⊠ *770 Auloa Rd., Kailua* ☎ *808/262–2139* ⊕ *www.royalhawaiiangolfclub.com* ⚑ *18 holes. 5,522 yds. Par 72. Greens fee: $125* ⚐ *Facilities: Driving range, putting green, golf carts, rental clubs, pro shop, restaurant, bar.*

NORTH SHORE

The North Shore sports both the cheapest and most expensive courses on the island. You can play nine holes in your bare feet, and you can chunk up the course played by both the LPGA and Champions Tour here, too. Don't try to go the barefoot route on the LPGA course, or the only course you may be allowed on in the Islands will be the Kahuku muni.

DID YOU KNOW?

The North Shore's Turtle Bay Resort attracts golfers who come for the prized Palmer Course.

Kahuku Municipal Golf Course. The only true links course in Hawaii, this 9-hole muni is not for everyone. Maintenance is an ongoing issue, and in summer it can look a bit like the Serengeti. It's walking-only (a few pull-carts are available for rent); there's no pro shop, just a starter who sells lost-and-found balls; and the 19th hole is a soda machine and a covered picnic bench. And yet the course stretches out along the blue Pacific where surf crashes on the shore, the turf underfoot is spongy, sea mist drifts across the links, and wildflowers bloom in the rough. ⊠ *56-501 Kamehameha Hwy., Kahuku* ☏ *808/293–5842* ⊕ *www1.honolulu.gov/ des/golf/kahuku.htm* ⅄ *9 holes. 2,699 yds. Par 35. Greens fee: $13.50 for 9 holes* ⌒ *Facilities: putting green, pull carts.*

★ **Turtle Bay Resort & Spa.** When the Lazarus of golf courses, the **Fazio Course** at Turtle Bay (George Fazio, 1971), rose from the dead in 2002, Turtle Bay on Oahu's rugged North Shore became a premier golf destination. Two holes had been plowed under when the **Palmer Course** at Turtle Bay (Arnold Palmer and Ed Seay, 1992) was built, while the other seven lay fallow, and the front nine remained open. Then new owners came along and re-created holes 13 and 14 using Fazio's original plans, and the Fazio became whole again. It's a terrific track with 90 bunkers. The gem at Turtle Bay, though, is the Palmer Course. The front nine is mostly open as it skirts Punahoolapa Marsh, a nature sanctuary, while the back nine plunges into the wetlands and winds along the coast. The short par-4 17th runs along the rocky shore, with a diabolical string of bunkers cutting diagonally across the fairway from tee to green. ⊠ *57-049 Kuilima Dr., Kahuku* ☏ *808/293–8574* ⊕ *www. turtlebaygolf.com* ⅄ *Fazio Course: 18 holes. 6,535 yds. Par 72. Greens fee: $125. Palmer Course: 18 holes. 7,199 yds. Par 72. Greens fee: $175* ⌒ *Facilities: Driving range, putting green, golf carts, rental clubs, pro shop, lessons, restaurant, bar.*

CENTRAL OAHU

Golf courses are densest here in Central Oahu, where plantations morphed into tract housing and golf courses were added to anchor communities. The vegetation is much sparser, but some of the best greens around can be found here. Play early to avoid the hot afternoons, but if you can handle the heat, note that most courses offer substantial discounts for twilight hours.

Hawaii Country Club. Also known as Kunia, but not to be confused with Royal Kunia a few miles away, this course is in the middle of sugarcane fields and dates to plantation times. Several par-4s are drivable, including the 9th and 18th holes. This is a fun course, but a bit rough around the edges. ⊠ *94-1211 Kunia Rd., Waipahu* ☏ *808/621–5654* ⊕ *www.hawaiicc.com* ⅄ *18 holes. 5,910 yds. Par 72. Greens fee: $65/$75* ⌒ *Facilities: Driving range, putting green, rental clubs, pro shop, restaurant, bar.*

Mililani Golf Course. Located on Oahu's central plain, Mililani is usually a few degrees cooler than downtown, 25 minutes away. The eucalyptus trees through which the course plays add to the cool factor, and stands of Norfolk pines give Mililani a mainland-course feel. Bob and Robert

L. Baldock (1966) make good use of an old irrigation ditch reminiscent of a Scottish burn. ✉ *95-176 Kuahelani Ave., Mililani* ☎ *808/623–2222* ⊕ *www.mililanigolf.com* ⛳ *18 holes. 6,239 yds. Par 72. Greens fee: $99* ☞ *Facilities: Driving range, putting green, golf carts, rental clubs, pro shop, lessons, restaurant, bar.*

Pearl Country Club. Carved in the hillside high above Pearl Harbor, the 18 holes here are really two courses. The front nine rambles out along gently sloping terrain, while the back nine zigzags up and down a steeper portion of the slope as it rises into the Koolau Mountains. ■ TIP➔ The views of Pearl Harbor are breathtaking. ✉ *98-535 Kaonohi St., Aiea* ☎ *808/487–3802* ⊕ *www.pearlcc.com* ⛳ *18 holes. 6,232 yds. Par 72. Greens fee: $120* ☞ *Facilities: Driving range, putting green, golf carts, rental clubs, pro shop, lessons, restaurant, bar.*

Royal Kunia Country Club. At one time the PGA Tour considered buying Royal Kunia Country Club and hosting the Sony Open there. It's that good. ■ TIP➔ Every hole offers fabulous views from Diamond Head to Pearl Harbor to the nearby Waianae Mountains. Robin Nelson's eye for natural sight lines and dexterity with water features adds to the visual pleasure. ✉ *94-1509 Anonui St., Waipahu* ☎ *808/688–9222* ⊕ *www.royalkuniacc.com* ⛳ *18 holes. 6,002 yds. Par 72. Greens fee: $150* ☞ *Facilities: Driving range, putting green, golf carts, rental clubs, pro shop, restaurant.*

Waikele Country Club. Outlet stores are not the only bargain at Waikele. The adjacent golf course is a daily-fee course that offers a private club-like atmosphere and a terrific Ted Robinson (1992) layout. The target off the tee is Diamond Head, with Pearl Harbor to the right. Robinson's water features are less distinctive here, but define the short par-4 fourth hole, with a lake running down the left side of the fairway and guarding the green; and the par-3 17th, which plays across a lake. The par-4 18th is a terrific closing hole, with a lake lurking on the right side of the green. ✉ *94-200 Paioa Pl., Waipahu* ☎ *808/676–9000* ⊕ *www.golfwaikele.com* ⛳ *18 holes. 6,261 yds. Par 72. Greens fee: $130* ☞ *Facilities: Driving range, putting green, golf carts, rental clubs, pro shop, lessons, restaurant, bar.*

WEST (LEEWARD) OAHU

On the leeward side of the mountains, shielded from the rains that drench the Kaneohe side, West Oahu is arid and sunny and has a unique kind of beauty. The Ewa area is dotted with golf courses and new development, so you'll have your pick of a number of different options—golfers generally choose courses in Ewa and Kapolei because they provide a totally different landscape from Waikiki or the North Shore. The resort courses on the west side are a long drive from town, but the beaches are magnificent, and you can find deals if you're combining a room with a round or two on the greens. At this writing the Makaha course was closed for renovations; check ⊕ *www.makaharesort.com* for updates.

★ **Coral Creek Golf Course.** On the Ewa Plain, 4 miles inland, Coral Creek is cut from ancient coral—left from when this area was still under water. Robin Nelson (1999) does some of his best work in making use of the coral, and of some dynamite, blasting out portions to create dramatic lakes and tee and green sites. They could just as easily call it Coral Cliffs, because of the 30- to 40-foot cliffs Nelson created. They include the par-3 10th green's grotto and waterfall, and the vertical drop-off on the right side of the par-4 18th green. An ancient creek meanders across the course, but there's not much water, just enough to be a babbling nuisance. ✉ *91-1111 Geiger Rd., Ewa Beach* ☎ *808/441–4653* ⊕ *www. coralcreekgolfhawaii.com* ⏳ *18 holes. 6,810 yds. Par 72. Greesn fee: $130* ☞ *Facilities: Driving range, putting green, golf carts, rental clubs, pro shop, lessons, restaurant, bar.*

Ewa Beach Golf Club. A private course open to the public, Ewa is one of the delightful products of the too-brief collaboration of Robin Nelson and Rodney Wright (1992). Trees are very much part of the character here, but there are also elements of links golf, such as a double green shared by the 2nd and 16th holes. ✉ *91-050 Fort Weaver Rd., Ewa Beach* ☎ *808/689–6565* ⊕ *www.ewabeachgc.com* ⏳ *18 holes. 5,861 yds. Par 72. Greens fee: $140* ☞ *Facilities: Putting green, golf carts, rental clubs, pro shop, restaurant.*

Hawaii Prince Golf Course. Affiliated with the Hawai'i Prince Hotel in Waikiki, the Hawaii Prince Golf Course (not to be confused with the Prince Course at Princeville, Kauai) has a links feel to it, and it is popular with local charity fund-raiser golf tournaments. Arnold Palmer and Ed Seay (1991) took what had been flat, featureless sugarcane fields and sculpted 27 challenging, varied holes. Mounding breaks up the landscape, as do 10 lakes. Water comes into play on six holes of the A course, three of B, and seven of C. The most difficult combination is A and C (A and B from the forward tees). ✉ *91-1200 Fort Weaver Rd., Ewa Beach* ☎ *808/944–4567* ⊕ *www.princeresortshawaii.com* ⏳ *A Course: 9 holes. 3,138 yds. Par 36. B Course: 9 holes. 3,099 yds. Par 36. C Course: 9 holes. 3,076 yds. Par 36. Greens fee: $160* ☞ *Facilities: Driving range, putting green, golf carts, pull carts, rental clubs, pro shop, golf academy/lessons, restaurant, bar.*

Kapolei Golf Course. This is a Ted Robinson water wonderland with waterfalls and four lakes—three so big they have names—coming into play on 10 holes. Set on rolling terrain, Kapolei is a serious golf course, especially when the wind blows. ✉ *91-701 Farrington Hwy., Kapolei* ☎ *808/674–2227* ⊕ *www.kapoleigolfcourse.com* ⏳ *18 holes. 6,136 yds. Par 72. Greens fee: $160/$170* ☞ *Facilities: Driving range, putting green, golf carts, rental clubs, pro shop, lessons, restaurant, bar.*

Ko Olina Golf Club. Hawaii's golden age of golf-course architecture came to O'ahu when Ko Olina Golf Club opened in 1989. Ted Robinson, king of the water features, went splash-happy here, creating nine lakes that come into play on eight holes, including the par-3 12th, where you reach the tee by driving behind a Disney-like waterfall. Tactically, though, the most dramatic is the par-4 18th, where the approach is a minimum 120 yards across a lake to a two-tiered green guarded on the left by a cascading waterfall. Today, Ko Olina, affiliated with the adjacent Ihilani Resort and Spa (guests receive discounted rates), has matured into one of Hawaii's top courses. You can niggle about routing

issues—the first three holes play into the trade winds (and ⌐_
ing sun), and two consecutive par-5s on the back nine play in
trades—but Robinson does enough solid design to make those of pa⌐
ing concern. ✉ *92-1220 Aliinui Dr., Kapolei* ☎ *808/676–5300* ⊕ *www.
koolinagolf.com* ⚐. *18 holes. 6,432 yds. Par 72. Greens fee: $179* ⚲ *Fa-
cilities: Driving range, putting green, golf carts, rental clubs, pro shop,
golf academy, restaurant, bar.*

Makaha Valley Country Club. This course (William F. Bell, 1968), known
locally as Makaha East, is indeed a valley course, taking great advantage of the steep valley walls and natural terrain. It's shorter than the
nearby West course, but offers plenty of challenge from the back tees.
The double-dogleg, downhill-uphill, par-5 18th is a doozy of a closer.
✉ *84-627 Makaha Valley Rd., Waianae* ☎ *808/695–7111* ⊕ *www.
makahavalleycc.com* ⚐. *18 holes. 6,091 yds. Par 71. Greens fee:
$65/$75* ⚲ *Facilities: Driving range, putting green, golf carts, rental
clubs, pro shop, restaurant, bar.*

West Loch Municipal Golf Course. The best of Honolulu's municipal
courses, this Robin Nelson (1991) design plays along Pearl Harbor's
West Loch. In the process of building the course, wetlands were actually
expanded, increasing bird habitat. ✉ *91-1126 Okupe St., Ewa Beach*
☎ *808/675–6076* ⊕ *www1.honolulu.gov/des/golf/westloch.htm* ⚐. *18
holes. 6,335 yds. Par 72. Greens fee: $49* ⚲ *Facilities: Driving range,
putting green, golf carts, rental clubs, restaurant.*

HIKING

The trails of Oahu cover a full spectrum of environments: desert walks
through cactus, slippery paths through bamboo-filled rain forest, and
scrambling rock climbs up ancient volcanic calderas. The only thing
you won't find is an overnighter, as even the longest of hikes won't take
you more than half a day. In addition to being short in length, many of
the prime hikes are within 10 minutes of downtown Waikiki, meaning
that you won't have to spend your whole day getting back to nature.

Hawaii State Department of Land and Natural Resources. To obtain a Oahu
recreation map that outlines the island's 33 major trails ($3.95), contact
this office. You can also obtain camping permits for state parks here.
✉ *1151 Punchbowl St., Rm. 130, Honolulu* ☎ *808/587–0307* ⊕ *www.
hawaii.gov.*

Na Ala Hele Trails and Access. Contact the Na Ala Hele ("Trails To Go
On") folks for a free hiking-safety guide. ☎ *808/973–9782* ⊕ *ha-
waiitrails.ehawaii.gov.*

BEST SPOTS

Diamond Head Crater. Every vacation has requirements that must be
fulfilled so that when your neighbors ask, you can say, "Yeah, did it."
Climbing Diamond Head is high on that list of things to do on Oahu.
It's a moderate hike if you're in good physical condition, due in part to
the many stairs along the way; be sure to bring a water bottle because
it's hot and dry. Only a mile up, a clearly marked trail with handrails
scales the inside of this extinct volcano. At the top, the fabled final

ake you up to the pillbox
ing the Pacific Ocean and
u. It's a breathtaking view
t cheaper than taking a heli-
ride for the same photo op.
mond Head Rd. at 18th Ave.
on east side of crater; there's
ed parking inside, most park
on street and walk in, Honolulu.

TIPS FOR THE TRAIL

■ When hiking the waterfall and rain-forest trails, use insect repellent. The dampness draws huge swarms of bloodsuckers that can ruin a walk in the woods.

■ Volcanic rock is very porous and therefore likely to be loose. Rock climbing is strongly discouraged, as you never know which little ledge is going to go.

■ Always let someone know where you're going and never hike alone. The foliage gets very dense, and, small as the island is, hikers have been known to get lost for a week or longer.

Fodor's Choice
★ **Kaena Point.** This hike is a little longer (a 5-mile round-trip) and hotter than the Makapuu Lighthouse Trail, but it is right next to the beach, and there are spots where you can get in and cool off. Sea-carved cliffs give way to lava-rock beaches and sea arches. Halfway to the point, there is a double blow-hole, which is a good indicator of sea conditions. If it is blowing good, stay out of the water. Though the area is hot and dry, there is still much wildlife here, as it is the only nesting ground for many rare sea birds. ■TIP→ Keep a lookout for the Laysan albatrosses; these enormous birds have recently returned to the area. Don't be surprised if they come in for a closer look at you, too. There has been a cave-in of an old lava tube, so be careful when crossing it, but enjoy the view in its enormous mouth. ⊠ *81-780 Farrington Hwy. Take Farrington Hwy. to its end at Yokohamas. Hike in on the old 4WD trail, Waianae.*

Fodor's Choice
★ **Manoa Falls.** Travel up into the valley beyond Honolulu to make the Manoa Falls hike. Though only a mile long, this path passes through so many different ecosystems that you feel as if you're in an arboretum (the beautiful Lyon Arboretum is right near the trailhead, if you want to make another stop). Walk among the elephant-ear ape plants, ruddy fir trees, and a bamboo forest straight out of China. At the top is a 150-foot falls with a small pool not quite suited for swimming but good for wading. This hike is more about the journey than the destination; make sure you bring some mosquito repellent because they grow 'em big up here. ⊠ *3998 Manoa Rd., West Manoa Rd. behind Manoa Valley in Paradise Park. Take West Manoa Rd. to end, park on side of road, and follow trail signs in, Honolulu.*

★ **Maunawili Falls.** Want to find a waterfall that you can actually swim in? Then Maunawili Falls is your trip. In fact, even if you don't want to get wet, you're going to have to cross Maunawili Stream several times to get to the falls. Along the 1½-mile trek enjoy the ginger, vines, and heliconia before greeting fern-shrouded falls that are made for swimming. The water is not the clearest, but it's cool and refreshing after battling the bugs to get here. ⊠ *1221 Kelewina St., take Pali Hwy., Rte. 61 from Honolulu through the tunnels, take 3rd right onto Auloa Rd.,*

DID YOU KNOW?

Manoa Falls is about 150 feet high, and is the gem at the end of a mile-long hike. At its top, you'll find a small pool perfect for wading.

then take left fork immediately. At dead end, climb over vehicle gate for trailhead, Kailua.

Makapuu Lighthouse Trail. For the less adventurous hiker and anyone looking for a great view, this paved trail that runs up the side of Makapuu Point in southeast Oahu fits the bill. Early on, the trail is surrounded by lava rock but, as you ascend, foliage—the tiny white *koa haole* flower and the cream-tinged spikes of the *kiawe*—begins taking over the barren rock. Once atop the point, you begin to understand how alone these Islands are in the Pacific. The easternmost tip of Oahu, this is where the island divides the sea, giving you a spectacular view of the cobalt ocean meeting the land in a cacophony of white caps. To the south are several tide pools and the lighthouse, while the eastern view looks down upon Rabbit and Kaohikaipu Islands, two bird sanctuaries just off the coast. The 2-mile round-trip hike is a great break on a circle-island trip. ⊠ *Makapuu Lighthouse Rd., Take Kalanianaole Hwy. to base of Makapuu Point. Look for asphalt strip snaking up mountain, Honolulu.*

Trails at Turtle Bay Resort. When on the North Shore, check out the Turtle Bay Resort, which has more than 12 miles of trails and oceanside pathways. You can pick up a trail and ocean guide for a self-led tour of the 5 miles of coastline and its exotic plants and trees. ⊠ *57-091 Kamehameha Hwy., Kahuku* ☎ *808/293–8811* ⊕ *www.turtlebayresort.com.*

GOING WITH A GUIDE

Hawaii Nature Center. A good choice for families, the center in upper Makiki Valley conducts a number of programs for both adults and children. There are guided hikes into tropical settings that reveal hidden waterfalls and protected forest reserves. They don't run tours every day so it's a good idea to get advance reservations. ⊠ *2131 Makiki Heights Dr., Honolulu* ☎ *808/955–0100* ⊕ *www.hawaiinaturecenter.org.*

Oahu Nature Tours. Guides explain the native flora and fauna that are your companions on glorious sunrise, hidden-waterfall, mountain-forest, rain-forest, and volcanic walking tours. Tours include pick-up at any Waikiki hotel. ☎ *808/924–2473* ⊕ *www.oahunaturetours.com.*

HORSEBACK RIDING

A great way to see the island is atop a horse, leaving the direction to the pack while you drink in the views of mountains or the ocean. It may seem like a cliché, but there really is nothing like riding a horse down a stretch of beach to put you in a romantic state of mind.

★ **Happy Trails Hawaii.** Take a guided horseback ride above the North Shore's Waimea Bay along trails that offer panoramic views from Kaena Point to the famous surfing spots. Rates for a 90-minute trail ride begin at $80; a two-hour ride costs $99. Reservations are required. ⊠ *59-231 Pupukea Rd., 1 mile mauka up Pupakea Rd. on right, Pupukea* ☎ *808/638–7433* ⊕ *happytrailshawaii.com.*

Kualoa Ranch. This ranch across from Kualoa Beach Park on the Windward side leads trail rides in the Kaaawa Valley. Rates for a one-hour trail ride begin at $65. Kualoa has other activities such as bus and Jeep tours, all-terrain-vehicle trail rides, and children's activities, which may be combined for half- or full-day package rates. ✉ *49-560 Kamehameha Hwy., Kaaawa* ☎ *808/237–8515* ⊕ *www.kualoa.com.*

Turtle Bay Stables. This is the only spot on the island where you can take horses on the beach. The stables here are part of the North Shore resort, but can be utilized by nonguests. The sunset ride is a definite must if you are a fan of our four-legged friends. Rates for a 45-minute trail ride begin at $65. ✉ *Turtle Bay Resort, 57-091 Kahemeha Hwy, Kahuku* ☎ *808/293–8811* ⊕ *www.turtlebayresort.com/activities/horseback.asp.*

JOGGING

In Honolulu, the most popular places to jog are the two parks, **Kapiolani** and **Ala Moana,** at either end of Waikiki. In both cases, the loop around the park is just under 2 miles. You can run a 4-mile ring around **Diamond Head crater,** past scenic views, luxurious homes, and herds of other joggers.

5

Hawaii State Department of Health Community Resources Section. This department provides a free "Honolulu Walking Map" and "The Fitness Fun Map," which list more than two dozen walking and jogging routes and suggested itineraries. ✉ *1250 Punchbowl St., Rm. 422, Honolulu* ☎ *808/586–4488* ⊕ *www.healthyhawaii.com/.*

Running Room. Once you leave Honolulu, it gets trickier to find places to jog that are scenic as well as safe. It's best to stick to the well-traveled routes, or ask the experienced folks at this store for advice. ✉ *819 Kapahulu Ave., Kapahulu, Honolulu* ☎ *808/737–2422* ⊕ *www. runningroomhawaii.com.*

TENNIS

While tennis has given way to golf as the biggest resort attraction, and many of the hotel courts have closed, there are still locations in Waikiki to get your tennis match on. Both sides of Waikiki are framed by tennis complexes, with Ala Moana Park containing a 12-court spread, and two different sets at Kapiolani Park. Play is free at public courts, with courts readily available during the day—but these tend to fill up after the sun goes down and the asphalt cools off.

Ala Moana Park. The closest public courts to the *ewa* (west) end of Waikiki are in Ala Moana Park. ✉ *1141 Ala Moana Blvd., Honolulu* ☎ *808/592–2288.*

Diamond Head Tennis Center. Near Kapiolani Park, this center has nine courts open to the public. ✉ *3908 Paki Ave., Honolulu* ☎ *808/971–7150.*

Kapiolani Tennis Courts. There are more than a dozen courts for play here. ✉ *2748 Kalakaua Ave., Waikiki, Honolulu* ☎ *808/971–2510.*

Waikiki Tennis Club. The Pacific Beach Hotel has rooftop tennis courts that are open to nonguests for a fee via the Waikiki Tennis Club. ✉ *Pacific Beach Hotel, 2490 Kalakaua Ave., Waikiki, Honolulu* ☎ *808/206–6735* ⊕ *www.thewaikikitennisclub.com.*

VOLLEYBALL

With no shortage of sand, beach volleyball is an extremely popular sport on the Islands.

BEST SPOTS

There are sand-volleyball courts in Waikiki near **Fort DeRussy**. These are open to the public, so talent levels vary. However, the winner-plays-on policy here guarantees a higher level of play as the day progresses. For more advanced play, go to **Queen's Beach**, where you must bring your own net (which can lead to court possessiveness). This is the area where college kids and pros come when they're in town.

Shops and Spas

WORD OF MOUTH

"We went to the Aloha stadium for the weekday swap meet. We got there early and found a parking spot in the shade. We walked around the area and bought a few items. Should have bought more, as the prices are really cheap compared to the shops in Waikiki."

—monicapileggi

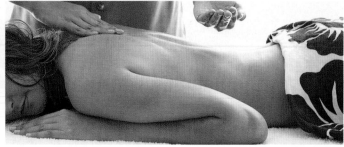

Updated
by Melissa
Chang

Eastern and Western traditions meet on Oahu, where savvy shoppers find luxury goods at high-end malls and scout tiny boutiques and galleries filled with pottery, blown glass, woodwork, and Hawaiian-print clothing by local artists. This blend of cultures is pervasive in the wide selection of spas as well. Hawaiian *lomilomi* and hot-stone massages are as omnipresent as the orchid and plumeria flowers decorating every treatment room.

Exploring downtown Honolulu, Kailua on the windward side, and the North Shore often yields the most original merchandise. Some of the small stores carry imported clothes and gifts from around the world—a reminder that, on this island halfway between Asia and the United States, shopping is a multicultural experience.

If you're getting a massage at a spa, there's a spiritual element to the *lomilomi* that calms the soul while the muscles release tension. During a hot-stone massage, smooth rocks, taken from the earth with permission from Pele, the goddess of volcanoes, are heated and placed at focal points on the body. Others are covered in oil and rubbed over tired limbs, feeling like powerful fingers. For an alternative, refresh skin with mango scrubs so fragrant they seem edible. Savor the unusual sensation of bamboo tapped against the arches of the feet. Indulge in a scalp massage that makes the entire body tingle. Day spas provide additional options to the self-indulgent services offered in almost every major hotel on the island.

SHOPS

There are two distinct types of shopping experiences for visitors: vast malls with the customary department stores and tiny boutiques with specialty items. Three malls in Honolulu provide a combination of the standard department stores and interesting shops showcasing original paintings and woodwork from local artists and craftsmen. Shoppers who know where to look in Honolulu will find everything from designer merchandise to unusual Asian imports.

Possibilities are endless, but a bit of scouting is usually required to get past the items you'll find in your own hometown. Industrious bargain hunters can detect the perfect gift in the sale bin of a slightly hidden store at every mall.

You'll find that shops stay open fairly late in Waikiki. Stores open at around 9 am and many don't close until 10 or even 11 pm.

HONOLULU

DOWNTOWN HONOLULU

Downtown shopping is an entirely different, constantly changing experience. Focus on the small galleries—which are earning the area a strong reputation for its arts and culture renaissance—and the burgeoning array of hip, home-decor stores tucked between ethnic restaurants. ■TIP→ Don't miss the festive atmosphere on the first Friday of every month, when stores, restaurants, and galleries stay open from 5 pm to 9 pm for the "Downtown Gallery Walk."

SHOPPING CENTERS

■TIP→ Getting to the Ala Moana shopping centers from Waikiki is quick and inexpensive thanks to TheBus and the Waikiki Trolley.

Ala Moana Shopping Center. The world's largest open-air shopping mall is five minutes from Waikiki by bus. More than 240 stores and 60 restaurants make up this 50-acre complex, which is a unique mix of national and international chains as well as smaller, locally owned shops and eateries—and everything in between. Thirty-five luxury boutiques in residence include Gucci, Louis Vuitton, Christian Dior, and Emporio Armani. All of Hawaii's major department stores are here, including the state's only Neiman Marcus and Nordstrom, plus Sears, and Macy's. To get to the mall from Waikiki, catch TheBus line 8, 19, or 20; a one-way ride is $2.50. Or hop aboard the Waikiki Trolley's Pink Line for $2 each way, which comes through the area every 12 minutes. ⊠ *1450 Ala Moana Blvd., Ala Moana* ☎ *808/955–9517* ⊕ *www. alamoanacenter.com.*

Ward Centers. Heading west from Waikiki toward downtown Honolulu, you'll run into a section of town with five distinct shopping-complex areas; there are more than 80 specialty shops and 40 eateries here. The Ward Entertainment Center features 16 movie theaters, including a state-of-the-art, 3-D, big-screen auditorium. For distinctive Hawaiian gifts, such as locally made muumuu, koa wood products, and Niihau shell necklaces, visit Nohea Gallery, Martin & MacArthur, and Native Books/Na Mea Hawaii. Island Soap and Candle Works makes all of its candles and soaps on-site with Hawaiian flower scents. Take TheBus routes 19, 20, and 42; fare is $2.50 one way. Or hop on the Waikiki Trolley Red Line, which comes through the area every 40 minutes. There also is free parking nearby and a valet service. ⊠ *1050–1200 Ala Moana Blvd., Ala Moana* ☎ *808/591–8411* ⊕ *www.wardcenters.com.*

BOOKS

★ **Native Books/Na Mea Hawaii.** In addition to clothing for adults and children and unusual artwork such as Niihau shell necklaces, this boutique's book selection covers Hawaiian history and language, and offers children's books set in the Islands. ⊠ *Ward Warehouse, 1050 Ala Moana Blvd.* ☎ *808/596–8885* ⊕ *www.nativebookshawaii.com.*

KOA KEEPSAKES

Items handcrafted from native Hawaiian wood make beautiful gifts. Koa and milo have a distinct color and grain. The scarcity of koa forests makes the wood extremely valuable. That's why you'll notice a large price gap between koa wood-veneer products and the real thing.

CLOTHING

★ **Anne Namba Designs.** Anne Namba combines the beauty of classic kimonos with contemporary styles to make unique pieces for work and evening. In addition to women's apparel, she's also designed a men's line and a wedding couture line. ⊠ *324 Kamani St., Downtown Honolulu* ☎ *808/589–1135* ⊕ *www. annenamba.com.*

Hilo Hattie. Busloads of visitors pour in through the front doors of the world's largest manufacturer of Hawaiian and tropical aloha wear. Once shunned by Honolulu residents for its three-shades-too-bright tourist wear, it has become a favorite source for Island gifts, macadamia nut and chocolate packages, and clothing for elegant Island functions. Free shuttle service is available from Waikiki. ⊠ *700 N. Nimitz Hwy., Iwilei* ☎ *808/535–6500* ⊕ *www.hilohattie.com.*

Reyn's. Reyn's is a good place to buy the aloha print fashions residents wear. Look for the limited-edition Christmas shirt, a collector's item manufactured each holiday season. Reyn's has eight locations statewide and offers styles for men, women, and children. ⊠ *Ala Moana Shopping Center, 1450 Ala Moana Blvd., Ala Moana* ☎ *808/949–5929* ⊕ *www.reynspooner.com* ⊠ *Kahala Mall, 4211 Waialae Ave., Kahala* ☎ *808/737–8313.*

FOOD SPECIALTIES

Honolulu Chocolate Company. To really impress those back home, pick up a box of gourmet chocolates here. They dip the flavors of Hawaii, from Kona coffee to macadamia nuts, in fine chocolate. ⊠ *Ward Centre, 1200 Ala Moana Blvd., Ala Moana* ☎ *808/591–2997* ⊕ *www. honoluluchocolate.com.*

Longs Drugs. For gift items in bulk, try one of the many outposts of Longs, the perfect place to stock up on chocolate-covered macadamia nuts—at reasonable prices—to carry home. ⊠ *Ala Moana Shopping Center, 1450 Ala Moana Blvd., 2nd level, Ala Moana* ☎ *808/941–4433* ⊠ *Kahala Mall, 4211 Waialae Ave., Kahala* ☎ *808/732–0784.*

GALLERIES

Jeff Chang Pottery & Fine Crafts. With locations around the island, Jeff Chang has become synonymous with excellent craftsmanship and originality in Raku pottery, blown glass, and koa wood. Gift ideas include petroglyph stoneware coasters, ceramic and glass jewelry, blown-glass penholders and business-card holders, and Japanese Aeto chimes. The owners choose work from 300 different local and national artists. ⊠ *Ward Center, 1200 Ala Moana Blvd.* ☎ *808/591–1440.*

★ **Nohea Gallery.** These shops are really galleries representing more than 450 artists who specialize in koa furniture, bowls, and boxes, as well as art glass and ceramics. Original paintings and prints—all with an Island theme—add to the selection. They also carry unique handmade Hawaiian jewelry with ti leaf, maile, and coconut-weave designs. ■**TIP→** **The koa photo albums in these stores are easy to carry home and make wonderful gifts.** ⊠ *Ward Warehouse, 1050 Ala Moana Blvd., Ala Moana* ☎ *808/596–0074* ⊕ *www.noheagallery.com.*

GIFTS
Blue Hawaii Lifestyle. The Ala Moana store carries a large selection of locally made products, including soaps, honey, tea, salt, chocolates, art, and CDs. Every item, in fact, is carefully selected from various Hawaii companies, artisans, and farms, from the salt fields of Molokai to the lavender farms on Maui to the single-estate chocolate on Oahu's North Shore. ⊠ *Ala Moana Center, 1450 Ala Moana Blvd.* ☎ *808/949–0808* ⊕ *www.bluehawaiilifestyle.com.*

HAWAIIAN ARTS AND CRAFTS
Hawaiian Quilt Collection. Traditional island comforters, wall hangings, pillows, and other Hawaiian-print quilt items are the specialty here. ⊠ *Ala Moana Center, 1450 Ala Moana Blvd., Ala Moana* ☎ *808/946–2233* ⊕ *www.hawaiian-quilts.com.*

Indich Collection. Bring home some aloha you can sink your bare feet into. Designs from this exclusive Hawaiian rug collection depict Hawaiian petroglyphs, banana leafs, heliconia, and other tropical plants or scenery. ⊠ *Gentry Pacific Design Center, 560 N. Nimitz Hwy., Iwilei* ☎ *808/524–7769* ⊕ *indichcollectionhawaii.com.*

My Little Secret. The word is out that this shop has a wonderful selection of Hawaiian arts, crafts, and children's toys. ⊠ *Ward Warehouse, 1050 Ala Moana Blvd., Ala Moana* ☎ *808/596–2990.*

Na Hoku. If you look at the wrists of *kamaaina* (local) women, you are apt to see Hawaiian heirloom bracelets fashioned in either gold or silver in a number of Island-inspired designs. Na Hoku sells jewelry in designs that capture the heart of the Hawaiian lifestyle in all its elegant diversity. ⊠ *Ala Moana Center, 1450 Ala Moana Blvd., Ala Moana* ☎ *808/946–2100* ⊕ *www.nahoku.com.*

HOME DECOR
Robyn Buntin Galleries. Chinese nephrite-jade carvings, Japanese lacquer and screens, and Buddhist sculptures are among the international pieces displayed here. ⊠ *848 S. Beretania St., Downtown Honolulu* ☎ *808/523–5913* ⊕ *www.robynbuntin.com.*

SPORTING GOODS
Boca Hawaii. This triathlon shop near the Bike Factory offers training gear, racing- and mountain-bike rentals ($40 per day with a two-day minimum, $175 per week), yoga and Spinning classes, and nutritional products. ■**TIP→** **Inquire directly about the latest schedule of fitness and strength sessions at the store, which is owned and operated**

6

by top athletes. ⊠ *330 Cooke St., Kakaako* ☎ *808/591–9839* ⊕ *www. bocahawaii.com.*

CHINATOWN

Chinatown offers the typical mix of the tacky and unique, depending on individual taste, but it is an experience not to be missed. The vital, bright colors of fresh fruits and vegetables blend with the distinct scent of recently killed pigs and poultry. Tucked in between are authentic shops with Asian silk clothing at reasonable prices. The bustling, ethnic atmosphere adds to the excitement. If you're hungry for a local experience you should at least walk through the area, even if you don't plan to purchase the mysterious herbs in the glass jars lining the shelves.

> **BUYING TROPICAL FLOWERS AND FRUIT**
>
> Bring home fresh pineapple, papaya, or coconut to share with friends and family. Orchids also will brighten your home and remind you of your trip to the Islands. By law, all fresh fruit and plant products must be inspected by the Department of Agriculture before export. Inquire at the shop about Department of Agriculture rules so a surprise confiscation doesn't spoil your departure. Shipping to your home usually is best.

SHOPPING CENTERS

Aloha Tower Marketplace. Billing itself as a festival marketplace, Aloha Tower cozies up to Honolulu Harbor. Along with restaurants and entertainment venues, it has about two-dozen shops and kiosks selling mostly visitor-oriented merchandise, from sunglasses to apparel to souvenir refrigerator magnets. You can also find a nice selection of locally crafted ukuleles at the Hawaiian Ukulele Company, or music CDs if you prefer to just listen. To get there from Waikiki take the E-Transit Bus, which goes along TheBus routes every 15 minutes. ⊠ *1 Aloha Tower Dr., at Piers 8, 9, and 10, Downtown Honolulu* ☎ *808/566–2337* ⊕ *www. alohatower.com.*

GALLERIES

Louis Pohl Gallery. Stop in this gallery to browse modern works from some of Hawaii's finest artists. In addition to pieces by resident artists, there are monthly exhibitions from visiting artists. ⊠ *1111 Nuuanu Ave., Downtown Honolulu* ☎ *808/521–1812* ⊕ *www.louispohlgallery.com.*

GREATER HONOLULU

Kapahulu, like many older neighborhoods, should not be judged at first glance. It begins at the Diamond Head end of Waikiki and continues up to the H1 freeway and is full of variety; shops and restaurants are located primarily on Kapahulu Avenue. The upscale residential neighborhood of Kahala, near the slopes of Diamond Head, is 10 minutes by car from Waikiki and has a shopping mall and some gift stores.

SHOPPING CENTERS

Kahala Mall. The upscale residential neighborhood of Kahala, near the slopes of Diamond Head, is 10 minutes by car from Waikiki. The only shopping of note in the area is located at the indoor mall, which has 90 stores and restaurants, including Macy's, Gap, Reyn's Aloha Wear, and

Continued on page 174

ALL ABOUT LEI

Lei brighten every occasion in Hawaii, from birthdays to bar mitzvahs to baptisms. Creative artisans weave nature's bounty—flowers, ferns, vines, and seeds—into gorgeous creations that convey an array of heartfelt messages: "Welcome," "Congratulations," "Good luck," "Farewell," "Thank you," "I love you." When it's difficult to find the right words, a lei expresses exactly the right sentiment.

WHERE TO BUY THE BEST LEI

The best selections and prices are at the lei shops in Honolulu's Chinatown. Three favorites are: **Cindy's Lei & Flower Shop** (1034 Maunakea St., 808/536-6538); **Lin's Lei Shop** (1017-A Maunakea St., 808/537-4112); and **Lita's Leis** (59 N. Beretania St., 808/521-9065). In Moiliili, a 10-minute drive from Waikiki, check out **Flowers by Jr., Lou & T** (2652 S. King St., 808/941-2022); and **Rudy's Flowers** (2357 S. Beretania St., 808/944-8844).

LEI ETIQUETTE

■ To wear a closed lei, drape it over your shoulders, half in front and half in back. Open lei are worn around the neck, with the ends draped over the front in equal lengths.

■ Pikake, ginger, and other sweet, delicate blossoms are "feminine" lei. Men opt for cigar, crown flower, and ti leaf, which are sturdier and don't emit as much fragrance.

■ Lei are always presented with a kiss, a custom that supposedly dates back to World War II when a hula dancer fancied an officer at a U.S.O. show. Taking a dare from members of her troupe, she took off her lei, placed it around his neck, and kissed him on the cheek.

■ You shouldn't wear a lei before you give it to someone else. Hawaiians believe the lei absorbs your *mana* (spirit); if you give your lei away, you'll be giving away part of your essence.

ORCHID

Growing wild on every continent except Antarctica, orchids—which range in color from yellow to green to purple—comprise the largest family of plants in the world. There are more than 20,000 species of orchids, but only three are native to Hawaii—and they are very rare. The pretty lavender vanda you see hanging by the dozens at local lei stands has probably been imported from Thailand.

MAILE

Maile, an endemic twining vine with a heady aroma, is sacred to Laka, goddess of the hula. In ancient times, dancers wore maile and decorated hula altars with it to honor Laka. Today, "open" maile lei usually are given to men. Instead of ribbon, interwoven lengths of maile are used at dedications of new businesses. The maile is untied, never snipped, for doing so would symbolically "cut" the company's success.

ILIMA

Designated by Hawaii's Territorial Legislature in 1923 as the official flower of the Island of Oahu, the golden ilima is so delicate it lasts for just a day. Five to seven hundred blossoms are needed to make one garland. Queen Emma, wife of King Kamehameha IV, preferred ilima over all other lei, which may have led to the incorrect belief that they were reserved only for royalty.

PLUMERIA

This ubiquitous flower is named after Charles Plumier, the noted French botanist who discovered it in Central America in the late 1600s. Plumeria ranks among the most popular lei in Hawaii because it's fragrant, hardy, plentiful, inexpensive, and requires very little care. Although yellow is the most common color, you'll also find plumeria lei in shades of pink, red, orange, and "rainbow" blends.

PIKAKE

Favored for its fragile beauty and sweet scent, pikake was introduced from India. In lieu of pearls, many brides in Hawaii adorn themselves with long, multiple strands of white pikake. Princess Kaiulani enjoyed showing guests her beloved pikake and peacocks at Ainahau, her Waikiki home. Interestingly, pikake is the Hawaiian word for both the bird and the blossom.

KUKUI

The kukui (candlenut) is Hawaii's state tree. Early Hawaiians strung kukui nuts (which are quite oily) together and burned them for light; mixed burned nuts with oil to make an indelible dye; and mashed roasted nuts to consume as a laxative. Kukui nut lei may not have been made until after Western contact, when the Hawaiians saw black beads from Europe and wanted to imitate them.

Barnes & Noble. Don't miss fashionable boutiques such as **Ohelo Road** (☎ *808/735–5525*), where contemporary clothing for all occasions fills the racks. You can also browse local foods and products at Whole Foods. Eight movie theaters provide post-shopping entertainment. ⊠ *4211 Waialae Ave., Kahala* ☎ *808/732–7736* ⊕ *www.kahalamallcenter.com.*

CLOTHING

Bailey's Antiques & Aloha Shirts. Vintage aloha shirts are the specialty at this kitschy store. Prices can start at $3.99 for the 10,000 shirts in stock, and the tight space and musty smell are part of the thrift-shop atmosphere. ■TIP→ Antiques hunters can also buy old-fashioned postcards, authentic military clothing, funky hats, and denim jeans from the 1950s. ⊠ *517 Kapahulu Ave., Kapahulu* ☎ *808/734–7628* ⊕ *alohashirts.com.*

GIFTS

Island Treasures. Local residents come here to shop for gifts that are both unique and within reach of almost every budget, ranging in price from $1 to $5,000. Next to Zippy's and overlooking the ocean, the store has handbags, toys, jewelry, home accessories, soaps and lotions, and locally made original artwork. Certainly the most interesting shop in Hawaii Kai's suburban-mall atmosphere, this store is also a good place to purchase CDs of some of the best Hawaiian music. ⊠ *Koko Marina Center, 7192 Kalanianaole Hwy., Hawaii Kai* ☎ *808/396–8827.*

SURF SHOPS AND SPORTING GOODS

Downing Hawaii. Look for old-style Birdwell surf trunks here, along with popular labels such as Quiksilver, Roxy, DaKine, and Billabong, which supplement Downing's own line of surf wear. ⊠ *3021 Waialae Ave., Kaimuki* ☎ *808/737–9696* ⊕ *www.downingsurf.com.*

Hawaiian Fire. Some of the best-looking firefighters in Honolulu teach surf lessons out of this tiny shop; they transport beginners to the less crowded southwest side of the island. The store also sells T-shirts and backpacks. ⊠ *3318 Campbell Ave., Kapahulu* ☎ *808/737–3473* ⊕ *www.hawaiianfire.com.*

Island Paddler. Fashionable beach footwear, clothing, bathing suits, fun beach bags, and rash guards supplement a huge selection of canoe paddles. ■TIP→ Check out the wooden steering paddles: they become works of art when mounted on the wall at home. ⊠ *716 Kapahulu Ave., Kapahulu* ☎ *808/737–4854* ⊕ *islandpaddlerhawaii.com.*

Island Triathlon & Bike. Another source for bikes, sports bathing suits, water bottles, and active clothing. However, they don't rent bicycles. ✉ *569 Kapahulu Ave., Kapahulu* ☎ *808/732-7227* ⊕ *itbhawaii.com.*

Snorkel Bob's. This is a good place to seek advice about the best snorkel conditions, which vary considerably with the season. The company, popular throughout the Islands, sells or rents necessary gear, including fins, snorkels, wet suits, and beach chairs, and even schedules activities with other suppliers. ✉ *700 Kapahulu Ave., Kapahulu* ☎ *808/735-7944* ⊕ *www.snorkelbob.com.*

WAIKIKI

Most hotels and shops are clustered along a relatively short strip in Waikiki, which can be convenient or overwhelming, depending on your sensibilities. Clothing, jewelry, and handbags from Europe's top designers sit across the street from the International Marketplace, a conglomeration of booths reminiscent of New York City's Canal Street—with a tropical flair. It's possible to find interesting items at reasonable prices in Waikiki, but shoppers have to be willing to search beyond the $4,000 purses and the tacky wooden tikis to find innovation and quality.

SHOPPING CENTERS

DFS Galleria Waikiki. Hermès, Cartier, Michael Kors, and Marc Jacobs are among the shops on the Waikiki Luxury Walk in this enclosed mall, as well as Hawaii's largest beauty and cosmetic store. The third floor caters to duty-free shoppers only and features an exclusive Watch Shop. The Kalia Grill and Starbucks offer a respite for weary shoppers. ✉ *Kalakaua and Royal Hawaiian Aves., Waikiki* ☎ *808/931-2655* ⊕ *www. dfsgalleria.com/en/hawaii/.*

Royal Hawaiian Center. An open and inviting facade has made this three-block-long center a garden of Hawaiian shops. There are more than 100 stores and restaurants, including local gems such as Aloha Aina Boutique, Honolulu Home Collection, and Koi Boutique. Bike buffs can check out the Harley-Davidson Honolulu store, while Bob's Ukulele may inspire musicians to learn a new instrument. Nine restaurants round out the dining options, along with the Paina Lanai Food Court and Five-O Bar & Lounge. ✉ *2201 Kalakaua Ave., Waikiki* ☎ *808/922-0588* ⊕ *www.shopwaikiki.com.*

2100 Kalakaua. Tenants of this elegant, town house–style center include Chanel, Coach, Tiffany & Co., Yves Saint Laurent, Gucci, and Tod's. ✉ *2100 Kalakaua Ave., Waikiki* ☎ *808/971-9011* ⊕ *www.2100kalakaua.com.*

Waikiki Beach Walk. This open-air shopping center greets visitors at the west end of Waikiki's Kalakaua Avenue with 70 locally owned

> **WORD OF MOUTH**
>
> "There is an interesting Farmer's Market in the parking lot of Kapiolani Community College, right across from the parking lot for Diamond Head. You might plan an early visit and get breakfast there (opens at 7 am on Saturday, and long lines form for the food booths right away), then go across the street for the hike up Diamond Head. —Leburta

6

stores and restaurants. Get reasonably priced, fashionable resort wear for yourself at Mahina or for your pet at Planet U2; find unique pieces by local artists at Under the Koa Tree; or browse locally made gifts and treats from Coco Cove. The mall also features free local entertainment on the fountain stage at least once a week. ⊠ *226 Lewers St., Waikiki* ☎ *808/931–3591* ⊕ *www.waikikibeachwalk.com.*

Waikiki Shopping Plaza. This five-floor shopping center is across the street from the Royal Hawaiian Shopping Center. Sephora, Armani Exchange, Guess, Alter Ego, and Tanaka of Tokyo Restaurant are some of its 50 shops and eateries. The Big Kahuna marketplace on the third floor has a bazaar-type feel to it with great, cheap souvenirs. The Visitor Aloha Society/Travelers Aid of Honolulu is also located here if you run into trouble while on vacation. ⊠ *2270 Kalakaua Ave., Waikiki* ☎ *808/923–1191* ⊕ *waikikishoppingplaza.com.*

Waikiki Town Center. Free hula shows liven up this open-air complex on Monday, Wednesday, Friday, and Saturday at 7 pm. Shops carry everything from fashions to jewelry. ⊠ *2301 Kuhio Ave., Waikiki* ☎ *808/922–2724.*

CLOTHING

Blue Ginger. Look inside this little shop across from The Yardhouse for beach-casual clothing and accessories, soft cotton prints, and alohawear. ⊠ *227 Lewers St.* ☎ *808/942–2829* ⊕ *www.blueginger.com.*

Newt at the Royal. Newt is known for high-quality, hand-woven Panama hats and tropical sportswear. ⊠ *The Royal Hawaiian Hotel, 2259 Kalakaua Ave., Waikiki* ☎ *808/949–4321* ⊕ *www.newtattheroyal.com.*

GALLERIES

Noeha Gallery. A smaller version of the stores located in Ward Center and Ward Warehouse carries koa bowls and boxes, ceramics, and art glass. ⊠ *Westin Moana Surfrider, 2365 Kalakaua Ave.* ☎ *808/923–6644* ⊕ *www.noheagallery.com.*

GIFTS

★ **Sand People.** This little shop stocks easy-to-carry gifts, such as fish-shaped Christmas ornaments, Hawaiian-style notepads, charms in the shape of flip-flops (known locally as "slippers"), soaps, and ceramic clocks. There's another branch in Kailua. ⊠ *Moana Surfrider, 2369 Kalakaua, Waikiki* ☎ *808/924–6773.*

JEWELRY

Bernard Hurtig's. Antique jade and 18-karat gold are the specialties at this fine jeweler. ⊠ *Hilton Hawaiian Village Alii Tower, 2005 Kalia Rd., Waikiki* ☎ *808/947–9399* ⊕ *www.4bernardhurtig.com.*

Philip Rickard. The heirloom design collection of this famed jeweler features custom Hawaiian wedding jewelry, sought by various celebrities. ⊠ *Royal Hawaiian Shopping Center, 2201 Kalakaua Ave., Waikiki* ☎ *808/924–7972.*

SURF SHOPS

Local Motion. If you plan on surfing or just want to look like a surfer, check out this outfitter's flagship store. They have it all—from surfboards to surf wear. ⊠ *2255 Kalakaua Ave., Waikiki* ☎ *808/254–7873* ⊕ *localmotionhawaii.com.*

Maui Divers Design Center. For a look into the harvesting and design of coral and black- pearl jewelry, visit this shop and its adjacent factory near the Ala Moana Shopping Center. ⊠ *1520 Liona St., Moiliili* ☎ *808/946–7979* ⊕ *www.mauidivers.com.*

WINDWARD OAHU

Shopping on the windward side is one of Oahu's best-kept secrets. The trip here takes a half hour by car or about an hour on TheBus. At Windward Mall in Kaneohe, stop by the Lomi Shop for authentic Tahitian oils and a 10-minute foot massage in the entrance built to resemble a voyaging canoe. The real treats, however, lie in the small boutiques and galleries in the heart of Kailua—the perfect place to gather unique gifts. After shopping, enjoy the outdoors in one of the most beautiful beach towns in the world. Kailua is the best place to rent kayaks and paddle out to the Mokulua Islands with a guide, take a windsurfing lesson, or watch the expert kiteboarders sailing across the bay.

6

■**TIP→** Stop by Kalapawai Market in Lanikai—the only shop in Lanikai, which is right next to Kailua—for sandwiches and cold drinks and souvenirs, and finish the day relaxing on a sparsely populated white-sand beach. The surf here is minimal, making it a perfect picnic spot with the kids, but not the place to learn to ride waves. Save that for Waikiki.

BOOKS

Fodor's Choice ★ **Bookends.** The perfect place to shop for gifts, or just take a break with the family, this bookstore feels more like a small-town library, welcoming browsers to linger for hours. The large children's section is filled with toys and books to read. ⊠ *600 Kailua Rd., Kailua* ☎ *808/261–1996.*

CLOTHING

Fodor's Choice ★ **Global Village.** Tucked into a tiny strip mall near Maui Tacos, this boutique features contemporary apparel for women, Hawaiian-style children's clothing, and unusual jewelry and gifts from all over the world. Look for Kula Cushions eye pillows (made with lavender grown on Maui), coasters in the shape of flip-flops, a wooden key holder shaped like a surfboard, and placemats made from lauhala and other natural fibers, plus accessories you won't find anywhere else. ⊠ *Kailua Village Shops, 539 Kailua Rd., Kailua* ☎ *808/262–8183* ⊕ *www.globalvillagehawaii.com.*

HOME DECOR

Fodor's Choice ★ **Under a Hula Moon.** Exclusive tabletop items and Pacific home decor, such as shell wreaths, shell nightlights, Hawaiian-print kitchen towels, and Asian silk clothing, define this eclectic shop. ⊠ *Kailua Shopping Center, 600 Kailua Rd., Kailua* ☎ *808/261–4252* ⊕ *www.hulamoonhawaii.com.*

THE NORTH SHORE

A drive to the North Shore takes about one hour from Waikiki, but allot a full day to explore the beaches and Haleiwa, a burgeoning attraction that has managed to retain its surf-town charm. The occasional makeshift stand selling delicious fruit or shrimp beside the road adds character to the beach, farm, and artist-colony atmosphere. Eclectic shops are the best place to find skin-care products made on the North Shore, Hawaiian music CDs, sea glass and shell mobiles, coffee grown in the Islands, and clothing items unavailable anywhere else. Be sure to chat with the owners in each shop. North Shore residents are an animated, friendly bunch with multiple talents. Stop in for coffee and the shop's owner might reveal a little about his or her passion for creating distinguished pieces of artwork.

SHOPPING CENTERS

North Shore Marketplace. While playing on the North Shore, check out this open-air plaza that includes North Shore Custom and Design Swimwear for mix-and-match bikinis off the rack, as well as Jungle Gems, where they make almost all of the precious and semiprecious gemstone jewelry on the premises. And don't miss the Silver Moon Emporium or Outrigger Trading Company upstairs. People drive out of their way for The Coffee Gallery, or for happy hour at Cholo's Homestyle Mexican Restaurant. ⊠ *66-250 Kamehameha Hwy., Haleiwa* ☎ *808/637–7000.*

CLOTHING

★ **The Growing Keiki.** Frequent visitors return to this store year after year for a fresh supply of original, hand-picked, Hawaiian-style clothing for youngsters. ⊠ *66-051 Kamehameha Hwy., Haleiwa* ☎ *808/637–4544* ⊕ *www.thegrowingkeiki.com.*

Fodor's Choice **Silver Moon Emporium.** This small boutique carries everything from Brigh-
★ ton accessories and fashionable T-shirts to Betsy Johnson formal wear, and provides attentive yet casual personalized service. Its stock changes frequently, and there's always something wonderful on sale. No matter what your taste, you'll find something for everyday wear or special occasions. ⊠ *North Shore Marketplace, 66-250 Kamehameha Hwy., Haleiwa* ☎ *808/637–7710.*

FOOD SPECIALTIES

Matsumoto Shave Ice. Actor Tom Hanks, sumo wrestler Konishiki, and ice skater Kristi Yamaguchi have all stopped in for a cold flavored cone at Matsumoto's. If you're going to the North Shore, it's a must to stop by this legendary shack established in 1951. On average, they produce 1,000 shave ices a day. Matsumoto's also has T-shirts and souvenirs. ⊠ *66-087 Kamehameha Hwy., Haleiwa* ☎ *808/637–4827* ⊕ *www.matsumotoshaveice.com.*

Tropical Fruits Distributors of Hawaii. Avoid the hassle of airport inspections. This company specializes in packing inspected pineapple and papaya; they will deliver to your hotel and to the airport check-in counter, or ship to the mainland United States and Canada. Think about ordering on the Web. ⊠ *64-1550 Kamehameha Hwy., Haleiwa*

☎ *808/847–3234* ⊕ *www.dolefruithawaii.com* ✉ *Ilalo St., Wahiawa* ☎ *800/697–9100.*

GIFTS

★ **Global Creations Interiors.** Look for Hawaiian bath products, pikake perfume, locally made jewelry, and a carefully chosen selection of Hawaiian music CDs. Fun gifts include chip-and-dip plates and spreaders shaped like ukuleles. ✉ *66-079 Kamehameha Hwy., Haleiwa* ☎ *808/637–1780* ⊕ *www.globalcreationscart.com.*

Island X Hawaii. This is a surprising, yet charming store in a section of the old Waialua Sugar Mill. The store carries gifts, clothes, and local food items—especially coffee and chocolate that is grown there. If you're lucky, you can get an unofficial tour of the coffee mill and trees. ✉ *Waialua Sugar Mill, 67-106 Kealohanui St., Waialua* ☎ *808/637–2624* ⊕ *www.islandxhawaii.com.*

North Shore Soap Factory. Housed in a converted silo in the old Waialua Sugar Mill, this is a working factory where you can watch the soap as it's made. The soaps are all natural and use as many local ingredients as possible. The factory also sells gift sets and T-shirts. ✉ *Waialua Sugar Mill, 67-106 Kealohanui St., Waialua* ☎ *808/637–8400* ⊕ *www.hawaiianbathbody.com.*

SURF SHOPS AND SPORTING GOODS

Surf 'N Sea. A North Shore water-sports store with everything under one roof. Purchase rash guards, bathing suits, T-shirts, footwear, hats, and shorts. Rent kayaks, snorkeling or scuba gear, spears for free diving, windsurfing equipment, surfboards, and body boards. Experienced surfing instructors will take beginners to the small breaks on the notoriously huge (winter) or flat (summer) North Shore beaches. Warning to fishing enthusiasts: a fishing pole is the one ocean apparatus they don't carry. ✉ *62-595 Kamehameha Hwy., Haleiwa* ☎ *808/637–9887* ⊕ *www.surfnsea.com.*

WEST (LEEWARD) OAHU

Shopping on this part of the island is at two extremes—an outdoor market that literally sells everything under the sun, and a high-end shopping outlet with all the big designer names.

SHOPPING CENTERS

Aloha Stadium Swap Meet. This thrice-weekly outdoor bazaar attracts hundreds of vendors and even more bargain hunters. Every Hawaiian souvenir imaginable can be found here, from coral shell necklaces to bikinis, as well as a variety of ethnic wares, from Chinese brocade dresses to Japanese pottery. There are also ethnic foods, silk flowers, and luggage in aloha floral prints. Shoppers must wade through the typical sprinkling of used and stolen goods to find value. Wear comfortable shoes, use sunscreen, and bring bottled water. The flea market takes place in the Aloha Stadium parking lot Wednesday and Saturday from 8 to 3; Sunday from 6:30 to 3. Admission is $1 per person ages 12 and up.

Several shuttle companies serve Aloha Stadium for the swap meet, including VIP Shuttle (☎ *808/839–0911*), Reliable Shuttle (☎ *808/924–9292*), and Hawaii Supertransit (☎ *808/841–2928*). The average cost is $12 per person, round-trip. For a cheaper but slower ride, take TheBus (⊕ *www.thebus.org*). ✉ *99-500 Salt Lake Blvd., Aiea* ☎ *808/486–6704* ⊕ *www.alohastadiumswapmeet.net*.

Waikele Premium Outlets. Anne Klein Factory, Donna Karan Company Store, Kenneth Cole, and Saks Fifth Avenue Outlet anchor this discount destination. You can take a shuttle to the outlets, but the companies do change over frequently. One to try: **P.G. Plover** (☎ *808/744–2836*); $10 round-trip. ✉ *94-790 Lumiaina St., Waipahu, Waikele* ☎ *808/676–5656*.

SPAS

Day spas provide additional options to the self-indulgent services offered in almost every major hotel on the island.

HONOLULU

Ampy's European Facials and Body Spa. This 30-year-old spa has kept its prices reasonable over the years thanks to their "no frills" way of doing business. All of Ampy's facials are 75 minutes (except for teens), and the spa has become famous for custom aromatherapy treatments. Call at least a week in advance because the appointment book fills up quickly here. It's in the Ala Moana Building, adjacent to the Ala Moana Shopping Center. ✉ *1441 Kapiolani Blvd., Suite 377, Ala Moana, Honolulu* ☎ *808/946–3838* ⊕ *www.ampys.com* ✂ *$95, 60-min lomilomi massage. Sauna. Services: body treatments, facials, hand and foot care, massage.*

Hoala Salon and Spa. This Aveda Concept spa has everything from Vichy showers to hydrotherapy rooms to customized aromatherapy. Ladies, they'll even touch up your makeup for free before you leave. ✉ *Ala Moana Shopping Center, 3rd fl., 1450 Ala Moana Blvd., Honolulu* ☎ *808/947–6141* ⊕ *www.hoalasalonspa.com* ✂ *$160, 75-min lomilomi massage. Hair salon, eucalyptus steam room. Services: body treatments, facials, massage, nail care, waxing.*

The Kahala Spa. Escape the hustle and bustle of metro Honolulu at the elegant yet homey Kahala property favored by celebrities and U.S. presidents. The two-story spa suites feature wooden floors, handmade Hawaiian quilts, Kohler infinity-edged whirlpool tubs, private vanity areas, and private gardens where clients can relax with a green-tea extract infused with various fruit. Custom-designed treatments merge Hawaiian, Asian, and traditional therapies. "Romance packages" are also available. ✉ *The Kahala, 5000 Kahala Ave., Kahala, Honolulu* ☎ *808/739–8938* ⊕ *www.kahalaresort.com* ✂ *$185, 60-min lomilomi massage. Hair salon, hot tub, "chi facility." Services: facials, massage, body treatments.*

WAIKIKI

Abhasa Spa. Natural organic skin and body treatments highlight this spa tucked away in the Royal Hawaiian Hotel's coconut grove. Vegetarian-lifestyle spa therapies, color-light therapy, an Ayurveda-influenced Bamboo Facial using Sundari products, and body cocooning are all available. You can choose to have your treatment in any of Abhasa's eight indoor rooms or in one of their three garden cabanas. ⊠ *Royal Hawaiian Hotel, 2259 Kalakaua Ave., Waikiki, Honolulu* ☎ *808/922– 8200* ⊕ *www.abhasa.com* ☞ *$135, 50-min lomilomi massage. Hair salon, indoor hot tub, sauna. Services: body cocoons and scrubs, facials, hydrotherapy, massage.*

Mandara Spa at the Hilton Hawaiian Village Beach Resort & Spa. From its perch in the Kalia Tower, Mandara Spa, an outpost of the chain that originated in Bali, overlooks the mountains, ocean, and downtown Honolulu. Fresh Hawaiian ingredients and traditional techniques headline an array of treatments. Try an exotic upgrade, such as reflexology or an eye treatment using Asian silk protein. The delicately scented, candlelit foyer can fill up quickly with robe-clad conventioneers, so be sure to make a reservation. There are spa suites for couples, a private infinity pool, and a boutique. ⊠ *Hilton Hawaiian Village Beach Resort and Spa, 2005 Kalia Rd., Waikiki, Honolulu* ☎ *808/949–4321* ⊕ *www. hiltonhawaiianvillage.com* ☞ *$130, 50-min lomilomi massage. Hair salon, hot tubs (indoor and outdoor), sauna, steam room. Gym with: cardiovascular machines, free weights, weight-training equipment. Services: aromatherapy, body wraps and scrubs, facials, massages.*

Na Hoola at the Hyatt Regency Waikiki Resort & Spa. Na Hoola is the premier resort spa in Waikiki, with 16 treatment rooms sprawling across the fifth and sixth floors of the Hyatt. Arrive early for your treatment to enjoy the postcard views of Waikiki Beach. Four packages identified by Hawaii's native healing plants—noni, kukui, awa, and kalo—combine various body, face, and hair treatments; they also have packages that last three to six hours. The Kele Kele body wrap employs a self-heating mud wrap to release tension and stress. The small exercise room is for use by hotel guests only. ⊠ *Hyatt Regency Waikiki Resort and Spa, 2424 Kalakaua Ave., Waikiki, Honolulu* ☎ *808/921–6097* ⊕ *www. waikiki.hyatt.com* ☞ *$139, 50-min lomilomi massage. Sauna. Gym with: cardiovascular machines. Services: aromatherapy, body scrubs and wraps, facials, hydrotherapy, massages.*

Paul Brown's Spa Olakino at the Waikiki Beach Marriott Resort & Spa. Paul Brown has created a spa facing Waikiki Beach. Linger with a cup of tea between treatments and gaze through 75-foot-high windows at the activity outside. Lush Hawaiian foliage, sleek Balinese teak furnishings, and a mist of ylang-ylang and nutmeg in the air inspire relaxation. Treatments incorporate Brown's Hapuna line of essential oils, as well as a thermal masking system using volcanic ash. The couples' experience lasts four hours and includes massage, massage instruction, and chocolate-covered strawberries at sunset. ⊠ *Waikiki Beach Marriott Resort & Spa, 2552 Kalakaua Ave., Waikiki, Honolulu* ☎ *808/922– 6611* ⊕ *www.marriottwaikiki.com* ☞ *$115, 50-min lomilomi massage.*

6

JW Marriott Ihilani Resort & Spa

SpaHalekulani

Hair salon, nail care, steam showers. Services: massage, facials, body treatments, waxing.

Serenity Spa Hawaii. Only steps off the beach, this renovated Aveda Concept spa provides aromatherapy treatments, massages, and facials. Each room is extra spacious not just to give therapists area to move, but to accommodate handicapped guests as well. ■TIP➔ **Book the last appointment of the day—usually 4, 5, or 6 pm—so you can watch the sunset as you're finishing your massage treatment.** ⊠ *Outrigger Reef on the Beach, 2169 Kalia Rd., Waikiki, Honolulu* ☎ *808/926–2882* ⊕ *www. serenityspahawaii.com* ☞ *$110, 50-min lomilomi massage. Hair salon. Services: body treatments, facials, makeup, massages, nail care, waxing.*

Fodor's Choice **SpaHalekulani.** SpaHalekulani mines the traditions and cultures of the
★ Pacific Islands with massages, body, and facial therapies. Try the Polynesian Nonu, which uses warm stones and healing gel. The exclusive line of bath and body products is scented by maile, lavender orchid, or coconut passion. Facilities specific to treatment but may include Japanese *furo* bath or steam shower. ⊠ *Halekulani Hotel, 2199 Kalia Rd., Waikiki, Honolulu* ☎ *808/931–5322* ⊕ *www.halekulani.com* ☞ *$180, 55-min lomilomi massage plus 20-min pre- and post-treatment work. Services: body treatments, facials, hair salon, massages, nail care.*

The Spa at Trump Waikiki. One of the newest in Waikiki, The Spa at Trump offers private changing and showering areas for each room, creating an environment of uninterrupted relaxation. No matter what treatment you choose, it is inspired by "personal intention," such as purify, balance, heal, revitalize, or calm, to elevate the senses throughout your time there. Don't miss the signature gemstone treatments, which feature products by Shiffa; or treat yourself to a Kate Somerville facial to emerge with younger-looking skin. The Hawaiian pineapple lime exfoliation massage is the most popular, as it is exclusive to this spa. ⊠ *Trump International Hotel Waikiki, 223 Saratoga Rd., Waikiki, Honolulu* ☎ *808/683–7466* ⊕ *www.trumpwaikikihotel.com* ☞ *$165, 50-min lomilomi massage. Services: aromatherapy, body scrubs and wraps, facials, hydrotherapy, lash extensions, massages, nail care, waxing.*

THE NORTH SHORE

The Spa Luana at Turtle Bay Resort. Luxuriate at the ocean's edge in this serene spa. Don't miss the tropical Pineapple Pedicure ($100 with polish; $85 without), administered outdoors overlooking the North Shore. Tired feet soak in a bamboo bowl filled with coconut milk before the pampering really begins with Hawaiian algae salt, island bee honey, kukui nut oil, and crushed pineapple. There are private spa suites, an outdoor treatment cabana that overlooks the surf, an outdoor exercise studio, and a lounge area and juice bar. ⊠ *Turtle Bay Resort, 57-091 Kamehameha Hwy., Kahuku* ☎ *808/447–6868* ⊕ *www.turtlebayresort. com* ☞ *$145, 50-min lomilomi massage. Hair salon, outdoor hot tub, steam room. Gym with: cardiovascular machines, free weights, weight-training equipment. Services: body treatments, facials, massages, waxing. Classes and programs: aerobics, Pilates, yoga.*

6

WEST (LEEWARD) OAHU

Fodor's Choice ★ **JW Marriott Ihilani Resort & Spa.** Soak in warm seawater among velvety orchid blossoms at this unique Hawaiian hydrotherapy spa. Thalassotherapy treatments combine underwater jet massage with color therapy and essential oils. Specially designed treatment rooms have a hydrotherapy tub, a Vichy-style shower, and a needle shower with 12 heads. The spa's Ohia Ai Mountain Apple line of natural aromatherapy products uses the essence of the mountain apple fruit in

WORD OF MOUTH

"My husband got a massage at the JW Marriott spa. . . . He said the massage was very good but he would not do it again based on the cost. Last time we were here, we got massages pool side at the vacation club (in private huts—no one could see in) and they were wonderful and more reasonable."
—MomDDTravel

lotions, bath salts, shampoos, and conditioners. ⊠ *JW Marriott Ihilani Resort, 92-1001 Olani St., Kapolei* ☎ *808/679–0079* ⊕ *www.ihilani. com* ☞ *$145, 50-min lomilomi massage. Hair salon, hot tubs (indoor and outdoor), sauna, steam room. Gym with: cardiovascular machines, free weights, weight-training equipment. Services: aromatherapy, body wraps and scrubs, facials, massage, thalassotherapy. Classes and programs: aerobics, body sculpting, dance classes, fitness analysis, guided walks, personal training, Pilates, tai chi, yoga.*

Laniwai Spa at Aulani, A Disney Resort & Spa. Every staff member at this spa, or "cast member," as they call themselves, is extensively trained in Hawaiian culture and history to ensure they are projecting the right *mana*, or energy, in their work. To begin each treatment, you select a special *pohaku* (rock) with words of intent, then cast it into a reflective pool. Choose from about 150 spa therapies, and indulge in Kulu Wai, the only outdoor hydrotherapy garden on Oahu—with private vitality pools, co-ed mineral baths, six different "rain" showers, whirlpool jet spas, and more. ⊠ *Aulani, A Disney Resort & Spa, 92-1185 Aliinui Dr., Ko Olina, Kapolei* ☎ *714/520–7001* ⊕ *resorts.disney.go.com/aulani-hawaii-resort* ☞ *$150, 50-min lomilomi massage. Hot tubs, sauna, steam room. Services: aromatherapy, body wraps and scrubs, facials, massage, Vichy shower treatment.*

Entertainment
and Nightlife

WORD OF MOUTH

"At night we walked the streets of Waikiki. Saw the spray paint artist and all the other street entertainers. It could have [been] San Francisco at the wharf, only warmer. It was fun."

—wbpiii

Updated by
Catherine E.
Toth

Many people arrive in Oahu expecting to find white-sand beaches, swaying palm trees, and the kind of picturesque scenery you'd see in postcards. If they think about nightlife at all, it's sunsets over Waikiki.

But Oahu does have an after-dark scene, ranging from torch-lit luau shows to hip bars to sleek nightclubs. Posh bars are found in many of the larger hotels, and smaller neighborhoods hide comfortable local watering holes. Every night of the week you can find musicians in venues from Kailua to Ko Olina—and everywhere in between. Or you can simply walk down Kalakaua Avenue to be entertained by Waikiki's street performers.

And if all-night dancing isn't for you, Oahu boasts a thriving arts and culture scene, with community-theater productions, stand-up comedy, outdoor concerts, film festivals, and chamber-music performances. Major Broadway shows, dance companies, rock stars, and comedians come through the Islands, too. Check local newspapers—the *Honolulu Star-Advertiser, Midweek, Honolulu Weekly*—for the latest events. Websites like ⊕ *www.nonstophonolulu.com* and ⊕ *www.honolulupulse. com* also have great information.

Whether you stay out all night or get up early to catch the morning surf, there's something for everyone on Oahu.

ENTERTAINMENT

DINNER CRUISES AND SHOWS
Dinner cruises depart either from the piers adjacent to the Aloha Tower Marketplace in downtown Honolulu or from Kewalo Basin, near Ala Moana Beach Park, and head along the coast toward Diamond Head. There's usually a buffet-style dinner with a local accent, dancing, drinks, and a sensational sunset. Except as noted, dinner cruises cost approximately $40 to $110, cocktail cruises $25 to $40. Most major credit cards are accepted. In all cases, reservations are essential. Check the websites for savings of up to 15%.

Alii Kai **Catamaran.** Patterned after an ancient Polynesian vessel, this 170-foot catamaran casts off from Aloha Tower with 1,000 passengers. The deluxe dinner cruise has two bars, a huge dinner, and an authentic Polynesian show with dancers, drummers, and chanters. The menu is varied, and the after-dinner show is loud and fun. Cost is $75.60 and includes round-trip transportation. Vegetarian meals are available. ✉ *Aloha Tower Marketplace, Aloha Tower Dr., Honolulu* ☎ *808/954–8652, 866/898–2519* ⊕ *www.aliikaicatamaran.com.*

WORD OF MOUTH

"The Polynesian Cultural Center has the best Polynesian entertainment of all the islands. it's an all day experience so come there right by the opening time to have time to visit seven villages, see the float parade, luau and the night show." —needsun

★ **Atlantis Cruises.** The sleekly high-tech *Navatek*, designed to sail smoothly in rough waters, powers farther along Waikiki's coastline than its competitors, sailing past Diamond Head. Enjoy sunset dinners or moonlight cruises aboard the 300-passenger boat, feasting on roast beef tenderloin or whole Maine lobster. Rates begin at $94 for a bountiful buffet; five-course dinners, which include three drinks, start at $126. ✉ *Aloha Tower Marketplace, 1 Aloha Tower Rd., Pier 6, Honolulu* ☎ *808/973–1311, 800/548–6262* ⊕ *www.atlantisadventures.com.*

Creation: A Polynesian Journey. A daring Samoan fire-knife dancer is the highlight of this show that traces Hawaii's culture and history, from its origins of discovery to statehood. The buffet dinner is priced at $95; a sit-down dinner with steak and lobster is $145. You can also choose to see the show without dinner for $55. ✉ *Ainahau Showroom, Sheraton Princess Kaiulani Hotel, 120 Kaiulani Ave., Honolulu* ☎ *808/931–4660* ⊕ *www.princess-kaiulani.com/dining/creation/* 🍴 *$55–$145* ◷ *Dinner shows Tues. and Thurs.–Sun. at 6; closed Mon. and Wed.*

★ **Magic of Polynesia.** Hawaii's top illusionist, John Hirokawa, displays mystifying sleight of hand in this highly entertaining show, which incorporates contemporary hula and Island music into its acts. It's held in the Holiday Inn Waikiki's $7.5 million showroom. Reservations are required for dinner and the show, which is priced at $125.10. Walk-ups are permitted if you just want the entertainment for $49.50. ✉ *Holiday Inn Waikiki Beachcomber Hotel, 2300 Kalakaua Ave., Waikiki, Honolulu* ☎ *808/971–4321, 866/898–2519* ⊕ *www.magicofpolynesia. com* ◷ *Nightly at 8.*

☻ **Polynesian Cultural Center.** Easily one of the best on the Islands, this show has soaring moments and an "erupting volcano." It's a long drive—about an hour from Waikiki—but you can take part in the popular Alii Luau or stay for the heralded "Ha: Breath of Life" show. General admission starts at $49.95. ✉ *55-370 Kamehameha Hwy., Laie* ☎ *808/293–3333, 800/367–7060* ⊕ *www.polynesia.com* ◷ *Mon.–Sat. 12:30–9:30.*

Society of Seven. This lively, popular cabaret show has great staying power and, after more than 30 years, continues to put on one of the most popular shows in Waikiki. The cast sings, dances, does

DID YOU KNOW?

The ancient art of hula is taught to *keiki* (children) on Oahu from a very young age. Catch a performance here, at Kapiolani Park.

impersonations, plays instruments, and, above all, entertains with its contemporary sound. ⊠ *Outrigger Waikiki on the Beach, 2335 Kalakaua Ave., Waikiki, Honolulu* ☎ *808/923–0711, 808/922–6408* ⊕ *www.outrigger.com.*

Star of Honolulu Cruises. The award-winning 1,500-passenger *Star of Honolulu* boasts four sunset dinner-cruise packages, from a roast beef buffet and Polynesian show for $79 to a romantic seven-course fine-dining excursion with live jazz for $175. The company also runs whale- and dolphin-watching lunch cruises. ⊠ *Aloha Tower Marketplace, 1 Aloha Tower Dr., Pier 8, Downtown Honolulu, Honolulu* ☎ *808/983– 7827* ⊕ *www.starofhonolulu.com.*

LUAU

The luau is an experience that everyone, both local and tourist, should have. Today's luau still offer traditional foods and entertainment, but there's often a fun, contemporary flair. With many, you can watch the roasted pig being carried out of its *imu,* a hole in the ground used for cooking meat with heated stones.

Luau average around $100 per person—some are cheaper, others twice that amount—and are held around the island, not just in Waikiki. Reservations—and a camera—are a must.

Fia Fia at the Ihilani. Just after sunset, on the resort's oceanfront lagoon lawn, the charismatic Chief Sielu Avea leads the Samoan-based Fia Fia, an entertaining show that takes guests on the journey through the South Pacific. Every show is different and unscripted, but always a good look at Polynesian culture. It's the only show with eight fire-knife dancers in a blazing finale. Admission includes buffet. ⊠ *JW Marriott Ihilani Resort & Spa, 92-1001 Olani St., Ko Olina, Kapolei* ☎ *808/679–0079, 888/236–2427* ⊕ *www.ihilani.com* ۩ *Thurs. at 4:30.*

Germaine's Luau. More than 3 million visitors have come to this luau, held about 40 minutes west of Waikiki. Widely considered one of the most folksy and local, it offers a tasty, multicourse, all-you-can-eat buffet. Admission, which starts at $72, includes buffet, three drinks, and shuttle transport from Waikiki. ⊠ *91-119 Olai St., Kapolei* ☎ *808/949– 6626, 800/367–5655* ⊕ *www.germaneisluau.com* ۩ *Daily at 6.*

★ **Paradise Cove Luau.** One of the largest shows on Oahu, the lively Paradise Cove Luau is held in Kapolei, about 40 minutes from Waikiki. Drink in hand, you can stroll through the authentic village, learn traditional arts and crafts, and play local games. The stage show includes a fire-knife dancer, singing emcee, and both traditional and contemporary hula and other Polynesian dances. Admission includes the buffet, activities, and the show, as well as shuttle transport from Waikiki. You pay extra for table service and box seating. The stunning sunsets are free. ⊠ *92-1089 Alii Nui Dr., Kapolei* ☎ *808/842–5911, 800/775–2683* ⊕ *www. paradisecove.com* ⌨ *$86–$149* ۩ *Daily at 5:30.*

Fodor's Choice ★ **Polynesian Cultural Center Alii Luau.** This elaborate luau has the sharpest production values but no booze (it's a Mormon-owned facility). It's held amid the seven re-created villages at the Polynesian Cultural Center in the North Shore town of Laie, about an hour's drive from Honolulu. The luau—considered one of the most authentic on Oahu—includes the

"Ha: Breath of Life" show that has long been popular with both residents and visitors. Rates start at $91 and go up depending on activities and amenities (personalized tours, reserved seats, or table service, for example). Waikiki transport is available. ⊠ *Polynesian Cultural Center, 55-370 Kamehameha Hwy., Laie* ☎ *808/293–3333, 800/367–7060* ⊕ *www.polynesia.com* ☽ *Mon.–Sat. at 5.*

Waikiki Starlight Luau. Waikiki's only luau is done spectacularly on the rooftop of the Hilton Hawaiian Village. There isn't an *imu* ceremony, but the live entertainment is top-notch and the views are unparalleled. It all costs less than $100. (Premier seating raises the price to $122.) The event includes traditional activities, such as hula lessons and conch blowing, but don't miss the fun of the pineapple-tossing contest. ⊠ *Hilton Hawaiian Village, 2005 Kalia Rd., Waikiki, Honolulu* ☎ *808/949–4321, 808/951–5458* ⊕ *www.hiltonhawaiianvillage.com/ luau* ☽ *Sun.–Thurs. at 5:15 pm.*

FILM

Hawaii International Film Festival. It may not be Cannes, but this festival is unique and exciting in its own right. During the weeklong event in the middle of October, top films from all over the world, as well as some by local filmmakers, are screened day and night to packed crowds. It's a must-see for film adventurers. ⊠ *Regal Dole Cannery Theaters, 680 Iwilei Rd., Honolulu* ☎ *808/792–1577* ⊕ *www.hiff.org.*

Honolulu Academy of Arts. Art, international, classic, and silent films are screened at the intimate 280-seat Doris Duke Theatre. Although small, the theater is still classy and comfortable. It also has a great sound system. ⊠ *Doris Duke Theatre, 900 S. Beretania St., Downtown Honolulu, Honolulu* ☎ *808/532–8768* ⊕ *www.honoluluacademy.org.*

★ **Sunset on the Beach.** It's like watching a movie at the drive-in, minus the car and the speaker box. Bring a blanket and find a spot on the sand to enjoy live entertainment, food from top local restaurants, and a movie on a 40-foot screen. Held twice a month on Queen's Surf Beach across from the Honolulu Zoo, Sunset on the Beach is a favorite event for both locals and visitors. If the weather is blustery, beware of flying sand. ⊠ *Queen's Surf Beach, Kalakaua Ave., Waikiki, Honolulu* ☎ *808/923–1094* ⊕ *www.waikikiimprovement.com.*

MUSIC

First Friday. Rain or shine, on the first Friday of every month, the downtown Honolulu and Chinatown districts come alive after dark with a lively street party. Art galleries and restaurants stay open late, and local musicians and DJs provide the soundtrack for the evening. Check the website for featured artists and musicians. ⊠ *Downtown Honolulu, Honolulu* ☎ *808/739–9797* ⊕ *www.firstfridayhawaii.com* 🖃 *Free.*

Hawaii Opera Theatre. Better known as "HOT," the Hawaii Opera Theatre has been known to turn the opera-challenged into opera lovers since 1960. All operas are sung in their original language with projected English translation. Tickets range from $34 to $125. ⊠ *Neal S. Blaisdell Center Concert Hall, 777 Ward Ave., Honolulu* ☎ *808/596–7372, 800/836–7372* ⊕ *www.hawaiiopera.org.*

Honolulu Zoo Concerts. For two decades, the Honolulu Zoo Society has sponsored hour-long evening concerts called the "Wildest Show in Town." They're held at 6 pm on Wednesday from June to August. Listen to local legends play everything from Hawaiian to jazz to Latin music. ■TIP➔ At just $3 admission, this is one of the best deals in town. Take a brisk walk through the zoo, or join in the family activities. This is an alcohol-free event, and there's food for those who haven't brought their own picnic supplies. ⊠ *Honolulu Zoo, 151 Kapahulu Ave., Waikiki, Honolulu* ☎ *808/971–7171* ⊕ *www.honoluluzoo.org* ✉ *$1* ⊙ *Gates open at 4:30.*

Waikiki Aquarium Concerts. Every other Thursday evening in June and July, the Waikiki Aquarium holds an oceanside concert series called "Ke Kani O Ke Kai." You can listen to top performers while enjoying food from local restaurants. The aquarium stays open throughout the night, so you can see the marine life in a new light. Bring your own beach chairs. Proceeds support the aquarium, the third oldest in the United States. ⊠ *Waikiki Aquarium, 2777 Kalakaua Ave., Waikiki, Honolulu* ☎ *808/923–9741* ⊕ *www.waquarium.org* ✉ *$30.*

THEATER

Hawaii can be an expensive gig for touring shows and music artists that depend on major theatrical sets. Not many manage to stop here, and those who do sell out fast. Oahu has developed several excellent local theater companies, which present first-rate entertainment on an amateur and semiprofessional level all year long. Community support for these groups is strong.

Diamond Head Theatre. The repertoire of the third-oldest community theater in the United States includes a little of everything: musicals, dramas, and experimental productions. ⊠ *520 Makapuu Ave., Diamond Head, Honolulu* ☎ *808/733–0274* ⊕ *www.diamondheadtheater.com.*

Hawaii Theatre Center. This beautifully restored theater, built in the 1920s in a Beaux Arts style, hosts a wide variety of events, including international theatrical productions and touring acts, festivals, and films. It's easily the loveliest theater in Hawaii. Tours cost $10 and are offered Tuesday at 11 am. Admission for performances varies. ⊠ *1130 Bethel St., Downtown Honolulu, Honolulu* ☎ *808/528–0506* ⊕ *www. hawaiitheatre.com.*

Ⓒ **Honolulu Theater for Youth.** This group stages delightful productions from September through May. Founded in 1955, it's one of the oldest children's theaters in the country, serving more than 5 million people through school and family performances and drama-education programs. ⊠ *Tenney Theatre, 229 Queen Emma Sq., Honolulu* ☎ *808/839–9885* ⊕ *www.htyweb.org.*

Kennedy Theatre. Eclectic programs—everything from musical theater to Kabuki to Chinese opera—are offered at this space at the Manoa campus of the University of Hawaii. The theater, which opened in 1963, was designed by internationally renowned architect I.M. Pei. ⊠ *1770 East-West Rd., Manoa, Honolulu* ☎ *808/956–7655* ⊕ *www.hawaii. edu/kennedy.*

Continued on page 196

HULA: MORE THAN A FOLK DANCE

Hula has been called "the heartbeat of the Hawaiian people" and also "the world's best-known, most misunderstood dance." Both are true. Hula isn't just dance. It is storytelling.

Chanter Edith McKinzie calls it "an extension of a piece of poetry." In its adornments, implements, and customs, hula integrates every important Hawaiian cultural practice: poetry, history, genealogy, craft, plant cultivation, martial arts, religion, protocol. So when 19th century Christian missionaries sought to eradicate a practice they considered depraved, they threatened more than just a folk dance.

With public performance outlawed and private hula practice discouraged, hula went underground for a generation, to rural villages. The fragile verbal link by which culture was transmitted from teacher to student hung by a thread. Even increasing literacy did not help because hula's practitioners were a secretive and protected circle.

As if that weren't bad enough, vaudeville, Broadway, and Hollywood got hold of the hula, giving it the glitz treatment in an unbroken line from "Oh, How She Could Wicky Wacky Woo" to "Rock-A-Hula Baby." Hula became shorthand for paradise: fragrant flowers, lazy hours. Ironically, this development assured that hundreds of Hawaiians could make a living performing and teaching hula. Many danced *auana* (modern form) in performance; but taught *kahiko* (traditional), quietly, at home or in hula schools.

Today, 30 years after the cultural revival known as the Hawaiian Renaissance, language immersion programs have assured a new generation of proficient—and even eloquent—chanters, songwriters, and translators. Visitors can see more, and more authentic, traditional hula than at any other time in the last 200 years.

Like the culture of which it is the beating heart, hula has survived.

Lei *poo*. Head lei. In kahiko, greenery only. In auana, flowers.

Face emotes appropriate expression. Dancer should not be a smiling automaton.

Shoulders remain relaxed and still, never hunched, even with arms raised. No bouncing.

Eyes always follow leading hand.

Lei. Hula is rarely performed without a shoulder lei.

Arms and hands remain loose, relaxed, below shoulder level—except as required by interpretive movements.

Traditional hula skirt is loose fabric, smocked and gathered at the waist.

Hip is canted over weight-bearing foot.

Knees are always slightly bent, accentuating hip sway.

Kupee. Ankle bracelet of flowers, shells, or—traditionally—noise-making dog teeth.

In kahiko, feet are flat. In auana, they may be more arched, but not tiptoes or bouncing.

BASIC MOTIONS

Speak or Sing

Moon or Sun

Grass Shack or House

Mountains or Heights

Love or Caress

At backyard parties, hula is performed in bare feet and street clothes, but in performance, adornments play a key role, as do rhythm-keeping implements.

In hula *kahiko* (traditional style), the usual dress is multiple layers of stiff fabric (often with a pellom lining, which most closely resembles *kapa*, the paperlike bark cloth of the Hawaiians). These wrap tightly around the bosom but flare below the waist to form a skirt. In pre-contact times, dancers wore only kapa skirts. Men traditionally wear loincloths.

Monarchy-period hula is performed in voluminous muumuu or high-necked muslin blouses and gathered skirts. Men wear white or gingham shirts and black pants.

In hula *auana* (modern), dress for women can range from grass skirts and strapless tops to contemporary tea-length dresses. Men generally wear aloha shirts, but sometimes grass skirts over pants or even everyday gear.

SURPRISING HULA FACTS

■ Grass skirts are not traditional; workers from Kiribati (the Gilbert Islands) brought this custom to Hawaii.

■ In olden-day Hawaii, *mele* (songs) for hula were composed for every occasion—name songs for babies, dirges for funerals, welcome songs for visitors, celebrations of favorite pursuits.

■ Hula *mai* is a traditional hula form in praise of a noble's genitals; the power of the *alii* (royalty) to procreate gave *mana* (spiritual power) to the entire culture.

■ Hula students in old Hawaii adhered to high standards: scrupulous cleanliness, no sex, daily cleansing rituals, certain food prohibitions, and no contact with the dead. They were fined if they broke the rules.

WHERE TO WATCH

■ House Without a Key: Live music, graceful solo hula, relaxed seaside stage. Halekulani, ☎ 808/923-2311.

■ Two worthwhile commercial shows: "Creation-A Polynesian Journey," Sheraton Princess Kaiulani, ☎ 808/931-4660; Polynesian Cultural Center, ☎ 808/293-3333.

■ Free hula shows: Bishop Museum, ☎ 808/847-3511. Frequent performances and free hula lessons: Royal Hawaiian Center, ☎ 808/922-2299.

■ Festivals and hoike: To find authentic amateur hula, check local media and the gohawaii.com calendar for annual hula school hoike (recital/fundraisers) and hula festivals and competitions.

Kumu Kahua Theatre. This is the only troupe that presents plays written by local playwrights. It stages five or six productions a year in a 100-seat auditorium that's perfect for getting up close and personal with the cast. ⊠ *46 Merchant St., Downtown Honolulu, Honolulu* ☎ *808/536–4441* ⊕ *www.kumukahua.org.*

Manoa Valley Theatre. From September through July, wonderful performances grace this intimate theater in lush Manoa Valley. ⊠ *2833 E. Manoa Rd., Manoa, Honolulu* ☎ *808/988–6131* ⊕ *www. manoavalleytheater.com.*

Paliku Theatre. On the campus of Windward Community College, the 300-seat Paliku Theatre features everything from dramatic productions to chamber music concerts to hula and dance performances. The sound system is exceptional. ⊠ *45-720 Keaahala Rd., Kaneohe* ☎ *808/235–7310* ⊕ *www.etickethawaii.com.*

NIGHTLIFE

Oahu is the best of all the Islands for nightlife. The locals call it *pau hana*, but you might call it "off the clock and ready for a cocktail." (The literal translation of the Hawaiian phrase means "done with work.") On weeknights, it's likely that you'll find the working crowd, still in their casual-business attire, downing chilled beers even before the sun goes down. Those who don't have to wake up in the early morning should change into a fresh outfit and start the evening closer to 10 pm.

On the weekends, it's typical to have dinner at a restaurant before hitting the clubs around 9:30. Some bar-hoppers start as early as 7, but partygoers typically don't patronize more than two establishments a night. That's because getting from one Oahu nightspot to the next usually requires packing your friends into the car and driving.

You can find a bar in just about any area on Oahu. Most of the clubs, however, are in Waikiki, near Ala Moana, and in and around downtown Honolulu. The drinking age is 21 on Oahu and throughout Hawaii. Many bars will admit younger people but will not serve them alcohol. By law, all establishments that serve alcoholic beverages must close by 2 am. The only exceptions are those with a cabaret license, which can stay open until 4 am. ■ TIP➔ Most places have a cover charge of $5 to $10, but with some establishments, getting there early means you don't have to pay.

HONOLULU

BARS

Chai's Island Bistro. Here you can see some of Hawaii's top entertainers, such as the Brothers Cazimero, Danny Couch, Jake Shimabukuro, and Melveen Leed. Chai's is the perfect place if you're looking to enjoy the signature sounds of Hawaii while dining on Pacific Rim cuisine. ⊠ *Aloha Tower Marketplace, 1 Aloha Tower Dr., Downtown Honolulu* ☎ *808/585–0011* ⊕ *www.chaisislandbistro.com.*

☾ **Dave & Buster's.** This restaurant features a fully stocked bar and lots of amusements ranging from classic billiards to shuffleboard and the latest in video arcade games. There's live Hawaiian music at the rooftop bar on Friday, hip-hop on Wednesday night, and a comedy–variety show in the showroom on the last Friday of the month. ⊠ *Ward Entertainment Complex, 1030 Auahi St., Ala Moana* ☎ *808/589–2215* ⊕ *www. daveandbusters.com.*

Gordon Biersch. This outdoor bar flanks Honolulu Harbor. Live bands serenade patrons with everything from funk to jazz to rock and roll. Those who feel inspired can strut their stuff in front of the stage, while others can enjoy a pint of the restaurant's own brew and some garlic fries. ⊠ *Aloha Tower Marketplace, 1 Aloha Tower Dr., Suite 1123, Downtown Honolulu* ☎ *808/599–4877* ⊕ *www.gordonbiersch.com.*

Fodor'sChoice
★

Mai Tai Bar. After a long day of shopping, the third-floor Mai Tai Bar is a perfect spot to relax. There's live entertainment and two nightly happy hours: one for food and another strictly for drinks. There's never a cover charge and no dress code. To avoid waiting in line, get here before 9 pm. ⊠ *Ala Moana Center, 1450 Ala Moana Blvd., Ala Moana* ☎ *808/947–2900* ⊕ *www.maitaibar.com.*

Murphy's Bar & Grill. On the edge of Chinatown, this 120-year-old bar has been serving drinks to locals and visitors since Hawaii's days as a territory. The kind of Irish pub you'd find in Boston, Murphy's is a break from all the colorful drinks garnished with slices of fruit, and it's definitely the place to be on St. Patrick's Day. On Friday it serves some of the best homemade fruit pies around. They're so good, they sell out during lunch. ⊠ *2 Merchant St., Downtown Honolulu* ☎ *808/531–0422* ⊕ *www.murphyshawaii.com.*

Nocturna Lounge. This is Hawaii's first self-described NextGen lounge, a stylish and sophisticated karaoke and gaming lounge at the Waterfront Plaza. It boasts a full bar, four private suites with state-of-the-art karaoke, and video-game consoles around the lounge featuring the latest in social gaming. Play "Street Fighter" in the open lounge, perfect your moves in "Dance Central" on the Xbox Kinect in a side room, or wander through the noisy club while sipping one of Nocturna's creative cocktails with names like "Sonic Boomtini" and "Yuzu Is About to Die." The crowd isn't as young as you'd expect at a club outfitted with video-game consoles. ⊠ *Waterfront Plaza, 500 Ala Moana Blvd., Downtown Honolulu* ☎ *808/521–1555* ⊕ *www.nocturnalounge.com.*

thirtyninehotel. This loft and art gallery is on the cutting edge of what's hot downtown. Every three months it gets a new "art installation," where a local artist repaints and reconfigures the entire space. The bartenders and their "market-fresh" cocktails have become the stuff of local legend, using Hawaiian produce to re-create classic turn-of-the-century libations. Entertainment varies from jazz combos to DJs spinning the latest hits. ⊠ *39 N. Hotel St., Downtown Honolulu* ☎ *808/599–2552* ⊕ *www.thirtyninehotel.com.*

Varsity Grill & Bar. This bar has had several names over the years but there's always been one constant: cheap beer. Located just south of the University of Hawaii, students flock to this open-air pub for the pizza, big-screen TVs, and 50 beers on tap. ⊠ *1019 University Ave., Moiliili* ☎ *808/447–9244* ⊕ *www.varsityhonolulu.com.*

7

CLUBS

The Dragon Upstairs. In the heart of Chinatown, this cool club—formerly a tattoo parlor, hence the dragon mural—serves up classic cocktails along with lounge-y jazz performances most nights of the week. You'll hear local vocalists, as well as small combos, in this unique venue upstairs from Hank's Cafe Honolulu. ⊠ *1038 Nuuanu Ave., Chinatown* ☎ *808/526–1411* ⊕ *www.thedragonupstairs.com.*

Pearl Ultralounge. A hip after-work crowd flocks here on weekdays to unwind at happy hour. Weekends it's packed with the see-and-be-seen set. ⊠ *Ala Moana Center, 1450 Ala Moana Blvd., 3rd fl., Ala Moana* ☎ *808/944–8000* ⊕ *www.pearlhawaii.com.*

Fodor's Choice ★ **Rumours.** It may not be the hippest club in town, but Rumours prides itself on its theme events and its retro vibe, spinning hits from the '70s and '80s. It's got free pupu to nibble on and cages to dance inside. ⊠ *Ala Moana Hotel, 410 Atkinson St., Ala Moana* ☎ *808/955–4811.*

The Standard. The newest nightclub in Honolulu, The Standard is an ultramodern venue with an urban, artsy vibe. White walls are illuminated with shades of lavender, pink, and turquoise, and the space is decked with three bars, VIP seating areas, and an elevated DJ booth spinning house music over a spacious dance floor. The Standard is big enough to host networking mixers and fashion shows, and its location in downtown lures the after-work crowd. The suggested dress code—collared shirts and shoes—makes this a more grown-up hipster spot. ⊠ *500 Ala Moana Blvd., Downtown Honolulu* ☎ *808/529–0010* ⊕ *www.thestandardhonolulu.com.*

The Villa. VIP tables with bottle service and nine different bars make The Villa a popular spot for nighttime prowling. There are lots of open spaces to groove to whatever the DJ is spinning that night, be it house or hip-hop or classic dance tracks. With lots of parking at Aloha Tower and in lots nearby, The Villa is popular with the local club kids and regular night-crawlers. Open only on Friday and Saturday nights, it has discounted drinks until midnight. Fashionable attire is required. ⊠ *Aloha Tower Marketplace, 1 Aloha Tower Dr., Downtown Honolulu* ☎ *808/525–5211* ⊕ *www.thevillahonolulu.com.*

WAIKIKI

BARS

★ **Duke's Waikiki.** Making the most of its spot on Waikiki Beach, Duke's presents live music every Friday, Saturday, and Sunday. Contemporary Hawaiian musicians like Henry Kapono and Maunalua have performed, as well as nationally known musicians like Jimmy Buffett. Solo Hawaiian musicians take the stage nightly, and it's not unusual for surfers to leave their boards outside to step in for a casual drink after a long day on the waves. ⊠ *Outrigger Waikiki, 2335 Kalakaua Ave., Suite 116* ☎ *808/922–2268* ⊕ *www.dukeswaikiki.com.*

Formaggio Wine and Cheese Bar. There's no flashy signage for this establishment on the outskirts of Waikiki—only the name painted on the door. This tinted door cloaks a dimly lighted bar, where young professionals enjoy live jazz Wednesday to Saturday. There are more than 40 wines by the glass and a Mediterranean menu featuring everything from pizzas to panini. ✉ *Market City Shopping Center, 2919 Kapiolani Blvd., lower level* ☎ *808/739–7719* ⊕ *www.formaggio808.com.*

Genius Lounge Sake Bar & Grill. Removed from the tourist traps along Kalakaua Avenue, the Genius Lounge is tucked away on the third floor of a former apartment building on Lewers Street. The extensive drink menu offers beer and wine, cocktails, house-made sangria and, of course, sake. Japanese-inspired dishes are also available. Though small, the space, furnished with dark woods and lit by candles, makes an intimate setting for small gatherings and Friday-night dates. The crowd is mostly Asian visitors and transplants, but the daily happy hour from 6 pm to 8 pm lures the office workers and pre-club prowlers. ✉ *347 Lewers St., 3rd fl.* ☎ *808/626–5362* ⊕ *www.geniusloungehawaii.com.*

Lewers Lounge. A great spot for predinner drinks or post-sunset cocktails, Lewers Lounge offers a relaxed but chic atmosphere in the middle of Waikiki. There are classic and contemporary cocktails, many created by Dale DeGroff, the "King of Cocktails" from New York City's Rainbow Room. He's ditched the soda guns and mixes and brought back the craft of cocktails, using fresh and natural ingredients. Some standouts include the Ginger Lychee Caipirissima and the Blackberry Julep. Enjoy your libation with live jazz and tempting desserts, such as the hotel's famous coconut cake. Or just sit back and relax in the grand setting of the luxurious lounge, which is decked in dramatic drapes and cozy banquettes. ✉ *Halekulani Hotel, 2199 Kalia Rd.* ☎ *808/923–2311* ⊕ *www.halekulani.com.*

Lobby Bar. It's tricky to find the Lobby Bar at the new Modern Honolulu—it's behind a huge, revolving bookcase in the lobby behind the registration desk. It's an überchic space, with intimate alcoves and oversized sofas that are both hip and inviting. The cocktails, like the "Deconstructed Mai Tai," are pricey but cool. ✉ *The Modern Honolulu Hotel, 1775 Ala Moana Blvd.* ☎ *808/943–5800.*

Lulu's Waikiki. Even if you're not a surfer, you'll love this place's retro vibe and the unobstructed second-floor view of Waikiki Beach. The open-air setting, casual dining menu, and tropical drinks are all you need to help you settle into your vacation. The venue transforms from a nice spot for lunch or dinner to a bustling, high-energy club with live music lasting into the wee hours. ✉ *Park Shore Waikiki Hotel, 2586 Kalakaua Ave.* ☎ *808/926–5222* ⊕ *www.luluswaikiki.com.*

★ **Mai Tai Bar.** The bartenders here sure know how to mix up a killer mai tai. This is, after all, the establishment that first concocted the famous drink. The umbrella-shaded tables at the outdoor bar are front-row seating for sunsets and also have an unobstructed view of Diamond Head. Contemporary Hawaiian musicians hold jam sessions onstage. ✉ *Royal Hawaiian Hotel, 2259 Kalakaua Ave.* ☎ *808/923–7311* ⊕ *www.royal-hawaiian.com.*

Fodor'sChoice **Moana Terrace.** Three floors up from Waikiki Beach, this casual, open-
★ air terrace is the home of the Keawe Ohana, a family comprised of some of Hawaii's finest musicians. Order a drink served in a fresh

7

pineapple and watch the sun dip into the Pacific Ocean. ⊠ *Waikiki Beach Marriott Resort, 2552 Kalakaua Ave.* ☎ *808/922–6611.*

Moose McGillycuddy's Pub and Cafe. Loud bands play for the beach-and-beer gang in a blue-jeans-and-T-shirt setting. Live bands play hits from the '80s and '90s, and happy hour extends until 7 pm every night. Major sporting events are broadcast on the bar's flat-screen TVs. ⊠ *310 Lewers St.* ☎ *808/923–0751* ⊕ *www.moosemcgillycuddys.com.*

Rumfire. Locals and visitors head here for the convivial atmosphere and the million-dollar view of Waikiki Beach and Diamond Head. Come early to get a seat for happy hour, which is nightly from 4 to 6 and 9:30 to 11. If you're feeling peckish, there's a menu of Asian-influenced dishes. Rumfire also features original cocktails, signature shots, and live music. ⊠ *Sheraton Waikiki, 2255 Kalakaua Ave.* ☎ *808/922–4422* ⊕ *www.rumfirewaikiki.com.*

Tiki's Grill & Bar. Tiki torches light the way to this restaurant and bar overlooking Kuhio Beach. A mix of locals and visitors head here on the weekend to get their fill of kitschy cool. There's nightly entertainment featuring contemporary Hawaiian musicians. Don't leave without sipping on the Lava Flow, served in a whole coconut, or noshing on the famous coconut shrimp. ⊠ *Aston Waikiki Beach Hotel, 2570 Kalakaua Ave.* ☎ *808/923–8454* ⊕ *www.tikisgrill.com.*

The Veranda. The Veranda at the Moana Surfrider—Waikiki's first hotel—has its own interesting history. From this location, the radio program *Hawaii Calls* first broadcast the sounds of Hawaiian music to a U.S. mainland audience in 1935. Hawaiian entertainers continue to provide the perfect accompaniment to the sounds of the waves. There's a small bar in the dining area—this space turns into the Beach House at the Moana for dinner—or mosey to The Beach Bar below and enjoy live Hawaiian music nightly. ⊠ *Moana Surfrider, 2365 Kalakaua Ave.* ☎ *808/922–3111, 808/921–4600* ⊕ *www.moana-surfrider.com.*

Waiolu Ocean View Lounge. Hawaiian bars should have two things: stellar views of the sunset over the ocean and equally awesome mai tais. Both are on offer at the Waiolu Ocean View Lounge at the posh Trump International Hotel. Not only does the bar boast what might be the best view in Waikiki, its resident mixologist Christina Maffei has created a version of the popular cocktail that earned it the title of "World's Best Mai Tai." Judge for yourself. There's live music, ranging from contemporary to Hawaiian to R&B, on Thursday, Friday, and Saturday

---

MAI TAIS

Hard to believe, but the cocktail known around the world as the mai tai has been around for more than 50 years. While the recipe has changed slightly over the years, the original formula, created by bar owner Victor J. "Trader Vic" Bergeron, included 2 ounces of 17-year-old J. Wray & Nephew rum over shaved ice, ½ ounce Holland Dekuyper orange curaçao, ¼ ounce Trader Vic's rock candy syrup, ½ ounce French Garier orgeat syrup, and the juice of one fresh lime. Done the right way, this tropical drink still lives up to the name "mai tai!" meaning, "out of this world!"

nights, with an attractive crowd showing up around 8 pm. It's busy but not suffocating. Seats are scarce once the music starts at 7:30 pm, so reserve a table in advance. ⊠ *Trump International Hotel, 223 Saratoga Rd.* ☎ *808/683–7777* ⊕ *www.trumpwaikikihotel.com.*

Wang Chung's Karaoke Bar. Dubbed the "Friendliest Bar in Waikiki," this charming (read: small) karaoke bar is a must-see on any trip to the island. The positive vibe comes from owner Dan Chang, who personally welcomes his guests. (He might even hug you.) The cocktails are innovative and the list of karaoke songs is extensive. Don't be surprised if the entire bar starts singing along. ⊠ *2410 Koa Ave.* ☎ *808/921–9176* ⊕ *www.wangchungs.com.*

CLUBS

Addiction Nightclub. This new nightclub at The Modern Honolulu was launched by the hotel's director of nightlife, Matt Bendik, who also manages and owns nightlife concepts in Los Angeles and Hollywood. Traditional banquettes offer intimate seating for VIP tables, and bottle service lends a New York City feel. Red-velvet ropes guide you in the entrance; once inside you can dance to house and hip-hop music under a stunning ceiling installation of 40,000 round lights. But Addiction comes with a price—there's a $20 cover and drinks aren't cheap. ⊠ *The Modern Honolulu, 1775 Ala Moana Blvd.* ☎ *808/943–5800* ⊕ *www. addictionnightclub.com.*

Apartment 3. Tucked away on the third floor of an office building on the edge of Waikiki, this cool club is a favorite among cosmopolitan locals and the occasional celebrity—Johnny Depp has been spotted here. There's something going on every night of the week, except Sunday. The food—traditional comfort eats with a modern twist—is great, too. ⊠ *Century Center, 1750 Kalakaua Ave.* ☎ *808/955–9300* ⊕ *www. apartmentthree.com.*

Hula's Bar and Lei Stand. Hawaii's oldest and best-known gay-friendly nightspot offers panoramic views of Diamond Head by day and high-energy club music by night. Check out the soundproof, glassed-in dance floor. Patrons have included Elton John, Adam Lambert, and Dolly Parton. ⊠ *Waikiki Grand Hotel, 134 Kapahulu Ave., 2nd fl.* ☎ *808/923–0669* ⊕ *www.hulas.com.*

Nashville Waikiki. Country music in the tropics? You bet! Dress up like a *paniolo* (Hawaiian cowboy) and mosey on out to the giant dance floor at Nashville Waikiki. There's line dancing and free dance lessons five nights a week. Look for wall-to-wall crowds on the weekend. Pool tables, dartboards, and Wii consoles keep them occupied. ⊠ *Ohana Waikiki West Hotel, 2330 Kuhio Ave.* ☎ *808/926–7911* ⊕ *www. nashvillewaikiki.com.*

Zanzabar. Traverse the winding staircase to make a grand entrance at Zanzabar, where DJs spin everything from hip-hop and soul to techno and trance. With three bars, it's easy to find a drink at this high-energy nightspot. Not sure how to get your groove on? Zanzabar offers free Latin dance lessons every Tuesday night. ⊠ *Waikiki Trade Center, 2255 Kuhio Ave.* ☎ *808/924–3939* ⊕ *www.zanzabarhawaii.com.*

SOUTHEAST OAHU

Kona Brewing Co. This massive restaurant and bar on the docks of Koko Marina has long been a hot spot in east Honolulu. In addition to serving the company's signature ales, this authentic pub offers live music most nights. It's a lively spot, especially on the weekends when it's standing-room-only at the bar. ⊠ *Koko Marina Center, 7192 Kalanianiole Hwy., Honolulu* ☏ *808/396–5662* ⊕ *www.konabrewingco.com.*

The Shack. This sports bar and restaurant is about the only late-night spot you can find in Southeast Oahu. After a day of snorkeling at Hanauma Bay, stop by to kick back, have a beer, eat a burger, or play a game of pool. ⊠ *Hawaii Kai Shopping Center, 377 Keahole St., Hawaii Kai* ☏ *808/396–1919* ⊕ *www.shackhawaiikai.com.*

WINDWARD OAHU

Boardrider's Bar & Grill. Tucked away in Kailua Town, Boardrider's has long been the place for local bands to strut their stuff. Look for live music—reggae to rock and roll—every Friday and Saturday night. The spruced-up space includes pool tables, dartboards, and eight TVs for watching the game. ⊠ *201-A Hamakua Dr., Kailua* ☏ *808/261–4600.*

THE NORTH SHORE

Breaker's Restaurant. Just about every surf competition post-party is celebrated at this family-owned establishment. (The owner's son, Benji Weatherly, is a pro surfer.) Surfing memorabilia, including longboards hanging from the ceiling, fill the space. A tasty late-night menu is available until midnight. There's live music on Saturday. ⊠ *Marketplace Shopping Center, 66-250 Kamehameha Hwy., Haleiwa* ☏ *808/637–9898.*

Where to Eat

WORD OF MOUTH

"I like Hau Tree Lanai as well. You are right on the beach, sitting under a canopy of gnarled trees. Watching people play beach volleyball, watching the sunset, and then enjoying your meal with the lights on the surf is magical."

—Kailani

Updated
by Melissa
Chang

Oahu, where the majority of the Islands' 2,000-plus restaurants are located, offers the best of all worlds: it has the exoticism and excitement of Asia and Polynesia, but when the kids need McDonald's, or when you just have to have a Starbucks latte, they're here, too.

Budget for a pricey dining experience at the very top of the restaurant food chain, where chefs Alan Wong, Roy Yamaguchi, George Mavrothalassitis, and others you've seen on the Food Network and Travel Channel put a sophisticated and unforgettable spin on local foods and flavors. Savor seared ahi tuna in sea urchin beurre blanc or steak marinated in Korean kimchee sauce.

Spend the rest of your food dollars where budget-conscious locals do: in plate-lunch places and small ethnic eateries, at roadside stands and lunch wagons, or at window-in-the-wall delis. Snack on a *musubi* (a handheld rice ball wrapped with seaweed and often topped with Spam), slurp shave ice with red-bean paste, or order up Filipino pork adobo with two scoops of rice and macaroni salad.

In Waikiki, where most visitors stay, you can find choices from gracious rooms with a view to surprisingly authentic Japanese noodle shops. But hop in the car, or on the trolley or bus, and travel just a few miles in any direction, and you can save your money and get in touch with the real food of Hawaii.

Kaimuki's Waialae Avenue, for example, offers one of the city's best espresso bars, a hugely popular Chinese bakery, a highly recommended patisserie, an exceptional Italian bistro, a dim-sum restaurant, Mexican food (rare here), and a Hawaii regional cuisine standout, 3660 on the Rise—all in three blocks, and 10 minutes from Waikiki. Chinatown, 10 minutes in the other direction and easily reached by the Waikiki Trolley, is another dining (and shopping) treasure, not only for Chinese but also Vietnamese, Filipino, Malaysian, and Indian food, and even a chic little tea shop.

OAHU DINING PLANNER

EATING-OUT STRATEGY

Where should we eat? With dozens of eateries competing for your attention, it may seem like a daunting question. But our writers and editors have done most of the legwork—the selections here represent the best dining Oahu has to offer. Search "Best Bets" for picks by price, cuisine, and experience. Or find a restaurant quickly—reviews are ordered alphabetically within their geographic area.

WITH KIDS

Hawaii is a kid-friendly destination in many regards, and that includes taking the little ones out to eat with you. That said, there are probably a few places in Waikiki where you're better off dining sans kids and taking advantage of your hotel's child care.

SMOKING

Smoking is prohibited except in places where liquor revenues exceed food sales.

PARKING

In Waikiki, walk or take a cab; it's cheaper than parking or valet rates. Elsewhere on Oahu, free, validated, and reasonably priced parking is widely available. Exceptions: parking downtown during the day is hideously expensive—take the trolley or TheBus; Chinatown at night is somewhat dicey—use valet parking or park in lighted lots such as Mark's Garage or municipal lots.

RESERVATIONS

If you expect to dine at Alan Wong's, Chef Mavro, or Roy's, book your table from home weeks in advance. Also beware the brand-new restaurants: they get slammed by migratory hordes for the first few weeks. Otherwise, reserve when you get into town.

WHAT TO WEAR

You'll find people dress up for dinner on Oahu—especially in Waikiki and Honolulu—more so than on any other Hawaiian island. Even so, casual reigns supreme here; most top restaurants abide by the "dressy casual" standard, where dark jeans are acceptable as long as they're not worn with sneakers.

HOURS AND PRICES

The most sought-after dinner reservations are between 6 and 7, but you can often have your pick of tables at 8. Exceptions: sushi bars and Japanese taverns, a few 24-hour diners, and some younger-spinning restaurants. Takeout places still open at dawn and close shortly after midday. Standard tipping for good service is 20%.

WHAT IT COSTS				
	$	$$	$$$	$$$$
AT DINNER	Under $17	$17–$26	$27–$35	over $35

Restaurant prices are for a main course at dinner.

HONOLULU

There's no lack of choices when it comes to dining in Honolulu, where everything from the haute cuisine of heavy-hitting top-notch chefs to a wide variety of Asian specialties to reliable and inexpensive American favorites can be found.

DOWNTOWN HONOLULU

$ ✗ **Akasaka.** Step inside this tiny sushi bar tucked behind the Ala Moana
JAPANESE Hotel, and you'll swear you're in an out-of-the-way Edo neighborhood in some indeterminate time. Don't be deterred by its location between strip clubs or its reputation for inconsistent service. Greeted with a cheerful *"Iraishaimase!"* (Welcome!), sink down at a diminutive table or perch at the handful of seats at the sushi bar. It's safe to let the sushi chefs here decide (*omakase*-style) or you can go for the delicious grilled specialties, such as scallop *battayaki* (grilled in butter). ✉ *1646 B Kona St., Ala Moana* ☎ *808/942–4466* ⊕ *www.akasakahawaii.com/home. html* ✆ No lunch Sun.

$ ✗ **Bac Nam.** Tam and Kimmy Huynh's menu is much more extensive
VIETNAMESE than most, ranging far beyond the usual *pho* (beef noodle soup) and *bun* (cold noodle dishes). Coconut milk curries, an extraordinary crab noodle soup, and other dishes hail from both North and South Vietnam. The atmosphere is welcoming and relaxed, and they'll work with you to make choices. Reservations are not accepted for groups fewer than six. ✉ *1117 S. King St., Downtown Honolulu* ☎ *808/597–8201.*

$ ✗ **Big City Diner.** Part of a chain of unfussy retro diners, Big City
AMERICAN offers a short course in local-style breakfasts—rice instead of potatoes, option of fish or Portuguese sausage instead of bacon, roasted macadamia nut pancakes smothered in haupia (coconut) sauce—with generous portions, low prices, and pronounced flavors. Lunch and dinner focus on local-style comfort food—baby back ribs, kimchee fried rice—and burgers. There are always daily specials. ✉ *Ward Entertainment Center, 1060 Auahi St., Ala Moana* ☎ *808/591–8891* ⊕ *www. bigcitydinerhawaii.com.*

$$$ ✗ **Chai's Island Bistro.** Chai Chaowasaree's stylish, light-bathed, and
ECLECTIC orchid-draped lunch and dinner restaurant expresses the sophisticated side of this Thai-born immigrant. He plays East against West on the plate in signature dishes such as *kataifi* (baked and shredded phyllo), macadamia-crusted prawns, ahi *katsu* (tuna steaks dredged with crisp Japanese bread crumbs and quickly deep-fried), crispy duck confetti spring rolls, and Japanese eggplant zucchini soufflé. Some of Hawaii's best-known contemporary Hawaiian musicians play brief dinner shows here every night. ✉ *Aloha Tower Marketplace, 1 Aloha Tower Dr., Downtown Honolulu* ☎ *808/585–0011* ⊕ *www.chaisislandbistro.com* ✆ No lunch.

$ ✗ **Contemporary Cafe.** This tasteful lunch spot in the Contemporary
AMERICAN Museum offers light and healthful food from a short but well-selected menu of housemade soups, crostini of the day, innovative sandwiches garnished with fruit, and a hummus plate with fresh pita. In the exclusive Makiki Heights neighborhood above the city, the restaurant spills

BEST BETS FOR
FOR OAHU DINING

Where can I find the best food the island has to offer? Fodor's writers and editors have selected their favorite restaurants by price, cuisine, and experience in the lists below. In the first column, the Fodor's Choice properties represent the "best of the best" across price categories. You can also search by area for excellent eats—just peruse our complete reviews on the following pages.

Fodor's Choice ★

Alan Wong's, $$$$, p. 218

Buzz's Original Steakhouse, $$, p. 236

Chef Mavro, $$$$, p. 220

Little Village Noodle House, $, p. 217

Ola at Turtle Bay Resort, $$$$, p. 239

By Price

$

Bac Nam, p. 206

Little Village Noodle House, p. 217

Kakaako Kitchen, p. 213

Keo's in Waikiki, p. 228

Ono Hawaiian Foods, p. 222

Pah Ke's Chinese Restaurant, p. 237

To Chau, p. 218

Wailana Coffee House, p. 232

$$

Buzz's Original Steakhouse, p. 236

Kalapawai Café and Deli, p. 237

Roy's, p. 235

$$$

3660 on the Rise, p. 223

Sam Choy's Breakfast Lunch & Crab and Big Aloha Brewery, p. 234

$$$$

Alan Wong's, p. 218

Chef Mavro, p. 220

Hoku's at the Kahala, p. 221

Nobu, p. 229

Ola at Turtle Bay Resort, p. 239

By Cuisine

HAWAIIAN

Alan Wong's, $$$$, p. 218

Chef Mavro, $$$$, p. 220

Hoku's at the Kahala, $$$$, p. 221

Roy's, $$, p. 235

PLATE LUNCH

Keneke's BBQ, $, p. 237

L&L Hawaiian Barbecue, $, p. 225

Ono Hawaiian Foods, $, p. 222

Ted's Bakery, $, p. 239

SUSHI

Mitch's Sushi Restaurant, $$$, p. 233

Nobu, $$$$, p. 229

Sushi Sasabune, $$$$, p. 222

Yanagi Sushi, $$, p. 216

By Experience

MOST KID-FRIENDLY

3660 on the Rise, $$$, p. 223

Big City Diner, $, pp. 206, 236

Ono Hawaiian Foods, $, p. 222

Sam Choy's Breakfast, Lunch & Crab and Brewery, $$$, p. 234

Wailana Coffee House, $, p. 232

MOST ROMANTIC

Hau Tree Lanai, $$$$, p. 227

Hoku's at the Kahala, $$$$, p. 221

La Mer, $$$$, p. 229

Michel's at the Colony Surf, $$$$, p. 229

Sarento's Top of the "I," $$$$, p. 231

BEST VIEW

La Mer, $$$$, p. 229

Orchids, $$$$, p. 230

Sarento's Top of the "I," $$$$, p. 231

Top of Waikiki, $$$$, p. 232

8

out of the ground floor of the museum onto the lawn. The cafe now offers a a "Lauhala and Lunch" picnic lunch for two, priced at $30, which includes a choice of sandwich or salad for each person, dessert bars, and choice of beverages all packed in a pretty picnic basket. ⊠ *The Contemporary Museum, 2411 Makiki Heights Dr., Makiki* ☏ *808/523–3362* ⌲ *Reservations not accepted* Ⓨ *$5 corkage* ⊘ *No dinner. Closed Mon.*

$ ✕ **Downtown @ the HiSam.** Chef-owner Ed Kenney, who presides over
AMERICAN the popular restaurant Town, has contributed this new restaurant at the Hawaii State Art Museum to the downtown business-lunch crowd. Contemporary furnishings and art provide a frame for the lunch options inspired by Kenney's philosophy of "local first, organic whenever possible, with aloha always." You'll find salads with organic local produce, Mediterranean-inspired sandwiches, and even filet mignon for those with a bit more time to linger at this casual, contemporary local favorite. The restaurant is open late only on first Fridays (5:30–8:30 pm). ⊠ *Hawaii State Art Museum, 250 Hotel St., Downtown Honolulu* ☏ *808/586–5900* ⌲ *Reservations essential* ⊘ *No dinner.*

$ ✕ **Hank's Haute Dogs.** Owner Henry "Hank" Adaniya may know a thing
HOT DOG or two about hot dogs, since he was once a prominent restaurateur in
ⓒ Chicago. As seen on *Diners, Drive-Ins & Dives*, his upscale hot dog stand is always busy despite having limited metered street parking. Even if you only have the Chicago Dog, which is made with all the traditional fixings, you won't be disappointed; but people love the lobster dog, bratwurst, and decadent "fat boy," a hot dog wrapped in bacon and deep-fried. Wash your choice down with a hibiscus lemonade or *lilikoi*-lime soda, and pair with fries and unique dipping sauces. The original restaurant is in industrial Kakaako, but you can find the same great dogs at the International Marketplace location in Waikiki at 2330 Kalakaua Avenue. ⊠ *324 Coral St., Kakaako* ☏ *808/532–4265* ⊕ *www. hankshautedogs.com* ⌲ *Reservations not accepted.*

$$ ✕ **Hiroshi Eurasion Tapas.** Built around chef Hiroshi Fukui's signature
ASIAN style of "West & Japan" cuisine, this sleek dinner house focuses on small plates to share (enough for two servings each), with an exceptional choice of hard-to-find wines by the glass and in flights. Do not miss Hiroshi's braised veal cheeks (he was doing them before everyone else), the locally raised *kampachi* fish carpaccio, or the best *misoyaki* (marinated in a rich miso-soy blend, then grilled) butterfish ever. For a decadent treat, try the foie gras *nigiri*. You can also order off the menu from Vino, next door, as they share a kitchen. ⊠ *Restaurant Row, 500 Ala Moana Blvd., Ala Moana* ☏ *808/533–4476* ⊕ *www.hiroshihawaii. com* ⊘ *No lunch.*

$ ✕ **Honolulu Museum of Art Café.** The cool courtyards and varied galleries
AMERICAN of the Honolulu Museum of Art are well worth a visit and, afterward, so is Mike Nevin's popular lunch restaurant. The café overflows onto a lanai from which you can ponder Asian statuary while you wait for your salade Niçoise or Piadina sandwich (fresh-baked flatbread rounds stuffed with arugula, tomatoes, basil, and cheese). ⊠ *Honolulu Museum of Art, 900 S. Beretania St., Downtown Honolulu* ☏ *808/532–*

Continued on page 213

LUAU: A TASTE OF HAWAII

The best place to sample Hawaiian food is at a backyard luau. Aunts and uncles are cooking, the pig is from a cousin's farm, and the fish is from a brother's boat.

But even locals have to angle for invitations to those rare occasions. So your choice is most likely between a commercial luau and a Hawaiian restaurant.

Some commercial luau are less authentic; they offer little of the traditional diet and are more about umbrella drinks, spectacle, and fun.

For greater authenticity, folksy experiences, and rock-bottom prices, visit a Hawaiian restaurant (most are in anonymous storefronts in residential neighborhoods). Expect rough edges and some effort negotiating the menu.

In either case, much of what is known today as Hawaiian food would be as foreign to a 16th-century Hawaiian as risotto or chow mien. The pre-contact diet was simple and healthy—mainly raw and steamed seafood and vegetables. Early Hawaiians used earth ovens and heated stones to cook seafood, taro, sweet potatoes, and breadfruit and seasoned their food with sea salt and ground kukui nuts. Seaweed, fern shoots, sweet potato vines, coconut, banana, sugarcane, and select greens and roots rounded out the diet.

Successive waves of immigrants added their favorites to the ti leaf–lined table. So it is that foods as disparate as salt salmon and chicken long rice are now Hawaiian—even though there is no salmon in Hawaiian waters and long rice (cellophane noodles) is Chinese.

AT THE LUAU: KALUA PORK

The heart of any luau is the *imu*, the earth oven in which a whole pig is roasted. The preparation of an imu is an arduous affair for most families, who tackle it only once a year or so, for a baby's first birthday or at Thanksgiving, when many Islanders prefer to imu their turkeys. Commercial luau operations have it down to a science, however.

THE ART OF THE STONE

The key to a proper imu is the *pohaku*, the stones. Imu cook by means of long, slow, moist heat released by special stones that can withstand a hot fire without exploding. Many Hawaiian families treasure their imu stones, keeping them in a pile in the backyard and passing them on through generations.

PIT COOKING

The imu makers first dig a pit about the size of a re-frigerator, then lay down *kiawe* (mesquite) wood and stones, and build a white-hot fire that is allowed to burn itself out. The ashes are raked away, and the hot stones covered with banana and ti leaves. Well-wrapped in ti or banana leaves and a net of chicken wire, the pig is lowered onto the leaf-covered stones. *Laulau* (leaf-wrapped bundles of meats, fish, and taro leaves) may also be placed inside. Leaves—ti, banana, even ginger—cover the pig followed by wet burlap sacks (to create steam). The whole is topped with a canvas tarp and left to steam for the better part of a day.

OPENING THE IMU

This is the moment everyone waits for: The imu is unwrapped like a giant present and the imu keep-ers gingerly wrestle out the steaming pig. When it's unwrapped, the meat falls moist and smoky-flavored from the bone, looking just like Southern-style pulled pork, but without the barbecue sauce.

WHICH LUAU?

Paradise Cove. Party-hearty atmosphere, kid-friendly.

Polynesian Cultural Center. The sharpest production values but no booze.

Waikiki Starlight Luau. The only luau in Waikiki is on the rooftop of the Hilton Hawaii Village.

MEA AI ONO:
GOOD THINGS TO EAT.

LAULAU
Steamed meats, fish, and taro leaf in ti-leaf bundles: fork-tender, a medley of flavors; the taro resembles spinach.

LOMI LOMI SALMON
Salt salmon in a piquant salad or relish with onions, tomatoes.

POI
Poi, a paste made of pounded taro root, may be an acquired taste, but it's a must-try during your visit.

Consider: The Hawaiian Adam is descended from *kalo* (taro). Young taro plants are called "keiki"– children. Poi is the first food after mother's milk for many Islanders. Ai, the word for food, is synonymous with poi in many contexts.

Not only that, we love it. "There is no meat that doesn't taste good with poi," the old Hawaiians said.

But you have to know how to eat it: with something rich or powerfully flavored. "It is salt that makes the poi go in," is another adage. When you're served poi, try it with a mouthful of smoky kalua pork or salty lomi lomi salmon. Its slightly sour blandness cleanses the palate. And if you don't like it, smile and say something polite. (And slide that bowl over to a local.)

Laulau

Lomi Lomi Salmon

Poi

8

E HELE MAI AI! COME AND EAT!

Hawaiian restaurants tend to be inconveniently located in well-worn storefronts with little or no parking, outfitted with battered tables and clattering Melmac dishes, but they personify aloha, invariably run by local families who welcome tourists who take the trouble to find them.

Many are cash-only operations and combination plates are a standard feature: one or two entrées, a side such as chicken long rice, choice of poi or steamed rice and—if the place is really old-style—a tiny portion of coarse Hawaiian salt and some raw onions for relish.

Most serve some foods that aren't, strictly speaking, Hawaiian, but are beloved of ka-maaina, such as salt meat with watercress (preserved meat in a tasty broth), or *akubone*

(skipjack tuna fried in a tangy vinegar sauce).

Our two favorite: **Ono Hawaiian Foods** and **Helena's Hawaiian Food**.

MENU GUIDE

Much of the Hawaiian language encountered during a stay in the Islands will appear on restaurant menus and lists of luau fare. Here's a quick primer.

ahi: *yellowfin tuna.*

aku: *skipjack, bonito tuna.*

amaama: *mullet; it's hard to get but tasty.*

bento: *a box lunch.*

chicken luau: *a stew made from chicken, taro leaves, and coconut milk.*

haupia: *a light, pudding-like sweet made from coconut.*

imu: *the underground oven in which pigs are roasted for luau.*

kalua: *to bake underground.*

kau kau: *food. The word comes from Chinese but is used in the Islands.*

kimchee: *Korean dish of pickled cabbage made with garlic and hot peppers.*

Kona coffee: *coffee grown in the Kona district of the Big Island.*

laulau: *literally, a bundle. Laulau are morsels of pork, chicken, butterfish, or other ingredients wrapped with young taro leaves and then bundled in ti leaves for steaming.*

lilikoi: *passion fruit, a tart, seedy yellow fruit that makes delicious desserts, juice, and jellies.*

lomi lomi: *to rub or massage; also a massage. Lomi lomi salmon is fish that has been rubbed with onions and herbs; commonly served with minced onions and tomatoes.*

luau: *a Hawaiian feast; also the leaf of the taro plant used in preparing such a feast.*

luau leaves: *cooked taro tops with a taste similar to spinach.*

mahimahi: *mild-flavored dolphinfish, not the marine mammal.*

mai tai: *potent rum drink with orange liqueurs and pineapple juice, from the Tahitian word for "good."*

malasada: *a Portuguese deep-fried doughnut without a hole, dipped in sugar.*

manapua: *steamed chinese buns filled with pork, chicken, or other fillings.*

mano: *shark.*

niu: *coconut.*

onaga: *pink or red snapper.*

ono: *a long, slender mackerel-like fish; also called wahoo.*

ono: *delicious; also hungry.*

opihi: *a tiny shellfish, or mollusk, found on rocks; also called limpets.*

papio: *a young ulua or jack fish.*

poha: *Cape gooseberry. Tasting a bit like honey, the poha berry is often used in jams and desserts.*

poi: *a paste made from pounded taro root, a staple of the Hawaiian diet.*

poke: *cubed raw tuna or other fish, tossed with seaweed and seasonings.*

pupu: *appetizers or small plates.*

saimin: *long thin noodles and vegetables in broth, often garnished with small pieces of fish cake, scrambled egg, luncheon meat, and green onion.*

sashimi: *raw fish thinly sliced and usually eaten with soy sauce.*

ti leaves: *a member of the agave family. The leaves are used to wrap food while cooking and removed before eating.*

uku: *deep-sea snapper.*

ulua: *a member of the jack family that also includes pompano and amberjack. Also called crevalle, jack fish, and jack crevalle.*

8734 ⊕ *www.honolulumuseum.org/394-pavilion_cafe* ⚓ *Reservations essential* ☽ *Closed Sun. and Mon. No dinner.*

$ ✕ **Kakaako Kitchen.** Russell Siu was the first of the local-boy fine dining
MODERN chefs to open a place of the sort he enjoys when he's off-duty, serv-
HAWAIIAN ing high-quality plate lunches (house-made sauce instead of from-a-
☺ mix brown gravy, for example). Here you can get your two scoops of
either brown or white rice, green salad instead of the usual macaroni
salad, grilled fresh fish specials, and vegetarian fare. Breakfast is especially good, with combos like corned-beef hash and eggs, and exceptional baked goods. ✉ *Ward Centre, 1200 Ala Moana Blvd., Kakaako*
☏ *808/596–7488* ⊕ *kakaakokitchen.com* ⚓ *Reservations not accepted.*

$$$ ✕ **Kincaid's Classic American Dining.** Known for Copper River salmon in
AMERICAN season, consistently well-made salads and seafood specials, efficient
☺ service, and appropriate pricing, Kincaid's, part of a wide-ranging albeit
small chain, is business-lunch central. But, with its window-fronted
room overlooking Kewalo Basin harbor, it's also a relaxing place for a
post-shopping drink or intimate dinner. They're known for their early-
or late-night happy hours, which is a great way to sample more of their
dishes. ✉ *Ward Warehouse, 2nd level, 1050 Ala Moana Blvd., Kakaako*
☏ *808/591–2005* ⊕ *kincaids.com.*

$$$ ✕ **Mariposa.** Yes, the popovers and the wee little cups of bouillon are
ASIAN there at lunch, but in every other regard, this Neiman Marcus restau-
rant menu departs from the classic model, incorporating a clear sense of
Pacific place. The veranda, open to the breezes and view of Ala Moana
Park, twirling ceiling fans, and life-size hula-girl murals say Hawaii.
The popovers at lunch come with a butter-pineapple-papaya spread;
the oxtail osso buco is inspired, and local fish are featured nightly in
luxurious specials. Make sure to leave room for the warm *lilikoi* pudding cake for dessert. ✉ *Neiman Marcus, Ala Moana Center, 1450 Ala
Moana, Ala Moana* ☏ *808/951–3420* ⚓ *Reservations essential.*

$ ✕ **Murphy's Bar & Grill.** Located in the heart of the financial district,
AMERICAN Murphy's boasts an All-American menu of award-winning burgers and
steaks without that Waikiki price tag. The restaurant has been featured
on Guy Fieri's *Diners, Drive-ins and Dives* on the Food Network as a
place that specializes in comfort food for the weary traveler. The Blarney
Burger with Guinness-infused cheddar cheese is a must. ✉ *2 Merchant
St., Downtown Honolulu* ☏ *808/531–0422* ⊕ *murphyshawaii.com.*

$$ ✕ **The Pineapple Room by Alan Wong.** This is not your grandmother's
MODERN department-store restaurant. It's überchef Alan Wong's more casual
HAWAIIAN second spot, where the chef de cuisine plays intriguing riffs on local
food themes. Warning: the spicy chili-fried soybeans are addicting.
Their house burger, made with locally raised grass-fed beef, bacon,
cheddar cheese, hoisin-mayonnaise spread, and avocado, won a local
tasting hands-down. Service is very professional; reservations are rec-
ommended. ✉ *Macy's, Ala Moana Center, 1450 Ala Moana Blvd., Ala
Moana* ☏ *808/945–6573.*

$$ ✕ **Royal Garden.** You know it's good if, despite being in a hotel, a Chi-
CHINESE nese restaurant still draws more locals than tourists as customers. Royal
Garden is known as one of the best dim sum spots in town, and people
don't mind paying a little more for the quality they get. Just point to

8

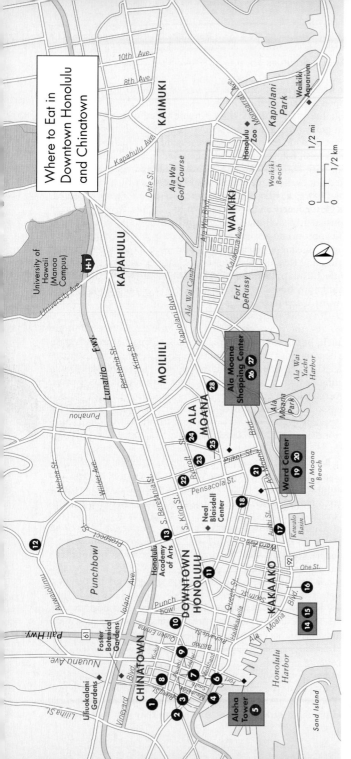

Where to Eat in Downtown Honolulu and Chinatown

1/2 mi

1/2 km

the steamed and baked morsels that look good; chances are, they're as good as they look. ⊠ *Ala Moana Hotel, 410 Atkinson Dr., Ala Moana* ☏ *808/942–7788.*

$ ✕ **Ryan's Grill at Ward Centre.** An all-purpose food and drink emporium, AMERICAN lively and popular Ryan's has an exceptionally well-stocked bar, with 20 beers on tap, an outdoor deck, and TVs broadcasting sports. Lunch, dinner, and small plates are served from 11 am to 2 am. The eclectic menu ranges from an addictive hot crab-and-artichoke dip with focaccia bread to grilled fresh fish, pasta, salads, and sophisticated versions of local favorites, such as the Kobe beef hamburger steak. ⊠ *Ward Centre, 1200 Ala Moana Blvd., Kakaako* ☏ *808/591–9132* ⊕ *ryansgrill.com.*

$$ ✕ **Sorabol.** The largest Korean restaurant in the city, this 24-hour eatery, KOREAN with its impossibly tiny parking lot and maze of booths and private rooms, offers a vast menu encompassing the entirety of day-to-day Korean cuisine, plus sushi. English menu translations are cryptic at best. Still, it's great for wee hour "grinds" (local slang for food): *bi bim bap* (veggies, meats, and eggs on steamed rice), *kal bi* and *bulgogi* (barbecued meats), meat or fish *jun* (thin fillets fried in batter), and kimchi pancakes. ⊠ *805 Keeaumoku St., Ala Moana* ☏ *808/947–3113* ⊕ *sorabolhawaii.com.*

$$ ✕ **Tangö.** Long lines of hungry locals are the telltale sign that you've ECLECTIC stumbled upon Tangö, a dining destination at the swanky Hokua condominiums. Unflappable restaurateur Göran Streng seems to have bypassed the usual growing pains of a new restaurant, instead rewarding his customers' palates with an unfussy menu and polished service. Minimalist yet contemporary decor comes in the form of blond and birch woods, earthy complements to the cloudlike white lampshades. Silver birch branches divide spaces. Streng's dishes pay homage to his Scandinavian background, with touches of Pacific Rim and Asian influences. Dinner standouts include Swedish gravlax with crispy skin, moi (or Pacific threadfin), a flaky white fish served with fennel coulis, and a burger that stands heads above usual unremarkable bovine renditions. Dinner prices are reasonable (especially by Hawaii standards), but for an additional $6.50, diners can tack on a soup or salad, and a dessert, like *lilikoi* (passion fruit) sorbet. Reservations are available only for dinner, and don't expect a super-touristy experience—Streng caters mostly to his discriminating city-dwelling clientele. ⊠ *Hokua Building, 1288 Ala Moana Blvd., Ala Moana* ☏ *808/593–7288* ⊕ *www.tangocafehawaii.com* ⌁ *Reservations essential.*

$$ ✕ **Vino.** Small plates of Italian-inspired appetizers, a wine list selected ITALIAN by the state's first master sommelier, a relaxed atmosphere, and periodic special tastings are the formula for success at this wine bar. You can order items from the adjacent Hiroshi's Eurasion Tapas, as they share a kitchen. ■ **TIP➔** Vino is well situated for stopping off between downtown sightseeing and a return to your Waikiki hotel. ⊠ *Restaurant Row, 500 Ala Moana Blvd., Downtown Honolulu* ☏ *808/524–8466* ⊕ *vinohawaii.com* ⌁ *Reservations essential* ⊙ *Closed Sun.–Tues.*

$ ✕ **Yakiniku Mikawon.** Korean is spoken here, in cooking style and in lan-KOREAN guage, but you can make yourself understood with the help of menu translations and pointing. Mikawon is one of few grill-it-yourself

8

CLOSE UP

Oahu's Best Takeout

For lunch at the beach, or a movie night in your hotel room, do as Islanders do: get takeout. (And in the Islands, incidentally, the proper term is always takeout or to-go, never take-away.)

The universality of takeout here stems from traditions imported by plantation workers from Asia. The Chinese had their bakeries, the Japanese *okazu-ya*, Asian-style delis. Honolulu is awash in Western-style fast-food joints, Islands-style plate-lunch places, and Asian drive-ins offering Japanese sushi, Korean barbecue, Thai noodles, and Vietnamese spring rolls.

But locals particularly cherish the old-style businesses, now into the third and fourth generation, usually inconveniently located, with no parking and ridiculously quirky hours—and each with a specialty or two that no one else can quite match.

Buy a cheap Styrofoam cooler, pack it with ice to keep the goodies cool, and stop by one of these places. And remember: you'll need cash.

Fukuya Delicatessen. This family operation on the main thoroughfare in charming Moiliili, a mile or so mauka out of Waikiki, offers take-out breakfasts and lunches, Japanese snacks, noodle dishes, even confections. Try *mochi* (sweet rice-flour cakes), *chow fun* (thick, flat noodles flecked with vegetables and barbecue pork), hash patties, garlic chicken, and Asian-style salads. The folks here are particularly patient and helpful to visitors. Open 6 am to 2 pm. ⊠ *2710 S. King St., Moiliili* ☎ *808/946–2073* ⊘ *Closed Mon. and Tues. No dinner* ▭ *No credit cards.*

Mitsu-Ken. Trust us: Ignore the downscale neighborhood just north of the city and the unpromising, battered exterior. Just line up and order the garlic chicken (either as a plate lunch, with rice and salad, or chicken only). Crispy, profoundly garlicky, and drizzled with some sweetish glaze that sets the whole thing off, Mitsu-Ken chicken will haunt your dreams. But go early; they open at 4 am, and by 1 pm they're washing down the sidewalks. It's in Kahili, not far from the Bishop Museum. ⊠ *1223 N. School St., Kapalama* ☎ *808/848–5573* ▭ *No credit cards* ⊘ *Closed Sun. and Mon. No dinner.*

---

restaurants to use real, charcoal-burning grills, considered the sine qua non of this Korean style of cooking which has been adopted by Japan. Their specialty is *wang galbi*—ribs seasoned in the style of Su Won, Korea, a mellower style than the usual soy sauce–soaked kal bi ribs. ⊠ *1726 Kapiolani Blvd., Ala Moana* ☎ *808/947–5454.*

$$
JAPANESE

✕ **Yanagi Sushi.** One of relatively few restaurants to serve the complete menu until 2 am (Sunday only until 10 pm), Yanagi is a full-service Japanese restaurant offering not only sushi and sashimi around a small bar, but also *teishoku* (combination menus), tempura, stews, and grill-it-yourself shabu-shabu. The fish here can be depended on for freshness and variety. ⊠ *762 Kapiolani Blvd., Downtown Honolulu* ☎ *808/597–1525* ⊕ *yanagisushi-hawaii.com.*

CHINATOWN

$ ✕ **Grand Café & Bakery.** This well-scrubbed, pleasantly furnished break
AMERICAN fast, brunch, and lunch spot is ideal for taking a break before or after
☺ a trek around Chinatown. Its period feel comes from the fact that chef
Anthony Vierra's great-grandfather had a restaurant of this name in
Chinatown nearly 100 years ago. The delicious and well-presented food
ranges from retro diner dishes (chicken pot pie) to contemporary creations such as beet-and-goat-cheese salad. ⌧ *31 N. Pauahi, Chinatown*
☎ *808/531–0001* ⊕ *www.grandcafeandbakery.com* ⌕ *Reservations
essential* ☯ *Closed Mon. No dinner Tues.–Thurs. and Sun.*

$ ✕ **Green Door.** Closet-size and fronted by a green door and a row of
ASIAN welcoming Chinese lanterns, this Chinatown café has introduced
Honolulu to budget- and taste bud–friendly Malaysian and Singapor-
ean foods, redolent of spices and crunchy with fresh vegetables. The
restaurant's owner gets mixed reviews, as she may be rude to customers who question her cooking. Just order from the flavorful menu of
fewer than 10 dishes, and you'll do fine. ⌧ *1110 Nuuanu Ave., Chinatown* ☎ *808/533–0606* ⌕ *Reservations not accepted* ▭ *No credit
cards* ☯ *Closed Mon.*

$$ ✕ **Indigo Eurasian Cuisine.** Indigo sets the right mood for an evening out
ECLECTIC on the town: the walls are redbrick, the ceilings are high, and from
the restaurant's lounge next door comes the sultry sound of late-night
jazz. Take a bite of goat-cheese wontons with four-fruit sauce followed
by rich Mongolian lamb chops. After dinner, duck into the hip Green
Room lounge for a nightcap. If you're touring downtown at lunchtime,
the Eurasian buffet with a trio of dim sum is an especially good deal at
around $16 per person. ⌧ *1121 Nuuanu Ave., Chinatown* ☎ *808/521–
2900* ⊕ *www.indigo-hawaii.com.*

$ ✕ **Legend Seafood Restaurant.** Do as the locals do: start your visit to
CHINESE Chinatown with breakfast dim sum at Legend. If you want to be able
to hear yourself think, get there before 9 am, especially on weekends.
And don't be shy: use your best cab-hailing technique and sign language
to make the cart ladies stop at your table and show you their wares.
The pork-filled steamed buns, hearty spare ribs, prawn dumplings, and
still-warm custard tarts are excellent pre-shopping fortification. ⌧ *Chi-
nese Cultural Plaza, 100 N. Beretania St., Chinatown* ☎ *808/532–1868*
⊕ *www.legendseafoodhonolulu.com* ⌕ *Reservations essential.*

$ ✕ **Little Village Noodle House.** Unassuming and budget-friendly, Little Vil-
CHINESE lage sets a standard of friendly and attentive service to which every
Fodor's Choice Chinese restaurant should aspire. We have roamed the large, pan-China
★ menu and found a new favorite in everything we've tried: shredded
beef, spinach with garlic, Shanghai noodles, honey-walnut shrimp,
orange chicken, dried green beans. Two words: go there. Reservations
are accepted for parties of five or more. ■ TIP➔ **Two hours of free parking
is available next door.** ⌧ *1113 Smith St., Chinatown* ☎ *808/545–3008*
⊕ *littlevillagehawaii.com.*

$ ✕ **Mei Sum Chinese Dim Sum Restaurant.** In contrast to the sprawling and
CHINESE noisy halls in which dim sum is generally served, Mei Sum is compact
and shiny bright. It's open daily, one of the few places that serves dim
sum from 7:45 am all the way to 8:45 pm. Be ready to guess and point

HU'S BEST SHAVE ICE

-style shave ice (never shaved a pidgin thing) is said to ..ve been born when neighborhood kids hung around the icehouse, waiting to pounce on the shavings from large blocks of ice, carved with ultrasharp Japanese planes that created an exceptionally fine-textured granita.

In the 1920s, according to the historian for syrup manufacturer Malolo Beverages Co., Chinese vendors developed sweet fruit concentrates to pour over the ice.

The evolution continued with mom-and-pop shops adding their own touches, such as hiding a nugget of sweet bean paste, Japanese-style, in the center; placing a small scoop of ice cream at the bottom; adding *li hing* powder (a sweet spice); or using multitoned cones.

There's nothing better on a sticky hot day. Here are two great places to try:

Waiola. Waiola Shave Ice, off Kapahulu Avenue, is known for its finely shaved ice and wide variety of flavors, and more recently has become famous through its regular appearances in the reboot of *Hawaii Five-O*. In real life, the service is a bit surly and the prices are slightly higher than for most other shave ice, but it's close to Waikiki. ⊠ *525 Kapahulu Ave., Kapahulu.*

Aoki's. If you're not in the mood to stand in the long line at the famous Matsumoto's Shave Ice, walk across the parking lot to Aoki's, which the locals prefer. Here the shave ice is just as good, if not better, with a variety of tropical flavors to cool you off. ⊠ *66-117 Kamehameha Hwy., Haleiwa.*

at the color photos of dim sum favorites as not much English is spoken, but the delicate buns and tasty bits are exceptionally well prepared and worth the charades. Other menu items and specials are also served. ⊠ *1170 Nuuanu Ave., Chinatown* ☎ *808/531–3268* ⊟ *No credit cards.*

$ ✕ **To Chau.** If you need proof that To Chau is highly regarded for its
VIETNAMESE   authentic *pho* (Vietnamese beef noodle soup), just check the lines that form in front every morning of the week. It's said that the broth is the key, and it won't break the bank for you to find out, as the average check is less than $10. The restaurant is open only until 2:30 pm, but you may be turned away if the food runs out earlier. ⊠ *1007 River St., Chinatown* ☎ *808/533–4549* ⚑ *Reservations not accepted* ⊟ *No credit cards* ⊙ *No dinner.*

GREATER HONOLULU

$$$$ ✕ **Alan Wong's Restaurant Honolulu.** This not-to-be-missed restaurant
MODERN   is like that very rare shell you stumble upon on a perfect day at the
HAWAIIAN   beach—well polished and without a flaw. We've never had a bad expe-
Fodor'sChoice   rience here, and we've never heard of anyone else having one either.
★   The "Wong Way," as it's not-so-jokingly called by his staff, includes an ingrained understanding of the aloha spirit, evident in the skilled but unstarched service, and creative and playful interpretations of Island cuisine. Try Da Bag (seafood steamed in an aluminum pouch), Chinatown Roast Duck Nachos, and ginger crusted *onaga* (snapper). With

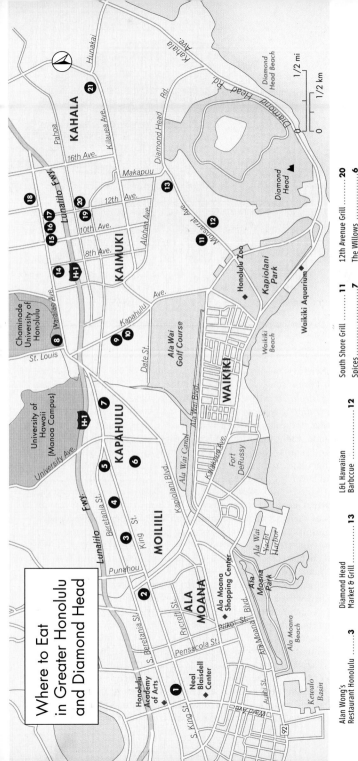

Alan Wong's is known for preparing creative Hawaiian dishes.

warm tones of koa wood, and *lauhala* grass weaving, you forget you're on the third floor of an office building. ⊠ *McCully Court, 1857 S. King St., 3rd fl., Moiliili* ☎ *808/949–2526* ⊕ *www.alanwongs.com* ⚔ *Reservations essential* ⊗ *No lunch*.

$
AMERICAN
✕ **Café Laufer.** Ten minutes from Waikiki, this is the Island version of a Viennese café. Light meals range from grilled sausage with sauerkraut to soups and salads. Try the classic apple tart, linzer torte, Black Forest cake, or chocolate macadamia-nut pastries. The café is open until 10 pm Friday and Saturday for a sweet nightcap. ⊠ *3565 Waialae Ave., Kaimuki* ☎ *808/735–7717* ⊕ *cafelaufer.com* ⚔ *Reservations not accepted*.

$$$$
MODERN
HAWAIIAN
Fodor's Choice
★
✕ **Chef Mavro.** George Mavrothalassitis, who took two hotel restaurants to the top of the ranks before founding this James Beard Award–winning restaurant, admits he's crazy. Crazy because of the care he takes to draw out the truest and most concentrated flavors, to track down the freshest fish, to create one-of-a-kind wine pairings that might strike others as mad. But for this passionate Provençal transplant, there's no other way. The menu changes quarterly, every dish (including dessert) matched with a select wine. Several options (three to six courses, including a vegetarian option) are offered at various price levels, with a supplement for wine pairings at each level. Etched-glass windows screen the busy street-corner scene and all within is mellow and serene with starched white tablecloths, fresh flowers, wood floors, and contemporary Island art. ⊠ *1969 S. King St., Moiliili* ☎ *808/944–4714* ⊕ *www. chefmavro.com* ⚔ *Reservations essential* ⊗ *No lunch*.

$
THAI
✕ **Chiang Mai.** Long beloved for its Thai classics based on family recipes, such as spicy curries and stir-fries and sticky rice in woven grass baskets, Chiang Mai is just a short cab ride from Waikiki. Some dishes,

like the signature Cornish game hen in lemongrass and spices, show how acculturation can create interesting pairings. The cozy space is decorated with Thai fabrics and artwork. ✉ *2239 S. King St., Moiliili* 🕾 *808/941–1151* ⊕ *808chiangmai.com* ⏲ *No lunch weekends.*

$ ✕ **Diego's Taco Shop.** Diego's is a no-frills, simple joint where the smell of
MEXICAN   masa cooking permeates the air, salsa comes in mini plastic containers, and the food is filling and reasonable. The ambience, if you can call it that, is laid-back with college students shuffling in after the beach and "grinding" (eating) at the drive-in style tables. Carne asada is the top pick for taco and burrito filling and the flavor is San Diego Mexican. ✉ *2239 S. King St., McCully* 🕾 *808/949–2239* ⌕ *Reservations not accepted* ▭ *No credit cards.*

$ ✕ **Good to Grill.** Specializing in grilled meats, this casual restaurant is a
AMERICAN   good choice for a full, quality meal at reasonable prices. From prime rib to melt-in-your-mouth short ribs to garlic shrimp pasta, you can count on a consistently good experience every time. It's modest but tasty and well-prepared food. The reasonable breakfasts on weekends and BYOB policy are definite pluses. No wonder Scott Caan of *Hawaii Five-0* is a repeat customer. ✉ *Safeway Center Kapahulu, 888 Kapahulu Ave., Kapahulu* 🕾 *808/734–7345* ⊕ *goodtogrill.com* ⌕ *Reservations not accepted* ⛛ *BYOB.*

$ ✕ **Hale Vietnam.** One of Oahu's first Vietnamese restaurants, this popular
ASIAN   neighborhood spot expresses its friendly character with its name: *hale* (hah-lay) is the Hawaiian word for house or home. If you're not sure what to order, just ask. The staff is known for their willingness to help those who don't know much about Vietnamese food. Be sure to try the piquant and crunchy green-papaya salad. Reservations are taken for groups only. ✉ *1140 12th Ave., Kaimuki* 🕾 *808/735–7581.*

$ ✕ **Himalayan Kitchen.** The sign claims to serve authentic Nepali and
ASIAN   Indian cuisine, but many dishes incorporate a blend of cultures, including Chinese and Hawaiian. Start with Himalayan spring rolls or garlic naan bread, try the mahi Nepali masala—which is a Nepalese curry with Hawaii mahimahi—and don't miss the mango *kulfi*, which is like a creamy mango dessert. The extensive menu appeals to a wide range of tastes—some that soothe the palate, others that excite—which may be why this little restaurant tucked away in a business/residential area is packed every night. Perhaps it helps that this place is BYOB, with no corkage fee, as well. ✉ *1137 11th Ave., Kaimuki* 🕾 *808/735–1122* ⊕ *himalayankitchen.net* ⌕ *Reservations essential.*

$$$$ ✕ **Hoku's at the Kahala.** Everything about this room speaks of quality and
MODERN   sophistication: the wall of windows with their beach views, the avant-
HAWAIIAN   garde cutlery and dinnerware, the solicitous staff, and border-busting Pacific Rim cuisine. The menu constantly changes, but you can count on Chef Wayne Hirabayashi to use fresh, local ingredients when possible in his innovative fusion flair. An excellent choice for special occasions. The dress code is collared shirts, no beachwear. ✉ *The Kahala Hotel & Resort, 5000 Kahala Ave., Kahala* 🕾 *808/739–8888* ⌕ *Reservations essential* ⏲ *No lunch Sat.*

$$$ ✕ **Morio's Sushi Bistro.** This small sushi bar is a favorite of locals, offer-
SUSHI   ing amazingly fresh sashimi and interesting cooked dishes at reasonable

8

prices. But more important, it's BYOB here, so you can bond with the gregarious owner-chef, Morio, by sharing what you're drinking. If you're able to get a reservation here, then count yourself lucky; most seats at the bar require a month's notice, but you may be able to get table seating. For a special treat, order the *omakase* (chef's choice) 24 hours in advance. ⊠ *1160-A S. King St., McCully* ☎ *808/741–5121* ⊕ *www.moriosushibistro.com* ⌲ *Reservations essential* 🍴 *BYOB* ⊘ *Closed Sun. No lunch.*

$$

MEDITERRANEAN

✕ **Olive Tree Café.** Mediterranean food is scarce in the Islands, so Olive Tree keeps insanely busy; expect a wait for your hummus, fish souvlaki, Greek egg-and-lemon soup, and other specialties at this small spot behind Kahala Mall. It's worth the wait—it's probably the best Greek food in these Islands. ⊠ *4614 Kiauea Ave., Kahala* ☎ *808/737–0303* ⌲ *Reservations not accepted* ▭ *No credit cards* 🍴 *BYOB* ⊘ *No lunch.*

$

HAWAIIAN

✕ **Ono Hawaiian Foods.** The adventurous in search of a real local food experience should head to this no-frills hangout. You know it has to be good if residents are waiting in line to get in. Here you can sample *poi* (a paste made from pounded taro root), *lomilomi* salmon (salmon massaged until tender and served with minced onions and tomatoes), *laulau* (a steamed bundle of ti leaves containing pork, butterfish, and taro tops), *kalua* pork (roasted in an underground oven), and *haupia* (a gelatinlike dessert made from coconut milk). Appropriately enough, the Hawaiian word *ono* means "delicious." ⊠ *726 Kapahulu Ave., Kapahulu* ☎ *808/737–2275* ⌲ *Reservations not accepted* ▭ *No credit cards* ⊘ *Closed Sun.*

$

SOUTHERN

✕ **Soul Cafe.** If you have a hankering for down-home Southern fare with a gourmet twist and Pacific flair, chef Sean Priester has it all. Must-tries include shrimp and cheesy grits with bacon gravy, crab cake on spring greens with an Asian black bean dressing, and the best fried chicken in town. Be prepared to order extra cornbread. It's that good. ⊠ *3040 Waialae Ave., Kaimuki* ☎ *808/947–3113* ⊕ *pacificsoulhawaii.com.*

$

MODERN ASIAN

✕ **Spices.** Created by a trio of well-traveled friends who enjoy the foods of Southeast Asia, Spices is alluringly decorated in spicelike oranges and reds and offers a lunch and dinner menu far from the beaten path, even in a city rich in the cuisine of this region. Leave room for dessert, as their exotic ice cream is to die for. They claim inspiration but not authenticity and use Island ingredients to everyone's advantage. The menu is vegetarian-friendly. ⊠ *2671 S. King St., Moiliili* ☎ *808/949–2679* ⊕ *spiceshawaii.com* ⌲ *Reservations essential* ⊘ *Closed Mon.*

$$$$

JAPANESE

✕ **Sushi Sasabune.** Meals here are unforgettable, though you may find the restaurant's approach exasperating and a little condescending. It's possible to order from the menu, but you're strongly encouraged to order *omakase*-style (oh-*mah*-ka-*say*, roughly, "trust me"), letting the chef send out his choices for the night. The waiters keep up a steady mantra to instruct patrons in the proper way to eat their delicacies: "Please, no shoyu on this one." "One piece, one bite." But any trace of annoyance vanishes with the first bite of California baby squid stuffed with Louisiana crab, or unctuous *toro* (ahi belly) smeared with a light soy reduction, washed down with a glass of the smoothest sake you've ever tasted. A caution: the courses come very rapidly—ask the server to slow down the pace a bit. An even bigger caution: the courses, generally two pieces of sushi or six to eight slices of sashimi, add up fast. ✉ *1419 S. King St., Moiliili* ☎ *808/947–3800* ⌒ *Reservations essential* ☽ *Closed Sun. No lunch Sat. and Mon.*

$$$
MODERN
HAWAIIAN
✕ **3660 on the Rise.** This casually stylish eatery is a 10-minute drive from Waikiki in the culinary mecca of Kaimuki. Sample Chef Russell Siu's New York Steak Alae (steak grilled with Hawaiian clay salt), the crab cakes, or the signature ahi katsu wrapped in nori and deep-fried with a wasabi-ginger butter sauce. Siu combines a deep understanding of local flavors with a sophisticated palate, making this place especially popular with homegrown gourmands. The dining room can feel a bit snug when it's full (as it usually is); go early or later. ✉ *3660 Waialae Ave., Kaimuki* ☎ *808/737–1177* ⊕ *3660.com.*

$$
INTERNATIONAL
✕ **town.** Pretty much everyone agrees that chef-owner Ed Kenney's Mediterranean eclectic menu ranges from just fine (pastas and salads) to just fabulous (polenta with egg and asparagus or buttermilk panna cotta). Town has become the place to see and be seen if you are a foodie and are looking to eat organic, local products. The restaurant serves an inexpensive Continental breakfast, as well as lunch and dinner. ✉ *3435 Waialae Ave., Kaimuki* ☎ *808/735–5900* ⊕ *www.townkaimuki.com* ⌒ *Reservations essential* ☽ *Closed Sun.*

$$
MODERN
HAWAIIAN
✕ **12th Avenue Grill.** At this clean, well-lighted place on a back street, chef Jason Schoonover dishes up diner chic, including macaroni-and-cheese glazed with house-smoked Parmesan and topped with savory breadcrumbs. The kimchi steak, a sort of teriyaki with kick, is a winner. Go early (5 pm) or late (8:30 pm). Enjoy wonderful, homey desserts. There's a small, exquisitely selected wine list. ✉ *1145C 12th Ave., Kaimuki* ☎ *808/732–9469* ⊕ *12thavegrill.com* ☽ *Closed Sun. No lunch.*

$$$
HAWAIIAN
✕ **The Willows.** An island dream, this buffet restaurant is made up of pavilions overlooking a network of ponds (once natural streams flowing from mountain to sea). The Island-style comfort food includes the trademark Willows curry along with Hawaiian dishes such as *laulau* and local favorites such as Korean barbecue ribs. ✉ *901 Hausten St., Moiliili* ☎ *808/952–9200* ⊕ *willowshawaii.com* ⌒ *Reservations essential.*

DIAMOND HEAD

$
AMERICAN
✕ **Diamond Head Market & Grill.** Kelvin Ro's one-stop spot is a plate-lunch place, a gourmet market, and deli, bakery, and espresso bar, too—and it's a five-minute hop from Waikiki hotels. A take-out window offers grilled sandwiches or plates ranging from teriyaki beef to portobello mushrooms. The market's deli case is stocked with a range of heat-and-eat entrées from risotto cakes to lamb stew; specials change daily. There are packaged Japanese bento lunchboxes, giant scones, enticing desserts, and even a small wine selection. ✉ *3158 Monsarrat Ave.,*

8

CLOSE UP

Izakaya

Japanese pub-restaurants, called *izakaya* (ee-ZAH-ka-ya), are sprouting up all over the Islands like *matsutake* mushrooms in a pine forest. They began as oases for homesick Japanese nationals but were soon discovered by adventurous locals, who appreciated the welcoming atmosphere, sprawling menus, and later dining hours.

Expect to be greeted by a merry, full-staff cry of "Irashaimase!" and offered an *oshibori* (hot towel), a drink, and handed a menu of dozens of small-plate, made-to-order dishes.

You can find *yakitori* (grilled dishes), tempura (deep-fried dishes), *donburi* (rice bowls), sushi and sashimi, *nabemono* and *shabu-shabu* (hot pots), noodles (both soup and fried), *okonomiyaki* (chop suey–type omelets), and a bizarre assortment of *yoshoku* dishes (Western foods prepared in Japanese style, such as hamburgers in soy-accented gravy, fried chicken with a mirin glaze, odd gratins, and even pizza).

Full bars are usual; a wide choice of lager-type beers and good-to-great sakes are universal. Many specialize in single-malt scotch, but wine lists are generally short.

Izakaya menus are often confusing, many staff speak marginal English, and outings can get expensive fast (liquor plus small-plate prices equals eyes bigger than stomach). Prices range from $5 for a basket of edamame (steamed and salted soybeans) to $20 or more for *wafu* (seasoned, grilled steak, sliced for sharing). Start by ordering drinks and edamame or silky-textured braised *kabocha* pumpkin. This will keep the waiter happy. Then give yourself a quarter of

an hour to examine the menu, ogle other people's plates, and seek recommendations. Start with one dish per person and one for the table; you can always call for more.

Imanas Tei. Go early to this cozy, out-of-the-way restaurant for its tasteful, simple decor and equally tasteful and simply perfect sushi, sashimi, *nabe* (hot pots prepared at the table), and grilled dishes; reservations are taken from 5 to 7 pm; after that, there's always a line. ✉ *2626 S. King St., Moiliili* ☎ *808/941–2626 or 808/934–2727* ✆ *$8–$25.*

Izakaya Nonbei. Teruaki Mori designed this pub to put you in mind of a northern inn in winter in his native Japan; dishes not to miss— *karei kara-age* (delicate deep-fried flounder) and *dobinmushi* (mushroom consommé presented in a teapot). ✉ *3108 Olu St., Kapahulu* ☎ *808/734–5573* ✆ *$7–$20.*

Tokkuri-Tei. This is a favorite of locals for the playful atmosphere that belies the excellence of the food created by chef Hideaki "Santa" Miyoshi, famous for his quirky menu names (Nick Jagger, Spider Poke); just say "Moriwase, kudasai" ("chef's choice, please"), and he'll order for you. ✉ *611 Kapahulu Ave., Kapahulu* ☎ *808/739–2800* ✆ *$13–$25.*

Also worth a visit:

Mr. Oji-san (✉ *1018 Kapahulu Ave., Kapahulu* ☎ *808/735–4455*) for family-style *izakaya* specialties.

Kaiwa (✉ *Waikiki Beachwalk, 2nd Floor, 226 Lewers St., Waikiki* ☎ *808/924–1555*) for Osaka-style omelets.

Diamond Head ☎ *808/732–0077* ⊕ *www.diamondheadmarket.com* ⚖ *Reservations not accepted.*

$ ✕ **L&L Hawaiian Barbecue.** On Monsarrat Avenue in Waikiki and at more
ECLECTIC   than 38 neighborhood locations on the island of Oahu, the Drive Inn
location serves up an impressive mix of Asian-American and Hawaiian-style plate lunches. Chicken *katsu* (cutlet), shrimp curry, and seafood mix plates include two scoops each of rice-and-macaroni salad. There are also "mini" versions of the large-portion plates that include just one scoop of each starch. It's a quick take-out place to pick up lunch before heading to the nearest beach or park. ⊠ *3045 Monsarrat Ave., Diamond Head* ☎ *808/735–1388* ⊕ *hawaiianbarbecue.com.*

$ ✕ **South Shore Grill.** Just a couple of minutes out of Waikiki proper
AMERICAN   on trendy Monsarrat, South Shore Grill is a great place to stoke up before or after sightseeing or beach time. It's inexpensive and portions are ample. The food, a cut above the usual plate lunch or burgers, includes ciabatta-bread sandwiches, entrée salads, and stuffed burritos. ⊠ *3114 Monsarrat Ave., Diamond Head* ☎ *808/734–0229* ⊕ *www. southshoregrillhawaii.com* ⚖ *Reservations not accepted.*

WAIKIKI

There are several notable steak houses and grills in Waikiki as well, serving upscale American cuisine. But thanks to the many Japanese nationals who stay here, Waikiki is blessed with lots of cheap, filling, authentic Japanese food, particularly noodle houses. Plastic representations of food in the window outside are an indicator of authenticity and a help in ordering. It's not uncommon for a server to accompany a guest outside so that the selection can be pointed to.

$$ ✕ **Arancino di Mare.** Arancino offers fresh seafood, hand-trimmed beef,
ITALIAN   pastas cooked to order, handmade pizza dough and bread, homemade desserts, and meats and cheeses imported from Italy. Locals as well as tourists come here to enjoy dishes that use only fresh, authentic ingredients. Customer favorites include Pescatore and a pizza with shrimp and Maui onions, which is the owner's favorite pizza. There's a Beachwalk location, too. ⊠ *2552 Kalakaua Ave., Waikiki* ☎ *808/931–6273* ⊕ *www.arancino.com* .

$$$$ ✕ **Bali Steak & Seafood.** This many-windowed, multilevel room takes
STEAKHOUSE   delightful advantage of the restaurant's perch above the beach, facing Diamond Head. The chef creates uncomplicated contemporary cuisine—grilled fish, steaks, and chops accented with East–West fusion flavors. The experienced staff, often called on to serve the VIPs who favor this hotel, extends unruffled and gracious service. ⊠ *Hilton Hawaiian Village, 2005 Kalia Rd., Waikiki* ☎ *808/941–2254* ⚖ *Reservations essential* ⊘ *Closed Sun. No lunch.*

$$$$ ✕ **Chart House Waikiki.** Enjoy the sunset views over the yacht harbor as
MODERN   you take in live local music nightly while sipping one of the signature
HAWAIIAN   "Guy-Tai" cocktails. Such offerings as ahi wontons, loco moco, and garlic chicken are perennial appetizer favorites with locals and tourists alike. For dinner, make sure you try specialties: prime rib, garlic steak, or bone-in New York steak from Kahua Ranch on the Big

8

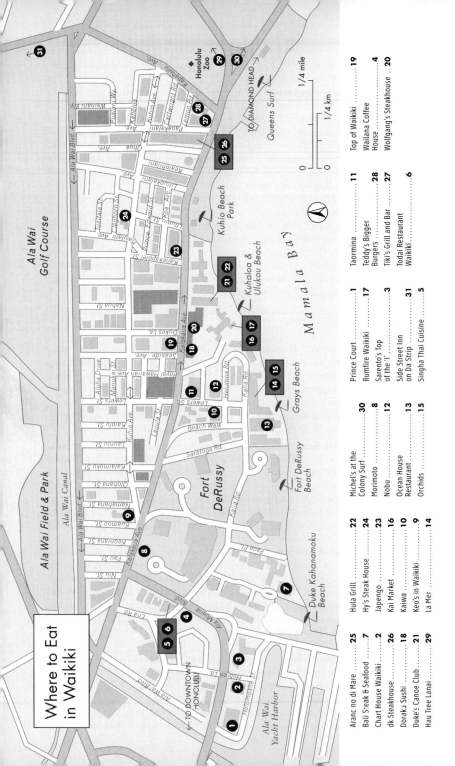

Where to Eat in Waikiki

Ala Wai Golf Course

Ala Wai Field & Park

Ala Wai Yacht Harbor

Fort DeRussy

Fort DeRussy Beach

Duke Kahanamoku Beach

Grays Beach

Kahaloa & Ulukou Beach

Kuhio Beach Park

Mamala Bay

Honolulu Zoo

Queens Surf

TO DIAMOND HEAD

TO DOWNTOWN HONOLULU

1/4 mile
1/4 km

Island. But fish is also a high point here, and while specials change regularly, they are always made with the freshest fish available from the market. ✉ *1765 Ala Moana Blvd., Waikiki* ☎ *808/941–6669* ⊕ *www. charthousehonolulu.com* ⊗ *No lunch.*

$$$$
STEAKHOUSE

✕ **dk Steakhouse.** Around the country, the steak house has returned to prominence as chefs rediscover the art of dry-aging beef and of preparing the perfect béarnaise sauce. D.K. Kodama's chic second-floor restaurant characterizes this trend with such presentations as a 22-ounce *paniolo* (cowboy) rib-eye steak, dry-aged 30 days on the bone with house-made rub, grilled local onions, and creamed corn. The restaurant shares space, but not a menu, with Kodama's Sansei Seafood Restaurant & Sushi Bar; sit at the bar perched between the two and you can order from either menu. ✉ *Waikiki Beach Marriott Resort and Spa, 2552 Kalakaua Ave., Waikiki* ☎ *808/931–6280* ⊕ *www.dksteakhouse. com* ⊗ *No lunch.*

$$
JAPANESE

✕ **Doraku Sushi.** This contemporary fusion sushi bar was started in Miami by Kevin Aoki, son of famous restaurateur Rocky Aoki. As a result, you'll find some Cuban-influenced fusion dishes on the mostly traditional sushi menu that are as exceptional as they are unique, like the nigiri with slices of Cuban beef or the spicy lobster roll with cucumber and a spicy cream sauce. Chef Hide Yoshimoto is constantly coming up with new creations to show off the freshness of Hawaii's fish and other island ingredients. This is a hot spot at night for local club goers and scensters, but for meals, it's outstanding. Be sure to try the Emperor Roll, which Hide created specifically for Kevin, and the New Style Doraku Roll, which is like a California roll topped with tuna, radish, shiso, and a special sauce. ✉ *Royal Hawaiian Center, 2233 Kalakaua Ave., Waikiki* ☎ *808/922–2268* ⊕ *www.dorakusushi.com* 🍴 *Reservations essential.*

$$
AMERICAN

✕ **Duke's Canoe Club.** Named for the father of modern surfing, and outfitted with much Duke Kahanamoku memorabilia, Duke's is both an open-air bar and a very popular steak-and-seafood grill. It's known for its slow-roasted prime rib, *huli huli* (rotisserie) chicken, and grilled catch of the day, as well as for a simple and economical Sunday brunch. Their cocktails are probably the best in Waikiki. A drawback is that it's often loud and crowded, and the live contemporary Hawaiian music often stymies conversation. ✉ *Outrigger Waikiki on the Beach, 2335 Kalakaua Ave., Waikiki* ☎ *808/922–2268* ⊕ *www.dukeswaikiki.com* 🍴 *Reservations essential.*

$$$$
SEAFOOD

✕ **Hau Tree Lanai.** The vinelike *hau* tree is ideal for sitting under, and it's said that the one that spreads itself over this beachside courtyard is the very one that shaded Robert Louis Stevenson as he mused and wrote about Hawaii. In any case, diners are still enjoying the shade and the island-casual food, but we like the place for late-afternoon or early-evening drinks, pupu, and people-watching. The *poi* pancakes at breakfast, papaya chicken salad at lunch, and fresh fish selection at dinner are all favorites. ✉ *New Otani Kaimana Beach Hotel, 2863 Kalakaua Ave., Waikiki* ☎ *808/921–7066* ⊕ *www.kaimana.com* 🍴 *Reservations essential.*

8

$$
HAWAIIAN

✗ **Hula Grill.** The placid younger sister of boisterous Duke's, downstairs, this restaurant and bar resembles a plantation-period summer home: open to the air, outfitted with kitschy decor, stone-flagged floors, warm wood, and floral prints. The food is carefully prepared and familiar—standard breakfast items, steaks and grilled seafood at dinner—but with local and Asian touches that add interest. There's a fabulous Diamond Head view. ⊠ *Outrigger Waikiki on the Beach, 2335 Kalakaua Ave., Waikiki* ☎ *808/923–4852* ⊕ *www.hulagrillwaikiki.com* ⊗ *No lunch.*

$$$$
STEAKHOUSE

✗ **Hy's Steak House.** If the Rat Pack reconvened for big steaks and a bigger red, they'd feel right at home at Hy's, which has changed little in the last 30 years. The formula: prime-grade beef, old-style service, a men's-club atmosphere (but ladies very welcome), and a wine list recognized for excellence by *Wine Spectator.* Specialties include Beef Wellington, Caesar salad, and those tableside flambéed desserts rarely seen these days. ⊠ *Waikiki Park Heights Hotel, 2440 Kuhio Ave., Waikiki* ☎ *808/922–5555* ⊕ *www.hyshawaii.com* ⌂ *Reservations essential* ⊗ *No lunch.*

$$$
JAPANESE
FUSION

✗ **Japengo.** The very trendy, spendy Japengo may set your bankroll back a bit for a night out on the town, but the food gets consistently high marks from everyone who comes here. If you like interesting flavor combinations, try the Tootsie roll, which has soft-shell crab, snow crab, avocado, shiitake mushroom, and lobster teriyaki covered in a sauce that will tease your taste buds. The fried chicken, a starter, and coconut crème brûlée are also must-tries. A kids' menu is available. ⊠ *Hyatt Regency Waikiki, 2424 Kalakaua Ave., Waikiki* ☎ *808/923–1234* ⌂ *Reservations essential* ⊗ *Closed Mon. and Tues. No lunch.*

$$$$
ASIAN

✗ **Kai Market.** This is the first "farm-to-table" buffet on Oahu (or the other Islands), and it's quite a surprise to find it in a hotel like the Sheraton Waikiki. Local chef Darren Demaya helped to bring this concept to life, creating recipes that use as much local produce as possible. The dinner menu changes daily, and you get the added bonus of an open-air luau-style show. Be sure to take a look at their "living wall" of herbs, which are plucked as needed during the preparation of very small buffet servings such as kurobuta pork loin with lehua honey mustard glaze or Chinese salt and pepper head-on Kahuku shrimp. Kai has created a following with locals as well as tourists for the high quality of food and friendliness of the service. ⊠ *Sheraton Waikiki Hotel, 2255 Kalakaua Ave., Waikiki* ☎ *808/922–4422* ⊗ *No lunch.*

$
JAPANESE

✗ **Kaiwa.** This casual little spot introduced Honolulu to *okonomiyaki,* the famous savory pancakes that are a specialty of Osaka, with mix-and-match ingredients scrambled together on a griddle, then drizzled with various piquant sauces. They also specialize in unusual appetizers such as fried lotus root with cheese and a crackerlike crust or a wasabi-tinged tossed salad with crab and avocado. The combinations may at times strike you as bizarre, but you can always order simpler grilled dishes such as sliced pork wrapped around enoki mushrooms, slices of Wagyu beef, or eggplant with shaved bonito (dried mackerel). ⊠ *Waikiki Beach Walk, 226 Lewers St., Waikiki* ☎ *808/924–1555.*

$
THAI

✗ **Keo's in Waikiki.** Many Islanders—and many Hollywood stars—got their first taste of pad thai noodles, lemongrass, and coconut milk curry at one of Keo Sananikone's restaurants. This one, perched right at the entrance to Waikiki, characterizes his formula: a bright, clean space awash in flowers with intriguing menu titles and reasonable prices. Evil Jungle Prince, a stir-fry redolent of Thai basil, flecked with chilis and rich with coconut milk, is a classic; also try the apple bananas (smaller, sweeter variety of banana) in coconut milk. The Eastern and Western breakfasts are popular. ⊠ *2028 Kuhio Ave., Waikiki* ☎ *808/951–9355* ⊕ *keosthaicuisine.com.*

$$$$
FRENCH

✕ **La Mer.** Like the hotel in which it's housed (Halekulani, "House Befitting Heaven"), La Mer is pretty much heavenly: a softly lighted, low-ceiling room has its windows open to the breeze, a perfectly framed vista of Diamond Head, and the faint sound of music from a courtyard below. The food captures the rich and yet sunny flavors of the south of France in one tiny, exquisite course after another. Four prix-fixe options are offered (from three to five or more courses), as well as several rather expensive supplements. We recommend the degustation menu; place yourself in the sommelier's hands for wine choices from the hotel's exceptional cellar. ⊠ *Halekulani, 2199 Kalia Rd., Waikiki* ☎ *808/923–2311* ⚞ *Reservations essential Jacket required* ◷ *No lunch.*

$$$$
FRENCH

✕ **Michel's at the Colony Surf.** With its wide-open windows so close to the water that you literally feel the soft mist at high tide, this is arguably the most romantic spot in Waikiki for a sunset dinner for two. Michel's is synonymous with fine dining in the minds of Oahuans who have been coming here for more than 40 years. The menu is très French with both classic choices (escargot, foie gras) and contemporary items (Hardy's Hawaiian Bouillabaisse—named after the chef who created a Hawaiian twist on a French classic). There's dinner nightly and Sunday brunch. ⊠ *Colony Surf, 2895 Kalakaua Ave., Waikiki* ☎ *808/923–6552* ⊕ *michelshawaii.com* ⚞ *Reservations essential* ◷ *No lunch.*

$$$$
JAPANESE

✕ **Morimoto.** Iron Chef Morimoto of Food Network fame is a big part of the dining scene in Honolulu. The menu is made up primarily of sushi and cooked seafood, with a couple of expensive cuts of steak thrown in as well as a wide selection of appetizers, all heavily weighted toward seafood. If you're adventurous, try the *omakase* (chef's choice) menu, which changes daily. You can choose to sit at the sushi bar, the regular bar, or at a table, but try to get a seat outside, as the room gets pretty noisy. This has become a popular spot for brunch, as well, with a view overlooking the yacht harbor. ⊠ *The Modern, 1775 Ala Moana Blvd., Waikiki* ☎ *808/943–5900* ⊕ *morimotowaikiki.com.*

$$$$
JAPANESE

✕ **Nobu.** Famed chef Nobu Matsuhisa is the master of innovative Japanese cuisine, and his Hawaiian outpost is definitely a Waikiki hot spot. Fish is the obvious centerpiece, with entrees such as Tasmanian ocean trout with crispy spinach and yuzu soy, seafood harumaki with caviar and Maui onion salsa, and even Nobu's version of fish-and-chips. Cold dishes include tuna tataki (seared raw fish slices) with ponzu, yellowtail sashimi with jalapeño, and whitefish sashimi with dried miso. The warm decor and sexy lighting mean there isn't a bad seat in the house. ⊠ *Waikiki Parc Hotel, 2233 Helumoa Rd., Waikiki* ☎ *808/237–6999* ⊕ *www.noburestaurants.com.*

8

Oahu Food Trucks

CLOSE UP

Lunch wagons, or "food trucks" as they are now known around the country, have been a staple for plate lunches around Hawaii for decades, even before they were trendy. But now, with the taco-truck craze and the emergence of social media, more food trucks are popping up, serving an amazing variety of local flavors.

You can check the trucks' locations and daily menus on Twitter, or try a sampling from more than two dozen vendors at the monthly Eat the Street food-truck rally or the weekly Tacoako Tuesdays. Visit ⊕ *www.Streetgrindz. com* for details.

Here are some of our favorite lunch wagons:

Camille's on Wheels (⊕ *Twitter.com/ Camillesonwheel*) combines Mexican, American, and Asian flavors in tacos and other dishes. Check out the shoyu chicken tacos, homemade salsas, and any of the homemade desserts. Camille's uses local ingredients whenever possible.

Elena's (⊕ *Twitter.com/ElenasFilipino*) is an extension of the popular, family-run Filipino restaurant in Waipahu.

There are three trucks, in Campbell, Mililani, and the airport area. Try the AFRO, an adobo–fried rice omelet, or the famous *lechón* (roast pork with onions and tomatoes) special.

Ono To Go (⊕ *Twitter.com/Onotogo*) has a regular spot on Sheridan Street off of King Street. It's open Monday through Saturday from 11 am until the food sells out—which is often, as the plate lunches are restaurant quality at lower prices. Best sellers are pork chops, teriyaki-citrus salmon, *pulehu* (fire-broiled) short ribs, poke, and roast turkey. Park on the street or at the car-repair shop next door.

Shogunai Tacos (⊕ *Twitter.com/ Shogunai_tacos*) serves up hearty tacos with unique fillings that have Greek, Korean, Italian, Indian, Mexican, Thai, and Japanese flavors. The most popular item is the Osaka Jo taco, which is brimming with pork marinated in ginger, shoyu, garlic, lemon, a special sauce, sprouts, and then sprinkled with *furikake* (shredded dried seaweed). Make it a meal with the Moroccan-inspired French fries.

$$$ ✕ **Ocean House Restaurant.** Guests are greeted on the front porch at this
SEAFOOD re-creation of a 1900s plantation home. Tables and booths are spaced for views. The menu puts forth the bounty of the Pacific with such dishes as crusted opah, coconut lobster skewers, and seared peppered scallops. For beef lovers, there's the slow-roasted prime rib. If you're an early riser, you can also enjoy their daily breakfast or Sunday brunch offerings. ✉ *Outrigger Reef on the Beach, 2169 Kalia Rd., Waikiki* ☎ *808/923–2277* ⊕ *www.oceanhousewaikiki.com* ☾ *No lunch.*

$$$$ ✕ **Orchids.** Perched along the seawall at historic Gray's Beach, Orchids
SEAFOOD is beloved by power breakfasters, ladies who lunch, and family groups celebrating at the elaborate Sunday brunch. La Mer, upstairs, is better known for the evening, but we have found dinner at Orchids equally enjoyable. The louvered walls are open to the breezes, the orchids add splashes of color, the seafood is perfectly prepared, and the wine list is

intriguing. Plus, it is more casual and a bit less expensive than La Mer. Whatever meal you have here, finish with the hotel's signature coconut layer cake. ☒ *Halekulani, 2199 Kalia Rd., Waikiki* ☎ *808/923–2311* ⊕ *www.halekulani.com/dining/orchids/* ⌂ *Reservations essential.*

$$$$ ✕ **Prince Court.** This restaurant overlooking Ala Wai Yacht Harbor is a
ECLECTIC multifaceted success, with exceptional high-end lunches and dinners, daily breakfast buffets, weekly dinner seafood buffets, and sold-out weekend brunches. With a truly global mix of offerings, the overall style is Eurasian. Their ever-changing prix-fixe menu includes offerings such as Australian rack of lamb, Kahuku prawns, and medallions of New York Angus beef. ☒ *Hawaii Prince Hotel, 100 Holomoana St., Waikiki* ☎ *808/944–4494* ⊕ *www.princeresortshawaii.com/hawaii-prince-court.php* ⌂ *Reservations essential.*

$$ ✕ **Rumfire Waikiki.** This beachfront restaurant offers indoor and out-
ASIAN door dining for the full oceanside dining experience; even while sitting indoors, you can view the horizon through floor-to-ceiling windows. You can get a full meal here, but it's the ideal setting for noshing on appetizers while you enjoy an exotic tropical drink: try the kalua pig quesadillas and the ahi *poke* (raw fish) chips, which come with freshly-made condiments, including guacamole, salsa, and a special hot sauce. At night, Rumfire is a popular club/lounge for young locals. ☒ *Sheraton Waikiki Hotel, 2255 Kalakaua Ave., Waikiki* ☎ *808/922–4422* ⊕ *www.rumfirewaikiki.com.*

$$$$ ✕ **Sarento's Top of the "I".** Among restaurants with the best views in
ITALIAN Honolulu, 30th-floor Sarento's, looking toward both the Koolau Mountains and the South Shore, is a favorite date-night venue. Regional Italian cuisine is the specialty, and the wild tiger shrimp–stuffed potato ravioli and osso buco are local favorites. The wine cellar contains some gems, and there may not be more attentive service staff in the city. For a less-spendy meal, you may want to opt for happy hour and order from their appetizer menu, which is filled with tasty choices. ☒ *Ilikai Waikiki Hotel, 1777 Ala Moana, top floor, Waikiki* ☎ *808/955–5559* ⊕ *www.sarentoswaikiki.com* ⌂ *Reservations essential* ☾ *No lunch.*

$ ✕ **Side Street Inn on Da Strip.** The original Hopaka Street pub is famous
HAWAIIAN as the place where celebrity chefs gather after hours; this second location, also run by local boy Colin Nishida, is on the bustling Kapahulu Avenue, closer to Waikiki. Local-style bar food comes in huge, share-plate portions, and Nishida's famous pork chops, fried rice, and *lilikoi* ribs make it worth the trip. This is a place to dress any way you like, nosh all night, and watch sports on TV. Pupu (in portions so large as to be dinner) are served from 4 pm to 12:30 am daily. ☒ *614 Kapahulu Ave., Waikiki* ☎ *808/739–3939* ⊕ *www.sidestreetinn.com* ⌂ *Reservations essential* ☾ *No lunch weekends.*

$$ ✕ **Singha Thai Cuisine.** Chai and Joy Chaowasaree's devotion to their
THAI native Thailand is evident in the gilt model of the Thai royal palace that graces the entryway of this restaurant just below street level on a busy Waikiki corner. This is also the only Thai restaurant in the city to showcase Thai dance each evening. We especially like Singha Thai's way with seafood—Siamese Fighting Fish, a whole fish sizzling in garlic-chili oil, or fish in Thai chili, ginger, and black-bean sauce—and

8

the contemporary additions to the menu, such as blackened ahi summer rolls. ✉ *1910 Ala Moana Blvd., Waikiki* ☎ *808/941–2898* ⊕ *www.singhathai.com* ⊙ No lunch.

$$$$ ✕ **Taormina.** Dishes inspired by the romantic Mediterranean resort
ITALIAN town of Taormina are served at this elegant restaurant on the Waikiki Beach Walk. In addition to Sicilian-inspired *primi piatti* (first-course dishes, usually pasta) such as *uni* (sea urchin) pasta and a light cream risotto with grilled scallops and prawns, the menu features a variety of local fish done with Italian flair. The artfully presented antipasti *misti* (mixed appetizers) should not be missed. Try the cannoli with a touch of coconut in the filling to round out your meal. The wine list is extensive. ✉ *Waikiki Beach Walk, 227 Lewers St., Waikiki* ☎ *808/926–5050* ⊕ *taorminarestaurant.com* ⬦ Reservations essential.

$ ✕ **Teddy's Bigger Burgers.** Though the focus at Teddy's is on the burgers,
AMERICAN fries, and shakes, their success has inspired them to add a chicken, veggie, and fish sandwich to their menu. But, for those who like a classic, the burgers are beefy, the fries perfectly crisp, the shakes rich and sweet. The original location in Waikiki combines burger-shack simplicity with surf-boy cool—there's even a place to store your surfboard while you have your burger. This popular location has given birth to several others around the state. ✉ *134 Kapahulu Ave., Waikiki* ☎ *808/926–3444.*

$$$ ✕ **Tiki's Grill and Bar.** On the second floor of a busy hotel, Tiki's is the kind
AMERICAN of place people come to Waikiki for: a retro–South Pacific spot designed for fun. It has a back-of-the-bar faux volcano, an open-air lounge with live local-style music, indoor-outdoor dining, and a view of the beach across the street. The menu of contemporary island cuisine, revamped by chef Ronnie Nasuti, includes Asian-influenced seven-spice salmon, sophisticated interpretations of plate-lunch standards, and exceptional desserts. Try their mai tais, which come in a variety of flavors. ✉ *Aston Waikiki Beach Hotel, 2570 Kalakaua Ave., Waikiki* ☎ *808/923–8454* ⊕ *tikisgrill.com.*

$$$ ✕ **Todai Restaurant Waikiki.** Bountiful buffets and menus that feature sea-
SEAFOOD food are popular with Islanders, so this Japan-based restaurant is a local favorite. It's popular with budget-conscious travelers as well, for the wide range of hot dishes, sushi, and the 160-foot seafood spread. The emphasis here is more on quantity than quality. ✉ *1910 Ala Moana Blvd., Waikiki* ☎ *808/947–1000* ⬦ Reservations essential.

$$$$ ✕ **Top of Waikiki.** The three-tiered Top of Waikiki has amazing 360-degree
MODERN views of Honolulu, but unlike many revolving restaurants it also has an
AMERICAN award-winning menu that features delicious new American cuisine with island flavor. The lobster–crab cake salad or the coconut shrimp are great ways to start the evening. For dinner, although they may sound basic, the seafood pasta and garlic rib eye are the most popular entrées because they're just that good. To get a sunset view, grab dinner from 5 to 6 pm and enjoy the added early-bird dishes starting at $17. ✉ *Waikiki Business Plaza, 2270 Kalakaua Ave., Waikiki* ☎ *808/923–3877* ⊕ *topofwaikiki.com.*

$ ✕ **Wailana Coffee House.** Despite the notoriously inattentive waitstaff,
AMERICAN budget-conscious snowbirds, night owls with a yen for karaoke, all-day drinkers of both coffee and the stronger stuff, hearty eaters, and

lovers of local-style plate lunches contentedly rub shoulders at this venerable diner and cocktail lounge at the edge of Waikiki. Most checks are under $9, and there's a $2.50 children's menu. It's open 24 hours a day (except Tuesday, when the restaurant closes from midnight to 6 am), seven days a week, 365

WORD OF MOUTH

"Just returned from Oahu and House Without a Key and Orchids at the Halekaulani were my absolute favorite places to spend an evening." —Ronda

days a year but the place fills up and a line forms around the corner at breakfast time, so arrive early or late. ⊠ *Wailana Condominium, 1860 Ala Moana Blvd., corner of Ena Rd. and Ala Moana, Waikiki* ☎ *808/955–1674* ⌦ *Reservations not accepted.*

$$$$
STEAKHOUSE

✕**Wolfgang's Steak House.** Diners can get a New York–style steak dinner with gruff New York–style service, but in a uniquely open-air, Waikiki-style restaurant. Located on the third floor of the Royal Hawaiian Center, this classic steak house serves up excellent steaks, thanks to an in-house dry-aging room. Even nonsteak items are of the highest quality; people come in just for crab cakes or the famous slabs of Canadian bacon. Stop by for happy hour to get some good deals. ⊠ *Royal Hawaiian Center, 2201 Kalakaua Ave., Waikiki* ☎ *808/922–3600* ⊕ *wolfgangssteakhouse.net.*

ELSEWHERE ON OAHU

Outside Honolulu and Waikiki there are fewer dining options, but restaurants tend to be filled with locals and are cheaper and more casual. Cuisine is mainly American—great if you're traveling with kids—but there are a handful of Italian and Asian places worth trying as well.

8

AIRPORT AREA AND IWILEI

$$
AMERICAN
☺

✕**La Mariana Restaurant & Sailing Club.** Just past downtown Honolulu, tucked away in the industrial area of Sand Island, is this friendly South Seas–style restaurant. Once you walk through the doors, you may think that it's still 1955. The owner, the late Annette Nahinu, bought up kitsch from many other restaurants, so it's tikis in here in a way that's so old-fashioned, it's cool. The food—grilled seafood, steaks—is just okay; but go for the sing-along fun and the feeling that Don the Beachcomber might walk in any minute. ⊠ *50 Sand Island Access Rd., Iwilei* ☎ *808/848–2800* ⊕ *www.lamarianasailingclub.com.*

$$$
JAPANESE

✕**Mitch's Sushi Restaurant.** This microscopic sushi bar (15 seats) is an adjunct of a wholesale seafood market operated by gregarious South African expatriate Douglas Mitchell, who oversees the sushi chefs and keeps customers chatting. The fish, air-freighted from around the world, is ultrafresh, well cut, and nicely presented. You can spend as much or as little as you like—$40 for a half-dozen pieces of prime bluefin tuna belly, or just a few dollars for pickled plum sushi. ⊠ *524 Ohohia St., near Honolulu International Airport, Airport Area* ☎ *808/837–7774* ⊕ *www.mitchsushi.com* ⌦ *Reservations essential* ⌁ *BYOB.*

YAKINIKU

A Korean technique with a Japanese name, *yakiniku* restaurants—where diners grill their own marinated meats and sliced vegetables on braziers set in the middle of the table—is one of the few happy results of the Japanese occupation of Korea.

A yakiniku restaurant may be a chic contemporary pub (like Yakiniku Toraji), but it can also be a homey family buffet. A few, like Yakiniku Mikawon, employ well-vented charcoal braziers to infuse the ingredients with rich, smoky flavor. Most, however, use gas grills.

Budget yakiniku places charge a flat rate; you serve yourself from a raw buffet. In upscale yakiniku, you order from a menu.

■TIP➔ Appoint one griller to prevent mid-table traffic jams. Order or fill your plate in stages to avoid waste and a big bill.

$ ✕ **Nico's at Pier 38.** Lyon-born chef Nico Chaiz opened Nico's in 2004
SEAFOOD in a small, takeout-style restaurant with limited seating just a few steps from the city's fish auction. The concept—and Nico's fresh, original dishes at reasonable prices—has been such a success that it has recently moved into a larger, cooler, more stylish space at the same pier. The restaurant's chief clientele is still rough-hewn dock workers and fishermen, but you'll also see a hip, young crowd here for the beers on tap and signature cocktails. You can still get upscale plate lunches (and dinners) such as seaweed-crusted tuna steaks, garlic shrimp, and *poke*, as well as soups, salads, sandwiches, burgers, and pizzas. A new fish market at Nico's is open from 6:30 am to 6 pm Monday through Saturday, and from 10 to 4 on Sunday. ⊠ *1133 N. Nimitz Hwy., Pier 38, Iwilei* ☎ *808/540–1377* ⊕ *nicospier38.com* ⤸ *Reservations not accepted.*

$$$ ✕ **Sam Choy's Breakfast, Lunch & Crab and Big Aloha Brewery.** In this fam-
SEAFOOD ily-friendly setting, diners can down crab and lobster—but since these
🕙 come from elsewhere, we recommend the catch of the day, the *char siu* (Chinese barbecue), baby back ribs, Sam's special fried *poke* (flash-fried tuna), or Papa Choy's beef-stew omelet. The warehouse size sets the tone for its *bambucha* (huge) portions. An on-site microbrewery brews five varieties of Big Aloha beer. Sam Choy's is in Iwilei past downtown Honolulu on the highway heading to Honolulu International Airport, making it convenient for long layovers. ⊠ *580 Nimitz Hwy., Iwilei* ☎ *808/545–7979* ⊕ *samchoyhawaii.com* ☾ *No dinner Mon.*

$ ✕ **Sugoi Bento & Catering.** Sugoi was among the first of a new wave of
AMERICAN plate-lunch places to take particular care with quality and to recognize that some plate-lunch eaters are interested in good health. They serve, for example, brown rice and green salad instead of the usual white rice and macaroni loaded with mayonnaise. Garlic chicken and *mochiko* (batter-dipped and fried) chicken, both adapted from traditional Japanese dishes, are specialties. Service is quick and cheerful. Primarily a take-out place, Sugoi is in a strip mall in industrial Kalihi, north of town. ⊠ *City Square Shopping Center, 1286 Kalani St., Iwilei* ☎ *808/841–7984* ⊕ *www.sugoihawaii.com* ⤸ *Reservations not accepted* ▭ *No credit cards* ☾ *No dinner. Closed Sun.*

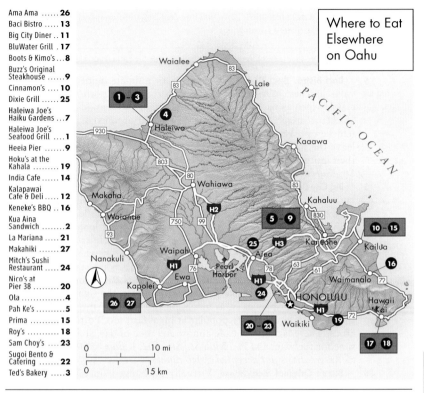

Where to Eat
Elsewhere
on Oahu

SOUTHEAST OAHU

$$ ✕ **BluWater Grill.** Time your drive through East Honolulu to allow for a
ECLECTIC stop at this relaxed restaurant on Kuapa Pond. The savvy chef-manager
team left a popular chain restaurant to found this "American eclectic"
eatery, serving wok-seared moi fish, mango and guava ribs, and lots of
other interesting small dishes. They're open until 10 pm Sunday through
Thursday, and until 11 pm Friday and Saturday. ✉ *Hawaii Kai Shop-
ping Center, 377 Keahole St.* ☎ *808/395–6224* ⊕ *bluwatergrill.com.*

$$ ✕ **Roy's.** Roy Yamaguchi's flagship restaurant across the highway from
ASIAN Maunalua Bay attracts food-savvy visitors as the North Shore attracts
surfers. But it also has a strong following among well-heeled Oahuans
from surrounding neighborhoods, who consider the place an extension
of their homes and Roy's team their personal chefs. For this reason,
Roy's is always busy and sometimes overly noisy. It's best to visit later in
the evening if you're sensitive to pressure to turn the table, or very early
to catch the sunset. The wide-ranging and ever-interesting Hawaiian-
fusion menu changes daily except for signature dishes like Szechuan
spiced barbecue baby back ribs, Roy's Original blackened ahi with soy-
mustard-butter sauce, and a legendary meat loaf. There's an exceptional
wine list. ✉ *Hawaii Kai Corporate Plaza, 6600 Kalanianaole Hwy.,*

Hawaii Kai, Honolulu ☎ *808/396–7697* ⊕ *www.roysrestaurant.com* 🥢 *Reservations essential.*

WINDWARD OAHU

$ ✕ **Baci Bistro.** Baci Bistro is a favorite for intimate dinners and good-
ITALIAN value lunches. Join Windward locals for generous portions of Italian classics such as pappardelle del campo (wide pasta noodles with veal, chicken, sausage, sun-dried tomatoes, and mushrooms) or pollo piccata (chicken breast in a lemon, white wine, and caper sauce). You won't leave the table hungry. Service is friendly, and dining is available in their intimate dining room or alfresco on their leafy lanai. ⊠ *30 Aulike St., Kailua* ☎ *808/262–7555* ⊕ *bacibistro.com* ⊗ *No lunch weekends.*

$ ✕ **Big City Diner.** This outlet of the popular retro diner chain has outdoor
AMERICAN lanai seating, a bar, and is across the street from a small bird sanctuary. It's a hot spot for breakfast; popular dinner items include grilled steak with onions and mushrooms, baby back ribs, meat loaf, and salads. ⊠ *108 Hekili St., Kailua* ☎ *808/263–8880* ⊕ *bigcitydinerhawaii.com.*

$ ✕ **Boots & Kimo's Homestyle Kitchen.** If you're wondering what aloha spirit
AMERICAN is all about, check out this family-owned, local-style restaurant in the industrial backwaters of Kailua where brothers Ricky and Jesse Kiakona treat their guests like family. At breakfast, the signature dish is macadamia-nut pancakes; at lunch, *pulehu* (grilled) ribs. Then again, the *pulehu* ribs are pretty popular at breakfast, too. Portions are generous. There is a line outside almost any time of day, so budget some time for the wait. ⊠ *151 Hekili St., Ste. 102, Kailua* ☎ *808/263–7929* 🥢 *Reservations not accepted* ⊗ *No dinner.*

$$ ✕ **Buzz's Original Steakhouse.** Virtually unchanged since it opened in
STEAKHOUSE 1967, this cozy maze of rooms opposite Kailua Beach Park is filled
Fodor's Choice with the enticing aroma of grilling steaks. It doesn't matter if you're a
★ bit sandy (but bare feet are not allowed). Stop at the salad bar, order up a steak, a burger, teri chicken, or the fresh fish special. If you sit at the bar, expect to make friends. And remember that this place is cash only. ⊠ *413 Kawailoa Rd., Kailua* ☎ *808/261–4661* ⊕ *buzzssteakhouse. com* ⊟ *No credit cards.*

$ ✕ **Cinnamon's Restaurant.** Known for uncommon variations on common
AMERICAN breakfast themes (pancakes, eggs Benedict, French toast, home fries, and eggs), this neighborhood favorite is tucked into a hard-to-find Kailua office park; call for directions. Lunch and dinner feature local-style plate lunch and a diner-style menu (meat loaf, baked beans) which are good, but the main attraction is breakfast. Don't miss the guava chiffon pancakes. ⊠ *315 Uluniu, Kailua* ☎ *808/261–8724* ⊕ *www. cinnamonsrestaurant.com* ⊗ *No dinner Sun.–Wed.*

$$ ✕ **Haleiwa Joe's Haiku Gardens.** Like the more famous restaurant on the
AMERICAN North Shore, Haleiwa Joe's serves standard surf-and-turf favorites in a casual and friendly atmosphere, but the view of the Haiku Gardens directly behind the restaurant makes the difference at this Kaneohe location. Come for an early dinner or fantastic Sunday brunch and enjoy the stunning views. Be sure to leave time for a stroll around the pond and through the garden. ⊠ *44-336 Haiku Rd., Kaneohe* ☎ *808/247–6671* ⊕ *www.haleiwajoes.com* 🥢 *Reservations not accepted.*

$ ✕**Heeia Pier General Store and Deli.** Step back in time to an era where

HAWAIIAN you could buy a traditional Hawaiian plate lunch and some ice cake from the store and sit on the pier as fishermen idly motored by. It doesn't feel like much more than a shack on the pier, but the food is pumped out by one of Oahu's hottest young chefs, Mark Noguchi. Try the guava barbecue chicken or the luau stew (a hearty stew made with taro leaves and beef), which are his specialties. If you're hungry, try the off-menu Cheekeater Burger, a beef burger topped with homemade Thousand Island dressing, Portuguese sausage, Spam, bacon, and a fried egg. This is well worth the drive—way, way off the beaten path. ✉ *Heeia Pier, 46-499 Kamehameha Hwy., Kaneohe* ☎ *808/235–2192* ⊕ *www. heeiapier.com* ⚓ *Reservations not accepted* ☾ *Closed Mon. No dinner.*

$ ✕**India Cafe.** At this restaurant owned by Indians of Malaysian origin,

INDIAN *dosai*, griddle breads made of rice and lentil flour, are filled variously with savory and sweet ingredients. Like most such restaurants, this one is very vegetarian-friendly, serving up *dals* (lentil stews), curries, and samosas. ✉ *600 Kailua Rd., #129, Kailua* ☎ *808/262–1800* ⊕ *www. indiacafehawaii.com* ☾ *No lunch Mon.–Thurs.*

$$ ✕**Kalapawai Café and Deli.** Rarely do you find a café that serves as a wine

ECLECTIC bar, breakfast spot, gourmet deli, tapas bar, and restaurant with a wide variety of Mediterranean entrées, but owner Don Dymond of Kala-pawai Café and Deli has established just that with this green-and-white landmark that is a central meeting spot for Windward residents. Come in on your way to the beach for a cup of coffee and bagel, stop back for a gourmet sandwich or salad at lunchtime. Happy-hour tapas plates include hummus and flatbread or bacon-wrapped figs. Dinner entrées have suggested wine pairings. ✉ *750 Kailua Rd., Kailua* ☎ *808/262– 3354* ⊕ *www.kalapawaimarket.com* ⚓ *Reservations not accepted.*

8

$ ✕**Keneke's Plate Lunch & BBQ.** When you're sightseeing between Hanauma

HAWAIIAN Bay and Makapuu, the food pickings are slim. But every day, 365 days a year, there's Keneke's in Waimanalo town. It's the home of inexpensive plate lunches, shave ice, and Scriptural graffiti on the walls (Keith "Keneke" Ward, the burly, weight-lifting, second-generation owner of the place, is a born-again Christian). The food is diet busting, piled high, and mostly pretty good, particularly the Asian-style barbecue (including teriyaki chicken or beef and Korean *kal bi* (barbecue), and Filipino *guisantes* (pork and peas in tomato gravy) and adobo (piquant pork stew). If you want a treat, try the shave ice with ice cream. ✉ *41-855 Kalanianaole Hwy., Waimanalo* ☎ *808/259–9800* ⊕ *www.kenekes.net.*

$ ✕**Pah Ke's Chinese Restaurant.** Chinese restaurants tend to be interchange-

CHINESE able, but this one—named for the local pidgin term for Chinese (literally translated this is Chinese's Chinese Restaurant)—is worth the drive from Honolulu for its focus on healthier cooking techniques and use of local ingredients, its seasonal specials such as cold soups and salads made from locally raised produce, and its exceptional East–West desserts. The menu offers all the usual suspects, but ask the owner and chef Raymond Siu, a former hotel pastry chef, if he's got anything different and interesting in the kitchen, or call ahead to ask for a special menu. ✉ *46-018 Kamehameha Hwy., Kaneohe* ☎ *808/235–4505* ⚲ *BYOB.*

Shrimp Snacks

No drive to the North Shore is complete without a shrimp stop. Shrimp stands dot Kamehameha Highway from Kahaluu to Kahuku. For about $12, you can get a shrimp plate lunch or a snack of chilled shrimp with cocktail sauce, served from a rough hut or converted van (many permanently parked), with picnic-table seating.

The shrimp-shack phenomenon began with a lost lease and a determined restaurateur. In 1994, when Giovanni and Connie Aragona couldn't renew the lease on their Haleiwa deli, they began hawking their best-selling dish—an Italian-style scampi preparation involving lemon, butter, and lots of garlic—from a truck alongside the road. About the same time, aquaculture was gaining a foothold in nearby Kahuku, with farmers raising sweet, white shrimp and huge, orange-whiskered prawns in shallow freshwater ponds. The ready supply and the success of the first shrimp truck led to many imitators.

Though it's changed hands, that first business lives on as Giovanni's Original Shrimp Truck, parked in Kahuku town. Signature dishes include the garlic shrimp and a spicy shrimp sauté, both worth a stop.

But there's plenty of competition—at least a dozen stands, trucks, or stalls are operating at any given time, with varying menus (and quality).

Not all of that shrimp comes fresh from the ponds; much of it is imported. The only way you can be sure you're buying local, farm-raised shrimp is if the shrimp is still kicking. Romy's Kahuku Prawns and Shrimp Hut (Kamehameha Hwy., near Kahuku) is an arm of one of the longest-running aquaculture farms in the area; it sells live shrimp and prawns and farm-raised fish along with excellent plate lunches. The award-winning Mackey's serves some of the juiciest, tastiest plates on the North Shore; if you're lucky, you'll be greeted by the gregarious Mackey Chan himself.

$$$ ✕ **Prima.** Owned by two of Hawaii's rising stars in the culinary industry—
MODERN ITALIAN   Aker Briceno and Lindsey Ozawa—Prima offers locavore dishes with Italian and Japanese twists. Our favorites include the savory fennel panna cotta, curry Bolognese on pappardelle with fried curry leaves, and any of the signature pizzas. Save room for Aker's homemade gelatos in an array of unique flavors. ⌧ *Kailua Shopping Center, 108 Hekili St., Kailua, Honolulu* ☎ *808/888–8933* ⊕ *primahawaii.com* ⌧ *Reservations essential* ⊘ *Closed Sun. and Mon.*

THE NORTH SHORE

$$ ✕ **Haleiwa Joe's Seafood Grill.** After the long drive to the North Shore,
AMERICAN   it's a treat to while away the afternoon on the covered open-air lanai at Haleiwa Joe's, scoring a couple of cute souvenir glasses, watching the boats and surfers in the harbor, and munching crunchy coconut shrimp, a mahi burger, or whatever's the freshest fish special. It's just past the Anahulu Stream Bridge. A Kaneohe location overlooks lush Haiku Gar-

The food is as good as the views at Ola at Turtle Bay Resort.

dens. ⊠ *66-011 Kamehameha Hwy., Haleiwa* ☎ *808/637–8005* ⊕ *www.haleiwajoes.com* ⌖ *Reservations not accepted.*

$
AMERICAN
✗**Kua Aina Sandwich.** A must-stop spot during a drive around the island, this North Shore eatery specializes in large, hand-formed burgers heaped with bacon, cheese, salsa, and pineapple; or try the grilled mahimahi sandwich. The crispy shoestring fries alone are worth the trip. Kua Aina also has a south-shore location in the Ward Centre in Honolulu. ⊠ *66-160 Kamehameha Hwy., Haleiwa* ☎ *808/637–6067* ⌖ *Reservations not accepted.*

$$$$
MODERN
HAWAIIAN
Fodor'sChoice
★
✗**Ola at Turtle Bay Resort.** In a pavilion literally on the sand, this casual but refined restaurant wowed critics from the moment it opened, both with its idyllic location on Kuilima Cove and with chef Fred DeAngelo's reliably wonderful food. Ola means "life, living, healthy," an apt name for a place that combines a commitment to freshness and wholesomeness with a discriminating and innovative palate in such dishes as a vegan risotto made with local mushrooms and orzo pasta, slow-poached salmon with caramelized cane sugar and Okinawan sweet potatoes. It is absolutely worth the drive. ⊠ *57-091 Kamehameha Hwy., Kahuku* ☎ *808/293–0801* ⊕ *olaislife.com.*

$
AMERICAN
✗**Ted's Bakery.** Across from Sunset Beach and famous for its chocolate *haupia* pie (layered coconut and chocolate puddings topped with whipped cream), Ted's Bakery is also favored by surfers and area residents for quick breakfasts, sandwiches, or plate lunches, to go or eaten at the handful of umbrella-shaded tables outside. ⊠ *59-024 Kamehameha Hwy., Haleiwa* ☎ *808/638–8207* ⊕ *www.tedsbakery.com* ⌖ *Reservations not accepted.*

CENTRAL OAHU

$ ✕ **Dixie Grill.** Casual and family-friendly, the Dixie Grill, just off the
AMERICAN freeway in Pearl City, brings a taste of the South to the islands with
barbecue (including a variety of spicy sauces to choose from), seafood
specialties (creole mahimahi, fried catfish), coleslaw, and hush puppies.
■ **TIP→ This place is convenient if you're visiting Pearl Harbor or the swap
meet.** ✉ *99-016 Kamehameha Hwy., Aiea* ☎ *808/485–2722* ⊕ *www.
dixiegrill.com* ⚔ *Reservations not accepted.*

WEST (LEEWARD) OAHU

$$$$ ✕ **Ama Ama.** It's not enough that this restaurant looks out upon the
MODERN Ko Olina lagoons and the vast Pacific Ocean—the food is wonder-
HAWAIIAN ful, too. Thanks to renowned local chef Kevin Chong, you can enjoy
modern as well as classic menu items made from local ingredients.
Even the Kahuku corn chowder tastes great on a warm day; other
favorites include the light and colorful goat-cheese ravioli, firecracker
chicken, and nori-wrapped ahi tuna. Save room for dessert: the Hawaiian Chocolate Cake is an amazing treat. If you're on a budget, skip
dinner—breakfast and lunch entrées are half the price (although menu
offerings vary). Make your reservations online at the Disney Resorts
website. ✉ *Aulani, a Disney Resort & Spa, 92-1185 Aliinui Dr., Ko
Olina, Kapolei* ☎ *714/520–7001* ⊕ *disneyparks.disney.go.com* ⚔ *Reservations essential.*

$$$$ ✕ **Makahiki—The Bounty of the Islands.** The buffet restaurant at Disney's
ECLECTIC Aulani resort offers a wide variety of locally produced items, as well as
familiar dishes from stateside and the rest of the world. A chef walking
the line can explain the various dishes, which always include sustainable Hawaiian seafood and Asian selections. You'll also always find
familiar grilled meats and vegetables, in addition to a kids' menu. If
you have children, plan months in advance to get a reservation for the
Character Breakfast, as it's offered only on select days and is always sold
out. ■ **TIP→ Arrive early for dinner and have a drink at the adjacent Olelo
Room, where the staff are fluent in Hawaiian; you can get a language lesson along with your libation.** ✉ *Aulani, a Disney Resort & Spa, 92-1185
Aliinui Dr., Ko Olina, Kapolei* ☎ *714/520–7001* ⚔ *Reservations essential* ☾ *No lunch.*

Where to Stay

WORD OF MOUTH

"It's truly about location, location, location. . . . The [kids] will totally enjoy surfing lessons at Waikiki Beach. [And] Waikiki is a short drive to Hanauma Bay for outstanding snorkeling."

—adventureseeker

Updated by
Catherine E.
Toth

As in real estate, location matters. And though Oahu is just 44 miles long and 30 miles wide—meaning you can circle the entire island before lunch—it boasts neighborhoods and lodgings with very different vibes and personalities. If you like the action and choices of big cities, consider Waikiki, a 24-hour playground with everything from surf to karaoke bars. Those who want an escape from urban life look to the island's leeward or windward sides, or the North Shore, whose surf culture creates a laid-back atmosphere.

Most of the island's major hotels and resorts are in Waikiki, which has a lot to offer within a small area, namely shopping, restaurants, nightlife, and nearly 3 miles of sandy beach. You don't need a car in Waikiki; everything is nearby, from the Honolulu Zoo and Waikiki Aquarium, the 300-acre Kapiolani Park, running and biking paths, grocery stores, and access to public transportation that can take you to museums, shopping centers, and historic landmarks around the island.

You'll find places to stay along the entire stretch of Kalakaua Avenue, with smaller and quieter hotels and condos at the eastern end, and more business-centric accommodations on the western edge of Waikiki, near the Hawaii Convention Center, Ala Moana Center, and downtown Honolulu.

The majority of tourists who come to Oahu stay in Waikiki, but choosing accommodations in downtown Honolulu affords you the opportunity to be close to shopping and restaurants at Ala Moana Center, the largest shopping mall in the state. It also provides easy access to the airport.

If you want to get away from the bustle of the city, consider a stay on Oahu's leeward coast—namely, at the Ko Olina resort area, about 20 minutes from the Honolulu International Airport and 40 minutes from Waikiki. Here, there are great golf courses and quiet beaches and coves that make for a relaxing getaway. But you'll need a car to get off the property if you want to explore the rest of the island.

Other more low-key options are on Windward Oahu or the North Shore. Both regions are rustic and charming, with quaint eateries and coffee shops, unique shops, and some of the island's best beaches—plus one of the top resorts, Turtle Bay, on the North Shore.

OAHU LODGING PLANNER

LODGING PROPERTY TYPES

HOTELS AND RESORTS

Oahu offers more accommodation choices than any other Hawaiian island, and for many visitors, staying at a top-notch resort or hotel here—such as the luxe Turtle Bay Resort on the North Shore or the posh Halekulani in Waikiki—is the ultimate island-style pampering experience.

Keep in mind that most Waikiki hotels charge $10 or more per day for parking. Consider renting a car only on the days that you wish to go exploring or factor the parking costs into your budget.

B&BS AND INNS

There are about a dozen B&Bs on Oahu, primarily located in Kailua, on the windward side of the island. Several are located within walking distance of world-famous Kailua Beach and a handful have pools. A few serve simple continental breakfasts with pastries, coffee, and fresh island fruit and juices, while others provide breakfast items in the units for guests to enjoy at their leisure during their stay. *In addition to the listings below, check the Oahu Visitors Bureau website (⊕ www.gohawaii.com/oahu) for additional B&B options.*

CONDOS AND VACATION RENTALS

Vacation rentals give you the convenience of staying at a home away from home—and you should be able to find the perfect getaway on Oahu. Properties managed by individual owners can be found at online vacation-rental directories, as well as on the Oahu Visitors Bureau website. There also are several Oahu-based management companies with vacation rentals. Compare companies, as some offer Internet specials and free nights when booking.

RESERVATIONS

After your online research but before you book a room, try calling the hotels directly. Sometimes on-property reservationists can get you the best deals, and they usually have the most accurate information about rooms and hotel amenities. If you use a toll-free number, ask for the location of the calling center you've reached. If it's not in Oahu, double-check information and rates by calling the hotel's local number.

PRICES

The lodgings we list are the cream of the crop in each price category. Assume that hotels have private bath, phone, and TV unless we state otherwise. We always list facilities but not whether you'll be charged

9

an extra fee to use them, so when pricing accommodations, find out what's included.

WHAT IT COSTS				
	$	$$	$$$	$$$$
For two people	Under $180	$180–$260	$261–$340	over $340

Hotel prices are for two people in a standard double room in high season, excluding taxes. Condo price categories reflect studio and one-bedroom rates.

HONOLULU

For expanded hotel reviews, visit Fodors.com.

GREATER HONOLULU

$$
HOTEL

Aston at the Executive Centre Hotel. Downtown Honolulu's only hotel is an all-suites high-rise in the center of the business district, within walking distance of the historic Capitol District and Honolulu's Chinatown and a 10-minute drive from Honolulu International Airport. **Pros:** central to downtown businesses, transportation, and sights; great restuarant—Hukilau—in the lobby. **Cons:** no beach within walking distance; area businesses shut down early on weekdays and usually close on weekends; parking is very expensive. ⊠ *1088 Bishop St., downtown Honolulu, Honolulu* ☎ *808/539–3000, 866/774–2924* ✉ *res.exc@ astonhotels.com* ⊕ *www.astonhotels.com* ⤶ *116 suites* ♿ *In-room: a/c, safe, kitchen. In-hotel: restaurant, pool, gym, laundry facilities, parking* ☉ *Breakfast.*

$$
HOTEL

Ala Moana Hotel. Shoppers might wear out their Manolos here: this renovated condo-hotel is connected to Oahu's largest mall, the Ala Moana Center, by a pedestrian ramp, and it's a four-block stroll away from the eclectic shopping at Ward Centers. **Pros:** adjacent to Ala Moana Center and all of its shops and restaurants; rooms nicely appointed; quick walk to the beach. **Cons:** outside the heartbeat of Waikiki; can feel a bit distant from the action; not right on the beach. ⊠ *410 Atkinson Dr., Ala Moana, Honolulu* ☎ *808/955–4811, 888/367–4811* ⊕ *www.alamoanahotel.com* ⤶ *1,150 studios, 67 suites* ♿ *In-room: a/c, safe, Internet, Wi-Fi. In-hotel: restaurant, bar, pool, gym, parking* ☉ *No meals.*

$$$$
HOTEL
Fodor's Choice
★

The Kahala Hotel & Resort. Hidden away in the upscale residential neighborhood of Kahala (on the other side of Diamond Head from Waikiki), this elegant oceanfront hotel has played host to both presidents and princesses as one of Hawaii's very first luxury resorts. **Pros:** away from hectic Waikiki; beautiful rooms and public spaces; heavenly spa; pet-friendly. **Cons:** Waikiki is a drive away. ⊠ *5000 Kahala Ave., Kahala, Honolulu* ☎ *808/739–8888, 800/367–2525* ⊕ *www. kahalaresort.com* ⤶ *345 rooms, 33 suites* ♿ *In-room: a/c, safe, Internet, Wi-Fi. In-hotel: restaurant, bar, pool, gym, spa, beach, children's programs, parking* ☉ *No meals.*

BEST BETS FOR OAHU LODGING

Fodor's writers and editors have selected their favorite hotels, resorts, condos, vacation rentals, and B&Bs by price and experience. Fodor's Choice properties represent the "best of the best" across price categories. You can also search by area for excellent places to stay—check out our reviews on the following pages.

Fodor's Choice ★

Halekulani, p. 253
The Kahala Hotel & Resort, p. 244
The Turtle Bay Resort, p. 259

By Price

$

Aqua Aloha Surf Waikiki, p. 246
Aqua Palms Waikiki, p. 249
The Breakers, p. 251
The Equus Hotel and Marina Tower, p. 252
Ke Iki Beach Bungalows, p. 259
Royal Grove Hotel, p. 256
Winston's Waikiki Condos, p. 257

$$

Ala Moana Hotel, p. 244
Aston Waikiki Beach Hotel, p. 249
Hilton Hawaiian Village Beach Resort and Spa, p. 253

Paradise Bay Resort, p. 258
Waikiki Parc, p. 257

$$$

Embassy Suites Hotel Waikiki Beach Walk, p. 252

$$$$

Halekulani, p. 253
JW Marriott Ihilani Resort & Spa, p. 261
The Kahala Hotel & Resort, p. 244
Marriott Ko Olina Beach Vacation Club, p. 261
Moana Surfrider, p. 254
Outrigger Reef on the Beach, p. 255
The Royal Hawaiian, p. 256

By Experience

MOST KID-FRIENDLY

Aqua Aloha Surf Waikiki, $, p. 246
Aston Waikiki Beach Hotel, $$, p. 249

Embassy Suites Hotel Waikiki Beach Walk, $$$, p. 252
Hilton Hawaiian Village Beach Resort and Spa, $$, p. 253
Marriott Ko Olina Beach Vacation Club, $$$$, p. 261

BEST FOR ROMANCE

Halekulani, $$$$, p. 253
JW Marriott Ihilani Resort & Spa, $$$$, p. 261
The Kahala Hotel & Resort, $$$$, p. 244
Moana Surfrider, $$$$, p. 254
The Royal Hawaiian, $$$$, p. 256

BEST HOTEL BAR

Hilton Hawaiian Village Beach Resort and Spa, $$, p. 253
JW Marriott Ihilani Resort & Spa, $$$$, p. 261
Moana Surfrider, $$$$, p. 254

Outrigger Waikiki on the Beach, $$$$, p. 256
The Royal Hawaiian, $$$$, p. 256

BEST SPA

Halekulani, $$$$, p. 253
Hilton Hawaiian Village Beach Resort and Spa, $$, p. 253
JW Marriott Ihilani Resort & Spa, $$$$, p. 261
The Kahala Hotel & Resort, $$$$, p. 244
Waikiki Beach Marriott Resort & Spa, $$$, p. 257

BEST B&BS & INNS

Diamond Head Bed and Breakfast, $, p. 252
Ke Iki Beach Bungalows $, p. 259
Paradise Bay Resort, $$, p. 258

BEST BEACH

JW Marriott Ihilani Resort and Spa, $$$$, p. 261
The Kahala Hotel & Resort, $$$$, p. 244
Marriott Ko Olina Beach Vacation Club, $$$$, p. 261
Moana Surfrider, $$$$, p. 254
The Turtle Bay Resort, $$$$, p. 259

9

WHERE TO STAY ON OAHU

Neighborhood	Local Vibe	Pros	Cons
Honolulu	Lodging options are limited in downtown Honolulu, but if you want an urban feel or to be near Chinatown, look no farther.	Access to a wide selection of art galleries, boutiques, and new restaurants as well as Chinatown.	No beaches within walking distance. If you're looking to get away from it all, this is not the place.
Waikiki	Lodgings abound in Waikiki, from youth hostels to five-star accommodations. The area is always abuzz with activity and anything you desire is within walking distance.	You can surf in front of the hotels, wander miles of beach and explore hundreds of restaurants and bars.	This is tourist central. Prices are high, and you are not going to get the true Hawaii experience.
Windward Oahu	More in tune with the local experience, here is where you'll find most of the island's B&Bs and enjoy the lush side of Oahu.	From beautiful vistas and green jungles, this side really captures the tropical paradise most people envision when dreaming of a Hawaiian vacation.	The lushness comes at a price—it rains a lot on this side. Also, luxury is not the specialty here; if you are looking to get pampered, stay elsewhere.
The North Shore	This is true country living, with one luxurious resort exception. It's bustling in the winter (when the surf is up) but pretty slow-paced in the summer.	Amazing surf and long stretches of sand truly epitomize the beach culture in Hawaii. Historic Haleiwa has enough stores to keep shopaholics busy.	There is no middle ground for accommodations; you're either in backpacker cabanas or $300-a-night suites. There is also zero nightlife, and traffic can get heavy during winter months.
West (Leeward) Oahu	This is the resort side of the rock; there is little outside of these resorts, but plenty on the grounds to keep you occupied for a week.	Ko Olina's lagoons offer the most kid-friendly swimming on the island, and the golf courses on this side are magnificent. Rare is the rainy day out here.	You are isolated from the rest of Oahu, with little in the way of shopping or jungle hikes.

WAIKIKI

For expanded hotel reviews, visit Fodors.com.

Hotels in Waikiki range from super-luxe resorts to the kind of small, beachy places where shirtless surfers hang out in the lobby. It's where the heart of the action is on Oahu. Those traveling with families might want to take into consideration easy access to the beach, restaurants, and other activities, as parking in the area can sometimes be difficult and pricey. For those looking to be slightly removed from the scene, choose accommodations on the *ewa* (west) end of Waikiki.

$ **Aqua Aloha Surf Waikiki.** This boutique property in the heart of
HOTEL   Waikiki is surfer chic with a lobby and interior spaces reflecting the

The Kahala

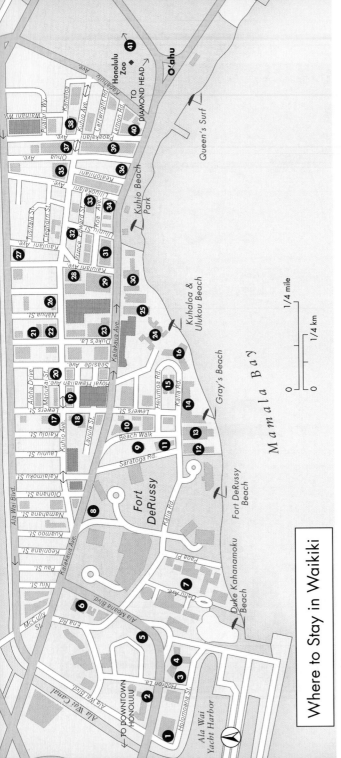

Where to Stay in Waikiki

O'ahu

1/4 mile

1/4 km

theme and is a great value to boot. **Pros:** fun lobby; great beachy decor and friendly atmosphere; pool with sundeck and cabanas; on-site coin-operated laundry facilities. **Cons:** no view; traffic noise; 10-minute walk to beach. ✉ *444 Kanekapolei St., Waikiki* ☎ *866/406–2782, 808/923–0222* ⊕ *www.aquaresorts.com* ↩ *202 rooms* ⅄ *In-room: a/c, safe, Internet. In-hotel: pool, spa, laundry facilities, parking* ¶⊙¶ *Breakfast.*

WORD OF MOUTH

". . . [T]he buzz of being in central Waikiki—so much to see and do. And you can get out on your own on feet, without all being tied together and having to use the rental car." —suze

$ **Aqua Palms Waikiki.** Across from the Hilton Hawaiian Village on Ala
RENTAL Moana Boulevard just as it curves toward Waikiki's Kalakaua Avenue, the 12-story Aqua Palms completed a $15-million transformation into a "condotel" in 2005 and now has studio and luxury one-bedroom-suite accommodations. **Pros:** excellent full kitchens in suites; comfortable furnishings; trolley stop directly in front of hotel; complimentary coffee and tea service in the lobby 24/7. **Cons:** closest beach access is through the Hilton Hawaiian Village across the street. ✉ *1850 Ala Moana Blvd., Waikiki* ☎ *808/947–7256, 866/406–2782* ⊕ *www.aquaresorts.com* ↩ *263 units* ⅄ *In-room: a/c, safe, kitchen. In-hotel: pool, gym, spa, laundry facilities, parking* ¶⊙¶ *No meals.*

$$ **Aston at the Waikiki Banyan.** The recreation deck at this family-oriented
RENTAL property has outdoor grills, a heated swimming pool, two hot tubs, a
☺ children's playground, a mini putting green, and volleyball, basketball and tennis courts. **Pros:** many rooms have great views; walking distance to shops and restaurants. **Cons:** trekking to the beach (a block away) with all of your gear; no on-site restaurant. ✉ *201 Ohua Ave., Waikiki* ☎ *808/922–0555, 877/997–6667* ⊕ *www.astonhotels.com* ↩ *876 units* ⅄ *In-room: a/c, safe, kitchen, Internet. In-hotel: tennis court, pool, spa, laundry facilities, parking* ¶⊙¶ *No meals.*

$$ **Aston Pacific Monarch.** One block from *ewa* end of Waikiki Beach,
RENTAL this 34-story high-rise condominium resort features a rooftop deck— with a freshwater pool, hot tub, and sauna—affords a panoramic view spanning the length of Waikiki. **Pros:** fantastic view from rooftop pool; hospitality lounge. **Cons:** stairs to the pool deck are fairly steep and may be difficult for some. ✉ *2427 Kuhio Ave., Waikiki* ☎ *808/923–9805, 877/997–6667* ⊕ *www.astonhotels.com* ↩ *152 units* ⅄ *In-room: safe, kitchen, Internet. In-hotel: restaurant, pool, laundry facilities, parking* ¶⊙¶ *No meals.*

$$ **Aston Waikiki Beach Hotel.** A good choice for families, this hotel is
HOTEL directly across the street from a protected stretch of Kuhio Beach, and
☺ near Kapiolani Park. **Pros:** fun for families; great beach access. **Cons:** active lobby area and crowded elevators; no self-parking. ✉ *2570 Kalakaua Ave., Waikiki* ☎ *808/922–2511, 877/997–6667, 800/877–7666* ⊕ *www.astonwaikikibeach.com* ↩ *644 rooms, 40 suites* ⅄ *In-room: a/c, safe, Internet, Wi-Fi. In-hotel: restaurant, pool, gym, laundry facilities, parking* ¶⊙¶ *Breakfast.*

9

Halekulani

$ ⊞ **Aston Waikiki Beach Tower.** You'll find the elegance of a luxury all-suites
RENTAL condominium combined with the intimacy and service of a boutique
hotel at this Kalakaua Avenue address. **Pros:** *very* large rooms—big
enough to move into. **Cons:** no on-site restaurants; you must cross a
busy street to the beach. ⊠ *2470 Kalakaua Ave., Waikiki* ☎ *808/926–*
6400, 877/997–6667 ⊕ *www.astonhotels.com* ⤵ *140 units* ♿ *In-room:*
a/c, safe, kitchen, Internet, Wi-Fi. In-hotel: tennis court, pool, spa, laun-
dry facilities, parking ¶⊙¶ *No meals.*

$ ⊞ **Aston Waikiki Circle Hotel.** This unusual 14-story circular hotel—built
HOTEL to resemble a Chinese lantern—is a Waikiki landmark, though the
rooms are small, with tiny bathrooms with showers only. **Pros:** great
location and views; on-site surfboard lockers and complimentary beach
gear. **Cons:** interior design, though charming to some, may feel dated
to others. ⊠ *2464 Kalakaua Ave., Waikiki* ☎ *808/923–1571, 877/997–*
6667 ⊕ *www.astonhotels.com* ⤵ *104 rooms* ♿ *In-room: a/c, safe, Inter-*
net. In-hotel: restaurant, laundry facilities, parking ¶⊙¶ *No meals.*

$ ⊞ **Aston Waikiki Joy Hotel.** A trellised open-air lobby of Italian marble,
HOTEL a koi pond, and a guava smoothie greet you on arrival at this Lewers
Street hideaway, about a five-minute stroll from Kalakaua Avenue and
through one of the many public-access ways to the beach. **Pros:** a bit of
old Waikiki; rooms are spotless; attentive staff; karaoke lounge in the
lobby. **Cons:** rooms are slightly dated; valet parking only. ⊠ *320 Lewers*
St., Waikiki ☎ *808/923–2300, 877/997–6667* ⊕ *www.astonhotels.com*
⤵ *50 rooms, 44 suites* ♿ *In-room: a/c, safe, kitchen, Internet. In-hotel:*
restaurant, bar, pool, gym, laundry facilities, parking ¶⊙¶ *Breakfast.*

$$ ⊞ **Aston Waikiki Sunset.** This 38-story high-rise condominium resort
RENTAL is near Diamond Head, one block from Waikiki Beach and on the
city's bus line. **Pros:** spectacular views; fully equipped kitchens; lots to
do within walking distance. **Cons:** noise from outdoor activities can
be a distraction. ⊠ *229 Paoakalani Ave., Waikiki* ☎ *808/922–0511,*
877/997–6667 ⊕ *www.astonhotels.com* ⤵ *307 units* ♿ *In-room: a/c,*
safe, kitchen, Internet. In-hotel: tennis court, pool, laundry facilities
¶⊙¶ *No meals.*

$ ⊞ **The Breakers.** Despite an explosion of high-rise construction all
RENTAL around it, the low-rise Breakers continues to offer a taste of '60s Hawaii
in this small complex a mere half block from Waikiki Beach. **Pros:**
intimate atmosphere; great location. **Cons:** parking space is limited.
⊠ *250 Beach Walk, Waikiki* ☎ *808/923–3181, 800/426–0494* ⊕ *www.*
breakers-hawaii.com ⤵ *64 units* ♿ *In-room: a/c, kitchen. In-hotel: res-*
taurant, bar, pool, business center, parking ¶⊙¶ *No meals.*

$$$ ⊞ **Castle Waikiki Shore.** Nestled between Fort DeRussy Beach Park and
RENTAL the Outrigger Reef on the Beach, this is the only condo situated right
on Waikiki Beach. **Pros:** great security; great views; great management;
free high-speed Internet access. **Cons:** beach out front is kind of thin;
two-night stay minimum. ⊠ *2161 Kalia Rd., Waikiki* ☎ *808/952–4500,*
800/367–5004 ⊕ *www.castleresorts.com* ⤵ *168 units* ♿ *In-room: a/c,*
safe, kitchen, Internet. In-hotel: restaurant, beach, laundry facilities,
parking ¶⊙¶ *No meals.*

9

$ ⊞ **Coconut Waikiki Hotel.** Overlooking the Ala Wai Canal, this reason-
HOTEL ably priced boutique hotel is more residential than a typical resort,
with a cobblestone driveway, a lobby with rattan living room–style
furnishings, and a wall of French doors that open up to a gazebo garden and a tiny swimming pool tucked in a backyard. **Pros:** a small
and economical hotel in Waikiki; free Wi-Fi throughout hotel. **Cons:**
the walk through busy Waikiki gets tiring when you're carrying all of
your beach equipment. ⊠ *450 Lewers St., Waikiki* ☎ *866/406–2782,
808/923–8828* ⊕ *www.coconutwaikikihotel.com* ⤳ *80 rooms* ⛄ *In-
room: safe, kitchen, Internet, Wi-Fi. In-hotel: pool, gym, laundry facilities, business center, parking* ¡○¡ *Breakfast.*

$ ⊞ **Diamond Head Bed and Breakfast.** Many travelers and residents would
B&B/INN love to own a home like this art-filled B&B at the base of Waikiki's
famous Diamond Head crater, one of the city's most exclusive neighborhoods; however, there are only three rooms available, so you may have
to work a bit to stay here. **Pros:** secluded and peaceful; very homey.
Cons: small and therefore difficult to book; doesn't accept credit cards;
no air-conditioning. ⊠ *3240 Noela Dr., Waikiki* ⊕ *Hawaii's Best Bed
and Breakfasts, Box 485, Laupahoehoe 96767* ☎ *808/923–3360,
800/262–9912 reservations* ⊕ *www.diamondheadbnb.com* ⤳ *2 rooms,
1 suite* ⛄ *In-room: no a/c. In-hotel: some pets allowed* ⊟ *No credit
cards* ¡○¡ *Breakfast.*

$$ ⊞ **Doubletree Alana Waikiki.** The location (a 10-minute walk from
HOTEL the Hawaii Convention Center), three phones in each room, and the
☾ 24-hour business center and gym meet the requirements of the Double-
tree's global business clientele, which also appeals to vacationers. **Pros:**
professional staff; pleasant public spaces; pet-friendly; walk-in glass
showers with oversized rain showerheads. **Cons:** beach is a bit of a
walk. ⊠ *1956 Ala Moana Blvd., Waikiki* ☎ *808/941–7275, 800/222–
8733* ⊕ *www.alana-doubletree.com* ⤳ *317 rooms, 385 suites* ⛄ *In-
room: a/c, safe, Internet. In-hotel: restaurant, bar, pool, gym, business
center, parking, some pets allowed* ¡○¡ *No meals.*

$$$ ⊞ **Embassy Suites Waikiki Beach Walk.** In a place where space is at a pre-
HOTEL mium, the only all-suites resort in Hawaii offers families and groups
☾ traveling together a bit more room to move about, with two 21-story
towers housing one- and two-bedroom suites. **Pros:** great location next
to Waikiki Beach Walk and all of its shops and restaurants; great vibe;
nice pool deck; complimentary hot breakfast served daily. **Cons:** no
direct beach access. ⊠ *201 Beachwalk St., Waikiki* ☎ *800/362–2779,
808/921–2345* ⊕ *www.embassysuiteswaikiki.com* ⤳ *353 1-bedroom
suites, 68 2-bedroom suites* ⛄ *In-room: a/c, safe, Wi-Fi. In-hotel: restaurant, bar, pool, gym, business center* ¡○¡ *Breakfast.*

$ ⊞ **The Equus Hotel and Marina Tower.** Formerly the Hawaii Polo Inn, this
HOTEL small hotel has been completely renovated with a Hawaiian country
theme that pays tribute to Hawaii's polo-playing history. **Pros:** casual;
fun atmosphere; attentive staff; nicely furnished rooms. **Cons:** on a
very busy road you must cross to get to the beach. ⊠ *1696 Ala Moana
Blvd., Waikiki* ☎ *808/949–0061, 800/669–7719* ⊕ *www.equushotel.
com* ⤳ *70 rooms* ⛄ *In-room: a/c, safe, Internet. In-hotel: pool, laundry
facilities, parking* ¡○¡ *Breakfast.*

$$$$
RESORT
Fodor's Choice
★
🏨 **Halekulani.** The luxurious Halekulani exemplifies the translation of its name—the "house befitting heaven"—and from the moment you step inside the lobby, the attention to detail and impeccable service wraps you in privilege. **Pros:** heavenly interior spaces and wonderful dining opportunities in-house; world-class service. **Cons:** might feel a bit formal for Waikiki; pricey. ✉ *2199 Kalia Rd., Waikiki* ☎ *808/923–2311, 800/367–2343* ⊕ *www.halekulani.com* ↙ *412 rooms, 43 suites* ⚒ *In-room: a/c, safe, Internet, Wi-Fi. In-hotel: restaurant, bar, pool, gym, spa, beach, business center, parking* ⊘*No meals.*

$$
HOTEL
🏨 **Hawaii Prince Hotel & Golf Club Waikiki.** This slim high-rise with 521 oceanfront rooms and 57 luxury suites fronts Ala Wai Yacht Harbor at the *ewa* (west) edge of Waikiki. **Pros:** fantastic views; all very elegant; easy exit from complicated-to-maneuver Waikiki. **Cons:** can feel a bit stuffy as it caters more to business travelers. ✉ *100 Holomoana St., Waikiki* ☎ *808/956–1111, 888/977–4623* ⊕ *www.hawaiiprincehotel. com* ↙ *521 rooms, 57 suites* ⚒ *In-room: a/c, safe. In-hotel: restaurant, bar, golf course, pool, gym, spa, business center, parking* ⊘*No meals.*

$$
RESORT
🏨 **Hilton Hawaiian Village Beach Resort and Spa.** Location, location, location: this megaresort and convention destination sprawls over 22 acres on Waikiki's widest stretch of beach, with the green lawns of neighboring Fort DeRussy creating a buffer zone to the high-rise lineup of central Waikiki. **Pros:** activities and amenities can keep you busy for weeks. **Cons:** temptation to stay on-site and not venture out; frequent renovations and construction; size of property can be overwhelming. ✉ *2005 Kalia Rd., Waikiki* ☎ *808/949–4321, 800/445–8667* ⊕ *www. hiltonhawaiianvillage.com* ↙ *3,432 rooms, 365 suites, 264 condominiums* ⚒ *In-room: a/c, safe, Internet. In-hotel: restaurant, bar, pool, gym, spa, beach, children's programs, parking* ⊘*No meals.*

$$
HOTEL
🏨 **Hilton Waikiki Beach Hotel.** You enter through a lobby of rich wood detailing, contemporary fabrics and magnificent tropical floral displays whose colors match the hibiscus reds of the carpeting. **Pros:** good value; central location; pleasant, comfortable public spaces. **Cons:** a bit of a distance to the beach; very few rooms with views. ✉ *2500 Kuhio Ave., Waikiki* ☎ *808/922–0811, 888/370–0980* ⊕ *www.hilton.com* ↙ *601 rooms* ⚒ *In-room: a/c, safe, Internet. In-hotel: restaurant, bar, pool, gym, business center, parking* ⊘*No meals.*

$
HOTEL
☺
🏨 **Holiday Inn Waikiki Beachcomber Resort.** The property is almost directly across from the upgraded Royal Hawaiian Center, next door to the International Marketplace, and 300 steps to the beach. **Pros:** lots of freebies; in the thick of Waikiki action. **Cons:** very busy area; no direct beach access; no on-site cultural activities. ✉ *2300 Kalakaua Ave., Waikiki* ☎ *808/922–4646, 877/317–5756* ⊕ *www. waikikibeachcomberresort.com* ↙ *500 rooms, 7 suites* ⚒ *In-room: a/c, Internet. In-hotel: restaurant, bar, pool, children's programs, laundry facilities, parking* ⊘*No meals.*

$$$
RESORT
☺
🏨 **Hyatt Regency Waikiki Resort and Spa.** Though it's across the street from Kuhio Beach, the recently renewed Hyatt is actually considered oceanfront, as there's no resort between it and the Pacific Ocean. **Pros:** public spaces are open; great little coffee shop, Kimo Bean, in the lobby; kid-friendly. **Cons:** in a very busy and crowded part of Waikiki; parking

9

and ballrooms are across the street. ⊠ *2424 Kalakaua Ave., Waikiki* ☏ *808/923–1234, 800/633–7313* ⊕ *www.hyattregencywaikiki.com* ✈ *1,230 rooms, 18 suites* ♿ *In-room: a/c, safe, Internet, Wi-Fi. In-hotel: restaurant, bar, pool, gym, spa, children's programs, parking* ⓘ *No meals.*

$$$$
RESORT

⚏ **Ilikai Hotel and Suites.** At the *ewa* (west) edge of Waikiki overlooking the Ala Wai Small Boat Harbor, this resort has both standard rooms and units with full kitchens, which can save you some money if you dine in occasionally. **Pros:** views of sunset from most rooms on the *ewa* side; comfortable beds; central location.

> **ASK FOR A LANAI**
>
> Islanders love their porches, balconies, and verandas—all wrapped up in a single Hawaiian word: lanai. You may not want to look at a parking lot, so when booking, ask about the lanai and be sure to specify the view (understanding that top views command top dollars). Also, check that the lanai is not merely a step-out or Juliet balcony, with just enough room to lean against a railing—you want a lanai that is big enough for patio seating.

Cons: very slow elevators; in need of renovations. ⊠ *1777 Ala Moana Blvd., Waikiki* ☏ *808/949–3811, 866/406–2782* ⊕ *www.ilikaihotel. com* ✈ *728 rooms, 51 suites* ♿ *In-room: kitchen. In-hotel: restaurant, bar, pool, gym, laundry facilities, parking* ⓘ *No meals.*

$$
RENTAL

⚏ **Ilima Hotel.** Tucked away on a residential side street near Waikiki's Ala Wai Canal, this locally owned 17-story condominium-style hotel is a gem. **Pros:** big rooms are great for families; free parking in Waikiki is a rarity; on-site coin-operated laundry facilities; smoking rooms available. **Cons:** limited hotel parking, and street parking can be difficult to find; not the most luxurious accommodations. ⊠ *445 Nohonani St., Waikiki* ☏ *808/923–1877, 800/684–2140* ⊕ *www.ilima.com* ✈ *99 units* ♿ *In-room: a/c, safe, kitchen, Internet. In-hotel: pool, gym, laundry facilities, parking* ⓘ *No meals.*

$$$$
RESORT

⚏ **Moana Surfrider, A Westin Resort & Spa.** Outrageous rates of $1.50 per night were the talk of the town when the "First Lady of Waikiki" opened her doors in 1901; today, this historic beauty—the oldest hotel in Waikiki—is still a wedding and honeymoon favorite with a sweeping main staircase and period furnishings in its historic main wing, the Moana. **Pros:** elegant; historic property; best place on Waikiki Beach to watch hula and have a drink; can't beat the location. **Cons:** you'll likely dodge bridal parties in the lobby. ⊠ *2365 Kalakaua Ave., Waikiki* ☏ *808/922–3111, 888/488–3535, 866/500–8313* ⊕ *www.moana-surfrider.com* ✈ *793 rooms, 46 suites* ♿ *In-room: a/c, safe, Internet, Wi-Fi. In-hotel: restaurant, bar, pool, spa, beach, parking* ⓘ *No meals.*

$$$$
HOTEL

⚏ **The Modern Honolulu.** It's a long story: formerly an annex of the iconic Ilikai Hotel, this first incarnation of Marriott International's boutique Edition chain was quickly converted into an Aqua property, but the modern touches of the former owner remain. **Pros:** newly refurbished; great bars and restaurants. **Cons:** not kid-friendly; on the outer edge of Waikiki; no direct beach access. ⊠ *1775 Ala Moana Blvd., Waikiki* ☏ *808/943–5800, 866/970–4161* ⊕ *www.themodernhonolulu.com*

⚓ *353 rooms* ⟠ *In-room: a/c, safe. In-hotel: restaurant, bar, pool, gym, spa, parking* ⦿ *No meals.*

$$$
HOTEL

⌨ **Ohana East.** If you want to be in central Waikiki and don't want to pay beachfront lodging prices, consider the flagship property for Ohana Hotels in Waikiki. **Pros:** close to the beach and reasonable rates; decent on-site eateries, including a piano bar. **Cons:** no lanai and very basic public spaces. ✉ *150 Kaiulani Ave., Waikiki* ☎ *808/922–5353, 866/956–4262* ⊕ *www.ohanahotels.com* ⚓ *420 rooms, 20 suites* ⟠ *In-room: a/c, safe, kitchen, Internet. In-hotel: restaurant, bar, pool, gym, laundry facilities, parking* ⦿ *No meals.*

$$
HOTEL

⌨ **Ohana Waikiki Malia.** Close to the *ewa* (west) end of Waikiki, this older hotel comprises a pair of buildings, one with standard rooms, the other with one-bedroom suites that have kitchenettes. **Pros:** central to shopping and dining in Waikiki; on-site coin-operated laundry facilities. **Cons:** views not much to speak of. ✉ *2211 Kuhio Ave., Waikiki* ☎ *808/923–7621, 866/956–4262* ⊕ *www.ohanahotels.com* ⚓ *285 rooms, 47 suites* ⟠ *In-room: safe, kitchen, Internet. In-hotel: restaurant, pool, laundry facilities, parking* ⦿ *No meals.*

$$
HOTEL

⌨ **Ohana Waikiki West.** Just behind the International Marketplace, this economical hotel offers a third-floor pool and sundeck overlooking all the action of busy Kuhio Avenue. **Pros:** clean rooms; centrally located. **Cons:** no bathtubs. ✉ *2330 Kuhio Ave., Waikiki* ☎ *808/922–5022, 866/956–4262* ⊕ *www.ohanahotels.com* ⚓ *645 rooms, 16 suites* ⟠ *In-room: safe, kitchen, Internet. In-hotel: restaurant, bar, pool, laundry facilities, parking* ⦿ *No meals.*

$$
HOTEL

⌨ **Outrigger Luana.** At the entrance to Waikiki near Fort DeRussy is this welcoming hotel offering both rooms and condominium units. **Pros:** two lanai in suites; barbecue area (rare for Waikiki); walking distance to shops and restaurants. **Cons:** no direct beach access. ✉ *2045 Kalakaua Ave., Waikiki* ☎ *808/955-6000, 866/956-4262* ⊕ *www.outrigger.com* ⚓ *218 units* ⟠ *In-room: a/c, safe, kitchen, Internet. In-hotel: pool, gym, laundry facilities, parking* ⦿ *No meals.*

$$$$
HOTEL

⌨ **Outrigger Reef on the Beach.** Recent renovations have drastically updated this beachfront property, adding a new entrance that incorporates a Hawaiian voyaging design theme; expanded guest rooms; larger and more contemporary bathrooms; and a new signature restaurant—the poolside Kani Ka Pila Grille, with nightly live music by legendary Hawaiian entertainers—though the Shore Bird Restaurant & Beach Bar and Ocean House Restaurant also remain. **Pros:** on beach; direct access to

---

HOTELS' CULTURAL PROGRAMS

Hotels, especially in Waikiki, are fueling a resurgence in Hawaiian culture, thanks to repeat visitors who want a more authentic island experience. In addition to lei-making and hula-dancing lessons, you can learn how to strum a ukulele, listen to Grammy Award–winning Hawaiian musicians, watch a revered master *kumu* (teacher) share the art of ancient hula and chant, chat with a marine biologist about Hawaii's endangered species, or get a lesson in the art of canoe-making. Check with the concierge for daily Hawaiian activities at the hotel or nearby.

9

Waikiki Beach Walk. **Cons:** views from non-oceanfront rooms are uninspiring; can be pricey. ✉ *2169 Kalia Rd., Waikiki* ☎ *808/923–3111, 866/956–4262* ⊕ *www.outrigger.com* ⤵ *631 rooms, 44 suites* ⚅ *In-room: a/c, Internet. In-hotel: restaurant, bar, pool, gym, spa, beach, laundry facilities, business center, parking* ⦿ *No meals.*

$$$$ ⊞ **Outrigger Waikiki on the Beach.**
RESORT This star of Outrigger Hotels & Resorts sits on one of the finest strands of Waikiki Beach. **Pros:** the best bar on the beach is downstairs;

free Wi-Fi in lobby. **Cons:** the lobby feels a bit like an airport with so many people using it as a throughway to the beach. ✉ *2335 Kalakaua Ave., Waikiki* ☎ *808/923–0711, 808/956–4262* ⊕ *www.outrigger.com* ⤵ *524 rooms, 30 suites* ⚅ *In-room: a/c, safe, kitchen, Internet. In-hotel: restaurant, bar, pool, gym, spa, beach, children's programs, laundry facilities, parking* ⦿ *No meals.*

$ ⊞ **Royal Grove Hotel.** Two generations of the Fong family have put their
HOTEL heart and soul into the operation of this tiny (by Waikiki standards), six-story hotel that feels like a throwback to the days of boarding houses, where rooms were outfitted for function, not style, and served up with a wealth of home-style hospitality at a price that didn't break the bank. **Pros:** very economical Waikiki option; lots of character. **Cons:** no a/c in some rooms; rooms are dated. ✉ *151 Uluniu Ave., Waikiki* ☎ *808/923–7691* ⊕ *www.royalgrovehotel.com* ⤵ *78 rooms, 7 suites* ⚅ *In-room: a/c, kitchen. In-hotel: restaurant, pool* ⦿ *No meals.*

$$$$ ⊞ **The Royal Hawaiian, a Luxury Collection Resort.** There's nothing like
HOTEL the legendary Pink Palace of the Pacific, and after a recent $85 million face-lift—which included removing the storefronts that clogged the lobby and opening up the public spaces—the iconic hotel on Waikiki Beach is a unique blend of luxury and tradition. **Pros:** can't be beat for history; mai tais and sunsets are amazing; there's a doctors-on-call service. **Cons:** history is not cheap; you'd better like pink. ✉ *2259 Kalakaua Ave., Waikiki* ☎ *888/488–3535, 808/923–7311, 866/500–8313* ⊕ *www.royal-hawaiian.com* ⤵ *528 rooms, 53 suites* ⚅ *In-room: a/c, Internet. In-hotel: restaurant, bar, pool, gym, spa, beach, business center, parking* ⦿ *No meals.*

$$$ ⊞ **Sheraton Princess Kaiulani.** This hotel sits across the street from its
HOTEL upscale sister property, the Moana Surfrider. **Pros:** in the heart of everything in Waikiki; on-site surfboard storage (for a fee). **Cons:** no direct beach access; kids' activities off-site; pool closes early; no spa. ✉ *120 Kaiulani Ave., Waikiki* ☎ *808/922–5811, 866/716–8109, 800/325–3535* ⊕ *www.princess-kaiulani.com* ⤵ *1,142 rooms, 14 suites* ⚅ *In-room: a/c, Internet. In-hotel: restaurant, bar, pool, gym* ⦿ *No meals.*

$$$$ ⊞ **Sheraton Waikiki.** If you don't mind crowds, this could be the place
HOTEL for you: towering over its neighbors on the prow of Waikiki's famous

sands, the Sheraton is center stage on Waikiki Beach. **Pros:** location in the heart of everything. **Cons:** busy atmosphere clashes with laid-back Hawaiian style. ⊠ *2255 Kalakaua Ave., Waikiki* ☎ *808/922–4422, 866/716–8109* ⊕ *www.sheraton-waikiki.com* ⊷ *1,695 rooms, 128 suites* ☐ *In-room: a/c, Internet. In-hotel: restaurant, bar, pool, gym, beach, children's programs, parking* ¶◎¶ *No meals.*

WORD OF MOUTH

"Kailua has a great beach. My family stayed at a house there a few years ago. We didn't snorkel there, but the windsurfing and kayaking were great. It is a beautiful beach and a wonderful little town." —lauren25

$$$$
HOTEL ⛾ **Trump International Hotel Waikiki Beach Walk.** One of the chicest hotels on the Waikiki scene, Trump has been drawing rave reviews since its opening in November 2009. **Pros:** beautifully appointed rooms; on the edge of Waikiki so a bit quieter; great views of Friday fireworks. **Cons:** must cross street to reach the beach; pricey. ⊠ *223 Saratoga Rd., Waikiki* ☎ *808/683–7777, 877/683–7401* ⊕ *www.trumpwaikikihotel. com* ⊷ *1,462 rooms* ☐ *In-room: a/c, Internet, Wi-Fi. In-hotel: restaurant, bar, pool, gym, spa, parking* ¶◎¶ *No meals.*

$$$
RESORT ⛾ **Waikiki Beach Marriott Resort & Spa.** On the eastern edge of Waikiki, this flagship Marriott sits across from Kuhio Beach and close to Kapiolani Park, the Honolulu Zoo, and Waikiki Aquarium. **Pros:** stunning views of Waikiki; professional service; airy tropical public spaces. **Cons:** noise from Kalakaua Avenue can drown out surf below. ⊠ *2552 Kalakaua Ave., Waikiki* ☎ *808/922–6611, 800/848–8110* ⊕ *www. marriottwaikiki.com* ⊷ *1,310 rooms, 13 suites* ☐ *In-room: a/c, Internet, Wi-Fi. In-hotel: restaurant, bar, pool, gym, spa, parking* ¶◎¶ *No meals.*

$$
HOTEL ⛾ **Waikiki Parc.** In contrast to the stately vintage-Hawaiian elegance of her sister hotel, the Halekulani, the Waikiki Parc makes a chic and contemporary statement to its Gen-X clientele, offering the same attention to detail in service and architectural design but lacking the beachfront location and higher prices. **Pros:** stunningly modern; high-design rooms; great access to Waikiki Beach Walk. **Cons:** no direct beach access. ⊠ *2233 Helumoa Rd., Waikiki* ☎ *808/921–7272, 800/422–0450* ⊕ *www.waikikiparc.com* ⊷ *297 rooms* ☐ *In-room: a/c, safe, Internet. In-hotel: restaurant, pool, gym, parking* ¶◎¶ *No meals.*

$
HOTEL ⛾ **Waikiki Sand Villa.** Families and others looking for an economical rate without sacrificing proximity to Waikiki's beaches, dining, and shopping return to the Waikiki Sand Villa year after year. **Pros:** fun bar; economical choice. **Cons:** the noise from the bar might annoy some; 10-minute walk to the beach. ⊠ *2375 Ala Wai Blvd., Waikiki* ☎ *808/922–4744, 800/247–1903* 🖷 *808/926–7587* ⊕ *www.sandvillahotel.com* ⊷ *214 rooms* ☐ *In-room: a/c, safe, Internet. In-hotel: restaurant, bar, pool, parking* ¶◎¶ *Breakfast.*

$
RENTAL ⛾ **Winston's Waikiki Condos.** This five-story condominium complex specializing in monthly rates is just off Kuhio Avenue near the International Marketplace and two blocks from Waikiki Beach. **Pros:** the owner is a slice of 1960s Hawaii; suites are all unique; careful attention to details.

9

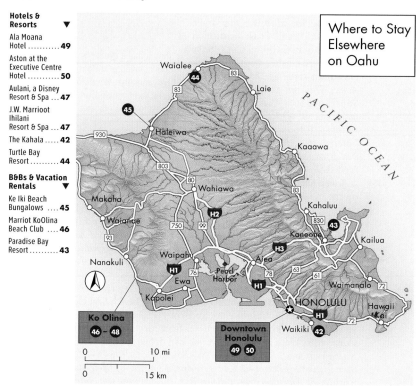

Cons: not many suites; credit cards not accepted for payment (only to hold reservations); two blocks from the beach; parking not available at the condo and can be pricey elsewhere. ⊠ *417 Nohonani St., Waikiki* ☎ *808/924–3332, 800/545–1948* ⊕ *www.winstonswaikikicondos.com* ⤳ *10 units* ⟳ *In-room: kitchen. In-hotel: pool, laundry facilities, parking* ⵏⵔⵍ *No meals.*

ELSEWHERE ON OAHU

For expanded hotel reviews, visit Fodors.com.

Away from the hopping scene of Waikiki or busy downtown, accommodations on the rest of Oahu range from quiet and romantic bed-and-breakfasts and cottages to less expensive hotels that are a great value. There are a few luxury resorts as well, where you'll truly feel like you're getting away from it all.

WINDWARD OAHU

$$ 🏠 **Paradise Bay Resort.** If you're looking for an alternative to staying in
B&B/INN   Waikiki and you aren't fussy about amenities, consider Paradise Bay Resort, located 30 minutes from both Waikiki and the North Shore.

Pros: great views of Kaneohe Bay; cooler temps on this side of the island. **Cons:** not all units are beside the bay; rental car is a necessity. ⊠ 47-039 Lihikai Dr., Kaneohe ☎ 800/735–5071, 808/239–5711 ⊕ www.paradisebayresort.com ⟿ 57 units ⊠ In-room: kitchen. In-hotel: pool ¶⊙¶ Breakfast.

THE NORTH SHORE

$ ⊡ **Ke Iki Beach Bungalows.** At this 1½-acre sloped beachfront lot with

RENTAL six duplex bungalows, you can choose from studios to one- or two-bedroom units outfitted with breezy beach-house furnishings, individual grills and picnic tables, and access to a 200-foot strand of creamy white-sand beach running between the North Shore's famous Waimea Bay and Ehukai Beach (Banzai Pipeline). **Pros:** helpful and friendly staff; great prices; steps to the beach. **Cons:** a bit far from restaurants and shopping. ⊠ 59-579 Ke Iki Rd., Haleiwa ☎ 808/638–8829, 866/638–8229 ⊕ www.keikibeach.com ⟿ 11 units ⊠ In-room: no a/c, kitchen. In-hotel: beach, laundry facilities, parking ¶⊙¶ No meals.

$$$$ ⊡ **The Turtle Bay Resort.** Sprawling over 880 acres of natural landscape

RESORT on the edge of Kuilima Point in Kahuku, the luxe Turtle Bay Resort

Fodor's Choice boasts spacious guest rooms averaging nearly 500 square feet, with

★ lanai that showcase stunning peninsula views. **Pros:** great open, public spaces in a secluded area of Oahu; world-class spa. **Cons:** very far from anything else—even Haleiwa is a 20-minute drive; hotel charges a $25 per night resort fee. ⊠ 57-091 Kamehameha Hwy., Box 187, Kahuku ☎ 808/293–8811, 800/203–3650 ⊕ www.turtlebayresort.com ⟿ 373 rooms, 40 suites, 42 beach cottages, 56 ocean villas ⊠ In-room: a/c, Wi-Fi. In-hotel: restaurant, bar, golf course, tennis court, pool, gym, spa, beach, children's programs ¶⊙¶ No meals.

WEST (LEEWARD) OAHU

9

$$$$ ⊡ **Aulani, A Disney Resort & Spa.** In

RESORT September 2011, Disney opened

 its first hotel and time-share develoment not connected to a theme park, and first property in Hawaii, in the resort area of Ko Olina, about a 40-minute drive from Waikiki on Oahu's leeward side. **Pros:** tons to do on premise; very kid-friendly; a 1,500-square-foot teens-only spa with a private entrance, yogurt bar, and teen-specific treatments. **Cons:** a long way from Waikiki; "character break-fasts" are often sold out; resort still under construction. ⊠ 92-1185 Aliinui Dr., Ko Olina, Kapolei ☎ 714/520–7001, 808/674–6200, 866/443–4763 ⊕ resorts.disney.

CONDO COMFORTS

The local **Foodland** (⊠ Market City, 2939 Harding Ave., near intersection with Kapahulu Ave. and highway overpass, Kai-muki ☎ 808/734–6303 ⊠ Ala Moana Center, 1450 Ala Moana Blvd., ground level, Ala Moana ☎ 808/949–5044) grocery-store chain has two locations near Waikiki. A smaller version of larger Foodland, **Food Pantry** (⊠ 2370 Kuhio Ave., across from Miramar hotel, Waikiki ☎ 808/923–9831) also has apparel, beach stuff, and tourist-oriented items.

Turtle Bay Resort

go.com/aulani-hawaii-resort ↩ 359 rooms, 481 villas ⚓ In-room: a/c, safe, kitchen, Internet, Wi-Fi. In-hotel: restaurant, bar, pool, gym, spa, beach, water sports, children's programs, laundry facilities, business center, parking ❍❙ No meals.

$$$$ ⚟ **JW Marriott Ihilani Resort & Spa.**
RESORT Forty-five minutes and a world
🕯 away from the bustle of Waikiki, this sleek, 17-story resort anchors the still-developing Ko Olina Resort and Marina on Oahu's leeward

WORD OF MOUTH

"I would suggest you stay up at the North Shore for a few nights and then maybe spend a few nights in lovely Kailua, or vice versa depending on the availability. You can drive from Kailua up the leeward side to North Shore in about an hour if you decided to just stay down there." —Tomsd

coastline. **Pros:** beautiful property; impeccable service; pool is stunning at night. **Cons:** a bit of a drive from Honolulu; rental car a must. ✉ *92-1001 Olani St., Ko Olina, Kapolei* ☎ *808/679–0079, 800/626–4446* ⊕ *www.ihilani.com ↩ 387 rooms, 36 suites ⚓ In-room: a/c. In-hotel: restaurant, golf course, tennis court, pool, spa, beach, children's programs* ❍❙ *No meals.*

$$$$ ⚟ **Marriott Ko Olina Beach Vacation Club.** If you have your heart set on
HOTEL getting away to Oahu's western shores, check out the Marriott, which
🕯 is primarily a vacation-ownership property, though it also offers nightly rental rates for its rooms, which range from hotel-style standard guest rooms to expansive and elegantly appointed one- or two-bedroom guest villa apartments. **Pros:** suites are beautifully decorated and have ample space for families; full kitchens; nice views; fairly private lagoon; on-site luau and dinner show. **Cons:** at least a half-hour drive to Honolulu; ongoing construction at other properties nearby. ✉ *92-161 Waipahe Pl., Ko Olina, Kapolei* ☎ *808/679–4900, 877/229–4484* ⊕ *www.marriottvacationclub.com ↩ 200 units ⚓ In-room: a/c, safe, kitchen, Wi-Fi. In-hotel: restaurant, bar, golf course, tennis court, pool, gym, beach, children's programs, parking* ❍❙ *No meals.*

9

HAWAIIAN VOCABULARY

Although an understanding of Hawaiian is by no means required on a trip to the Aloha State, a *malihini*, or newcomer, will find plenty of opportunities to pick up a few of the local words and phrases. Traditional names and expressions are widely used in the Islands. You're likely to read or hear at least a few words each day of your stay.

With a basic understanding and some uninhibited practice, anyone can have enough command of the local tongue to ask for directions and to order from a restaurant menu. One visitor announced she would not leave until she could pronounce the name of the state fish, the *humuhumunukunukuāpua'a*.

Simplifying the learning process is the fact that the Hawaiian language contains only eight consonants—H, K, L, M, N, P, W, and the silent *'okina*, or glottal stop, written '—plus one or more of the five vowels. All syllables, and therefore all words, end in a vowel. Each vowel, with the exception of a few diphthongized double vowels such as *au* (pronounced "ow") or *ai* (pronounced "eye"), is pronounced separately. Thus *'Iolani* is four syllables (ee-oh-la-nee), not three (yo-la-nee). Although some Hawaiian words have only vowels, most also contain some consonants, but consonants are never doubled.

Pronunciation is simple. Pronounce *A* "ah" as in *father*; *E* "ay" as in *weigh*; *I* "ee" as in *marine*; *O* "oh" as in *no*; *U* "oo" as in *true*.

Consonants mirror their English equivalents, with the exception of *W*. When the letter begins any syllable other than the first one in a word, it is usually pronounced as a *V*. *'Awa*, the Polynesian drink, is pronounced "ava," *'ewa* is pronounced "eva."

Almost all long Hawaiian words are combinations of shorter words; they are not difficult to pronounce if you segment them. *Kalaniana'ole*, the highway running east from Honolulu, is easily understood as *Kalani ana 'ole*. Apply the standard pronunciation rules—the stress falls on the next-to-last syllable of most two- or three-syllable Hawaiian words—and Kalaniana'ole Highway is as easy to say as Main Street.

Now about that fish. Try *humu-humu nuku-nuku āpu a'a*.

The other unusual element in Hawaiian language is the *kahakō*, or macron, written as a short line (ˉ) placed over a vowel. Like the accent (´) in Spanish, the kahakō puts emphasis on a syllable that would normally not be stressed. The most familiar example is probably *Waikīkī*. With no macrons, the stress would fall on the middle syllable; with only one macron, on the last syllable, the stress would fall on the first and last syllables. Some words become plural with the addition of a macron, often on a syllable that would have been stressed anyway. No Hawaiian word becomes plural with the addition of an *S*, since that letter does not exist in the language.

The Hawaiian diacritical marks are not printed in this guide.

'a'ā: rough, crumbling lava, contrasting with *pāhoehoe*, which is smooth.

'ae: yes.

aikane: friend.

āina: land.

akamai: smart, clever, possessing savoir faire.

akua: god.

ala: a road, path, or trail.

ali'i: a Hawaiian chief, a member of the chiefly class.

aloha: love, affection, kindness; also a salutation meaning both greetings and farewell.

'ānuenue: rainbow.

'a'ole: no.

'apōpō: tomorrow.

'auwai: a ditch.

auwē: alas, woe is me!

'ehu: a red-haired Hawaiian.

'ewa: in the direction of 'Ewa plantation, west of Honolulu.

hala: the pandanus tree, whose leaves (*lau hala*) are used to make baskets and plaited mats.

hālau: school.

hale: a house.

hale pule: church, house of worship.

ha mea iki or **ha mea 'ole:** you're welcome.

hana: to work.

haole: ghost. Since the first foreigners were Caucasian, *haole* now means a Caucasian person.

hapa: a part, sometimes a half; often used as a short form of *hapa haole*, to mean a person who is part-Caucasian.

hau'oli: to rejoice. *Hau'oli Makahiki Hou* means Happy New Year. *Hau'oli lā hānau* means Happy Birthday.

heiau: an outdoor stone platform; an ancient Hawaiian place of worship.

holo: to run.

holoholo: to go for a walk, ride, or sail.

holokū: a long Hawaiian dress, somewhat fitted, with a yoke and a train. Influenced by European fashion, it was worn at court, and at least one local translates the word as "expensive mu'umu'u."

holomū: a post–World War II cross between a *holokū* and a mu'umu'u, less fitted than the former but less voluminous than the latter, and having no train.

honi: to kiss; a kiss. A phrase that some tourists may find useful, quoted from a popular hula, is *Honi Ka'ua Wikiwiki:* Kiss me quick!

honu: turtle.

ho'omalimali: flattery, a deceptive "line," bunk, baloney, hooey.

huhū: angry.

hui: a group, club, or assembly. A church may refer to its congregation as a *hui* and a social club may be called a *hui*.

hukilau: a seine; a communal fishing party in which everyone helps to drive the fish into a huge net, pull it in, and divide the catch.

hula: the dance of Hawai'i.

iki: little.

ipo: sweetheart.

ka: the. This is the definite article for most singular words; for plural nouns, the definite article is usually *nā*. Since there is no *S* in Hawaiian, the article may be your only clue that a noun is plural.

kahuna: a priest, doctor, or other trained person of old Hawai'i, endowed with special professional skills that often included prophecy or other supernatural powers; the plural form is kāhuna.

kai: the sea, saltwater.

kalo: the taro plant from whose root *poi* (paste) is made.

kamā'aina: literally, a child of the soil; it refers to people who were born in the Islands or have lived there for a long time.

kanaka: originally a man or humanity, it is now used to denote a male Hawaiian or part-Hawaiian, but is occasionally taken as a slur when used by non-Hawaiians. *Kanaka maoli,* originally a full-blooded Hawaiian person, is used by some native Hawaiian rights activists to embrace part-Hawaiians as well.

kāne: a man, a husband. If you see this word on a door, it's the men's room. If you see *kane* on a door, it's probably a misspelling; that is the Hawaiian name for the skin fungus tinea.

kapa: also called by its Tahitian name, *tapa,* a cloth made of beaten bark and usually dyed and stamped with a repeat design.

kapakahi: crooked, cockeyed, uneven. You've got your hat on *kapakahi*.

kapu: keep out, prohibited. This is the Hawaiian version of the more widely known Tongan word *tabu* (taboo).

kapuna: grandparent; elder.

kēia lā: today.

keiki: a child; *keikikāne* is a boy, *keikiwahine* a girl.

kona: the leeward side of the Islands, the direction (south) from which the *kona* wind and *kona* rain come.

kula: upland.

kuleana: a homestead or small plot of ground on which a family has been installed for some generations without necessarily owning it. By extension, *kuleana* is used to denote any area or department in which one has a special interest or prerogative. You'll hear it used this way: If you want to hire a surfboard, see Moki; that's his *kuleana*.

lā: sun.

lamalama: to fish with a torch.

lānai: a porch, a balcony, an outdoor living room. Almost every house in Hawaii has one. Don't confuse this two-syllable word with the three-syllable name of the island, Lāna'i.

lani: heaven, the sky.

lau hala: the leaf of the *hala*, or pandanus tree, widely used in handicrafts.

lei: a garland of flowers.

limu: sun.

lolo: stupid.

luna: a plantation overseer or foreman.

mahalo: thank you.

makai: toward the ocean.

malihini: a newcomer to the Islands.

mana: the spiritual power that the Hawaiian believed inhabited all things and creatures.

manō: shark.

manuwahi: free, gratis.

mauka: toward the mountains.

mauna: mountain.

mele: a Hawaiian song or chant, often of epic proportions.

Mele Kalikimaka: Merry Christmas (a transliteration from the English phrase).

Menehune: a Hawaiian pixie. The *Menehune* were a legendary race of little people who accomplished prodigious work, such as building fishponds and temples in the course of a single night.

moana: the ocean.

mu'umu'u: the voluminous dress in which the missionaries enveloped Hawaiian women. Now made in bright printed cottons and silks, it is an indispensable garment. Culturally sensitive locals have embraced the Hawaiian spelling but often shorten the spoken word to "mu'u." Most English dictionaries include the spelling "muumuu."

nani: beautiful.

nui: big.

ohana: family.

'ono: delicious.

pāhoehoe: smooth, unbroken, satiny lava.

Pākē: Chinese. This *Pākē* carver makes beautiful things.

palapala: document, printed matter.

pali: a cliff, precipice.

pānini: prickly pear cactus.

paniolo: a Hawaiian cowboy, a rough transliteration of *español*, the language of the Islands' earliest cowboys.

pau: finished, done.

pilikia: trouble. The Hawaiian word is much more widely used here than its English equivalent.

puka: a hole.

pupule: crazy, like the celebrated Princess Pupule. This word has replaced its English equivalent in local usage.

pu'u: volcanic cinder cone.

waha: mouth.

wahine: a female, a woman, a wife, and a sign on the ladies' room door; the plural form is *wāhine*.

wai: freshwater, as opposed to saltwater, which is *kai*.

wailele: waterfall.

wikiwiki: to hurry, hurry up (since this is a reduplication of *wiki*, quick, neither W is pronounced as a V).

Note: Pidgin is the unofficial language of Hawaii. It is a Creole language, with its own grammar, evolved from the mixture of English, Hawaiian, Japanese, Portuguese, and other languages spoken in 19th-century Hawaii, and it is heard everywhere.

Travel Smart Oahu

GETTING HERE AND AROUND

Yes, Oahu is a wonderful tourist destination, and on any given day there are more than 100,000 visitors on the island. It's also home to about 75% of the 1.4 million people who live in Hawaii. And, as the capital of the state and the financial crossroads to Asia and the Pacific, Honolulu is among the nation's largest cities. So, needless to say, you'll find lots of cars and traffic, especially during the morning and afternoon drive times. Visitors may be able to navigate more easily by orienting themselves to a few major landmarks. Oahu is made up of two extinct volcanoes, which form what is today the island's two mountain ranges: Waianae and Koolau. The Waianae range curves from Kaena State Park, on the island's westernmost point, past Makaha, Waianae, and Nanakuli to Ko Olina, a growing resort town on the sunny leeward shore. The extinct craters of Diamond Head and Koko Head are usually visible from anywhere along the island's leeward coast. The Koolau Range forms a jagged spine that runs from the island's eastern tip along the windward coast to the famous surfing center on the North Shore.

The island's volcanic origins have limited Oahu's developments to tidal flats and ridgelines, and as a result the city and county have many one-way streets and limited public parking. Honolulu's public transportation system, TheBus, is a stress-free, affordable, and convenient way to get around. There are routes that will take you to all of the major attractions, neighborhoods, and sightseeing locations around the island.

■ AIR TRAVEL

Flying time to Oahu is about 10 hours from New York, 8 hours from Chicago, and 5 hours from Los Angeles.

All of the major airline carriers serving Hawaii fly direct to Honolulu; some also offer nonstops to Maui, Kauai, and the Big Island. Honolulu International Airport, although open-air and seemingly more casual than most major airports, can be very busy. Allow extra travel time during busy mornings and afternoons.

Plants and plant products are subject to regulation by the Department of Agriculture, both on entering and leaving Hawaii. Upon leaving, you'll have to have your bags x-rayed and tagged at the airport's agricultural inspection station before you proceed to check-in. Pineapples and coconuts with the packer's agricultural inspection stamp pass freely; papayas must be treated, inspected, and stamped. All other fruits are banned for export to the U.S. mainland. Flowers pass except for gardenia, rose leaves, jade vine, and mauna loa. Also banned are insects, snails, soil, cotton, cacti, sugarcane, and all berry plants.

You'll have to leave dogs and other pets at home. A 120-day quarantine is imposed to keep out rabies, which is nonexistent in Hawaii. If specific pre- and postarrival requirements are met, animals may qualify for a 30-day or 5-day-or-less quarantine.

Airline Security Issues Transportation Security Administration ☎ *808/831–2755* ⊕ *www.tsa.gov.*

Air-Travel Resources in Oahu State of Hawaii Airports Division Offices ☎ *808/836–6413* ⊕ *www.hawaii.gov/dot/airports.*

AIRPORTS

Honolulu International Airport (HNL) is 20 minutes (9 miles) west of Waikiki, and is served by most of the major domestic and international carriers. To travel to other Islands from Honolulu, you can depart from either the interisland terminal or the commuter-airline terminal, located in two separate structures adjacent to the main overseas terminal building. A free Wiki Wiki shuttle bus operates between terminals.

If you have time after you've checked in for your flight home, visit the Pacific Aerospace Museum, open daily, in the main terminal. It includes a 1,700-square-foot, three-dimensional, multimedia theater presenting the history of flight in Hawaii, and a full-scale space-shuttle flight deck. Hands-on exhibits include a mission-control computer program tracing flights in the Pacific.

Airport Information Honolulu International Airport (HNL) ☎ *808/836-6413* ⊕ *www. hawaii.gov/dot/airports.*

GROUND TRANSPORTATION

Some hotels have their own pickup service, so check when you book accommodations.

Taxi service is available on the center median just outside baggage-claim areas. Look for the taxi dispatchers wearing green shirts who will radio for a taxi. The fare to Waikiki runs approximately $35 to $40, plus 50¢ per bag, and tip. If your baggage is oversized, there is an additional charge of $4.60.

Roberts Hawaii, a major bus company, launched a shuttle service that will greet you at the arrival gate, escort you to baggage claim, and take you to your hotel. Call ahead for the service, which costs $12 for one-way service, $20 round-trip.

TheBus, the municipal bus, will take you into Waikiki for only $2, but you are allowed only one bag, which must fit on your lap.

Contacts Roberts Hawaii ☎ *808/539-9400* ⊕ *www.robertshawaii.com.* **TheBus** ☎ *808/848-5555* ⊕ *www.thebus.org.*

FLIGHTS

From the U.S. mainland, Alaska Airlines, Continental, Delta, Hawaiian, and United serve Honolulu.

Airline Contacts Alaska Airlines ☎ *800/252-7522* ⊕ *www.alaskaair.com.* **Delta Airlines** ☎ *800/221-1212 for U.S. reservations, 800/241-4141 for international reservations* ⊕ *www.delta.com.* **Hawaiian Airlines** ☎ *800/367-5320* ⊕ *www.hawaiianair.com.*

United Airlines ☎ *800/864-8331 for U.S. reservations, 800/538-2929 for international reservations* ⊕ *www.united.com.*

CHARTER FLIGHTS

Three companies provide charter flights between the Islands. In business since 1998, go! Mokulele Airlines offers nonstop charter service from Oahu to Lanai and Maui. The company also serves the Big Island, Kauai, and Molokai. Pacific Wings serves Oahu, Lanai, Maui, Molokai, and the Big Island. Premiere (sameday departures) and premium (24-hour notice) service is available. Paragon Air offers 24-hour private charter service from any airport in Hawaii. In business since 1980, the company prides itself on its perfect safety record and such celebrity passengers as Bill Gates, Michael Douglas, and Kevin Costner. You also can arrange a customized tour of neighboring islands.

Charter Companies go! Mokulele Airlines ☎ *808/326-7070* ⊕ *www.iflygo.com.* **Pacific Wings** ☎ *888/575-4546* ⊕ *www.pacificwings. com.*

INTERISLAND FLIGHTS

If you've allotted more than a week for your vacation, you may want to consider visiting a Neighbor Island. From Honolulu, flights depart almost hourly from early morning until evening. Since each flight lasts only 30 to 60 minutes, you can watch the sunrise on Oahu and sunset on the Big Island, Kauai, Lanai, Maui, or Molokai. To simplify your vacation, schedule your return flight to Oahu so that it coincides with your flight home.

Hawaiian Airlines, Island Air, go! Mokulele Airlines, and Pacific Wings offer regular service between the Islands, so be sure to compare prices. All have frequent-flyer programs that entitle you to rewards and upgrades. A number of wholesalers offer Neighbor Island packages including air, hotel, rental car, and even visitor attractions or activities.

Interisland Flights go! Mokulele Airlines ☎ *808/326-7070* ⊕ *www.iflygo.com.* **Hawaiian Airlines** (☎ *800/367-5320* ⊕ *www.*

hawaiianair.com). **IslandAir** ☎ *800/323–3345* ⊕ *www.islandair.com.*

▌ BOAT TRAVEL

CRUISES

For information about cruises, see Chapter 1, Experience Oahu.

▌ BUS TRAVEL

Getting around by bus is a convenient and affordable option on Oahu. In addition to TheBus and the Waikiki Trolley, Waikiki has brightly painted private buses, many of them free, that shuttle you to such commercial attractions as dinner cruises, garment factories, and the like.

You can travel around the island or just down Kalakaua Avenue for $2.50 on Honolulu's municipal transportation system, affectionately known as TheBus. It's one of the island's best bargains. Buses make stops in Waikiki every 15 minutes to take passengers to nearby shopping areas.

You're entitled to one free transfer, so ask for one when boarding. Exact change is required, and dollar bills are accepted. A four-day pass for visitors costs $25 and is available at ABC convenience stores in Waikiki and in the Ala Moana Shopping Center. Monthly passes cost $60.

There are no official bus-route maps, but you can find privately published booklets at most drugstores and other convenience outlets. The important route numbers for Waikiki are 2, 4, 8, 19, 20, 58, and City Express Route B. If you venture farther afield, you can always travel back on one of these buses.

Bus Information TheBus ☎ *808/848–5555* ⊕ *www.thebus.org.*

▌ CAR TRAVEL

Except for one area around Kaena Point, major highways follow Oahu's shoreline and traverse the island at two points. Rush-hour traffic (6:30 to 9:30 am and 3:30 to 6 pm) can be frustrating around Honolulu and the outlying areas. Winter swells also bring traffic to the North Shore, as people hoping to catch some of the surfing action clog the two-lane Kamehameha Highway. Parking along many streets is curtailed during these times, and tow-away zones are strictly enforced. Read curbside signs before leaving your vehicle, even at a meter.

Asking for directions will almost always produce a helpful explanation from the locals, but you should be prepared for an island term or two. Instead of using compass directions, remember that Hawaii residents refer to places as being either *mauka* (toward the mountains) or *makai* (toward the ocean). Other directions depend on your location: in Honolulu, for example, people say to "go Diamond Head," which means toward that famous landmark, or to "go *ewa,*" meaning in the opposite direction. A shop on the *mauka*–Diamond Head corner of a street is on the mountain side of the street on the corner closest to Diamond Head. It all makes perfect sense once you get the lay of the land.

GASOLINE

You can pretty much count on having to pay more at the pump for gasoline on Oahu than on the U.S. mainland.

ROAD CONDITIONS

Oahu is relatively easy to navigate. Roads, although their names are often a challenge for the tongue, are well marked; just watch out for the many one-way streets in Waikiki and downtown Honolulu. Keep an eye open for the Hawaii Visitors and Convention Bureau's red-caped King Kamehameha signs, which mark major attractions and scenic spots. Ask for a map at the car-rental counter. Free publications containing helpful maps are found at most hotels throughout Waikiki.

ROADSIDE EMERGENCIES

In case of an accident, pull over if you can. If you have a cell phone, call the roadside assistance number on your car-rental contract or AAA Help. If your car has been broken into or stolen, report it immediately to your rental-car company. If it's an emergency and someone is hurt, call 911 immediately.

Emergency Services AAA Help ☎ *800/222–4357* ⊕ *www.hawaii.aaa.com.*

RULES OF THE ROAD

Be sure to buckle up, as Hawaii has a strictly enforced seat-belt law for front-seat passengers. Children 18 and under, riding in the backseat, are required by state law to use seat belts. Children under four must be in a car seat (available from car-rental agencies). The highway speed limit is usually 55 mph. In-town traffic moves from 25 to 40 mph. Jaywalking is not uncommon, so watch for pedestrians, especially in congested areas such as Waikiki and downtown Honolulu. Unauthorized use of a parking space reserved for persons with disabilities can net you a $150 fine.

Oahu's drivers are generally courteous, and you rarely hear a horn. People will slow down and let you into traffic with a wave of the hand. A friendly wave back is customary. If a driver sticks a hand out the window in a fist with the thumb and pinky sticking straight out, this is a good thing: it's the *shaka,* the Hawaiian symbol for "hang loose," and is often used to say "thanks."

CAR RENTAL

Hotel parking garages charge upwards of $20 per day, so if you're staying in Waikiki you may want to rent a car only when you plan to sightsee around the island. You can easily walk or take public transportation to many of the attractions in and around the area.

If you are staying outside of Waikiki, your best bet is to rent a car. Even though the city bus is a wonderfully affordable way to get around the island, you'll want the flexibility of having your own transportation, especially if you're planning lots of stops.

■ **TIP➔ Make sure that a confirmed reservation guarantees you a car. Agencies**

sometimes overbook, particularly for busy weekends and holiday periods.

You can rent anything from an econobox and motorcycle to a Ferrari while on Oahu. Rates are usually better if you reserve through a rental agency's website. It's wise to make reservations far in advance, especially if visiting during peak seasons.

Rates in Honolulu begin at about $25 a day for an economy car with air-conditioning, automatic transmission, and unlimited mileage. This does not include the airport concession fee, general excise tax, rental-vehicle surcharge or vehicle-license fee. When you reserve a car, ask about cancellation penalties and drop-off charges, should you plan to pick up the car in one location and return it to another. Many rental companies offer coupons for discounts at various attractions that could save you money later on in your trip.

In Hawaii you must be 21 years of age to rent a car, and you must have a valid driver's license and a major credit card. Those under 25 will pay a daily surcharge of $15 to $25. Request car seats and extras such as GPS when you make your reservation. Hawaii's Child Restraint Law requires that all children three years and younger be in an approved child safety seat in the backseat of a vehicle. Children ages four to seven must be seated in a rear booster seat or child restraint such as a lap and shoulder belt. Car seats and boosters range from $8 to $12 a day.

In Hawaii your unexpired mainland driver's license is valid for rental for up to 90 days.

Be sure to allow plenty of time to return your vehicle so that you can make your flight. Traffic in Honolulu is terrible during morning and afternoon rush hours. Give yourself about 3½ to 4 hours before departure time to return your vehicle if you're traveling during these peak times; otherwise plan on about 2½ to 3 hours.

Car Rental Resources

Automobile Associations

U.S.: American Automobile Association	☎ 315/797–5000	⊕ www.aaa.com
National Automobile Club	☎ 650/294–7000	⊕ www.thenac.com; CA residents only

Major Agencies

Alamo	☎ 800/462–5266	⊕ www.alamo.com
Avis	☎ 800/331–1212	⊕ www.avis.com
Budget	☎ 800/527–0700	⊕ www.budget.com
Hertz	☎ 800/654–3131	⊕ www.hertz.com
National Car Rental	☎ 800/227–7368	⊕ www.nationalcar.com
Thrifty Car Rental	☎ 888/400–8877	⊕ www.thrifty.com

▌TAXI TRAVEL

Taxis can be found at the airport, in the more popular resort areas, or by calling local taxi companies. Rates are $3.10 at the drop of the flag and each additional mile is $3.20. Drivers are generally courteous and the cars are in good condition, many of them air-conditioned. In addition, taxi and limousine companies can provide a car and driver for half-day or daylong island tours, and a number of companies also offer personal guides. Remember, however, that rates are quite steep for these services, ranging from $100 to $200 or more per day.

Taxi Companies Carey Hawaii Chauffeured Services ☎ *888/563–2888, 808/572–3400* ⊕ *www.careyhawaii.com.* **Charley's Taxi & Limousine** ☎ *808/233–3333* ⊕ *www. charleystaxi.com.* **Elite Limousine Service** ☎ *800/776–2098, 808/735–2431* ⊕ *www. elitelimohawaii.com.* **The Cab Hawaii** ☎ *808/422–2222* ⊕ *www.thecabhawaii.com.*

▌TROLLEY TRAVEL

The Waikiki Trolley has four lines and dozens of stops that allow you to plan your own itinerary while riding on brass-trimmed, open-air trolleys. The Honolulu City Line (Red Line) travels between Waikiki and the Bishop Museum and includes stops at Aloha Tower, Ala Moana, and downtown Honolulu. The Ocean Coast Line (Blue Line) provides a tour of Oahu's southeastern coast, including Diamond Head Crater, Hanauma Bay, and Sea Life Park. The Blue Line also has a twice-daily express trolley to Diamond Head. The Ala Moana Shuttle Line (Pink Line) departs from the DFS Galleria Waikiki or Hilton Hawaiian Village and stops at Ward Warehouse, Ward Centers, and Ala Moana Shopping Center. The Local Shopping and Dining Line (Yellow Line) starts at Ala Moana Center and has stops at Ward Farmers' Market, Ward Warehouse, and Ward Centers. A one-day pass costs $25, and four-day passes are $43. There are often money-saving online deals.

Information Waikiki Trolley ☎ *808/593–2822, 800/824–8804* ⊕ *www.waikikitrolley. com.*

ESSENTIALS

■ BUSINESS SERVICES AND FACILITIES

The Hawaii Convention Center, located at the entrance to Waikiki, is a gorgeous facility that captures the spirit of Hawaii through its open-air spaces, tropical gardens, and soaring forms that resemble Polynesian canoes. The center also boasts a $2 million art collection featuring the work of dozens of local artists. The Hawaii Visitors & Convention Bureau's website has a directory of products and services.

Contacts Hawaii Convention Center
⊠ *1801 Kalakaua Ave., Waikiki, Honolulu* 🖷 *808/943-3500* ⊕ *www.hawaiiconvention. com.* **Hawaii Visitors & Convention Bureau** ⊕ *www.meethawaii.com.*

■ COMMUNICATIONS

INTERNET

Most of the major hotels and resorts offer high-speed access in rooms and lobbies. Check with your hotel in advance to confirm that access is wireless; if not, ask whether in-room cables are provided. In some cases there will be an hourly or daily charge. If you're staying at a small inn or B&B that doesn't have Internet access, ask about the nearest café or coffee shop that does.

Contacts Cybercafés. Cybercafés lists more than 4,000 Internet cafés worldwide. ⊕ *www. cybercafes.com.* **JiWire.** JiWire features a directory of Wi-Fi hotspots around the world. ⊕ *www.jiwire.com.*

■ EMERGENCIES

To reach the police, fire department, or an ambulance in an emergency, dial 911.

A doctor, laboratory-radiology technician, and nurses are always on duty at Doctors on Call. Appointments are not necessary. Dozens of medical insurance plans are accepted, including Medicare, Medicaid, and most kinds of travel insurance.

Kuhio Pharmacy is Waikiki's only pharmacy and handles prescriptions only until 4:30 pm. Longs Drugs is open evenings at its Ala Moana location and 24 hours at its South King Street location (a 15-minute drive from Waikiki). Pillbox Pharmacy, located in Kaimuki, will deliver prescription medications for a small fee.

Doctors and Dentists Doctors on Call ⊠ *Sheraton Princess Kaiulani Hotel, 120 Kaiulani Ave., Waikiki, Honolulu* 🖷 *808/971-6000.*

General Emergency Contacts Coast Guard Rescue Center 🖷 *808/535-3333.*

Hospitals and Clinics Castle Medical Center ⊠ *640 Ulukahiki St., Kailua* 🖷 *808/263-5500* ⊕ *castlemed.org.* **Kapiolani Medical Center for Women and Children** ⊠ *1319 Punahou St., Makiki Heights, Honolulu* 🖷 *808/983-6000.* **Queen's Medical Center** ⊠ *1301 Punchbowl St., Downtown Honolulu, Honolulu* 🖷 *808/538-9011.* **Saint Francis Medical Center-West** ⊠ *91-2141 Fort Weaver Rd., Ewa Beach* 🖷 *808/678-7000.* **Straub Clinic** ⊠ *888 S. King St., Downtown Honolulu, Honolulu* 🖷 *808/522-4000.*

Pharmacies Longs Drugs ⊠ *Ala Moana Shopping Center, 1450 Ala Moana Blvd., 2nd level, near Sears, Ala Moana, Honolulu* 🖷 *808/949-4010* 🖷 *2470 S. King St., Moiliili, Honolulu* 🖷 *808/947-2651.* **Kuhio Pharmacy** ⊠ *Outrigger West Hotel, 2330 Kuhio Ave., Waikiki, Honolulu* 🖷 *808/923-4466.* **Pillbox Pharmacy** ⊠ *1133 11th Ave., Kaimuki, Honolulu* 🖷 *808/737-1777.*

■ HEALTH

Hawaii is known not only as the Aloha State, but also as the Health State. The life expectancy here is 80.8 years, the longest in the nation. Balmy weather makes it easy to remain active year-round, and the low-stress attitude contributes to the general well-being. When visiting the Islands, however, there are a few health issues to keep in mind.

The Hawaii State Department of Health recommends that you drink 16 ounces of water per hour to avoid dehydration when hiking or spending time in the sun. Use sunblock, wear UV–reflective sunglasses, and protect your head with a visor or hat. If you're not acclimated to warm, humid weather, you should allow plenty of time for rest stops and refreshments. When visiting freshwater streams, be aware of the tropical disease leptospirosis, spread by animal urine and carried into streams and mud. Symptoms include fever, headache, nausea, and red eyes. If left untreated it can cause liver and kidney damage, respiratory failure, internal bleeding, and even death. To avoid this, don't swim or wade in freshwater streams or ponds if you have open sores and don't drink from any freshwater streams or ponds.

On the Islands, fog is a rare occurrence, but there can often be "vog," an airborne haze of gases released from volcanic vents on the Big Island. During certain weather conditions such as "Kona Winds," the vog can settle over the Islands and wreak havoc with respiratory and other health conditions, especially asthma or emphysema. If susceptible, stay indoors and get emergency assistance if needed.

The Islands have their share of insects. Most are harmless but annoying. When planning to spend time outdoors in hiking areas, wear long-sleeve clothing and pants and use mosquito repellent containing DEET. In damp places you may encounter the dreaded local centipedes, which are brown and blue and measure up to eight inches long. Their painful sting is similar to those of bees and wasps. When camping, shake out your sleeping bag and check your shoes, as the centipedes like cozy places. When hiking in remote areas, always carry a first-aid kit.

▌ HOURS OF OPERATION

Even people in paradise have to work. Generally local business hours are weekdays 8 to 5. Banks are usually open Monday to Thursday 8:30 to 3 and until 6 on Friday. Some banks have Saturday-morning hours.

Many self-serve gas stations stay open around the clock, with full-service stations usually open from around 7 am until 9 pm. U.S. post offices are open weekdays 8:30 to 4:30 and Saturday 8:30 to noon. On Oahu, the Ala Moana post office is the only branch, other than the main Honolulu International Airport facility, that stays open until 4 pm on Saturday.

Most museums generally open their doors between 9 and 10 and stay open until 5 Tuesday to Saturday. Many museums operate with afternoon hours only on Sunday and close on Monday. Visitor-attraction hours vary, but most sights are open daily with the exception of major holidays such as Christmas. Check the local newspaper upon arrival for attraction hours and schedules if visiting over holiday periods. The local daily carries a listing of "What's Open/What's Not" for those time periods.

Stores in resort areas sometimes open as early as 8, with shopping-center opening hours varying from 9 to 10 on weekdays and Saturday, a bit later on Sunday. Bigger malls stay open until 9 weekdays and Saturday and close at 5 on Sunday. Boutiques in resort areas may stay open as late as 11.

▌ MONEY

Prices here are given for adults. Substantially reduced fees are almost always available for children, students, and senior citizens.

ATMS AND BANKS

Automatic-teller machines, for easy access to cash, can be found at many locations throughout Oahu, including shopping centers, convenience and grocery stores, and hotels and resorts, as well as outside most bank branches. For a directory of locations, call ☎ *800/424–7787* for the MasterCard/Cirrus/Maestro network or ☎ *800/843–7587* for the Visa/Plus network.

CREDIT CARDS

It's a good idea to inform your credit-card company before you travel. Otherwise, the credit-card company might put a hold on your card owing to unusual activity—not a good thing halfway through your trip. Record all your credit-card numbers—as well as the phone numbers to call if your cards are lost or stolen—in a safe place, so you're prepared should something go wrong. Both MasterCard and Visa have general numbers you can call (collect if you're abroad) if your card is lost, but you're better off calling the number of your issuing bank, since MasterCard and Visa usually just transfer you to your bank; your bank's number is usually printed on your card.

Reporting Lost Cards American Express ☎ *800/528–4800 in the U.S., 336/393–1111 collect from abroad* ⊕ *www.americanexpress. com.* **Diners Club** ☎ *800/234–6377 in the U.S., 303/799–1504 collect from abroad* ⊕ *www.dinersclub.com.* **Discover** ☎ *800/347–2683 in the U.S., 801/902–3100 collect from abroad* ⊕ *www.discover.com.* **MasterCard** ☎ *800/627–8372 in the U.S., 636/722–7111 collect from abroad* ⊕ *www.mastercard.com.* **Visa** ☎ *800/847–2911 in the U.S., 410/581–9994 collect from abroad* ⊕ *www.visa.com.*

TRAVELER'S CHECKS

Some consider this the currency of the cave man, and it's true that fewer establishments accept traveler's checks these days. Nevertheless, they're a cheap and secure way to carry extra money, particularly on trips to urban areas. Both Citibank (under the Visa brand) and American Express issue traveler's checks in the United States, but Amex is better known and more widely accepted; you can also avoid hefty surcharges by cashing Amex checks at Amex offices. Whatever you do, keep track of all the serial numbers in case the checks are lost or stolen.

Contacts American Express ☎ *800/528–4800 in the U.S., 801/945–9450 collect outside of the U.S. to speak to customer service* ⊕ *www.americanexpress.com.*

▮ PACKING

Oahu is casual: sandals, bathing suits, and comfortable, informal clothing are the norm. In summer synthetic slacks and shirts, although easy to care for, can be uncomfortably warm.

There's a saying that when a man wears a suit during the day, he's either going for a loan or he's a lawyer trying a case. Only a few upscale restaurants require a jacket for dinner. The aloha shirt is accepted dress on Oahu for business and most social occasions. Shorts are acceptable daytime attire, along with a T-shirt or polo shirt. There's no need to buy expensive sandals on the mainland—here you can get flip-flops for a couple of dollars and off-brand sandals for $20. Golfers should remember that many courses have dress codes requiring a collared shirt; call courses you're interested in for details. If you're not prepared, you can pick up appropriate clothing at resort pro shops. If you're visiting in winter or planning to visit a high-altitude area, bring a sweater or light- to medium-weight jacket. A polar fleece pullover is ideal, and makes a great impromptu pillow. If you're planning on doing any hiking, a good pair of boots is essential.

SHIPPING LUGGAGE AHEAD

Imagine globe-trotting with only a carry-on in tow. Shipping your luggage in advance via an air-freight service is a great way to cut down on backaches, hassles, and stress—especially if your packing list includes strollers, car seats, etc. There are some things to be aware of, though.

First, research carry-on restrictions; if you absolutely need something that isn't practical to ship and isn't allowed in carry-ons, this strategy isn't for you. Second, plan to send your bags several days in advance to U.S. destinations and as much as two weeks in advance to some international destinations. Third, plan to spend some money: it will cost at least $100 to send a small piece of luggage, a golf bag, or a pair of skis to a domestic destination, much more to places overseas.

Some people use Federal Express to ship their bags, but this can cost even more than air-freight services. All these services insure your bag (for most, the limit is $1,000, but you should verify that amount); you can, however, purchase additional insurance for about $1 per $100 of value.

Contacts **Luggage Concierge** ☎ *800/288–9818* ⊕ *www.luggageconcierge.com*. **Luggage/Sports Express.** Luggage/Sports Express ships luggage and sports equipment including golf clubs and surfboards. ☎ *800/357–4174* ⊕ *www.sportsexpress.com*. **Luggage Free** ☎ *800/361–6871* ⊕ *www. luggagefree.com*.

■ SAFETY

Oahu is generally a safe tourist destination, but it's still wise to follow the same common-sense safety precautions you would normally follow in your own hometown. Rental cars are magnets for break-ins, so don't leave any valuables in the car, not even in a locked trunk. Avoid poorly lighted areas, beach parks, and isolated areas after dark as a precaution. When hiking, stay on marked trails, no matter how alluring the temptation might be to stray. Weather conditions can cause landscapes to become muddy, slippery, and tenuous, so staying on marked trails will lessen the possibility of a fall or getting lost.

Be wary of those hawking "too good to be true" prices on everything from car rentals to attractions. Many of these offers are just a lure to get you in the door for time-share presentations. When handed a flyer, read the fine print before you make your decision to participate.

Women traveling alone are generally safe on the Islands, but always follow the safety precautions you would use in any major destination. When booking hotels, request rooms closest to the elevator, and always keep your hotel-room door and balcony doors locked. Stay away from isolated areas after dark; camping and hiking solo are not advised. If you stay out late visiting nightclubs and bars, use caution when exiting nightspots and returning to your lodging.

■ **TIP→** Distribute your cash, credit cards, I.D.s, and other valuables between a deep front pocket, an inside jacket or vest pocket, and a hidden money pouch. Don't reach for the money pouch once you're in public.

Safety **Transportation Security Administration** (*TSA*). ⊕ *www.tsa.gov*.

■ TAXES

Since July 1, 2010, there is a 9.25% tax added onto your hotel bill. A $3-per-day road tax is also assessed on each rental vehicle.

■ TIME

Hawaii is on Hawaiian Standard Time, five hours behind New York, and two hours behind Los Angeles.

When the U.S. mainland is on daylight saving time, Hawaii is not, so add an extra hour of time difference between the Islands and U.S. mainland destinations. You may also find that things generally move more slowly here. That has nothing to do with your watch—it's just the laid-back way called Hawaiian time.

TIPPING GUIDELINES FOR OAHU

Bartender	$1 to $5 per round of drinks, depending on the number of drinks
Bellhop	$1 to $5 per bag, depending on the level of the hotel and whether you have bulky items like golf clubs and surfboards
Hotel Concierge	$5 or more, depending on the service
Hotel Doorman	$1 to $5 if s/he helps you get a cab or helps with bags, golf clubs, etc.
Hotel Maid	$1 to $3 a day (either daily or at the end of your stay, in cash)
Hotel Room-Service Waiter	$1 to $2 per delivery, even if a service charge has been added
Porter at Airport or Train Station	$1 per bag
Skycap at Airport	$1 to $3 per bag checked
Taxi Driver	15% to 20%, but round up the fare to the next dollar amount
Tour Guide	10% of the cost of the tour
Valet Parking Attendant	$1 to $3, each time your car is brought to you
Waiter	15% to 20%, with 20% being the norm at high-end restaurants; nothing additional if a service charge is added to the bill

■ TIPPING

As this is a major vacation destination and many of the people who work in the service industry rely on tips to supplement their wages, tipping is not only common, but expected.

■ TOURS

GUIDED TOURS

Whenever you book a guided tour, find out what's included and what isn't. A "land-only" tour includes all your travel (by bus, in most cases) in the destination, but not necessarily your flights. In most cases prices in tour brochures don't include fees and taxes. And remember that you'll be expected to tip your guide (in cash) at the end of the tour.

Globus has four Hawaii itineraries that include Oahu, one of which is an escorted cruise on Norwegian Cruise Line's *Pride of America* that includes two days on the island. Tauck and Trafalgar offer several land-based Hawaii itineraries that include two or three nights on Oahu. Both companies offer similar itineraries with visits to the USS *Arizona* Memorial National Park and plenty of free time to explore the island. Tauck offers 7- and 11-night multi-island tours, including a "Magic Hawaii" trip for families. Highlights of the Tauck tours include a catamaran sail along Waikiki Beach and hula and surf lessons. Trafalgar has 7-, 9-, 10-, and 12-night multi-island tours.

EscortedHawaiiTours.com, owned and operated by Atlas Cruises & Tours, sells more than a dozen Hawaii trips ranging from 7 to 12 nights operated by various guided tour companies including Globus, Tauck, and Trafalgar.

Recommended Companies Atlas Cruises & Tours ☎ *800/942–3301* ⊕ *www.escortedhawaiitours.com.* **Globus** ☎ *866/755–8581* ⊕ *www.globusjourneys.com.* **Tauck Travel** ☎ *800/788–7885* ⊕ *www.tauck. com.* **Trafalgar** ☎ *866/544–4434* ⊕ *www. trafalgar.com.*

SPECIAL-INTEREST TOURS
BIRD-WATCHING

More than 150 species of birds live in the Hawaiian Islands. For about $4,200 per person, Field Guides has a three-island (Oahu, Kauai, and the Big Island), 11-day, guided bird-watching trip that includes accommodations, meals, ground transportation, and interisland air.

Victor Emanuel Nature Tours, the largest company in the world specializing in birding tours, has a nine-day "Fall Hawaii" trip to Oahu, Kauai, and the Big Island that costs around $4,000 and includes accommodations, meals, interisland air, ground transportation, and guided excursions.

Contacts Field Guides ☎ 800/728–4953 ⊕ *www.fieldguides.com.* **Victor Emanuel Nature Tours** ☎ 800/328–8368 ⊕ *www. ventbird.com.*

CULTURE
Elderhostel, a nonprofit educational travel organization running tours under the name Road Scholar, offers several guided Hawaii tours for adults 50 and over that provide in-depth looks into the culture, history, and beauty of the Islands.

Contacts Road Scholar ☎ 800/454–5768 ⊕ *www.roadscholar.org.*

ECOTOURS
Imagine the thrill of working alongside marine biologists and helping with conservation efforts on Oahu's west coast. Wild Side Specialty Tours offers seven-day "Under the Sea Ocean Trekker Expeditions" where you can do just that. You'll also visit Hawaiian historical and cultural sites along the coast and learn about the people who settled on these shores. Priced at about $1,900 per person, the trip includes accommodations at Makaha Golf Resort, meals, and all activities.

Contacts Wild Side Specialty Tours ☎ 808/306–7273 ⊕ *www.sailhawaii.com.*

HIKING
Want to hike through lush rain forests, snorkel at Shark's Cove, discover quiet beaches, and visit historical monuments? Check out the 10-night "It's Not Just Waikiki: Hiking and Touring Oahu" tour offered by Sierra Club Outings, priced at about $2,000 per person, including condominium accommodations in Honolulu and the North Shore; vegetarian-friendly

meals with fresh, local seafood, produce, and fruit; ground transportation; and activities. The 12 travelers on this tour will also be able to participate in a community-service project on the island.

Contacts Sierra Club Outings ☎ 808/538–6616 ⊕ *www.sierraclubhawaii.com.*

▌TRIP INSURANCE

Comprehensive trip insurance is valuable if you're booking a very expensive or complicated trip (particularly to an isolated region) or if you're booking far in advance. Comprehensive policies typically cover trip cancellation and interruption, letting you cancel or cut your trip short because of illness, or, in some cases, acts of terrorism in your destination. Such policies might also cover evacuation and medical care. Some also cover you for trip delays because of bad weather or mechanical problems, as well as for lost or delayed luggage.

Another type of coverage to consider is financial default—that is, when your trip is disrupted because a tour operator, airline, or cruise line goes out of business. Generally you must buy this when you book your trip or shortly thereafter, and it's available to you only if your operator isn't on a list of excluded companies.

Always read the fine print of your policy to make sure that you're covered for the risks that most concern you. Compare several policies to be sure you're getting the best price and range of coverage available.

Insurance Comparison Info Insure My Trip ☎ 800/487–4722 ⊕ *www.insuremytrip.com.* **Square Mouth** ☎ 800/240–0369 ⊕ *www. squaremouth.com.*

Comprehensive Insurers **Access America**
☎ *800/284-8300* ⊕ *www.accessamerica.*
com. **Travel Guard** ☎ *800/826-4919* ⊕ *www.*
travelguard.com. **CSA Travel Protection**
☎ *800/873-9855, 800/711-1197* ⊕ *www.*
csatravelprotection.com. **Travelex Insurance**
☎ *888/228-9792, 888/457-4602* ⊕ *www.*
travelexinsurance.com. **Travel Insured**
International ☎ *800/243-3174* ⊕ *www.*
travelinsured.com.

❚ VISITOR INFORMATION

Before you go, contact the Oahu Visitors Bureau (OVB) for a free vacation planner and map. The OVB website has online listing of accommodations, activities and sports, attractions, dining venues, services, transportation, travel professionals, and wedding information. For general information on all of the Islands, contact the Hawaii Visitors & Convention Bureau. The HVCB website has a calendar of local events that will be taking place during your stay.

Contacts Hawaii Visitors & Convention
Bureau ✉ *2270 Kalakaua Ave., Suite 801,*
Honolulu ☎ *808/923-1811, 800/464-2924*
for brochures ⊕ *www.gohawaii.com.* **Oahu**
Visitors Bureau ✉ *733 Bishop St., Suite 1520,*
Downtown Honolulu, Honolulu ☎ *877/525-*
6248 ⊕ *www.gohawaii.com/oahu.*

ONLINE RESOURCES

Contacts Hawaii Beach Safety
⊕ *oceansafety.ancl.hawaii.edu.* **Hawaii**
Department of Land and Natural Resources
⊕ *hawaii.gov/dlnr.* **Hawaii Tourism Authority**
⊕ *www.travelsmarthawaii.com.*

INDEX

PHOTO CREDITS

1, Douglas Peebles/eStock Photo. 3, cunningham- photos.com. Chapter 1: Experience Oahu: 6-7, Grant Studios/eStock Photo. 8 (top), Ken Ross/vies- tiphoto.com. 8 (bottom), Oahu Visitors Bureau. 9 (top left), Oahu Visitors Bureau. 9 (top right), Corbis. 9 (bottom), Michael S. Nolan/age fotostock. 11 (left and right), SuperStock/age fotostock. 14 (left), Douglas Peebles Photography/Alamy. 14 (top right), David Franzen/Doris Duke Foundation for Islamic Art. 14 (bottom center), Tor Johnson/Photo Resource Hawaii/Alamy. 14 (bottom right), Deborah Davis/Alamy. 15 (top left), Oahu Visitors Bureau. 15 (bottom left), David L. Moore/Alamy. 15 (right), Ann Cecil/Photo Resource Hawaii/Alamy. 16 (left), Hawaii Tourism Authority (HTA)/Tor Johnson. 16 (top right), Ablestock.com/Thinkstock. 16 (bottom right), IMG_6266 by takaokun (http://www.flickr.com/photos/takaokun/5017244988/) (Attribution License). 17 (left), Hawaii Tourism Authority (HTA) / Tor Johnson. 17 (right), Photo Resource Hawaii/Alamy. 19, Corbis. 20, Jay Spooner/iStockphoto. 25, Oahu Visitors Bureau. 26, Stephanie Horrocks/iStockphoto. 29, iStockphoto. 30, Andre Seale/Alamy. 31, Tor Johnson/Photo Resource Hawaii/ Alamy. 33 (left), Skip ODonnell/iStockphoto. 33 (right), Douglas Peebles/ age fotostock. 35 (left), Oahu Visitors Bureau. 35 (right), Starwood Hotels & Resorts. 36, Michael Brake/iStockphoto. Chapter 2: Exploring Oahu: 37, iStockphoto. 38, lmaronic/Shutterstock. 39, Tor Johnson/Photo Resource Hawaii/ Alamy. 44, Ken Ross/viestiphoto.com. 48, Corbis. 52, David L. Moore/Alamy. 55, J.D. Heaton/Picture Finders/age fotostock. 56, Oahu Visitors Bureau. 57 (left and center), Walter Bibikow/viestiphoto. com. 57 (right), Douglas Peebles/age fotostock. 58, Stuart Westmorland/age fotostock. 59 (left), The Royal Hawaiian. 59 (center), Atlantide S.N.C./age fotostock. 59 (right), Liane Cary/age fotostock. 67, Giovanni Simeone/SIME/eStock Photo. 69, Doug- las Peebles/eStock Photo. 71, Library of Congress Prints & Photographs Division. 73 (top), Corbis. 73 (bottom), USS Arizona Memorial Photo Collection/ NPS. 74, Army Signal Corps Collection in the U.S. National Archives. 74 (inset), USS Missouri Memorial Association. 75, USS Bowfin Submarine Museum & Park. 82, Kenny Williams/Alamy. 84, Blaine Harrington/age fotostock. 85, Pierre Tostee. 86 and 87, ASP Tostee. 88, cunninghamphotos. com. 92, Alan Seiden/Oahu Visitors Bureau. Chapter 3: Beaches: 95, J.D. Heaton/age fotostock. 96, Dhoxax/ Shutterstock. 100, David Schrichte/Photo Resource Hawaii/Alamy. 103, 105, and 106, SuperStock/age fotostock. 109, Chuck Babbitt/iStock Photo. 110 and 112, Photo Resource Hawaii/Alamy. Chapter 4: Water Sports & Tours: 115, Dave Bjorn/Photo Resource Hawaii/Alamy. 116, Kato Inowe/Shutterstock. 118 and 120, Photo Resource Hawaii/Alamy. 124, Douglas Peebles/cStock Photo. 128, Photo Resource Hawaii/Alamy. 131, Ron Dahlquist/ HVCB. 132, SuperStock/age fotostock. 134 (top), SPrada/iStockphoto. 134 (bottom), Gert Vrey/iStockphoto. 135, sweetlifephotos/iStockphoto. 137, Photo Resource Hawaii/Alamy. 140, Douglas Peebles/ eStock Photo. Chapter 5: Golf, Hiking & Outdoor Activities: 143, Photo Resource Hawaii/Alamy. 144, Preferred Hotel Group. 145, Jon McLean/Alamy. 146, Blue Hawaiian Helicopters. 149, Luca Tettoni/viestiphoto.com. 150, KauaI Visitors Bureau. 151, Jack Jeffrey. 155, Tor Johnson/Aurora Photos. 161, Photo Resource Hawaii/ Alamy. Chapter 6: Shops & Spas: 165, Beauty Photo Studio/age fotostock. 166, The Leading Hotels of the World. 171 (top), Linda Ching/HVCB. 171 (bottom), Sri Maiava Rusden/ HVCB. 172, Michael Soo/Alamy. 173 (top), leisofhawaii.com. 173 (2nd from top), kellyalexanderpho- tography.com. 173 (3rd, 4th, and 5th from top), leisofhawaii.com. 173 (bottom), kellyalexanderpho- tography.com. 182 (top), JW Marriott Ihilani Resort & Spa. 182 (bottom), The Leading Hotels of the World. Chapter 7: Entertainment & Nightlife: 185, Polynesian Cultural Center. 186, Jose Gil/Shutterstock.188, Ann Cecil/ Photo Resource Hawaii/Alamy. 192, Hawaii Visitors & Convention Bureau. 193, Thinkstock LLC. 195, Hawaii Visitors & Convention Bureau. Chapter 8: Where to Eat: 203, David L. Moore/ Alamy. 204, Joshua Rainey Photography/Shutterstock. 209, Polynesian Cultural Center. 210 (top), Douglas Peebles Photography. 210 (top center), Douglas Peebles Photography/Alamy. 210 (center), Dana Edmunds/Polynesian Cultural Center. 210 (bottom center), Douglas Peebles Photography/Alamy. 210 (bottom), Purcell Team/Alamy. 211 (top, top center, and bottom center), HTJ/HVCB. 211, Oahu Visitors Bureau. 220, Alan Wong's Restaurant Honolulu by Benjamin. 239, Preferred Hotel Group. Chapter 9: Where to Stay: 241, Waikiki Parc Hotel. 242, The Kahala. 247 (top and bottom), Kahala. 250 (top and bottom), Halekulani. 260 (top and bottom), Turtle Bay Resort.

ABOUT OUR WRITERS

Melissa Chang is a lifelong Honolulu resident and has worked in public relations for more than 20 years, representing a range of travel, retail, and restaurant clients. She is also a food reviewer for Honolulu's Metromix.com and is a regular contributor to the *Honolulu Advertiser,* the state's most popular daily newspaper. Melissa updated the Where to Eat and Shops and Spas chapters.

Michael Levine is a reporter-host for ⊕ *CivilBeat.com*, a Honolulu-based investigative news service. He covers city government, politics, and local issues, with a focus on the City Council and the mayor. For this book, he updated the Exploring; Beaches; Golf, Hiking, and Outdoor Activities; and Travel Smart sections.

Born and raised on Oahu, **Catherine E. Toth** has worked as a newspaper reporter in Hawaii for 10 years and continues to freelance—in between surfing, hiking, and eating everything in sight—for such print and online publications as *Haute Living, Modern Luxury Hawaii, HAWAII,* and *Alaska Airlines Magazine.* For this edition, she updated the Experience, Water Sports, Entertainment and Nightlife, and Where to Stay sections.

NOTES

Turtle Bay Resort

Hell ... Joe's

Pat's

NOTES